A Laboratory Manual for
Forensic Anthropology

A Laboratory Manual for
Forensic Anthropology

Angi M. Christensen
Federal Bureau of Investigation Laboratory,
Quantico, VA USA

Nicholas V. Passalacqua
Anthropology and Sociology Department,
Western Carolina University, Cullowhee,
NC USA

ACADEMIC PRESS
An imprint of Elsevier

Academic Press is an imprint of Elsevier
125 London Wall, London EC2Y 5AS, United Kingdom
525 B Street, Suite 1800, San Diego, CA 92101-4495, United States
50 Hampshire Street, 5th Floor, Cambridge, MA 02139, United States
The Boulevard, Langford Lane, Kidlington, Oxford OX5 1GB, United Kingdom

Notices
Knowledge and best practice in this field are constantly changing. As new research and experience broaden our understanding, changes in research methods, professional practices, or medical treatment may become necessary.

Practitioners and researchers must always rely on their own experience and knowledge in evaluating and using any information, methods, compounds, or experiments described herein. In using such information or methods they should be mindful of their own safety and the safety of others, including parties for whom they have a professional responsibility.

To the fullest extent of the law, neither the Publisher nor the authors, contributors, or editors, assume any liability for any injury and/or damage to persons or property as a matter of products liability, negligence or otherwise, or from any use or operation of any methods, products, instructions, or ideas contained in the material herein.

Library of Congress Cataloging-in-Publication Data
A catalog record for this book is available from the Library of Congress

British Library Cataloguing-in-Publication Data
A catalogue record for this book is available from the British Library

ISBN 978-0-12-812201-3

For information on all Academic Press publications
visit our website at https://www.elsevier.com/ books-and-journals

Working together
to grow libraries in
developing countries

www.elsevier.com • www.bookaid.org

Publisher: Mica Haley
Acquisition Editor: Elizabeth Brown
Editorial Project Manager: Pat Gonzalez
Production Project Manager: Anusha Sambamoorthy
Cover Designer: Miles Hitchen

Typeset by SPi Global, India

Last digit is the print number: 9 8 7 6 5 4

Contents

Preface

Forensic anthropology is an applied science, typically involving direct hands-on examination and analysis of skeletal remains and related evidence. Developing the skills to effectively practice forensic anthropology requires significant training, mentorship, experience, and practice using actual skeletal material, instruments, software, and other reference materials. This lab manual will introduce and guide students through various methods used by forensic anthropologists in the recovery and analysis of skeletal remains.

The principle rationale for writing this manual was a perceived need for a comprehensive introductory laboratory manual that introduces students and aspiring practitioners to the practice of forensic anthropology using up-to-date, validated, and accepted methods. The content of the chapters in this manual corresponds to material found in the textbook *Forensic Anthropology: Current Methods and Practice* (Christensen et al., 2014). It therefore may be used in accompaniment with that text, facilitating understanding of the content of each chapter through hands-on learning. It is not, however, designed to be used exclusively with that text and may also be used as a stand-alone volume or to supplement other texts or course materials. If used with that text, some overlap and updates in content will be noted. While this laboratory manual emphasizes more procedural information and concepts, the textbook provides more in-depth topic coverage and literature review.

Each chapter of this laboratory manual begins with an *Objectives* section, describing what information or procedures the student will learn or skills that should be demonstrated upon completion of the chapter. The text of each chapter provides necessary background information, figures, instructions, tables, and diagrams for reference. For each chapter, a series of *Exercises* are provided, giving students the opportunity to apply newly acquired knowledge from each topic area. Each exercise includes a list of *Materials needed*, as well as a *Note to instructor* to facilitate preparation and (where applicable) *Instructions/Procedures* to follow. All exercises are case-based, and each exercise includes a *Case Scenario* so that students have an understanding of the context in which the activities may be applied. A series of *Appendices* can be found at the end of the manual, consisting primarily of reference materials such as data tables, as well as various forms and charts for data recording.

We enjoyed and learned from each other during our collaboration on this laboratory manual, and hope that instructors and students will find it to be comprehensive, practical, and relevant to current practices in the discipline of forensic anthropology. While we appreciate the value of color images, we also made every effort to keep the cost of this laboratory manual down, and therefore most of the figures are printed in black and white. We recognize that backgrounds, experiences, and views of those teaching and practicing forensic anthropology differ, and understand that teaching the principles of forensic anthropology is improved through sharing and discussing different perspectives. We therefore welcome any comments, feedback, or suggestions from our colleges as well as students utilizing this text.

We appreciate the contributions of several of our colleagues who provided materials (such as images and data) related to this laboratory manual, including Lisa Bailey, Eric Bartelink, Robyn Capobianco, Christian Crowder, Dennis C. Dirkmaat, Megan Gilpin, Gary Hatch, Alexandra Klales, Lyniece Lewis, Marin Pilloud, James Pokines, Christopher W. Rainwater, Brian Spatola and the National Museum of Health and Medicine, Mohammed Swaraldahab, Steven A. Symes, and Norman Sauer. We also appreciate the feedback we received on structure and content from Derek Boyd, Christian Crowder, Suzanne Daly, Alexandra Klales, Krista Latham, Marin Pilloud, Christine Pink, and Christopher W. Rainwater.

Authors' Biography

Angi M. Christensen is a Forensic Anthropologist with the Federal Bureau of Investigation (FBI) Laboratory in Quantico, Virginia. She is also an adjunct professor in the Forensic Science Program at George Mason University. She received her Ph.D. in Anthropology from The University of Tennessee in 2003 and was certified by the American Board of Forensic Anthropology in 2012.

She is a coauthor of the award-winning textbook *Forensic Anthropology: Current Methods and Practice*, as well as a cofounder and an editor of the journal *Forensic Anthropology*. Her research interests include methods of personal identification, skeletal trauma analysis, and skeletal imaging. She has published numerous research papers in journals including the *Journal of Forensic Sciences, American Journal of Physical Anthropology, Journal of Forensic Radiology and Imaging, Journal of Forensic Identification, Forensic Science International, Forensic Science Medicine & Pathology,* and the *Journal of Anatomy*.

Nicholas V. Passalacqua is an Assistant Professor and the Forensic Anthropology Program Coordinator at Western Carolina University. Prior to arriving at WCU, he worked as a deploying forensic anthropologist with the Defense POW/MIA Accounting Agency—Laboratory. He received his Ph.D. in Anthropology from Michigan State in 2012 and was certified by the American Board of Forensic Anthropology in 2016.

He is a cofounder and the current editor-in-chief of the journal *Forensic Anthropology*. His research interests include age at death estimation, skeletal trauma analysis, and ethics. He is also a coauthor of the award-winning textbook *Forensic Anthropology: Current Methods and Practice*, as well as numerous publications in journals such as *The Journal of Forensic Sciences, The International Journal of Osteoarchaeology,* and *The American Journal of Physical Anthropology*, as well as chapters in books such as *Skeletal trauma analysis: Case studies in context, The analysis of burned human remains, Age estimation of the human skeleton*, and *A companion to forensic anthropology*.

Note to Instructors

The practice of forensic anthropology requires extensive hands-on experience and training using actual skeletal remains and other materials and instruments that are used in real forensic casework. It is recognized, however, that not all instructors are directly involved in casework and may not have the resources to procure or access all of the materials suggested in this laboratory manual. Here we offer a few notes and suggestions that may facilitate the effective use of this manual.

- The chapters in this lab manual largely correspond in content to those in the textbook *Forensic Anthropology: Current Methods and Practice* (Christensen et al., 2014), and this manual therefore makes a practical and easy accompaniment to that text. It is not, however, required that students have that particular text in order to use this manual, which may be used to accompany other texts or course materials.
- Each exercise begins with a list of *Materials needed* as well as a *Note to instructors*. Materials may include tables, figures, diagrams, appendices, skeletal material, instruments, or other materials or equipment that will be needed for that exercise. For most chapters, variations of exercises are included that can be suited to instructor/institution resource availability. For example, chapters that cover Fordisc include exercises that require the software; however, exercise options are also included for those who do not have a copy of the software (such as Fordisc outputs for students to interpret). Instructor notes contain details regarding exercise preparation, where to find/access certain materials, options/alternatives, and other information. It is suggested that instructors review the exercises for each chapter/topic in advance to determine which exercises will be used and what preparation may be necessary. Where specific steps should be followed, the exercise also includes *Instructions/Procedures*.
- The use of real human skeletal remains is ideal when available. Handling real skeletal material will give students the best sense of the nature of skeletal material including texture, weight, and quality, as well as the opportunity to appreciate subtle variations between different skeletons. Real skeletal material may be available in institutions with donated or curated human remains. Real skeletal material can also be purchased from certain anatomical supply companies (such as The Bone Room).
- Plastic skeletal replicas and casts are also widely available (though companies such as Bone Clones and France Casting) and are a good substitute if real skeletal material is not an option. Note that some features (such as osteometric landmarks) on replica material may not be as easy to locate and identify as on real skeletal remains. Although diagrams and images are provided in the manual and may be used exclusively if necessary, the use of some kind of hands-on material for many of the exercises is strongly recommended.
- The use of nonhuman skeletal material is also suggested in several of the chapters. These materials are useful for identifying differences between human and nonhuman skeletons but may also be substituted for human remains in some exercises. For example, nonhuman skeletal material can be used to show taphonomic changes such as weathering and scavenging and may also be used to demonstrate skeletal trauma. As with human skeletal material, these may be readily available in certain institutions and can also be purchased from biological supply companies. Nonhuman skeletal material may also be procured through agreements with local wildlife conservation offices or animal shelters. Local laws regarding the recovery and retention of certain nonhuman skeletons should be understood.
- Most of the instruments used in forensic anthropological analyses and in these exercises are relatively easy to obtain and at a fairly low cost. Calipers used in the measurement of skeletal material, for example, are affordable and are strongly recommended. Not every student needs their own calipers; they can be shared between students and among groups. Similarly, Fordisc is an important software tool in the analysis of human skeletal measurements. It is available through the University of Tennessee's Department of Anthropology and is relatively inexpensive, and site licenses are available for use by large groups in a laboratory setting.

- Other instruments will greatly facilitate learning and are recommended for courses that are intended to specifically prepare students for careers in forensic anthropology. The availability of histological slides and microscopes, for example, will be of great utility to aspiring practitioners. Other instruments are useful teaching tools if available but are used in only a small number of forensic anthropology laboratories. For example, instruments such as radiological devices (e.g., X-rays and CT scanners), 3-dimensional printers, and X-ray fluorescence spectrometers are probably not available in most academic institutions. Access to radiologic images including X-rays or CT scans, however, is likely to be less costly and more achievable and will greatly facilitate learning.

- Several of the exercises (such as searching, mapping, and recovering) are best performed in an outdoor setting since this is where they would most often be performed in a forensic context. While some institutions may have dedicated areas for outdoor student activities, any grassy or wooded area will suffice in most cases. In the event that such areas are unavailable (or in the event of bad weather), these exercises can also be modified to a classroom or other indoor setting.

- Some exercises involve equipment, materials, or activities that may present hazards including physical, chemical, biological, or radiological hazards. Universities and laboratories should have safety requirements and documented procedures for dealing with these types of hazards. It is recommend that instructors be familiar with these requirements and procedures for institutions in which they work and provide relevant information to students and/or have them complete applicable safety training.

- Exercises in this manual are provided as guides, options, and suggestions for instructor and student use, and not all exercises in this manual need to be completed. Instructors may omit exercises or entire chapters based on available time or resources, student knowledge and ability, or instructor preference. Many of the exercises can also be modified to suit the needs of the course. In addition to the general guidance provided here, many chapters also contain suggestions for alternatives and possible modifications, but instructors are also free to modify in their own way as needed.

Disclaimer

The views expressed in this book are those of the authors and do not necessarily represent the views of the Federal Bureau of Investigation (FBI), U.S. Government, or Western Carolina University (WCU). Names of commercial manufacturers are provided for identification or reference purposes only, and inclusion does not imply endorsement of the manufacturer or its products or services by the FBI, WCU, or the authors.

Chapter 1

Introduction to Forensic Anthropology

OBJECTIVES

Membership in, or at least familiarity with, various professional organizations is critical to the successful practice of forensic anthropology. Aspiring practitioners should also be aware of the variety of career paths available for forensic anthropologists. Upon completion of the exercises in this chapter, you will be familiar with various employment options for forensic anthropologists, as well as some of the professional organizations most relevant to the field of forensic anthropology.

INTRODUCTION TO FORENSIC ANTHROPOLOGY

Anthropology is a broad field, defined as the study of humankind (from the Greek *anthropos* "man" and *logia* "study"), and is generally considered to consist of four primary subdisciplines: cultural anthropology, linguistic anthropology, archaeology, and biological anthropology. Forensic anthropology is a specialized subfield primarily based on biological anthropology and archaeological methods and involves the application of anthropological method and theory to matters of legal concern, particularly those that relate to the recovery and analysis of the skeleton.

FORENSIC ANTHROPOLOGY PROFESSIONAL ORGANIZATIONS

Forensic anthropology is still considered a relatively young scientific discipline, beginning with anatomists, physicians, and biological anthropologists providing occasional assistance to law enforcement prior to the 1940s and becoming significantly more professionalized in the 1970–90s. Part of the development of the discipline included the establishment of the Physical Anthropology Section of the American Academy of Forensic Sciences (www.aafs.org) in 1972 (renamed the Anthropology Section in 2012 to better reflect the broader scope of present-day forensic anthropology) and the creation of the American Board of Forensic Anthropology (www.theabfa.org) in 1977. Today, forensic anthropology is a well-established forensic discipline that has experienced a recent and significant expansion in attention and breadth, facilitated in large part by increased public, media, and professional interest. There has been an enormous increase in research and publications in the field, coupled with the development of numerous graduate programs with curricula specifically tailored to prepare students for careers in forensic anthropology. Especially in the current era of forensic anthropology, a forensic anthropologist needs to have a specialized and advanced education. Mentorship, collaboration, and hands-on training are also considered essential.

In recent years, anthropologists and other forensic science practitioners (as well as policy-makers) have recognized the need for the standardization of methods and adherence to best-practice principles. In the 1990s, the Federal Bureau of Investigation (FBI) Laboratory began sponsoring Scientific Working Groups (SWGs) in partnership with the National Institute of Justice (NIJ) to improve practices and build consensus with their federal, state, and local forensic community partners. Scientific working groups consist of representatives from forensic, industrial, commercial, and academic communities, including international participants, who assist in the development of standards and guidelines and improve communications throughout their respective disciplines. The Scientific Working Group for Forensic Anthropology (SWGANTH) was formed in 2008 under the joint sponsorship of the FBI Laboratory and the Department of Defense Central Identification Laboratory. Like many of the other SWGs, the primary objectives of SWGANTH were to develop and disseminate best practice guidelines and standards for the discipline.

Most SWGs have now become part of the Organization for Scientific Area Committees (OSAC), an initiative of the National Institute of Standards and Technology (NIST) and Department of Justice (DOJ) (www.nist.gov/forensics/osac). The OSAC coordinates the development of draft standard and guideline documents, which then proceed through a Standards Development Organization (SDO) to ensure transparency and equity. Once through the SDO process, these documents can then be recommended for publication on the OSAC registry of approved guidelines and standards. The

A Laboratory Manual for Forensic Anthropology. https://doi.org/10.1016/B978-0-12-812201-3.00001-3

OSAC Anthropology Subcommittee is part of the Crime Scene and Death Investigation Committee and focuses on standards and guidelines related to application of anthropological methods and theory, particularly those relating to the recovery and analysis of human remains. Although voluntary in most cases, following consensus guidelines and standards is generally considered best practice, and such guidelines are increasingly recognized and considered by courts. Many of the techniques and approaches described in this manual follow guidelines promulgated by SWGANTH and the Anthropology Subcommittee of the OSAC.

Other organizations dedicated to forensic anthropology include the Society of Forensic Anthropologists (www.sofainc.org), the Forensic Anthropology Society of Europe (www.forensicanthropology.eu), and the Asociación Latinoamericana de Antropología Forense (alafforense.org). Many other organizations exist related to biological anthropology and forensic science and may occasionally address forensic anthropology topics.

FORENSIC ANTHROPOLOGY PROFESSIONS

Forensic anthropologists are employed in a wide variety of professional settings. Most are university professors who provide forensic anthropological consultations as a matter of public service. Over the past few decades, several university anthropology programs have developed laboratories where practitioners perform casework as well as train and mentor students. Examples include the Forensic Anthropology Center at the University of Tennessee, the C.A. Pound Human Identification Laboratory at the University of Florida, the Forensic Anthropology Center at Texas State University, and the Human Identification Laboratory at California State University, Chico. For many forensic anthropologists in universities, their primary job duties include teaching, research, and service, but they may also have other responsibilities. Courses taught may range from forensic anthropology, to general biological anthropology, to anatomy and human variation.

Medical examiners' and coroners' offices are increasingly employing forensic anthropologists not only to assist with skeletal remains cases but also to apply their expertise to recently deceased individuals, especially in regard to the analysis of skeletal trauma. In larger jurisdictions, there may be full-time work for a forensic anthropologist. In other jurisdictions, anthropologists in these offices may perform forensic anthropological analyses as one of their roles and may also fill additional roles such as medicolegal investigator or identification specialist.

Museums also employ forensic anthropologists, some of whom may also provide forensic anthropological services as consultants. The Smithsonian Institution's National Museum of Natural History (NMNH), for example, has a long history of providing forensic anthropological services, including to the FBI, and several of the anthropologists employed by the NMNH continue to provide this public service. The National Museum of Health and Medicine (NMHM) employs forensic anthropologists in various roles who also provide their services on casework. In addition to forensic casework, responsibilities of forensic anthropologists in museums may include collections management, teaching, research, outreach, and mentoring.

Forensic anthropologists are also employed by federal laboratories that recover and analyze skeletal remains for identification as part of their primary mission. The Defense POW/MIA Accounting Agency (DPAA), with laboratories in Honolulu, Hawaii and Omaha, Nebraska, was initially established to assist in the identification of deceased military personnel in the Pacific region. Today, the laboratory is congressionally mandated to have the capacity to identify a minimum number of service members annually and employs numerous full-time forensic anthropologists and archaeologists. The Armed Forces Medical Examiner System (AFMES), which is responsible for the examination and identification of recently deceased military personnel as well as US citizens who died abroad, has forensic anthropologists who assist with morgue operations, particularly in cases involving fragmentary remains. The FBI Laboratory employs anthropologists who assist in the detection, recovery, and analysis of skeletal material in support of federal, state, and local investigations.

Forensic anthropologists have taken on important roles in the identification of victims of mass disasters. Many forensic anthropologists are members of the Disaster Mortuary Operation Response Team (DMORT), a federal response team of numerous specialists that assists local jurisdictions (e.g., coroners, medical examiners, and law enforcement) in the event of a mass disaster. Such work is typically sporadic and rarely a career in and of itself. Forensic anthropologists may, however, serve in mass disaster roles as part of their other responsibilities, such as being the mass fatality planner/coordinator in a medical examiner's office. The National Transportation Safety Board (NTSB) is charged with investigating civil aviation accidents as well as certain highway, pipeline, marine, and rail incidents. The NTSB employs several forensic anthropologists to assist with mass fatality medicolegal operations.

Anthropologists have become increasingly involved in humanitarian, human rights, and armed conflict investigations abroad. Among the first was the use of forensic anthropology to investigate conflicts in Latin America (especially Argentina) in the 1970s and 1980s. Many forensic anthropologists have also assisted in the excavation and analysis of skeletal remains in the Balkans since the 1990s. Such investigations continue today, and forensic anthropologists can find work in association with these investigations with organizations such as Physicians for Human Rights (PHR), the International Commission on Missing Persons (ICMP), and the International Committee for the Red Cross (ICRC).

In looking for careers in forensic anthropology, students and aspiring practitioners should bear in mind that actual position titles are most often not "Forensic Anthropologist." Effectively, the roles often involve performing forensic anthropological analyses, but job titles might be "Professor," "Criminalist," "Physical Scientist," "Curator," "Collections Manager," "Medicolegal Investigator," "Autopsy Technician," or "Independent Contractor." Even if not performing skeletal examination casework, a forensic anthropologist's skill set is often well suited to other positions within the medical, legal, forensic science, or crime scene disciplines. Examples include roles in laboratory management, biomechanical engineering, medicolegal death investigation, and crime scene investigation.

EXERCISE 1.1   The American Academy of Forensic Sciences

Materials needed:
- Internet access

Note to instructors: This exercise can be carried out individually or in groups, in class, or as a take-home exercise.

Case scenario: Given that you have decided to pursue a career in forensic anthropology, and that the American Academy of Forensic Sciences is the largest forensic science organization in the world, you decide to do some research to see what benefits the organization might provide for a student like you.

Instructions/Procedure:
- Visit the website of the American Academy of Forensic Sciences (www.aafs.org).
- Navigate to the "Students" tab and select "Choosing a Career" and "Types of Forensic Scientists" from the dropdown menu. Review the section on Forensic Anthropology.
- Next, from the "Students" tab, select Young Forensic Scientists Forum and review the contents of this page.

When was the AAFS founded and what are its objectives?

_____

_____

_____

Identify some of the organizations, offices, and places where forensic anthropologists may work:

_____

_____

What is the Young Forensic Scientists Forum?

_____

_____

EXERCISE 1.2   The American Academy of Forensic Sciences

Materials needed:
- Internet access

Note to instructors: This exercise can be carried out individually or in groups, in class, or as a take-home exercise. If you are a member of AAFS and/or have attended any AAFS meetings, discuss them with students and share your experience.

Case scenario: You have decided to become a Student Affiliate Member of the AAFS and attend the next AAFS meeting.

Instructions/Procedure:
- Navigate to the Membership page clicking "Membership" at the top of the page and review the contents of this page.
- Next, navigate to the Anthropology Section membership requirements by clicking (on the left side of the page) "Student Affiliate, Trainee Affiliate, or Associate Member." Review the basic AAFS Membership Requirements as well as the Individual Section Requirements for the Anthropology Section.
- Click "Apply Now" on the navigation pane on the left to download the application and reference forms.
- Next, navigate to the Meetings page by clicking "Meetings" at the top of the page, select next year's meeting, and review the contents of this page.

What are the requirements to apply as a Student Affiliate in the Anthropology Section? Do you meet the requirements? If not, what goals can you set to meet them in the future?

_____
_____
_____

When and where will the next AAFS meeting be held? Will you be able to attend? Consider whether you might have some research to present, or whether there are funding resources available at your institution. Note that you can also work at the meeting as a volunteer for free registration. If you hope to attend, outline some goals or steps that you will need to take.

_____
_____
_____

EXERCISE 1.3 The Organization of Scientific Area Committees

Materials needed:
• Internet access

Note to instructors: This exercise can be carried out individually or in groups, in class, or as a take-home exercise. If you are a member of the OSAC and/or have attended any OSAC meetings, discuss them with students and share your experience.

Case scenario: Given your understanding of the importance of standards in forensic science, you decide to familiarize yourself with the activities of NIST's OSACs, especially the Anthropology Subcommittee.

Instructions/Procedure:
• Visit the website of NIST's OSACs (www.nist.gov/forensics/osac).
• Review the contents of the Home Page.
• Navigate to the OSAC Registries page and review the contents of this page.
• Navigate to the "OSAC Subcommittees" page and select "Anthropology."

How many OSAC Subcommittees are there currently?

_____
_____
_____

What is the difference between a *standard* and a *guideline*?

_____
_____

What is the purpose of the Anthropology Subcommittee?

_____
_____

Are there any posted documents on which you would like to provide feedback? If so, how would you proceed?

_____
_____

EXERCISE 1.4 The American Board of Forensic Anthropology

Materials needed:
• Internet access

Note to instructors: This exercise can be carried out individually or in groups, in class, or as a take-home exercise. If you are ABFA certified, discuss the process and your experience with students.

Case Scenario: Having received your PhD in anthropology, you are considering whether you should become board certified to increase your chances for employment and follow best practices for forensic anthropology practitioners.

Instructions/Procedure:
• Visit the website of the American Board of Forensic Anthropology (www.theabfa.org).
• Review the contents of the Home Page.
• Select "ABFA Applicants" to see more information about the application process for ABFA certification.

- Access the Policies and Procedures page by clicking "Policies and Procedures" and locate the ABFA Reference Manual.
- Next, navigate to the Frequently Asked Questions by selecting "Students" from the FAQ tab on the Home Page and review the contents of the pate.

By whom is the ABFA accredited?

Historically, who was the first certified Diplomate of the ABFA?

Who is the current Vice President of the ABFA?

What are the minimum requirements to apply for ABFA certification?

If you are considering ABFA certification, outline some goals and milestones that you will need to achieve before applying.

EXERCISE 1.5   Forensic Anthropology as a Career

Materials needed:
- Internet access

Note to instructors: This exercise can be carried out as a take-home exercise. Encourage students to be patient when awaiting responses from interviewees since many likely have busy schedules.

Case scenario: You want to know more about what it is like to have a career in forensic anthropology. One way to learn more is to contact a practicing forensic anthropologist.

Instructions/Procedure:
- Identify a practicing forensic anthropologist and their email address via an internet search. Keep in mind the different career options, and which you think might interest you most.
- Compose a list of five questions that will help you get an idea of how this anthropologist came to this career and what their day-to-day work is like.
- Write an email to your selected anthropologist requesting their responses to your questions as part of this assignment.
- Alternatively, see if the answers to your questions can be found on the FAQ/Students page of the ABFA website.

Did you learn anything from your interviewee that you did not already know about working as a forensic anthropologist? If so, what?

What aspect of this forensic anthropologist's work is most appealing to you? Least appealing?

EXERCISE 1.6   Education and Career Paths in Forensic Anthropology

Materials needed:
- Internet access

Note to instructors: This exercise can be carried out as a take-home exercise. If you have a *Curriculum Vitae* (CV), consider sharing it with your students as an example.

Case scenario: You want to know more about the educational backgrounds and career paths of practicing forensic anthropologists. A CV will often tell you a great deal about a professional's educational background, employment history, research interests, accomplishments, and other professional activities.

Instructions/Procedure:
- Perform an internet search and locate the CVs of 2 or 3 forensic anthropologists, preferably working in different types of employment (e.g., university, museum, government lab). Many CVs are available online through university or employer websites, or other professional sites such as academia.edu.
- Compare and contrast their education, employment, and other professional activities.

Are there any patterns apparent in the CVs you compared?

_____

_____

_____

Are you able to identify any new education or career goals for yourself?

_____

_____

_____

Do you have a CV? If so, are there elements/components that you would like to add to your own CV? If you do not have one, start one now!

_____

_____

_____

Chapter 2

Osteology and Odontology

OBJECTIVES

The practice of forensic anthropology requires intimate knowledge of the human skeleton including various anatomical planes of reference, the features of skeletal tissue at various structural levels, the names of bones and teeth and locations of certain features, and the ability to differentiate between left and right bones (for paired bones). In the following exercises, you will use your knowledge of human osteology and odontology to identify bones and other features of skeletal anatomy, and document skeletal and dental inventories.

PRINCIPLES OF HUMAN OSTEOLOGY AND ODONTOLOGY

Osteology is the study of bones, and odontology is the study of teeth. Together, bones and teeth comprise the skeleton or skeletal system (Fig. 2.1) which serves a number of functions (Table 2.1). Osteology and odontology primarily focus on the study of morphology (shape) and the names of bones (as well as their parts and features), related anatomical terminology, and internal composition. The study of growth and development provides the background to understanding why bones are shaped the way that they are. Forensic anthropologists must have an intimate knowledge of the human skeleton, with the ability to recognize and identify not only complete bones, but also fragmentary remains, which are commonly encountered in forensic casework.

BONE HISTOLOGY

Osteons represent the basic structural unit of compact bone and are organized parallel to the long axis of the bone. Osteons are roughly cylindrical structures measuring approximately 300 µm in diameter and approximately 3–5 mm in length. Each osteon has a central canal called a Haversian canal which contains the blood and nerve supply. This central canal is surrounded by concentric rings of bone called lamellae. Perpendicular to the Haversian canal are smaller canals called Volkmann's canals which serve as a link between Haversian canals. Located within the lamellae are small cavities called lacunae which house the osteocytes. Individual osteocytes are connected by a series of small channels called canaliculi. When bone is examined histologically, it is usually sectioned transversely relative to the orientation of osteons, resulting in the ability to view osteon cross sections (Fig. 2.2).

REFERENCE TERMINOLOGY

Anatomical directions and planes are used in reference to bones, body parts, their portions, and their relative positions. All of these terms are relative to a standard anatomical position, which for humans is standing, facing with the feet pointing forward, the palms of the hands facing forward, and the thumbs pointed laterally (Fig. 2.3 and Table 2.2). In anatomical position, none of the bones is crossed when the body is viewed from the front. When the terms *left* and *right* are used, they refer to the left and right sides of the individual or bone being studied with respect to anatomical position, not from the perspective of the observer.

SKELETAL ANATOMY

Bones are categorized as being long bones (which are characterized by being mostly tubular, such as limb bones), flat bones (such as those of the cranium), or irregular bones (such as the bones of the vertebral column, wrist, and ankle). Long bones are characterized by a central medullary cavity surrounded by compact and sometimes trabecular bone (see Fig. 2.4). Bones also have various projections, depressions, and foramina which serve as the attachment sites for muscles, the passage of blood vessels and nerves, and other reflections of adjacent anatomy. Some of these general feature terms are defined in Table 2.3.

A Laboratory Manual for Forensic Anthropology. https://doi.org/10.1016/B978-0-12-812201-3.00002-5

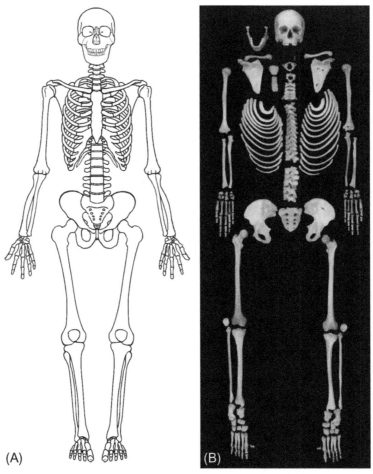

(A)   (B)

FIG. 2.1 Human skeleton—a schematic/homunculus (left) and skeletal remains (right). *((right) Image courtesy of Dennis C. Dirkmaat and Alexandra Klales.)*

TABLE 2.1 Function of the Skeletal System

Functions of the Skeletal System	
1. Protection	Protects organs such as the brain, spinal cord, lungs, and heart
2. Support	Provides a framework to support the body and attachment sites for muscles, tendons, and ligaments
3. Movement	Acts as a system of levers operated by muscles to move the body
4. Blood cell production	Bone marrow is the site of blood cell development
5. Mineral storage	Stores fat and minerals such as calcium and iron
6. Endocrine regulation	Bone cells release hormones involved in the regulation of blood sugar and fat deposition

The *cranial skeleton* refers to the bones of the skull, while the *postcranial skeleton* (or infracranial skeleton) refers to everything inferior to the skull. The postcranial skeleton can be further subdivided into the *axial skeleton*, which consists of bones along and near the body's midline, and the *appendicular skeleton*, which consists of the bones of the limbs as well as their supporting structures where they connect with the axial skeleton.

The skull consists of the entire bony head including the bones of the *cranium* (Fig. 2.5 and Table 2.4) and the *mandible* (Fig. 2.6) for a total of 28 bones. These include the *frontal*, two *parietals*, two *temporals* (each of which contain three

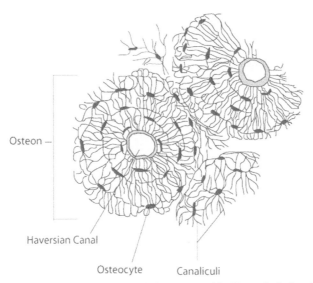

FIG. 2.2 Transverse cross section of human osteons. *(From Gray, H., 1918. Anatomy of the Human Body, Lea & Febiger, Philadelphia, PA.)*

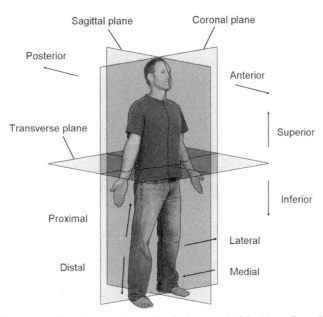

FIG. 2.3 Anatomical planes of reference and directions, relative to *Standard Anatomical Position. (From Christensen, A.M., Passalacqua, N.V., Bartelink, E.J., 2014. Forensic Anthropology: Current Methods and Practice, Academic Press.)*

auditory ossicles: the *malleus, incus,* and *stapes*), the *occipital,* the *sphenoid,* two *maxillae,* two *palatines,* two *inferior nasal conchae,* the *ethmoid,* the *vomer,* two *lacrimals,* two *nasals,* two *zygomatics,* and the mandible. The bones of the cranium can be divided into two groups: the cranial vault or *neurocranium,* consisting of the bones that form the sides, top, and back of the brain case, and the *splanchnocranium* or facial skeleton, consisting of the bones of the face. Several of the bones of the cranium contain *sinuses* (or paranasal sinuses), which are air pockets that are linked to the nasal cavity. Sinuses can be found in the frontal bone, the maxillae, the ethmoid, and the sphenoid, and the mastoid processes of the temporal bone contain sinus-like air cells. Table 2.5 describes several selected features of the skull.

The *axial skeleton* refers to bones on or near the body's midline including the skull as well as the thorax or trunk. Bones of the thorax include the *hyoid, sternum, vertebrae,* and *ribs,* and these bones and some of their features are described in Table 2.6. The hyoid (Fig. 2.7) is the only bone in the body that does not articulate with any other bone. It is located in the anterior neck and serves as a connection point for various structures of the neck and throat. The sternum or breastbone (Fig. 2.8) anchors the anterior ends of ribs 1–7 and also connects with the shoulder girdle. It consists of three major portions: the *manubrium* (the most superior portion), the *body* or corpus sterni (the central portion), and the *xiphoid process* (the most inferior portion).

TABLE 2.2 Anatomical Planes of Reference and Directional Terms

	Standard anatomical position	Standing, facing with the feet pointing forward, the palms of the hands facing forward, and the thumbs pointed laterally. In anatomical position, none of the bones is crossed when the body is viewed from the front
Planes of reference	Sagittal	A plane through the body from front to back that divides the body into left and right halves. Any planar slice through the body that parallels the sagittal plane is called a parasagittal plane; also called mid-sagittal, median, or midline
	Coronal	A plane at right angles to the sagittal plane that divides the body into front and back halves; also called frontal
	Transverse	A plane that slices through the body perpendicular to the sagittal and frontal planes; also called horizontal
	Frankfort	A plane running through the bottom of the left orbit (orbitale) and the upper margin of the left and right external auditory meati (porion); also called Frankfort Horizontal
Directional terms	Superior	Up or toward the head; also called cranial for quadrupeds
	Inferior	Down or away from the head; also called caudal for quadrupeds
	Anterior	Toward the front of the body; also called ventral for quadrupeds
	Posterior	Toward the back of the body; dorsal is used for quadrupeds
	Medial	Toward the midline of the body
	Lateral	Away from the midline of the body
	Proximal	Closest to an articular point; nearest the axial skeleton
	Distal	Farthest from an articular point; away from the axial skeleton
	External	Outer/outside
	Internal	Internal/inside
	Ectocranial	The outer surface of the cranial vault
	Endocranial	The inner surface of the cranial vault
	Superficial	Closest to the surface
	Deep	Farther from the surface
	Subcutaneous	Below the skin
	Palmar	The palm side of the hands
	Plantar	The sole side of the foot
	Dorsal	The top of the foot or back of the hand

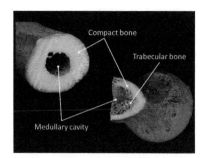

FIG. 2.4 Two femoral cross sections, one from near midshaft (left) and one more proximal (right) showing the relationship of the medullary cavity to the surrounding cortical and trabecular bone. *(Images courtesy of Eric Bartelink.)*

TABLE 2.3 Gross Anatomical Features of Bones

Projections	Articulation	An area where two bones contact at a joint
	Boss	A smooth, broad eminence
	Condyle	A rounded articular process
	Crest	A prominent, sharp ridge of bone
	Eminence	A bony projection, less prominent than a process
	Epicondyle	A nonarticular projection near a condyle
	Facet	A small articular surface
	Hamulus	A hook-shaped projection
	Head	A large rounded articular end of a bone
	Line	A raised linear surface
	Malleolus	A rounded protuberance of the ankle
	Neck	The section of a bone between the head and the shaft
	Process	A bony prominence
	Ridge	A linear bony elevation
	Spine	A long, thin process
	Torus	A bony thickening
	Trochanter	A large blunt process of the femur
	Tuberosity	A large roughened eminence
	Tubercle	A small roughened eminence
	Alveolus	A tooth socket
	Canal	A tunnel-like foramen
Depressions and holes	Fontanelle	A cartilaginous space between cranial bones of an infant
	Foramen	A hole through a bone
	Fossa	A broad, shallow depressed area
	Fovea	A pit-like depression
	Groove	A long pit or furrow
	Meatus	A short canal
	Sinus	A cavity within a cranial bone
	Sulcus	A long, wide groove
	Suture	A fibrous, interlocking joint of the cranial bones

Modified from White, T.D., Black, M.T., Folkens, P.A., 2011. Human Osteology, third ed. Academic Press, San Diego, CA.

There are 24 moveable (unfused) vertebrae of three different types in different regions of the *vertebral column* or *spinal column* (Fig. 2.9). The 7 *cervical vertebrae* are the most superior, forming the neck. The 12 *thoracic vertebrae* make up the upper and middle back, and the 5 *lumbar vertebrae* make up the lower back. Vertebrae are typically referred by their type and number counting from superior to inferior. For example, cervical vertebra number 5, or C5, is the fifth of the cervical vertebra from the top; thoracic vertebra number 10, or T10, is the tenth of the thoracic vertebrae; and lumbar vertebra number 3, or L3, is the third of the lumbar vertebrae. All vertebrae have a central foramen called the *vertebral foramen* through which the spinal cord passes.

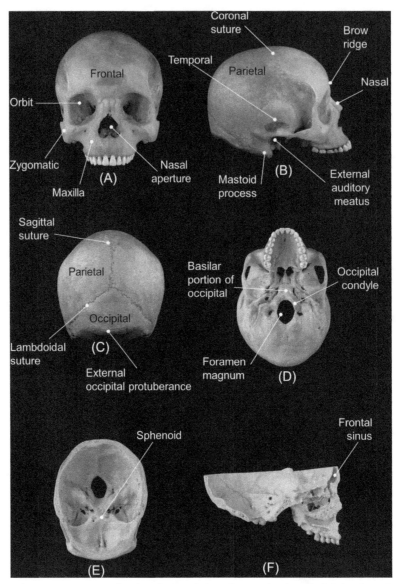

FIG. 2.5 Bones and features of the cranium: (A) anterior view, (B) lateral view, (C) posterior view, (D) inferior view, (E) superior view, and (F) lateral view along mid-sagittal plane. *(Photos by Rebecca Meeusen; Specimens courtesy of the National Museum of Natural History; From Christensen, A.M., Passalacqua, N.V., Bartelink, E.J., 2014. Forensic Anthropology: Current Methods and Practice, Academic Press.)*

Cervical vertebrae (Fig. 2.10) are the smallest of the vertebrae and are characterized by small *vertebral bodies* and a foramen through each of their *transverse processes* (called *transverse foramina*). The first two vertebrae are especially distinctive (Fig. 2.11). The first cervical vertebra (also called the *atlas*) is ring shaped, with large superior facets for articulation with the occipital bone. The second cervical vertebra (also called the *axis*) is characterized by a superior projection called the dens (also called the *odontoid process*) which allows the head to pivot on the spine.

Thoracic vertebrae make up the middle portion of the spinal column and can be distinguished by their facets for articulation with the ribs, one on each side of the vertebral body, and one on each transverse process (Fig. 2.12). Though the typical number of thoracic vertebrae is 12, accessory thoracic vertebrae (usually accompanied by accessory ribs) are not uncommon. Lumbar vertebrae are the most inferior of the moveable vertebra and are characterized by large vertebral bodies due to their greater weight-bearing function (Fig. 2.13).

At the distal end of the vertebral column is the *sacrum* which is formed of four to six (typically five) fused vertebral segments (Fig. 2.14). This bone also serves as the posterior portion of the pelvis. Inferior to the sacrum is the variably fused *coccyx* which represents the vestigial human tail and consists of three to five variably fused segments.

TABLE 2.4 Bones and Features of the Skull

Bones of the skull and associated features	Frontal bone	Bone comprising the front-most portion of the neurocranium and the superior portions of the orbits
	Frontal squama	The vertical portion making up the forehead
	Horizontal portion	The portion comprising the orbital roofs
	Superciliary arches	The bony tori over the orbits (also called the brow ridge)
	Parietal bones	Paired bones forming the sides and roof of the cranial vault
	Parietal eminence	The large, rounded eminence in the center of the bone
	Meningeal grooves	Vascular grooves on the endocranial surface from the middle meningeal arteries
	Temporal bones	Paired bones forming the lateral cranial vault and part of the cranial base; also house the auditory ossicles
	Temporal squama	The vertical plate-like portion
	Petrous pyramid	The dense endocranial portion
	External auditory meatus (EAM)	The opening of the ear canal
	Mastoid process	The roughened inferior projection
	Auditory ossicles	Small bones housed in the temporal bone; each side has three—the malleus, incus, and stapes
	Occipital bone	Bone forming the back of the cranial vault and base
	Squamous portion	The vertical portion that is part of the cranial base
	Basilar portion	The thick anterior/inferior projection
	Foramen magnum	The large hole for the passage of the brain stem
	External occipital protuberance	The variably pronounced projection on the posterior ectocranial surface
	Occipital condyles	The articular surfaces for the first cervical vertebra
	Maxillae	Paired bones forming a majority of the face
	Alveolar process	The portion that holds the teeth
	Alveoli	Holes for the roots of the teeth
	Anterior nasal spine	Projection forming the inferior portion of the nasal aperture
	Palatines	Paired L-shaped bones forming the posterior palate
	Vomer	Small thin bone that divides the nasal cavity
	Inferior nasal conchae	Paired bones forming the lateral walls of the nasal cavity
	Ethmoid	Spongy bone located between the orbits
	Lacrimals	Thin rectangular bones of the medial walls of the orbits
	Nasals	Paired bones that form the bridge of the nose
	Zygomatics	Paired bones of the cheeks
	Sphenoid	Bone situated between the cranial vault and the face
	Body	The robust portion on the midline
	Greater wings	The laterally extending segments
	Lesser wings	Posterior projections on the endocranial surface
	Mandible	Lower jaw
	Body	Thick anterior portion that holds the teeth
	Ramus	Thin vertical portion that articulates with the cranial base

Modified from White, T.D., Black, M.T., Folkens, P.A., 2011. Human Osteology, third ed. Academic Press, San Diego, CA.

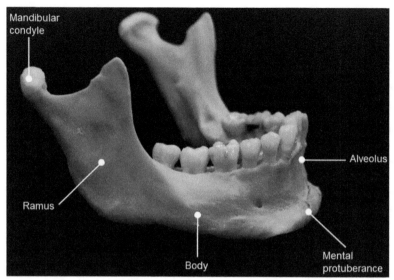

FIG. 2.6 Features of the mandible. *(From Christensen, A.M., Passalacqua, N.V., Bartelink, E.J., 2014. Forensic Anthropology: Current Methods and Practice, Academic Press.)*

TABLE 2.5 Sutures and Other Features of the Skull

Sutures	Sagittal suture	The articulation between the two parietal bones
	Coronal suture	The articulation between the frontal and parietal bones
	Lambdoidal suture	The articulation between the occipital and the parietals and temporals
	Metopic suture	The articulation between the left and right frontal halves, only occasionally retained into adulthood
	Basilar suture	The articulation between the sphenoid and the basilar portion of the occipital bone; also called the spheno-occipital synchondrosis
Other features of the skull	Orbits	The sockets for the eyes, formed by numerous cranial bones
	Nasal aperture	The hole for the nose, formed by portions of the nasal bones and maxillae
	Sinuses	Air pockets, located in the frontal, maxillae, ethmoid, and sphenoid bones
	Temporal line	Raised line that anchors the temporalis muscle, which crosses the frontal and parietal bones
	Temporomandibular joint	The joint where the temporal bones articulate with the mandible

Modified from White, T.D., Black, M.T., Folkens, P.A., 2011. Human Osteology, third ed. Academic Press, San Diego, CA.

There are 12 ribs on each side (24 in total) which form the *rib cage* (Fig. 2.15). Each rib articulates posteriorly with the vertebrae, and the first 10 ribs (ribs 1–10) articulate anteriorly with *costal cartilage* connected to the sternum. Ribs 11 and 12 do not connect to the sternum in this way and are therefore called "floating ribs." Ribs 1 and 2 can be distinguished because they are flatter and more tightly curved. Sequentially, ribs 1–7 increase in length and then decrease in length from ribs 8 to 12. Also, with each sequential rib, the angle becomes more obtuse.

The appendicular skeleton consists of the bones of the arms and legs as well as their supporting structures where they articulate with the axial skeleton. The supporting structure of the upper limb is referred to as the *shoulder girdle*, consisting of the *clavicle* and *scapula*, which connects the trunk to the arm (Fig. 2.16). The upper limb consists of the arm, wrist, and hand. The bones of the arm include the *humerus* (Fig. 2.17), which makes up the upper arm, and the *radius* (Fig. 2.18) and *ulna* (Fig. 2.19), which make up the lower arm (also called the forearm). The wrist consists of eight small irregular bones called *carpals*. The hand consists of five *metacarpals*, one for each digit or ray. The metacarpals are numbered one through five counting from lateral (the thumb side) to medial (the little finger side). The fingers consist of bones called

TABLE 2.6 Bones and Features of the Axial Skeleton

Bones of the axial skeleton and associated features	Hyoid bone	U-shaped bone of the anterior neck
	Sternum	The breast bone, which connects the shoulder girdle to the thorax, and anchors anterior ribs 1–7
	Manubrium	The wide, superior portion of the sternum
	Corpus sterni	The thin central portion of the sternum
	Xiphoid	The variably fused inferior tip of the sternum
	Vertebrae	Bones of the spinal column
	Body	The anterior and primary weight-bearing portion
	Vertebral arch	The posterior portion, enclosing the spinal cord
	Vertebral foramen	The hole through which the spinal cord passes; comprised of the body and the vertebral arch
	Spinous process	The most posterior projection
	Transverse process	The laterally directed projections
	Articular facets	Projections for articulation with adjacent vertebrae
	Cervical vertebrae	The most superior vertebrae in the spinal column, normally seven total
	C1 (Atlas)	The first (most superior) cervical vertebra, which articulates with the occipital bone
	C2 (Axis)	The second cervical vertebra, which forms a pivot with the atlas
	Transverse foramen	Foramen through the transverse process
	Thoracic vertebrae	The middle vertebrae in the spinal column, normally 12 total
	Costal fovea	Articular facets for the ribs
	Lumbar vertebra	The most inferior vertebrae in the spinal column, normally five total
	Mammillary process	Superior projection for the articular facets
	Sacrum	The most inferior portion of the spinal column and the posterior portion of the pelvis, formed of 4–6 fused segments
	Coccyx	The variably fused 3–5 segments of the vestigial tail
	Ribs	Long slender bones of the rib cage, normally 12 on each side or 24 total
	Head	The most proximal portion which articulates with the thoracic vertebral body
	Shaft	The curved main part of the rib
	Sternal end	The most anterior portion which articulates with the costal cartilage
Other features of the axial skeleton	Vertebral column	Comprised of the cervical, thoracic, and lumbar vertebra as well as the sacrum and coccyx
	Rib cage	The protective structure formed by the 24 ribs

Modified from White, T.D., Black, M.T., Folkens, P.A., 2011. Human Osteology, third ed. Academic Press, San Diego, CA.

manual phalanges; the first digit (the thumb) consists of two phalanges (a proximal and a distal), while digits two through five each consist of three (a proximal, intermediate, and distal) (Fig. 2.20). Often, accessory bones of the hand and wrist occur and are called *sesamoid* bones. Some features of the upper limb are described in Table 2.7.

The *pelvic girdle*, consisting of the two *innominates* [also called *ossa coxa* (singular *os coxae*)] along with the sacrum, connects the trunk to the lower limb (Fig. 2.21). The innominates form from three fused portions called the *ilium, ischium,* and *pubis*. The lower limb consists of the leg, ankle, and foot. The bones of the leg include the *femur* (Fig. 2.22), which makes up the upper leg, the *patella* or kneecap (Fig. 2.23), and the *tibia* (Fig. 2.24) and *fibula* (Fig. 2.25) which make up the lower leg. The ankle consists of seven irregular bones called *tarsals*. The foot consists of five *metatarsals*, one for each digit. The first toe (or "big toe") consists of two *pedal phalanges*, while digits 2–5 consist of three. Sesamoid bones may also occur in the ankle and foot (Fig. 2.26). Some features of the lower limb are described in Table 2.8.

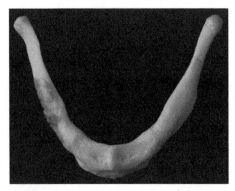

FIG. 2.7 Hyoid. *(Photo by Re becca Meeusen; Specimen courtesy of the National Museum of Natural History; From Christensen, A.M., Passalacqua, N.V., Bartelink, E.J., 2014. Forensic Anthropology: Current Methods and Practice, Academic Press.)*

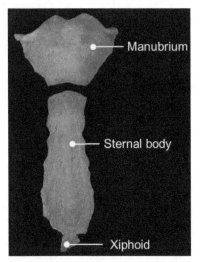

FIG. 2.8 Sternum. *(Photo by Rebecca Meeusen; Specimen courtesy of the National Museum of Natural History; From Christensen, A.M., Passalacqua, N.V., Bartelink, E.J., 2014. Forensic Anthropology: Current Methods and Practice, Academic Press.)*

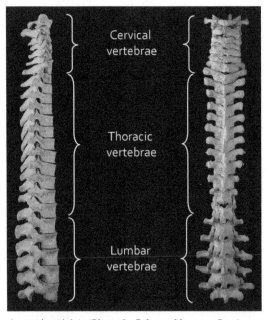

FIG. 2.9 Vertebral column: lateral (left) and posterior (right). *(Photos by Rebecca Meeusen; Specimens courtesy of the National Museum of Natural History; From Christensen, A.M., Passalacqua, N.V., Bartelink, E.J., 2014. Forensic Anthropology: Current Methods and Practice, Academic Press.)*

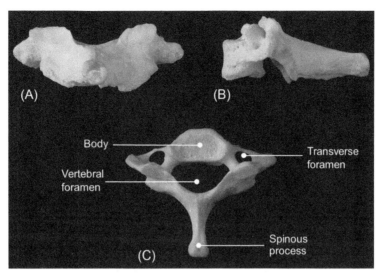

FIG. 2.10 Cervical vertebrae: (A) posterior, (B) lateral, and (C) superior. *(Photos by Rebecca Meeusen; Specimens courtesy of the National Museum of Natural History; From Christensen, A.M., Passalacqua, N.V., Bartelink, E.J., 2014. Forensic Anthropology: Current Methods and Practice, Academic Press.)*

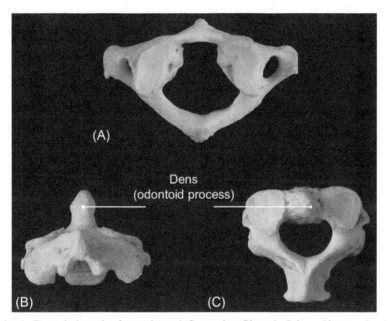

FIG. 2.11 (A) cervical vertebra 1, (B) cervical vertebra 2 posterior, and (C) superior. *(Photos by Rebecca Meeusen; Specimens courtesy of the National Museum of Natural History; From Christensen, A.M., Passalacqua, N.V., Bartelink, E.J., 2014. Forensic Anthropology: Current Methods and Practice, Academic Press.)*

DENTITION

The dentition consists of the teeth of the cranium and the mandible. Teeth articulate with bone via the *alveoli* or tooth sockets. For the upper dentition, the tooth sockets occur in the maxillae; in the lower dentition they are in the mandible. Due to their placement and orientation within the skeletal system, the dentition has its own set of directional terms (Table 2.9 and Fig. 2.27).

Teeth have two major portions (Fig. 2.28 and Table 2.10). The *crown* is the portion of the tooth that lies above the gumline (typically the visible portion in the mouth), and the *root*, which is the portion below the gumline that anchors the tooth in the alveolus. Teeth contain three different tissue types. *Dentin* forms the main part of the inner tooth. *Enamel* covers the external surface of the *crown* and is the hardest tissue on the body. *Cementum* covers the external surface of the root. Within a small cavity in the tooth is the *pulp*, consisting of blood vessels, nerves, connective tissue, and odontoblasts.

Teeth take four basic forms that are related to their functions. *Incisors* are the blade-like anterior teeth that are used for cutting. *Canines* are conical teeth lying just posterior to the incisors and are used for gripping and tearing. *Premolars* (also

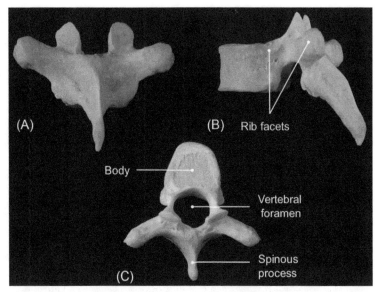

FIG. 2.12   Thoracic vertebrae: (A) posterior, (B) lateral, and (C) superior. *(Photos by Rebecca Meeusen; Specimens courtesy of the National Museum of Natural History; From Christensen, A.M., Passalacqua, N.V., Bartelink, E.J., 2014. Forensic Anthropology: Current Methods and Practice, Academic Press.)*

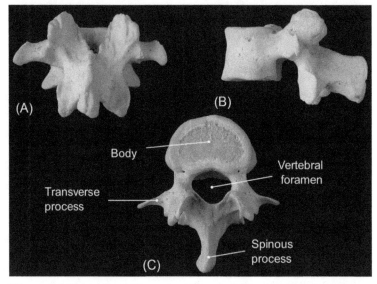

FIG. 2.13   Lumbar vertebrae: (A) posterior, (B) lateral, and (C) superior. *(Photos by Rebecca Meeusen; Specimens courtesy of the National Museum of Natural History; From Christensen, A.M., Passalacqua, N.V., Bartelink, E.J., 2014. Forensic Anthropology: Current Methods and Practice, Academic Press.)*

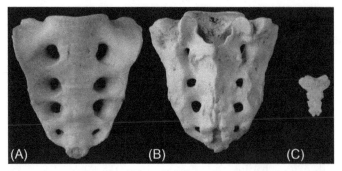

FIG. 2.14   Sacrum: (A) anterior, (B) posterior, and (C) coccyx. *(Photos by Rebecca Meeusen; Specimens courtesy of the National Museum of Natural History; From Christensen, A.M., Passalacqua, N.V., Bartelink, E.J., 2014. Forensic Anthropology: Current Methods and Practice, Academic Press.)*

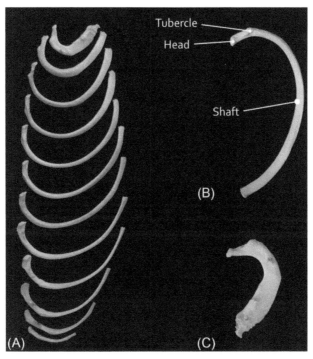

FIG. 2.15 Ribs: (A) ribs 1–12, (B) typical rib, and (C) first rib. *(Photos by Rebecca Meeusen; Specimens courtesy of the National Museum of Natural History; From Christensen, A.M., Passalacqua, N.V., Bartelink, E.J., 2014. Forensic Anthropology: Current Methods and Practice, Academic Press.)*

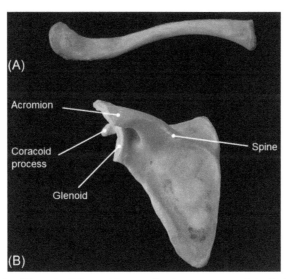

FIG. 2.16 (A) Clavicle and (B) scapula. *(Photos by Rebecca Meeusen; Specimens courtesy of the National Museum of Natural History; From Christensen, A.M., Passalacqua, N.V., Bartelink, E.J., 2014. Forensic Anthropology: Current Methods and Practice, Academic Press.)*

called *bicuspids*) are two-cusped teeth that are used for tearing and crushing, and they are transitional in form and function between the anterior and posterior teeth. *Molars* are the most posterior teeth which are used for grinding. The distal-most (third) molars are sometimes called *wisdom teeth* and are the most variable teeth in the human dentition.

A dental formula is a system for summarizing the number of each type of tooth (incisor, canine, premolar, molar) in each quadrant of the mouth for a species. In humans, the deciduous dentition consists of 20 total teeth, with the dental formula 2102 (or 2102/2102), indicating two incisors, one canine, zero premolars, and two molars in each quadrant. The permanent dentition consists of 32 teeth in total, with the dental formula 2123 (or 2123/2123), indicating two incisors, one canine, two premolars, and three molars in each quadrant.

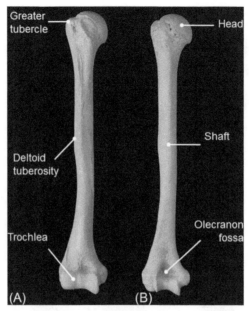

FIG. 2.17 Humerus: (A) anterior and (B) posterior. *(Photos by Rebecca Meeusen; Specimens courtesy of the National Museum of Natural History; From Christensen, A.M., Passalacqua, N.V., Bartelink, E.J., 2014. Forensic Anthropology: Current Methods and Practice, Academic Press.)*

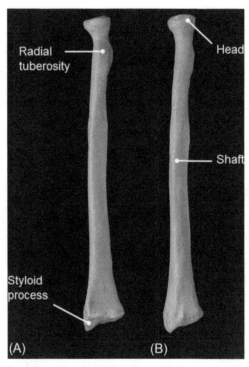

FIG. 2.18 Radius: (A) anterior and (B) posterior. *(Photos by Rebecca Meeusen; Specimens courtesy of the National Museum of Natural History; From Christensen, A.M., Passalacqua, N.V., Bartelink, E.J., 2014. Forensic Anthropology: Current Methods and Practice, Academic Press.)*

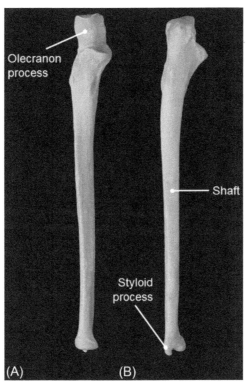

FIG. 2.19 Ulna: (A) anterior and (B) posterior. *(Photos by Rebecca Meeusen; Specimens courtesy of the National Museum of Natural History; From Christensen, A.M., Passalacqua, N.V., Bartelink, E.J., 2014. Forensic Anthropology: Current Methods and Practice, Academic Press.)*

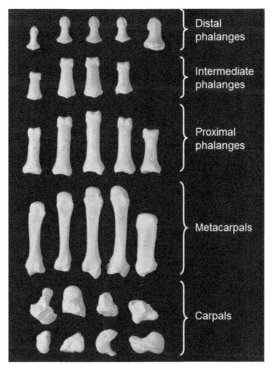

FIG. 2.20 Bones of the wrist, hand, and fingers. *(Photos by Rebecca Meeusen; Specimens courtesy of the National Museum of Natural History; From Christensen, A.M., Passalacqua, N.V., Bartelink, E.J., 2014. Forensic Anthropology: Current Methods and Practice, Academic Press.)*

TABLE 2.7 Bones and Features of the Upper Limb

Bones of the upper limb and associated features	Clavicle	S-shaped bone that articulates with the sternum and scapula; also called the collar bone
	Scapula	Flat, triangular-shaped bone; also called the shoulder blade
	Spine	The raised posterior ridge
	Acromion process	The lateral most projection of the spine
	Coracoid process	The anterolateral projection
	Glenoid fossa	Shallow cavity that articulates with the humerus
	Humerus	The bone of the upper arm
	Head	Rounded portion that articulates with the scapula
	Greater and lesser tubercles	Blunt eminences on the anterior aspect of the proximal humerus
	Deltoid tuberosity	Eminence on the lateral shaft for insertion of the deltoid muscle
	Trochlea	Spool-shaped distal region, for articulation with the ulna
	Capitulum	Dome-shaped distal region, for articulation with the radius
	Olecranon fossa	Posterior hollow, articulates with the olecranon process
	Radius	The lateral bone of the forearm
	Head	Rounded proximal end, for articulation with the humerus
	Radial tuberosity	Eminence on the proximal anteromedial for insertion of the biceps muscle
	Interosseous crest	Pointed medial aspect of the shaft which serves as the attachment for the interosseous ligament which connects to the interosseous crest of the ulna
	Styloid process	The sharp projection on distal end
	Ulnar notch	Concave articulation with the ulna
	Ulna	The medial bone of the forearm
	Olecranon process	The proximal projection which is the insertion for the triceps muscle
	Interosseous crest	Pointed lateral aspect of the shaft which serves as the attachment for the interosseous ligament which connects to the interosseous crest of the radius
	Styloid process	The sharp projection on the distal end
	Carpals	The eight bones of the wrist, consisting of the scaphoid, lunate, triquetral, pisiform, trapezium, trapezoid, capitate, and hamate
	Metacarpals	The five bones of the hand
	Manual phalanges	The bones of the fingers; on each side there are five proximal phalanges, four intermediate phalanges, and five distal phalanges (singular: phalanx)
Other features of the upper limb	Shoulder girdle	Supporting structure of the upper limb, consisting of the clavicle and scapula
	Elbow	The joint between the humerus and the radius/ulna
	Sesamoid bone	Variable accessory bone of the hand or wrist found in a tendon
	Nutrient foramen	Present on the anterior surfaces the humerus, radius, and ulna; provides passage for vascular supply

Modified from White, T.D., Black, M.T., Folkens, P.A., 2011. Human Osteology, third ed. Academic Press, San Diego, CA.

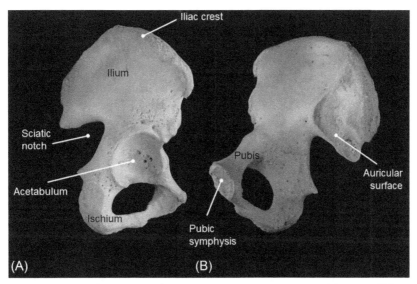

FIG. 2.21 Innominate: (A) lateral and (B) medial. *(Photos by Rebecca Meeusen; Specimens courtesy of the National Museum of Natural History; From Christensen, A.M., Passalacqua, N.V., Bartelink, E.J., 2014. Forensic Anthropology: Current Methods and Practice, Academic Press.)*

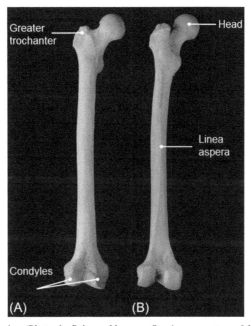

FIG. 2.22 Femur: (A) anterior and (B) posterior. *(Photos by Rebecca Meeusen; Specimens courtesy of the National Museum of Natural History; From Christensen, A.M., Passalacqua, N.V., Bartelink, E.J., 2014. Forensic Anthropology: Current Methods and Practice, Academic Press.)*

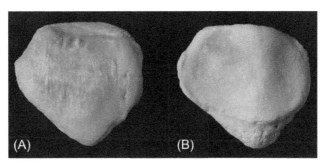

FIG. 2.23 Patella: (A) anterior and (B) posterior. *(Photos by Rebecca Meeusen; Specimens courtesy of the National Museum of Natural History; From Christensen, A.M., Passalacqua, N.V., Bartelink, E.J., 2014. Forensic Anthropology: Current Methods and Practice, Academic Press.)*

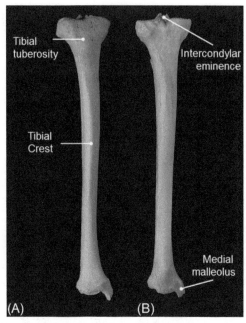

FIG. 2.24 Tibia: (A) anterior and (B) posterior. *(Photos by Rebecca Meeusen; Specimens courtesy of the National Museum of Natural History; From Christensen, A.M., Passalacqua, N.V., Bartelink, E.J., 2014. Forensic Anthropology: Current Methods and Practice, Academic Press.)*

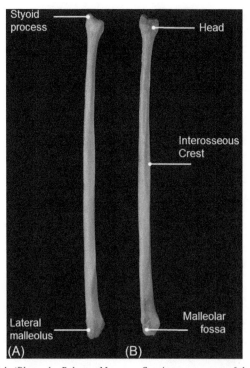

FIG. 2.25 Fibula: (A) lateral and (B) medial. *(Photos by Rebecca Meeusen; Specimens courtesy of the National Museum of Natural History; From Christensen, A.M., Passalacqua, N.V., Bartelink, E.J., 2014. Forensic Anthropology: Current Methods and Practice, Academic Press.)*

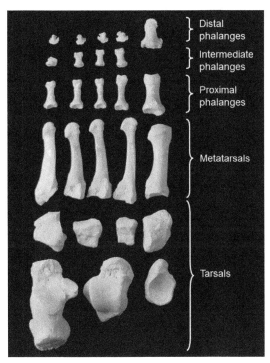

FIG. 2.26 Bones of the ankle, foot, and toes. *(Photos by Rebecca Meeusen; Specimens courtesy of the National Museum of Natural History; From Christensen, A.M., Passalacqua, N.V., Bartelink, E.J., 2014. Forensic Anthropology: Current Methods and Practice, Academic Press.)*

TABLE 2.8 Bones and Features of the Lower Limb

Bones of the lower limb and associated features	Innominate	Hip bone; also called *os coxa*
	Ilium	The blade-like superior portion
	Ischium	The posteroinferior portion
	Pubis	The anterior portion
	Acetabulum	The round hollow which forms the hip socket and articulates with the femoral head
	Greater sciatic notch	Wide notch on the ilium
	Pubic symphysis	The anterior surface where the left and right os coxae meet
	Auricular surface	The posterior surface of the ilium which articulates with the sacrum
	Femur	The bone of the upper leg
	Femoral head	The round proximal part that articulates with the os coxae
	Linea aspera	The raised ridge on the posterior shaft
	Condyles	The large protrusions on the posterior distal portion
	Trochanters	Blunt prominences on the proximal posterior surface
	Patella	The knee cap
	Tibia	The major of the two lower leg bones; also called the shin bone
	Tibial tuberosity	The roughened area on the anterior surface of the proximal end
	Medial malleolus	The projection on the medial surface of the distal end
	Anterior crest	The sharp ridge forming the shin

(Continued)

TABLE 2.8 Bones and Features of the Lower Limb—Continued

	Fibula	The smaller, lateral bone of the lower leg
	Malleolus	The projection on the lateral surface of the distal end
	Tarsals	The seven bones of the ankle, consisting of the talus, calcaneus, navicular, cuboid, medial cuneiform, intermediate cuneiform, and lateral cuneiform
	Metatarsals	The five bones of the foot
	Pedal phalanges	The bones of the toes; on each side there are five proximal phalanges, four intermediate phalanges, and five distal phalanges
Other features of the lower limb	Pelvic girdle	Supporting structure of the lower limb, consisting of the os coxae
	Knee	The joint between the femur and tibia and also including the patella
	Sesamoid bone	Variable accessory bone of the foot or ankle found in a tendon
	Nutrient foramen	Present on the posterior surfaces the femur, tibia, and fibula; provides passage for vascular supply

Modified from White, T.D., Black, M.T., Folkens, P.A., 2011. Human Osteology, third ed. Academic Press, San Diego, CA.

TABLE 2.9 Directional Terms of the Dentition

Dental directional terms	Mesial	Toward the point on the midline where the central incisors contact each other
	Distal	Away from the point on the midline where the central incisors contact each other
	Lingual	Toward the tongue
	Labial	Toward the lips (for anterior teeth)
	Buccal	Toward the cheeks (for posterior teeth)
	Interproximal	In contact with adjacent teeth in the same jaw
	Occlusal	Facing the opposite dental arch, usually the chewing surface
	Incisal	The biting or occlusal edge of incisors
	Mesiodistal	Axis running from medial to distal
	Buccolingual	Axis running from buccal or labial to lingual; also called labiolingual

Modified from White, T.D., Black, M.T., Folkens, P.A., 2011. Human Osteology, third ed. Academic Press, San Diego, CA.

SKELETAL INVENTORY PROCEDURE

A skeletal inventory is a documented record of each skeletal element present (including teeth). This should include, at a minimum, the name of the bone, whether the bone is from the left side or the right side, and whether the bone is complete or incomplete. For most bones (and even many bone fragments) it is possible to use certain features to determine from which side (left or right) the bone originates. Some siding and orientation techniques for bones and teeth can be found in Appendix A: Skeletal Siding and Orientation Guide. An inventory may also include the presence of any nonhuman skeletal bones, as well as nonskeletal material present (such as soft tissue, insects, clothing, or other artifacts). An inventory can be completed in narrative form, but often tables or charts are used (see, e.g., Appendix B: Skeletal Inventory Form and Appendix C: Dental Charting Forms).

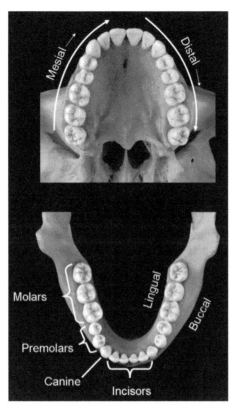

FIG. 2.27 Features and directions of the dentition. *(Photos by Rebecca Meeusen; Specimens courtesy of the National Museum of Natural History; From Christensen, A.M., Passalacqua, N.V., Bartelink, E.J., 2014. Forensic Anthropology: Current Methods and Practice, Academic Press.)*

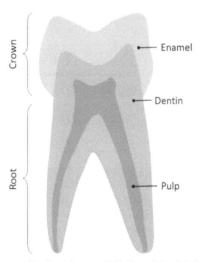

FIG. 2.28 Features of the teeth. *(From Christensen, A.M., Passalacqua, N.V., Bartelink, E.J., 2014. Forensic Anthropology: Current Methods and Practice, Academic Press.)*

TABLE 2.10 Teeth and Features of the Dentition

Tooth types	Incisors	Blade-like teeth of the anterior dentition used for cutting; each jaw contains four
	Canines	Conical teeth distal to the incisors used for grabbing; each jaw contains two
	Premolars	Two-cusped, transitional teeth between the canines and molars; each jaw contains four
	Molars	Four- to five-cusped distal teeth used for grinding; each jaw contains six
Tooth features	Crown	The part of the tooth above the gumline and covered with enamel
	Neck	The junction of the crown and the root
	Root	The part below the gumline that anchors the tooth in the alveolus
	Cusp	A projection on the occlusal surface of a crown
	Enamel	The tissue that covers the crown
	Dentin	The tissue that forms the core of the crown and root
	Cemento-enamel junction	Where the enamel meets the root
	Cementum	The tissue on the external surface of the roots
Other features of the dentition	Alveoli	The tooth sockets, where the teeth articulate with the maxillae and the mandible (singular: alveolus)
	Calculus	A calcified deposit resulting from plaque often found on tooth crowns
	Carious lesion	A lesion or hole from tooth decay
	Deciduous dentition	The first set of teeth to develop; also called primary dentition or "baby teeth"
	Permanent dentition	The second set of teeth to develop; also called secondary dentition or adult teeth
	Crypt	Alveolar pocket where tooth development occurs

Modified from White, T.D., Black, M.T., Folkens, P.A., 2011. Human Osteology, third ed. Academic Press, San Diego, CA.

EXERCISE 2.1   Anatomical Reference Planes and Directions

Materials needed:
- None

Note to instructors: This exercise can be carried out individually, in groups, or as an instructor-led class exercise.

Case scenario: Knowing that you would like to be a forensic anthropologist, you understand that being familiar with anatomical reference terminology is critical to being a well-trained osteologist.

Instructions/Procedure:
- Stand (or imagine yourself standing) in standard anatomical position.

Which plane divides your body into left and right halves?

_____

Relative to your *sternum*, where is your *cranium* positioned? Your *second thoracic vertebra?*

_____

Relative to your *humerus*, where is your *ulna* positioned? Your *scapula*?

_____

Why is having a standard anatomical position necessary?

_____
_____
_____

EXERCISE 2.2   Bone Microstructure Identification

Materials needed:
- Image provided in this exercise

Note to instructors: This exercise can be supplemented or replaced with histological slides of human bone, if available. Histology slides can be acquired from anatomical supply sources, or (if you have access to a histology laboratory and trained personnel), may be prepared specifically for your course.

Case scenario: A small fragment of suspected bone was found in the trunk of the abandoned car of a homicide suspect. Because there were no morphological features present to identify the material as bone or as being of human origin, the following histological slide was created from that bone fragment and sent to you from a medical examiner's office.

Instructions/Procedure:
- Identify the features indicated by the arrows on the lines provided.
   - If bone histology slides and a microscope are available, locate the following structures on the sample: Osteon, Haversian canal, Volkmann's canal, osteocyte, canaliculi.

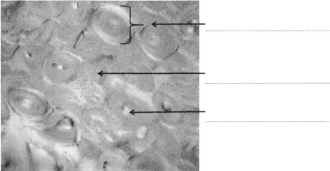

In which plane was this bone sectioned?

_____

Why might you not see any Volkmann's canals in this image?

_____
_____

EXERCISE 2.3   Bone and Feature Identification and Siding

Materials needed:
- Images provided in this exercise
- Figures and Tables in this chapter
- Appendix A: Skeletal Siding and Orientation Guide

Note to instructors: This exercise can be supplemented or replaced with real or replica human bones. Comparative exemplars (such as an articulated or disarticulated skeleton) can also be used for reference if available.

Case scenario: You have received some skeletal remains from law enforcement for analysis, which they believe to be from a homicide victim. One of the first things you will need to determine is which bones are present, and from which side they originate. In addition, the identification of certain features will be needed for your examination.

Instructions/Procedure:
- Using the figures and tables in this chapter (and optional skeletal material or replicas), identify and learn the bones and features described.
- For each of the bones below, identify the name of the bone, the side, and the feature indicated.

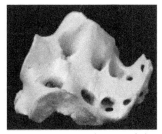

(Image courtesy of Eric Bartelink.)

Bone: _____

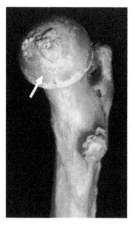

(Image courtesy of Eric Bartelink.)

Bone: _____

Side: _____

Feature: _____

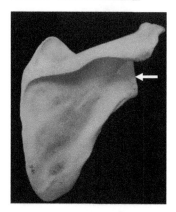

(Image courtesy of Eric Bartelink.)

Bone: _____

Side: _____

Feature: _____

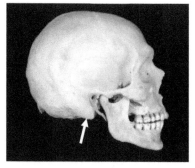

(Image courtesy of Eric Bartelink.)

Bone: _____

Side: _____

Feature: _____

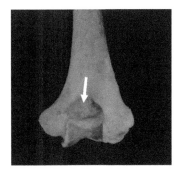

(Image courtesy of Eric Bartelink.)
Bone: _____
Side: _____
Feature: _____

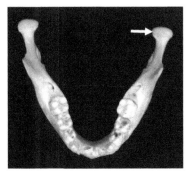

(Image courtesy of Eric Bartelink.)
Bone: _____
Side: _____
Feature: _____

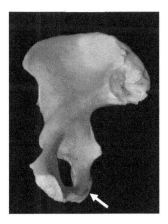

(Image courtesy of Eric Bartelink.)
Bone: _____
Side: _____
Feature: _____

Were there certain bones for which siding and feature identification were more challenging? If so, which bones and why?

_____

What issues may be involved in performing an inventory (particularly siding) based only on photographs?

_____
_____
_____

EXERCISE 2.4   Skeletal Inventory

Materials needed:
- Images provided in this exercise
- Appendix B: Skeletal Inventory Form

Note to instructors: This exercise can be supplemented or replaced with real or replica human bones if available.

Case scenario: Investigators have delivered a partial human skeleton to you for analysis. They believe that the victim was dismembered and that other parts of the skeleton may be found later in other locations. You have decided to start by documenting an inventory of the evidence received so far.

Instructions/Procedure:
- Using Appendix B, document a skeletal inventory for the following assemblage of skeletal material.

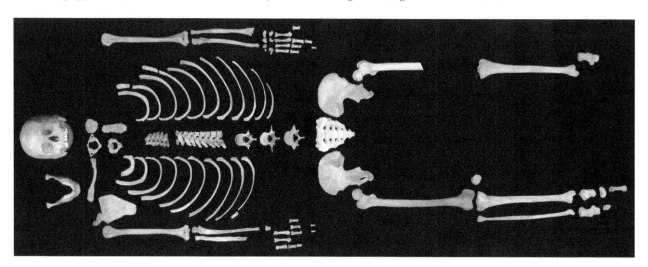

(Image courtesy of Dennis C. Dirkmaat.)

Why is a skeletal inventory important?

_____

_____

_____

In addition to an Inventory Form, what other types of documentation may be used to record which parts of the skeleton were recovered/received?

_____

_____

EXERCISE 2.5   Other Siding Techniques

Materials needed:
- Real or replica human skeletal material

Note to instructors: This exercise can be supplemented with bones in addition to those listed here. If time allows, encourage students to complete the exercise for all or most of the skeleton.

Case scenario: In addition to the siding techniques described in Appendix A, there are many other features and methods that can be used to determine which side of the body a bone is from. Especially since bones can often be fragmentary in casework, a good osteologist will be familiar with a number of different methods for siding various portions of bones.

Instructions/Procedure:
- For each of the following bones, describe a feature or method (other than those in Appendix A, or any supplementary textbook you may be using) that can be used to differentiate the left and right.
- For bilateral bones (i.e., those for which there is one left and one right) you will want to identify differences between left and right sides of the body. For single bones (i.e., midline bones for which there are not separate left and right bones) you will want to identify differences between the left and right halves.

Bone	Siding Method
Scapula	
Clavicle	
Humerus	
Radius	
Femur	
Tibia	
Mandible	
Lumbar vertebra	

EXERCISE 2.6 Charting Dentition

Materials needed:
- Images provided in this exercise
- Appendix C: Dental Charting Forms

Note to instructors: This exercise can be supplemented or replaced with real or replica human dentition if available.

Case scenario: As part of a skeletal inventory from a case involving an isolated cranium, you decide that it would also be helpful to chart the dentition.

Instructions/Procedure:
- Using Appendix C, chart the maxillary dentition of the cranium based on the image below.

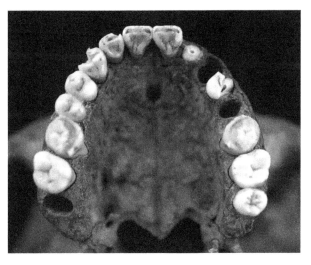

(Image courtesy of Eric Bartelink.)

Why is it important to document which teeth are present with skeletal remains?

_____

_____

For additional practice, chart your own dentition and/or the dentition of a classmate. Did you find this easier or more challenging than charting the dentition of skeletal remains?

_____

_____

EXERCISE 2.7 Anatomical Reference Directions

Materials needed:
- Table provided in this exercise

Note to instructors: This exercise can be supplemented or replaced with real or replica human bones.

Case Scenario: When siding and describing bones in a skeletal inventory, especially when bones are fragmentary, is important to know the positions of certain features with respect to the overall bone.

Instructions/Procedure:
- For each of the following features, use appropriate anatomical reference terminology to describe the location/orientation of this feature on the bone.

Feature	Description of Location
Mastoid process of the temporal bone	
Head of the femur	
Spinous process of a vertebra	
Acromion process of the scapula	
Pubic symphysis of the innominate	
Styloid process of the radius	

Chapter 3

Examination Methods

OBJECTIVES

A variety of methods are used in skeletal examinations, including macroscopic (visual) observation, microscopic observation, metric analysis, radiology, histology, and elemental analyses. The most appropriate method selected for a particular case depends on a number of factors including what is being asked, and the type and amount of skeletal material present. In this chapter, exercises will emphasize data collection and analysis based on various examination methods.

MACROSCOPIC APPROACHES

Macroscopic analyses of bones and teeth are methods of visually observing the presence/absence, configuration, or degree of expression of features with the unaided eye (i.e., without the use of instruments like microscopes or X-rays). Macroscopic analysis is used in conducting an inventory of the remains; assessing the overall condition of the material; describing taphonomic changes; estimating sex, age, and ancestry; and interpreting pathology and trauma. Many conclusions can be drawn based on macroscopic analysis alone, including determining whether bones are human or nonhuman and estimating the sex, ancestry, or age of the individual. Some macroscopic observations are scored in some manner or compared to charts or exemplars such as photographs or casts. Traits analyzed in this way are called *morphoscopic* or nonmetric traits. While macroscopic analysis has many advantages including ease of application and no need for sophisticated equipment, it also has limitations. Macroscopic analysis is typically considered more subjective, less standardized, and more prone to bias than some other types of analysis, such as metric analysis or examinations involving analytical instrumentation. By their nature, macroscopic interpretations are often less amenable to error analysis and sometimes rely heavily upon experience and training, but can still be highly reliable and valid and, in some cases, may be the only means of analysis possible.

METRIC ANALYSIS

Metric analysis in forensic anthropological cases involves recording and analyzing skeletal measurements, also referred to as *osteometrics*. Metric analysis can often help to reveal skeletal differences that are difficult to detect and interpret by macroscopic methods alone, such as differences in size between males and females and differences in cranial shape between ancestral groups. Measurements are also used in the calculation of certain parameters such as stature. Some advantages of metric analyses are that they add statistical weight to estimate and eliminate certain errors associated with more observational methods. Although fairly straightforward in most cases, metric analysis requires knowledge and training in the use of measurement instrumentation, locating particular landmarks on the remains, performing the relevant calculations, and interpreting the results.

Sliding calipers, spreading calipers, measuring tapes, and osteometric boards (Fig. 3.1) are the foundation for most metric analyses in forensic anthropology and are used to take two-dimensional, linear skeletal measurements. Calipers measure from one specific point on a bone to another, measuring tapes are typically used for long bone circumference measurements, and the osteometric board is used to measure the maximum lengths or breadths of long bones or to take other larger measurements which would exceed the maximum measuring capacity for standard calipers. Other methods for quantifying human remains, bony features, and human variation exist, including digitizers, laser scanners, and radiographic techniques, some of which can take measurements in three-dimensional space.

While some measurements are very specialized and tailored to particular types of analyses, many forensic anthropologists employ some or all of a suite of relatively standardized skeletal measurements. Many of these measurements, especially those of the skull, are taken from a set of specified osteometric landmarks; those located on the skull are called *craniometric landmarks*. Descriptions of these landmarks can be found in Appendix D: Craniometric Landmarks. The standard measurements that can be taken from craniometric landmarks as well as for postcranial elements are described in

A Laboratory Manual for Forensic Anthropology. https://doi.org/10.1016/B978-0-12-812201-3.00003-7

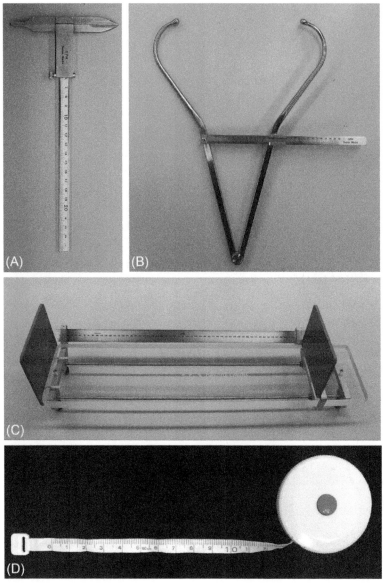

FIG. 3.1 (A) Sliding calipers, (B) spreading calipers, (C) osteometric board, and (D) measuring tape. *((A, B, C) From Christensen, A.M., Passalacqua, N.V., Bartelink, E.J., 2014. Forensic Anthropology: Current Methods and Practice, Academic Press).*

Appendix E: Skeletal Measurements. Many guides, including *Data Collection Procedures for Forensic Skeletal Material* (Moore-Jansen et al., 1994; Langley et al., 2016) and *Standards for Data Collection from Human Skeletal Remains* (Buikstra and Ubelaker, 1994), offer more detailed definitions, considerations, and recommendations for which instruments are most appropriate for each measurement.

RADIOLOGY

Radiology is the study of high-energy radiation used to examine and diagnose internal structures. The process of using radiology to make images is called radiography. Radiology in forensic anthropology is useful for documentation as well as detection and diagnostic applications and may include traditional two-dimensional radiography or computed tomography (CT). It can be used to produce a record of the condition of the remains at the time of examination, detect the presence of foreign material such as a bullet, and visualize internal skeletal structures that are not visible to the naked eye such as paranasal sinuses or developing dentition. It can also be used to diagnose conditions such as antemortem fractures or pathological conditions, or to see the placement of surgical implants.

Examination Methods **Chapter | 3** **37**

Taking and examining radiographs requires some knowledge of the relative radiodensities of various materials. Keeping thickness as well as other technical parameters constant, the radiographic appearance of materials will vary as a function of their attenuation properties (Fig. 3.2). This explains, for example, why it is possible to detect foreign material such as projectiles within bone or dental restorations using radiology—bullet lead and dental implements attenuate more X-rays (i.e., appears more radiopaque) than bone, making them appear distinct from bone (which attenuates more X-rays than soft tissues but less than lead) in a radiologic images (Fig. 3.3).

HISTOLOGY

Histology is the study of the microscopic structure of tissues. A histological analysis of skeletal material can be used in forensic anthropological examinations to determine whether or not the bone can be excluded as being human in origin, and

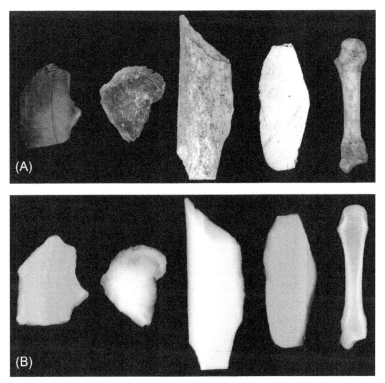

FIG. 3.2 Radiographic appearance of various materials—left to right: ceramic, fossilized shell, nonhuman long bone fragment, plastic, human metacarpal.

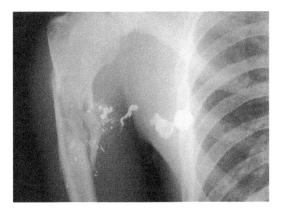

FIG. 3.3 Radiograph showing fractured humerus and projectile fragments. *(Image courtesy of B.G. Brogdon, M.D.; From Christensen, A.M., Passalacqua, N.V., Bartelink, E.J., 2014. Forensic Anthropology: Current Methods and Practice, Academic Press.)*

in the assessment of skeletal age on the basis of bone remodeling. In addition, it can be useful in the diagnosis of disease or recognizing the early stages of bone healing.

In order to observe the microscopic structures of osseous tissue, the bone must be prepared as thin sections (50–100 μm thick). This is typically accomplished by cutting sections of the bone into ~1 mm wafers using a sectioning saw and then grinding and polishing the wafer until it is suitably thin for microscopic examination (which means that it must transmit light and that there are ideally few if any overlapping structures). In some cases, particularly if bone fragments are very small or taphonomically compromised (e.g., burned, ancient, or highly weathered), the bone may need to be embedded in resin to stabilize it during cutting. The thin section is then mounted on a glass microscope slide and examined using light microscopy, sometimes with the aid of tissue staining and/or polarized light. Using this approach, the microstructure of the bone can be visualized, imaged, measured, and interpreted. Because histological examination is a destructive process, it should only be used when necessary and should follow thorough macroscopic and other nondestructive analyses.

ELEMENTAL ANALYSIS

Elemental analysis is the analysis of a material for its elemental or isotopic composition. It requires the use of specialized equipment such as scanning electron microscopy/energy dispersive spectroscopy (SEM/EDS), X-ray fluorescence spectrometry (XRF), or X-ray diffraction (XRD). These instruments are quite expensive and require extensive training, and therefore elemental analysis is only performed in a few anthropology laboratories. This equipment, however, is generally available in analytical chemistry and biology laboratories, as well as in many major crime laboratories.

Elemental analysis may be used in the determination of whether a material is bone or some other material based on whether or not it contains bone's signature levels of calcium and phosphorus. This approach is especially useful when pieces of unknown (but suspected to be skeletal) material are very fragmented and/or taphonomically compromised. Elemental analysis may also be used in stable isotopic profiling of human tissues such as bones, teeth, hair, and fingernails as a means of identifying an individual's likely dietary or residence pattern based on food and water consumed or tracking an individual's migration history and residence patterns based on signatures that reflect a particular drinking water source or geological region where food is grown. This information can be particularly useful in cases where a body is recovered a significant distance from where the individual last resided.

STATISTICS AND FORDISC

Skeletal examination and analysis methods often involve the use of statistics, and the use of statistical analysis in conjunction with qualitative descriptions in forensic anthropological casework is recommended. Definitions of various basic statistical terms that are commonly used in forensic anthropological analyses are shown in Table 3.1.

Two of the more commonly employed statistical analyses in forensic anthropology are *regression analysis* and *discriminant function analysis*. Regression analysis is a statistical approach that assesses the relationship between two or more variables. The simplest form of regression analysis is a linear, bivariate (two-variable) regression that describes the relationship between the two variables of interest. Such analyses are often used in forensic anthropology when determining the relationship between the length of a bone and an individual's known stature. This mathematical relationship then allows for the estimation of an unknown stature based on a known bone length (or vice versa).

Discriminant function analysis is a statistical approach that is used to predict group membership based on a set of variables. In forensic anthropology, this type of analysis is often used to estimate ancestry and sex based on a series of cranial and postcranial measurements. Discriminant function analysis proceeds by inserting the appropriate measurements into discriminant function equations and assessing where the resulting calculation falls with respect to various sectioning points which are developed based on a reference sample of individuals of known sex and ancestry. The most common program used for discriminant function analysis of skeletal measurements is Fordisc Personal Computer Forensic Discriminant Functions (or, "Fordisc"), an interactive computer program that calculates custom discriminant function analyses (Jantz and Ousley, 2005). Fordisc is built on a large database of individuals of known sex, ancestry, and stature and can provide classifications based on any combination of standard measurements. Because Fordisc will always provide a classification, there is significant responsibility on the user including proper data collection, entry, analysis, and interpretation.

When using Fordisc, the measurements are recorded and entered into an electronic form (Fig. 3.4) and then a series of skeletal populations to be included in the analysis are selected (Ousley and Jantz, 2012). After selecting the "Process" button, Fordisc classifies group membership by maximizing between-group differences using the sum of the numerical weights calculated for each measurement (Ousley and Jantz, 2012). Importantly, Fordisc always classifies the measurements of the skeleton into the closest selected group, even if the individual belongs to a group that is not selected (or may not even exist

TABLE 3.1 Basic Statistical Terms

Term	Definition
	Measures of central tendency
Mean	The arithmetic average of all values
Median	A numerical value that separates the lower half from the upper half of the distribution; for an odd number of values, it is the middle value; for an even number of values, it is the mean of the two middle values
Mode	The most common value represented in a data set
	Measures of variation
Variance	A measure of the spread of values in a data set
Standard deviation	A measure of how much variation exists in a range of values, expressed in the same unit of measurement as the mean
Range	The difference between the highest and lowest value of a given set of values
Standard Error	The standard deviation of a distribution of samples, used to measure uncertainty of the true population mean and standard deviation
	Measures of sources of error
Error	The difference between an estimated quantity and its true value
Precision	The degree of accuracy with which a parameter is estimated by an estimator, usually measured by the standard deviation of the estimator and known as the standard error
Reliability	The ability to obtain the same result using the same methods and instrument
Validity	The degree to which an observation or result reflects empirical reality
Bias	A systematic (not random) deviation from the true value

within the reference database). Interpretation of the results is therefore critical and is described in the following in more detail. Appendix G: Fordisc DFA Flowchart also provides an overview of the recommended steps for using Fordisc.

Fordisc uses Mahalanobis's D^2, a multivariate measure of the difference between groups, to measure the average differences between groups for each analysis. Fordisc's output provides the D^2 values (labeled as "Distance from") for the unknown set of measurements relative to all groups used in the analysis, with the smallest D^2 value representing the group most similar to the measurements of the unknown skeleton (Fig. 3.5). The unknown individual will always be classified into the population with the smallest Mahalanobis distance. In some instances, a few of the selected populations will have very similar Mahalanobis distances, requiring close examination by the analyst to interpret the results.

Next in the Fordisc output is the posterior probability value, which provides a measure of the *relative* distance of the unknown skeleton to each group, compared to the other groups selected for comparison. Note that all posterior probabilities will always sum to 1.0 (with the default setting having the probabilities ranked from highest to lowest for each group included in the analysis), and that the unknown skeleton is assumed to belong to one of the groups selected. Groups with posterior probabilities <0.1 can usually be excluded from consideration and further analyses. After the posterior probability is the typicality value (labeled as "Typ F"), which is a measure of the *absolute* distance of the unknown skeleton to each group centroid, or how "typical" the skeleton is of each group (Fig. 3.6). High typicality values suggest that the skeleton is similar to the other skeletons in that reference group, while low values suggest that it is atypical. Groups with typicality probabilities <0.05 can usually be excluded. Fordisc also generates two- and three-dimensional graphical representations of the results, which can assist the analyst in interpretation (Fig. 3.7).

Fordisc analyses can be run initially by choosing to include all measurements and all groups. Fordisc will notify the user if any measurements seem especially atypical (too large or too small), which may be the result of measurement or recording errors that can be caught and fixed early in the analysis. Analyses should be repeated, eliminating groups with posterior probabilities of <0.1 and typicality probabilities of <0.05. Analyses ideally result in two to four remaining classification groups. The user should also ensure that all selected populations have large enough samples based on the number of variables selected. If the sample sizes are too small, a large number of variables will over-fit the model, resulting in

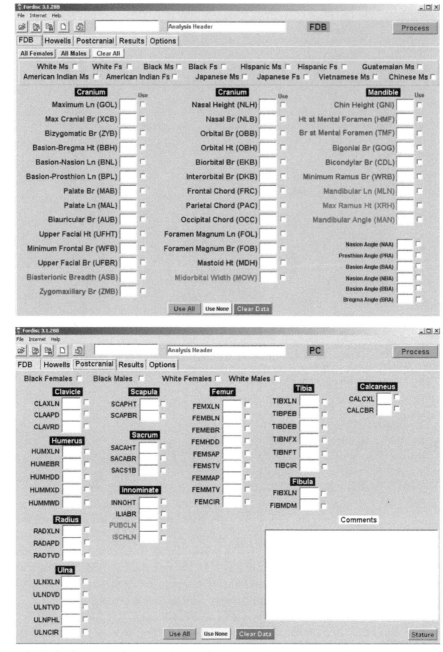

FIG. 3.4 Fordisc electronic Fordisc forms—cranial (top) and postcranial (bottom) (Jantz and Ousley, 2005).

Multigroup Classification of Current Case

Group	Classified into	Distance from	Probabilities Posterior	Typ F	Typ Chi	Typ R	
WF	**WF**	5.5	0.990	0.915	0.905	0.851	(38/249)
AF		15.9	0.005	0.497	0.144	0.226	(25/31)
HF		17.7	0.002	0.230	0.089	0.123	(51/57)
BF		18.4	0.002	0.161	0.072	0.143	(67/77)
JF		19.3	0.001	0.160	0.056	0.063	(60/63)

Current Case is closest to WFs

FIG. 3.5 Fordisc ancestry results for a White female skull. Note that the posterior probability of 0.915 indicates that the skull is more similar to White Females than any of the other groups selected, and the typicality of 0.915 indicates that the skull is highly typical of other White Female skulls (Jantz and Ousley, 2005).

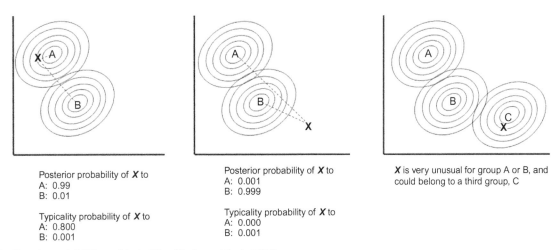

Posterior probability of **X** to
A: 0.99
B: 0.01

Typicality probability of **X** to
A: 0.800
B: 0.001

Posterior probability of **X** to
A: 0.001
B: 0.999

Typicality probability of **X** to
A: 0.000
B: 0.001

X is very unusual for group A or B, and
could belong to a third group, C

FIG. 3.6 Posterior probabilities and typicalities (Ousley and Jantz, 2012).

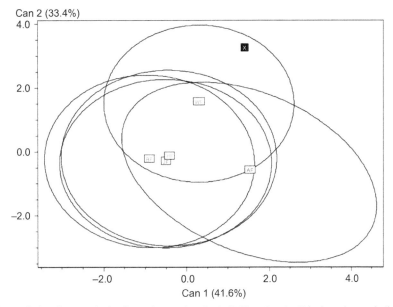

FIG. 3.7 Fordisc graph of canonical variates analysis of an unknown female skull. Note that the X is the unknown individual, which falls within the ellipse of the White female (WF) group and outside of the ellipses for the other selected groups (Jantz and Ousley, 2005).

potential misclassifications. A general rule is to have one variable (measurement) for every three individuals in the smallest population; for example, in an analysis with multiple populations where the smallest population has a sample size of 45, the maximum number of variables used should be 15. Overfitting can be avoided using the stepwise variable selection (available under "Options") and/or by removing measurements.

Fordisc's primary reference samples are based on modern human skeletons and thus are not appropriate for classifying archaeological or ancient material. Fordisc does, however, include W.W. Howells' craniometric database, consisting of measurements of historic and prehistoric crania from various parts of the world (Ousley and Jantz, 2012). This may be applicable for comparisons with historic or prehistoric skulls for remains which may be of questionable medicolegal significance but should be used cautiously due to the large number of groups represented.

ERROR AND UNCERTAINTY

Error can be defined in a number of ways, including deviation from what is correct, having false knowledge, a mistake, or the difference between an observed value or measurement and the true value. Error can result from a number of different causes in forensic science, and the concept is often vague and subject to a variety of interpretations. *Practitioner error* refers to human error or mistakes and may be unintentional or related to negligence or incompetence. Such practitioner errors may include blunders like transposing numbers when recording data (such as on a measurement form), incorrect instrument use, selection of inappropriate methods (such as selection of a particular age estimation method when another might be more appropriate), or improper method application. Practitioner error may also be intentional, such as fraudulent behavior. Practitioner error can be reduced through quality assurance systems, training, proficiency testing, peer review, and adhering to validated protocols and discipline best practices.

Instrument (or technological) error is the difference between an indicated instrument value and the actual (true) value and can be minimized largely by proper maintenance and calibration of instruments. Instruments used in forensic anthropology may include measurement tools such as calipers and osteometric boards, analytical instruments such as XRF and XRD, and diagnostic equipment such as radiology devices. All should be maintained properly and calibrated regularly to minimize instrument error.

Statistical error refers to random variation or deviation from actual and predicted values. Statistical error is generally represented by the standard error or the statistical probability of error, for example, when a prediction interval with an explicit probability is specified. This "error," which often merely expresses normal variability, is inherent in measurements and estimates because they are based on the properties of a sample. In forensic anthropology, this may be seen in calculations such as stature estimation. Regression formulae are based on the characteristics of a large sample which may or may not have the exact same properties as the case at hand; this is why these estimations are best expressed as intervals rather than point estimates.

Lastly, *technique (or methodological) error* relates to inherent limitations (or method sensitivity or resolving power) which are sources of potential error and which have nothing to do with practitioner or instrument error. Method limitations in forensic anthropology are often a function of how measurements or traits overlap among different groups or to the frequency of the observed trait(s) in the population at large. For example, femoral head size may be used to estimate sex, but because there is some overlap between males and females (i.e., some males have small femoral heads, and some females have large ones), there is a chance that any given sex estimate based on femoral head size may be incorrect. This type of error exists as a function of inherent limits in the material itself (in this case, inherent biological variation in femoral head size) and cannot be minimized through certain practices the way other error sources can. Such limitations, however, should be acknowledged and communicated in reports and testimony.

EXERCISE 3.1   Macroscopic Analysis

Materials needed:
- Images provided in this exercise

Note to instructors: This exercise can be supplemented or replaced with real or replica skeletal materials from case work or reference collections. Note that some features may be difficult to assess on replica materials.

Case scenario: A collection of skeletal materials was delivered to your laboratory by a medical examiner who found the remains in a box without an associated case ID or other information. After documenting an inventory, you perform a visual/macroscopic analysis of some of the features present on the bones.

Instructions/Procedure:
- For each image below, indicate whether the specified features are present or absent. If present, describe the anatomical location, configuration, or degree of expression of the feature, i.e., is its expression minimal, moderate, or pronounced? (See Appendix L for an example of degrees of cranial trait expression.)

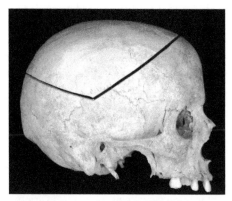

(Image courtesy of Eric Bartelink.)

Supraorbital ridge?_____

External occipital protuberance?_____

Extra sutural bone(s)?_____

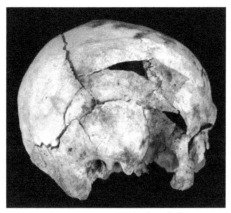

(Image courtesy of Eric Bartelink.)

Mastoid process?_____

Staining?_____

Fractures?_____

Other than those features noted earlier, what other macroscopic observations can you make from the pictured crania?

_____

_____

_____

EXERCISE 3.2 Radiologic Examination

Materials needed:

• Image provided in this exercise

Note to instructors: This exercise can be supplemented or replaced with radiologic images from case work or reference materials. Images may also be located using an internet search.

Case scenario: In the course of your examination of unidentified skeletal remains, you take an X-ray of the cranium, which is pictured below.

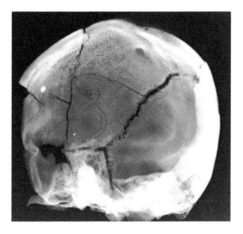

(Image courtesy of Eric Bartelink.)

Describe the features you see in this radiograph in terms of their relative radiodensities. Consider features such as normal anatomy, missing bone/fractures, and nonskeletal material.

_____

_____

_____

EXERCISE 3.3   Identification of Osteometric Landmarks

Materials needed:
- Image provided in this exercise
- Appendix D: Craniometric Landmarks

Note to instructors: This exercise can be supplemented or replaced with real or replica human bones. Small dot stickers can be used to designate which landmarks you would like students to identify.

Case scenario: You received the below unidentified skull for anthropological examination, and you have decided that metric analysis would be the most accurate way to assess the individual's sex and ancestry. The skull has been modified by scavengers and not all landmarks are present.

Instructions/Procedure:
- Identify the anterior craniometric landmarks that will be available for your analysis
- Use the space on the left to write the name or abbreviation of the landmark(s) and mark their location(s) on the cranium

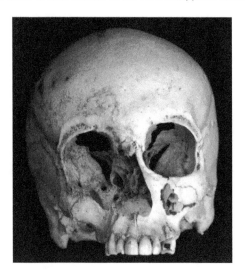

Anterior landmarks present:
- _____
- _____
- _____
- _____
- _____
- _____
- _____
- _____
- _____
- _____

(From Christensen, A.M., Passalacqua, N.V., Bartelink, E.J., 2014. Forensic Anthropology: Current Methods and Practice, Academic Press.)

EXERCISE 3.4 Taking and Recording Skeletal Measurements

Materials needed:
- Real or replica human skeletal material
- Sliding calipers
- Spreading calipers
- Osteometric board
- Appendix D: Craniometric Landmarks
- Appendix E: Cranial and Postcranial Measurements
- Appendix F: Skeletal Measurement Form

Note to instructors: Calipers and osteometric boards can be shared between students or groups. It may be useful to provide additional copies of Appendix F for students to use during this exercise. Some landmarks may be more difficult to locate/identify on replica material.

Case scenario: You have been asked to examine unidentified skeletal remains in order to help determined to whom the remains may belong. As part of your assessment, you decide to estimate a biological profile for the remains to include estimation of sex, ancestry, age, and stature. As part of your estimation of sex and ancestry, you decide to perform an osteometric analysis, which will require you to take standard skeletal measurements of the remains.

Instructions/Procedure:
- Take and record all available skeletal measurements following Appendices D and E and record them on Appendix F: Skeletal Measurement Form

Which measurements did you find most challenging to take? Why?

_____
_____
_____

Were there any measurements you could not take? Why?

_____

EXERCISE 3.5 Interpretation of Fordisc Results

Materials needed:
- Fordisc result provided in this exercise

Note to instructors: The results below can be replaced or supplemented with the results from the previous exercise, or with Fordisc results from casework or reference materials.

Case scenario: You entered a series of skeletal measurements into Fordisc, with the following results:

```
Multigroup Classification of Current Case
-----------------------------------------------------------------------
Group    Classified    Distance              Probabilities
         into          from     Posterior   Typ F    Typ Chi    Typ R
-----------------------------------------------------------------------
  BF       **BF**         9.8      0.518      0.919    0.910    0.904 (7/73)
  HF                     11.7      0.200      0.837    0.815    0.745 (12/47)
  JF                     11.8      0.199      0.833    0.814    0.661 (20/59)
  WF                     15.8      0.026      0.556    0.536    0.387 (111/191)
  BM                     16.2      0.021      0.534    0.509    0.638 (38/105)
  HM                     16.9      0.015      0.482    0.461    0.516 (90/186)
  CHM                    18.4      0.007      0.397    0.365    0.243 (53/70)
  GTM                    18.6      0.007      0.385    0.353    0.229 (54/70)
  VM                     19.3      0.005      0.349    0.311    0.286 (35/49)
  JM                     21.3      0.002      0.240    0.215    0.259 (63/85)
  WM                     24.2      0.000      0.127    0.114    0.233 (230/300)
  AF                     26.0      0.000      0.103    0.075    0.103 (26/29)
  AM                     35.8      0.000      0.007    0.005    0.096 (47/52)
-----------------------------------------------------------------------
Current Case is closest to BFs
-----------------------------------------------------------------------
```

What does "Classified into **BF**" mean?

_____

Discuss and provide an interpretation for the "Distance from" for the selected groups.

_____

_____

_____

Discuss and provide an interpretation for the "Posterior Probabilities" for the selected groups.

_____

_____

_____

Discuss and provide an interpretation for the "Typ F Probabilities" for the selected groups.

_____

_____

_____

Would this be the information on which you would make your final conclusion from your metric analysis? If not, describe what steps you would take next.

_____

_____

_____

EXERCISE 3.6 Analysis of Measurements Using Fordisc

Materials needed:
- Measurements provided in this exercise
- Fordisc
- PC computer

Note to instructors: The measurements provided below can be replaced or supplemented with the measurements from the previous exercise or from a forensic case or reference collection if available.

Case scenario: Skeletal remains recovered from an abandoned house were submitted to your laboratory for analysis. The house was known to be utilized by a number of homeless individuals in the area, and the identity of the skeletal remains is unknown. In order to estimate a biological profile to help narrow the pool of possible decedents, you took and recorded a series of standard skeletal measurements.

Instructions/Procedure:
- Enter the cranial and mandibular measurements into the "FDB" tab screen in Fordisc, selecting all male and female groups for comparison
- Follow the recommended procedure for eliminating groups until an appropriate number remains
- View the Graph tab to see your results in graphical form
- Repeat the above steps using the postcranial measurements, entering them in the "Postcranial" tab screen

------------------------------ CRANIAL MEASUREMENTS ------------------------------

		left	right
1. MAXIMUM CRANIAL LENGTH (g-op):	174		
2. NASIO-OCCIPITAL LENGTH (n-op):	_____		
3. MAXIMUM CRANIAL BREADTH (eu-eu)	152		
4. BIZYGOMATIC BREADTH (zy-zy):	131		
5. BASION-BREGMA HEIGHT (ba-b):	137		
6. CRANIAL BASE LENGTH (ba-n):	_____		
7. BASION-PROSTHION LENGTH (ba-pr):	_____		
8. MAXILLO-ALVEOLAR BREADTH (ecm-ecm):	60		
9. MAXILLO-ALVEOLAR LENGTH (pr-alv):	_____		
10. BIAURICULAR BREADTH (ra-ra):	129		
11. NASION-PROSTHION HEIGHT (n-pr):	_____		
12. MINIMUM FRONTAL BREADTH (ft-ft):	99		
13. UPPER FACIAL BREADTH (fmt-fmt):	_____		
14. NASAL HEIGHT:	48		

	left	right
15. NASAL BREADTH:	24	
16. ORBITAL BREADTH (d-ec):	39	39
17. ORBITAL HEIGHT:	32	32
18. BIORBITAL BREADTH (ec-ec):	98	
19. INTERORBITAL BREADTH (d-d):	21	
20. FRONTAL CHORD (n-b):	110	
21. PARIETAL CHORD (b-l):	103	
22. OCCIPITAL CHORD (l-o):	95	
23. FORAMEN MAGNUM LENGTH:	36	
24. FORAMEN MAGNUM BR:	30	
25. MASTOID HEIGHT (po-ms):	29	_____
26. BIASTERIONIC BR. (ast-ast):	_____	
27. ZYGOMAXILLARY BR. (zym-zym):	_____	
28. ZYGOORBITALE BR. (zo-zo):	_____	

------------------------------ MANDIBULAR MEASUREMENTS ------------------------------

	left	right
29. CHIN. HEIGHT (id-gn):		31
30. MANDIBULAR BODY HEIGHT:	29	29
31. MANDIBULAR BODY BREADTH:	12	13
32. BIGONIAL BREADTH (go-go):		90
33. BICONDYLAR BR. (cdl-cdl):		120

	left	right
34. MAX. RAMUS HEIGHT:	35	35
35. *MAX. RAMUS HEIGHT:	_____	
36. *MAND. LENGTH:	_____	
37. *MAND. ANGLE:	_____	

*Record only if mandibulometer is used

------------------------------ POSTCRANIAL MEASUREMENTS ------------------------------

CLAVICLE:	left	right
38. MAXIMUM LENGTH:	161	158
39. MAX. MIDSHAFT DIAM:	15	16
40. MIN. MIDSHAFT DIAM:	11	10
SCAPULA:		
41. HEIGHT:	149	152
42. BREADTH:	102	101
43. GLENOID CAVITY BREADTH:	_____	_____
44. GLENOID CAVITY HEIGHT:	_____	_____
HUMERUS:		
45. MAXIMUM LENGTH:	326	326
46. EPICONDYLAR BREADTH:	62	61
47. MAX. VERT. HEAD DIAM.:	47	48
48. MAX. MIDSHAFT DIAM.:	24	25
49. MIN. MIDSHAFT DIAM.:	17	17
RADIUS:		
50. MAXIMUM LENGTH:	246	248
51. MAX. MIDSHAFT DIAM.:	14	13
52. MIN. MIDSHAFT DIAM.:	17	17
53. MAX. HEAD DIAMETER:	_____	_____
ULNA:		
54. MAXIMUM LENGTH:	266	268
55. MAX. MIDSHAFT DIAM.:	14	13
56. MIN. MIDSHAFT DIAM.:	20	20
57. PHYSIOLOGICAL LENGTH:	233	234
58. MIN. CIRCUMFERENCE:	37	37
59. OLECRANON BREADTH:	_____	_____
SACRUM:		
60. ANTERIOR HEIGHT:	110	
61. ANTERIOR BREADTH:	96	
62. TRANSVERSE DIAM. S1:	_____	
63. A-P DIAMETER S1:	_____	

INNOMINATE:	left	right
64. MAXIMUM HEIGHT:	207	209
65. MAX. ILIAC BREADTH:	147	147
66. MIN. ILIAC BREADTH:	_____	_____
67. MAX. PUBIS LENGTH:	_____	_____
68. MIN. PUBIS LENGTH:	_____	_____
69. ISCHIAL LENGTH:	_____	_____
70. MIN. ISCHIAL LENGTH:	_____	_____
71. MAX. ISCHIOPUB RAM L.:	_____	_____
72. ASIS – SYMPHYSION:	_____	_____
73. MAX. PSIS – SYMPHYSION:	_____	_____
74. MIN. APEX – SYMPHYSION:	_____	_____
FEMUR:		
75. MAXIMUM LENGTH:	464	465
76. BICONDYLAR LENGTH:	462	463
77. EPICONDYLAR BREADTH:	84	84
78. MAX. HEAD DIAMETER:	46	46
79. TRANS. SUBTROCH DIAM:	33	34
80. A-P SUBTROCH DIAM:	28	28
81. MAX. MIDSHAFT DIAM.	31	30
82. MIN. MIDSHAFT DIAM.	26	26
83. MIDSHAFT CIRCUM.	88	88
84. MAX AP L. LAT. CONDYLE:	_____	_____
85. MAX AP L. MED. CONDYLE:	_____	_____
TIBIA:		
86. CONDYLO-MALLEOLAR L.:	393	396
87. MAX. PROX. EPIP. BR.:	78	79
88. DISTAL EPIP. BREADTH:	56	56
89. MAX. MIDSHAFT DIAM.:	_____	_____
90. MIN. MIDSHAFT DIAM.:	_____	_____
91. MIDSHAFT CIRCUM.:	_____	_____
FIBULA:		
92. MAXIMUM LENGTH:	387	392
93. MAX. MIDSHAFT DIAM.:	16	16
CALCANEUS:		
94. MAXIMUM LENGTH:	86	86
95. MIDDLE BREADTH:	44	44

What result did Fordisc provide regarding the likely sex and ancestry of the remains?

_____

What Posterior Probability and Typicality Probability did Fordisc provide? What do these numbers mean?

_____

_____

Did the graph view clarify the numeric results? Why or why not?

_____

_____

Did the cranial measurements result in the same ancestry estimate as the postcranial measurements? How/why might these results differ?

_____

_____

_____

Were there anything in the analysis that raised any red flags (such as very small or large measurements, or very small or large probabilities)? How did (or would) you handle these issues?

_____

_____

_____

EXERCISE 3.7   Analysis of Observer Error

Materials needed:
- Measurements you took in Exercise 3.2

Note to instructors: This exercise can be carried out in pairs or small groups.

Case scenario: In Exercise 3.2 you used Appendix F to record skeletal measurements. Given that you have relatively little experience taking skeletal measurements, you are curious how accurate your measurements are and how they may vary from others who took the same measurements.

Instructions/Procedure:
- Compare your measurements with those obtained by a classmate who also measured the same skeleton

Are there any measurements for which there are discrepancies of greater than 2 mm? What do you think might account for these differences?

_____

_____

_____

Based on any discrepancies, are there measurements that you believe should be double-checked or retaken?

_____

_____

Identify the measurement with the greatest discrepancy and then demonstrate how you took that measurement and have your classmate do the same. Were you taking the measurement the same way? If not, explain where the differences in measuring between observers arose.

_____

_____

After discussing and remeasuring, were you each able to arrive at the same measurement?

_____

EXERCISE 3.8   Statistical and Error Terminology

Materials needed:
- Chart provided in this exercise
- Tables and definitions in this chapter

Note to instructors: This exercise can be carried out in class or as a take-home exercise.

Case scenario: You are aware of how important statistics and quantitative methods are in forensic anthropology and want to be sure you have a good understanding of basic terminology.

Instructions/Procedure:

- Match the following statistical and error terms with their corresponding definition

Standard deviation	A numerical value that separates the lower half from the upper half of the distribution
Bias	The difference between an estimated quantity and its true value
Precision	The difference between an indicated instrument value and the actual (true) value
Error	A systematic (not random) deviation from the true value
Practitioner error	A measure of how much variation exists in a range of values
Discriminant function analysis	Human error; mistake
Median	The degree of accuracy with which a parameter is estimated by an estimator
Instrument error	A statistical approach that is used to predict group membership based on a set of variables

Chapter 4

Medicolegal Significance

OBJECTIVES

In order to be considered medicolegally significant to the forensic anthropologist, the evidence must be: (1) skeletal (bone or tooth) versus some other material, (2) human versus nonhuman in origin, and (3) recent (i.e., contemporary, modern) in origin versus nonrecent (i.e., historic, prehistoric, ancient). In the following exercises you will determine whether material is medicolegally significant by identifying the elemental profile of skeletal material, differentiating human from nonhuman bones and teeth based on morphology and histology, and differentiating recent from nonrecent remains based on taphonomy and context.

THE MEDICOLEGAL CONTEXT

It is sometimes necessary for a forensic anthropologist to first determine whether remains or items in question actually fit the criteria of being recent human skeletal material. This type of analysis is typically referred to as determining the medicolegal significance, or whether the material is of interest to the medicolegal death investigation system (usually involving the identification of unknown individuals or the investigation of unnatural deaths). In order to be considered of medicolegal significance to a forensic anthropologist, three questions must be answered in the affirmative:

- Is the material skeletal (bone or tooth) versus some other material?
- Is the skeletal material human versus nonhuman in origin?
- Is the human skeletal material recent versus nonrecent (historic, prehistoric, or ancient)?

SKELETAL VERSUS NONSKELETAL

Sometimes the determination of medicolegal significance is difficult due to fragmentation or taphonomic processes (such as burning or scavenging) that may destroy or obscure many of the gross morphological features that normally make bones and teeth readily recognizable. As Figs. 4.1 and 4.2 demonstrate, materials such as rocks, ceramic, building materials, and even plastic and metal can easily be confused with bone to the untrained eye, especially when samples are very small or resemble bone morphology.

The type of analysis used to determine whether such materials are skeletal in origin will depend on the size and condition of the material in question. Often a determination can be made by closer visual examination, usually by a trained forensic anthropologist in a laboratory setting. Visual or microscopic indicators may include the presence of gross bone structures such as trabeculae or an overall shape that includes morphology and landmarks that are consistent with bones. If a determination cannot be made based on a visual analysis, other methods typically include radiology and elemental analysis. Table 4.1 highlights the main criteria forensic anthropologists use for determining whether material is skeletal or nonskeletal in origin.

Using radiology (including X-rays and CT scans), most plastics and floral debris will typically appear less radiodense than bone, while metals will appear more radiodense. This can also be assessed quantitatively on CT scans using a measure of the material's radiodensity on the Hounsfield unit (HU) scale. Distilled water at standard pressure and temperature (STP) has a HU of zero, and air has a HU of −1000. The HU for trabecular bone is +100 and for cortical bone is +3000. The internal structures such as trabeculae and tooth pulp chambers may also be identifiable using X-rays or CT scans.

Possible skeletal material can also be examined using elemental analysis such as X-ray fluorescence spectrometry (XRF), since bones and teeth possess a specific elemental composition that includes both calcium and phosphorus (Fig. 4.3). Advantages of XRF include that it requires no sample destruction or preparation, and it can be used regardless of sample size, antiquity, or state of presentation. Skeletal material may also be identified using an alternate light source (ALS). Bone usually fluoresces under shortwave light due to its collagen content, so the intensity of fluorescence may be affected by time and/or taphonomy (Fig. 4.4).

A Laboratory Manual for Forensic Anthropology. https://doi.org/10.1016/B978-0-12-812201-3.00004-9

FIG. 4.1 Examples of materials that may initially be mistaken for bone. From top left to bottom right: lava rock, ceramic, tubing, and drywall.*(From Christensen, A.M., Passalacqua, N.V., Bartelink, E.J., 2014. Forensic Anthropology: Current Methods and Practice. Academic Press.)*

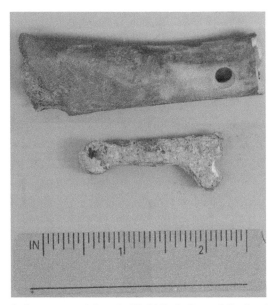

FIG. 4.2 Examples of materials mistaken for bone recovered from the World Trade Center following the 9/11/01 attack in New York. Top: plastic; bottom: metal door hinge.*(From Christensen, A.M., Passalacqua, N.V., Bartelink, E.J., 2014. Forensic Anthropology: Current Methods and Practice. Academic Press.)*

HUMAN VERSUS NONHUMAN

Assessment of human versus nonhuman animals can usually be accomplished using macroscopic or microscopic approaches. Biochemical methods such as DNA and pRIA may also be used to determine human or nonhuman origin, though other techniques are typically equally effective and more economical, and these analyses are not usually employed by forensic anthropologists themselves. It is not usually necessary to determine the species of nonhuman remains, and significant training in nonhuman osteology is needed to make conclusions regarding the identification of nonhuman species.

Methods may also include visual or radiographic assessment of skeletal and dental morphology, with particular attention to the bone architecture (shape) as well as size and stage of growth and development (i.e., immature versus skeletally mature adult) (Table 4.2). The presence of elements not found in the human skeleton such as a tail, claws, horns, baculum (a bone in the penis of many mammals) or metapodials (Fig. 4.5) can make the determination of nonhuman origin rather

TABLE 4.1 Features That Can Be Used to Differentiate Skeletal From Nonskeletal Material

	Skeletal	Nonskeletal
Morphology	• Trabecular and cortical bone • Evidence of vascular component • Skeletal landmarks	• Other morphology or features depending on origin
Microscopy	• Haversian systems • Trabecular and cortical bone • Cellular structures • Enamel prisms • Cement layers	• Other morphology or features depending on origin
Radiology	• Radiodensity (~3000 Hounsfield units for cortical bone) • Skeletal tissue features such as trabeculae	• May be more radiodense than bone • May be more radiolucent than bone
Elemental analysis	• Calcium and phosphorus	• Other elemental profile depending on origin
Alternate light source (ALS)	• May fluoresce under ALS	• May not fluoresce under ALS

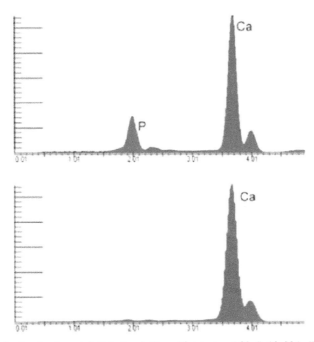

FIG. 4.3   Elemental profiles of bone (top) and gastropod shell (bottom). *(From Christensen, A.M., Smith, M.A., Thomas, R.M., 2012. Validation of X-ray fluorescence spectrometry for determining osseous or skeletal origin of unknown material. J. Forensic Sci. 57(1), 6–11.)*

FIG. 4.4   A clavicle fluorescing under ALS. *(Image courtesy of Mohamed Swaraldahab, specimen courtesy of National Museum of Natural History.)*

TABLE 4.2 Differences Between Human and Nonhuman Skeletons

	Human	Nonhuman
Skull	• Rounded and globular • Small, nonprojecting (orthognathic) face • The foramen magnum is anteriorly located to balance the head over the spinal column • Muscle attachment sites on the inferior surface are relatively gracile	• Elongated front to back • Projecting (prognathic) snout • Posteriorly positioned foramen magnum • Several prominent crests to anchor large muscles
Dentition	• Low, rounded molar cusps reflecting an omnivorous diet • Vertically implanted anterior teeth • Small canines that lack a diastema (gap)	• May have a diastema between the incisor and canine teeth • May have carnassial teeth
Vertebral column	• S-shaped curve that forms along the cervical, thoracic, and lumbar spine • Increase in size from the neck to the lower back due to increased weight bearing • Spinous processes show little variation in length, are often bifurcated in cervical vertebrae, and tend to be sharp and point inferiorly in thoracic vertebrae	• Little variation in vertebrae size, as body weight is distributed more evenly along the length of the spinal column • Some mammals have very elongated spinous processes on their thoracic vertebrae, which form the shoulder "hump"
Thorax	• Broad and shallow • Greater degree of curvature • Well-defined costal groove, located on the internal and inferior aspect	• Narrower and deeper • Costal groove absent or less pronounced
Shoulder girdle	• Elongated clavicle (collar bone) • Scapula (shoulder blade) is triangular and elongated superoinferiorly • Acromian and coracoid processes are more well defined and show a greater degree of projection	• Clavicle reduced or absent in nonhuman mammals • Scapula is longest mediolaterally
Pelvic girdle	• Pelvis is wide and broad, forming a basin to hold the internal organs • Ilium is short and flaring (curving medially) • Pelvis connects through a fibrocartilaginous joint along the pubic symphysis	• Ilium more narrow and elongated • In some nonhuman mammals, the pelvis is fused along the pubic symphysis
Long bones	• More gracile with smoother, less complex joint surfaces • Femoral and humeral heads more rounded and enlarged relative to overall size • Femoral neck elongated to position the legs under the body's center of gravity • Knee joint is valgus (medially oriented), reflecting the angle where the distal femur and proximal tibia intersect	• More defined joint surface morphology reflecting adaptations for specific forms of quadrupedal locomotion and the need for high-joint stability • In many nonhuman mammals, the radius and ulna and/or the tibia and fibula are fused together instead of being separate elements
Hands and feet	• Nails on terminal digits • Grasping hand, along with other primates • Elongated compared to nonhumans	• Claws on terminal digits

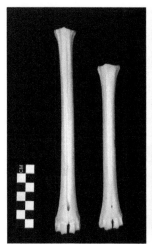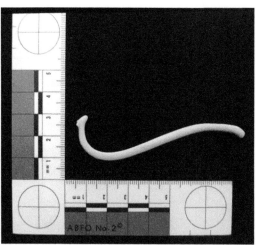

FIG. 4.5 Metapodials of a mule deer (left) and raccoon baculum (right). *(Left image from Christensen, A.M., Passalacqua, N.V., Bartelink, E.J., 2014. Forensic Anthropology: Current Methods and Practice. Academic Press.)*

obvious. If a skull is present, even most untrained investigators can typically determine whether or not it is human in origin (Fig. 4.6). For postcranial elements, however, especially those of similarly sized animals, more advanced training is typically required to make the correct determination (Figs. 4.7 and 4.8). There are a number of detailed atlases and reference guides to nonhuman bone identification (e.g., Adams and Crabtree, 2012; France, 2011), but identification is ideally performed using extensive training in comparative skeletal anatomy and access to a comparative skeletal collection.

Terrestrial mammals such as bear, deer, pig, and raccoon are most likely to be confused with human remains due to their greater similarity in bone size and morphology (Fig. 4.9). An additional source of confusion sometimes involves growth and developmental stages of the human skeleton compared to nonhuman animals (Fig. 4.10). Yet another feature that could initially confuse investigators is the presence of surgical hardware (typically associated with human remains) found associated with nonhuman remains (Fig. 4.11).

In cases where bones are fragmented, weathered, or burned, microscopy may be useful for determining human or nonhuman origin (Fig. 4.12). Although nonhuman bone is primarily fibrolamellar, Haversian systems may be present, especially near muscle attachment sites (entheses) in larger mammals, such as horses, cows, sheep, pigs, and goats. Alternating osteon and lamellar banding patterns may occur in nonhuman mammalian bone, and only rarely in human bone. For readers interested in this and other applications of bone histology, see *Bone Histology* by Crowder and Stout (2012).

RECENT VERSUS NONRECENT

If the remains are not recent in origin, then they likely fall outside of the purview of the medicolegal system, either because identification of the individual is not possible to establish or because the individual has already been previously processed through the medicolegal system (e.g., in the case of a disturbed historic burial). Examples of nonmedicolegally significant human remains include those from archaeological contexts, disturbed cemeteries, anatomical teaching specimens, and "trophy skulls." The primary indicators used to assess whether human remains are recent include taphonomic, contextual, and biocultural (Table 4.3).

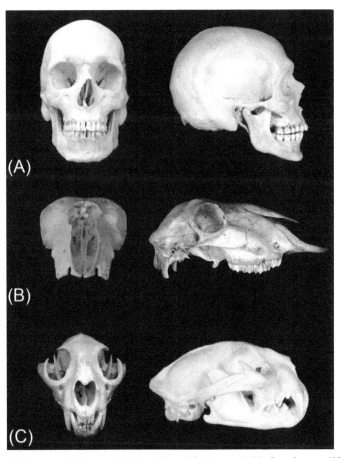

FIG. 4.6 Skulls of: (A) human, (B) deer, and (C) mountain lion. *(From Christensen, A.M., Passalacqua, N.V., Bartelink, E.J., 2014. Forensic Anthropology: Current Methods and Practice. Academic Press.)*

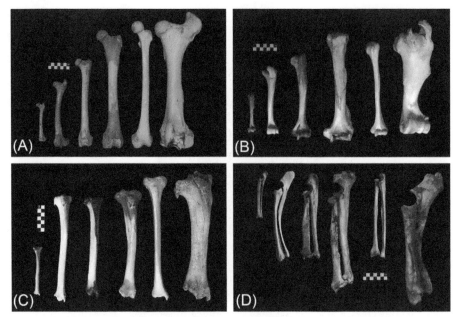

FIG. 4.7 (A) Left femur, (B) right humerus, (C) right tibia, and (D) right radius and ulna of various species. Left to right for each bone: dog (*Canis familiaris*), mule deer (*Odocoileus hemionus*), mountain lion (*Felis concolor*), bear (*Ursus americanus*), human (*Homo sapiens*), and Cow (*Bos taurus*). *(From Christensen, A.M., Passalacqua, N.V., Bartelink, E.J., 2014. Forensic Anthropology: Current Methods and Practice. Academic Press.)*

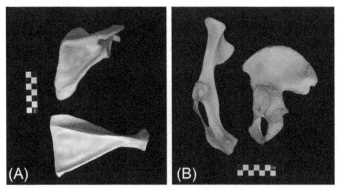

FIG. 4.8 (A) Right scapula of human (*Homo sapiens*) (top) and mule deer (*Odocoileus hemionus*) (bottom); (B) left innominate of mule deer (*Odocoileus hemionus*) (left) and human (*Homo sapiens*) (right). *(From Christensen, A.M., Passalacqua, N.V., Bartelink, E.J., 2014. Forensic Anthropology: Current Methods and Practice. Academic Press.)*

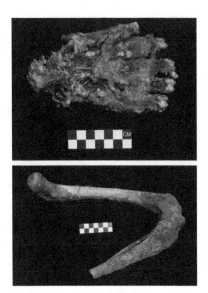

FIG. 4.9 Bear paw (above) and bear knee (below), often initially mistaken for human remains. *(From Christensen, A.M., Passalacqua, N.V., Bartelink, E.J., 2014. Forensic Anthropology: Current Methods and Practice. Academic Press.)*

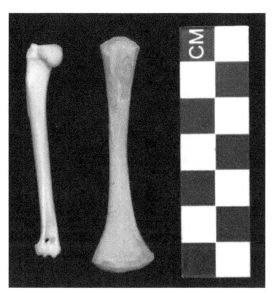

FIG. 4.10 Mature nonhuman humerus (left) and infant human humerus (right). *(From Christensen, A.M., Passalacqua, N.V., Bartelink, E.J., 2014. Forensic Anthropology: Current Methods and Practice. Academic Press.)*

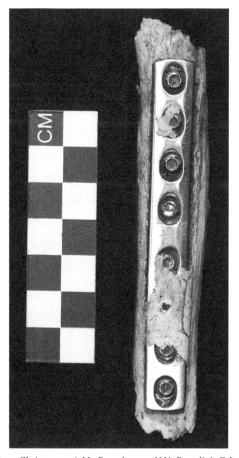

FIG. 4.11 Dog bone with surgical implant. *(From Christensen, A.M., Passalacqua, N.V., Bartelink, E.J., 2014. Forensic Anthropology: Current Methods and Practice. Academic Press.)*

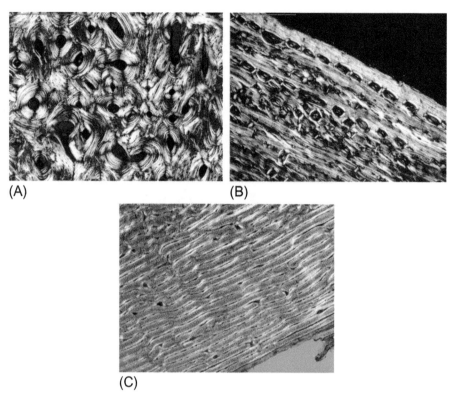

(A)   (B)

(C)

FIG. 4.12 (A) Human femur, showing Haversian bone (100×, polarized light), (B) nonhuman (horse) femur showing multiple rows of secondary osteo "banding" (40×, polarized light), and (C) nonhuman (pig) humerus showing fibrolamellar bone with the organization pattern typically classified as "plexiform" bone (40×, semipolarized light). *(Images courtesy of C. Crowder and A. Berensheim; From Christensen, A.M., Passalacqua, N.V., Bartelink, E.J., 2014. Forensic Anthropology: Current Methods and Practice. Academic Press.)*

TABLE 4.3 Features That Can Be Used to Differentiate Recent From Nonrecent Human Skeletal Material

	Recent	Nonrecent
Taphonomic	• Soft tissue and viscera may be present • Better preservation/less diagenesis • Brighter white colored bone • Lack of deliberate postmortem treatment	• Soft tissue usually absent • Diagenesis/poor preservation • Darker brown (stained) colored bone • Hardware, drill holes, bleaching, and shelf wear associated with curation • Presence of autopsy or anatomical preparation saw marks
Contextual	• Location, such as remote wooded area • Association with modern personal effects and grave goods	• Location, such as cemetery • Association with historic/ancient personal effects and grave goods
Biocultural	• Surgical devices and dental restorations • Lack of burial treatment	• Skeletal adaptations to prehistoric diets (e.g., dental attrition) • Cranial deformation • Dental mutilation • Cultural burial arrangement • Trephination
Radiocarbon dating	• Radiocarbon or bomb curve date that indicates more recent origin	• Radiocarbon or bomb curve date that indicates historic or prehistoric origin

Taphonomic indicators are those that affect the appearance, quality, and preservation of the remains. Recent remains will typically be more well preserved than remains that are older, especially if they were buried. Even when soft tissues have decomposed, well-preserved bone, such as bone that is still hydrated or greasy, is more likely to be more recent than poorly preserved bone, such as bone that is highly weathered, dried, decalcified, or friable. Deliberate postmortem treatment of the remains, such as embalming, autopsy, or processing for skeletal curation or analysis, may also give indications regarding medicolegal significance. For example, the presence of anatomical hardware, drill holes, bleaching, and shelf-wear maybe be indicators that remains were specially prepared and used as teaching skeletons before being re-discovered (Fig. 4.13). Embalming and postmortem grooming practices have changed over the years, including variation in the procedures, the chemicals used, and associated cultural and religious customs. These too may be indicators of the contemporaneity of the remains.

Understanding the context in which the remains were found is often the key to determining the medicolegal significance. For example, remains scattered in a remote wooded area are likely to be medicolegally significant, while those discovered in a known cemetery are likely not to be. Artifacts associated with remains such as clothing, jewelry, wallet, and other belongings directly associated with the decedent often provide contextual evidence of when the remains were deposited. Other artifacts may include grave goods such as coffin hardware, currency, or other directly dateable items that may provide clues to the time period of origin. Artifacts may also include materials such as stone tools and pottery which are likely indications of a nonrecent burial.

Biocultural factors may also assist in the determination of medicolegal significance. For example, nonrecent individuals may exhibit dental or skeletal adaptations or modifications that are not typically seen in modern populations. Notably, prehistoric Native Americans can often be distinguished from contemporary Americans by the dramatic degree of occlusal attrition often observed on their dentition, which resulted from the introduction of grit into the diet from food grinding implements, as well as use of the dentition in the processing of hides and basketry. Certain cultural modifications such as cranial deformation and dental mutilation may also be clues to the cultural affiliation and contemporaneity of the remains.

Interment conditions may also provide contextual clues to contemporaneity. For example, clandestine burial or body disposal is more likely to lack any pretreatment or care typically seen in normal burial circumstances. Certain cultural burial arrangements, such as flexed and semiflexed positions, were used by some prehistoric societies (Fig. 4.14), whereas modern burials are most often in an extended position. Medical and dental treatments may present a quick and obvious way to determine whether human remains are recent (Fig. 4.15). On the other hand, evidence of trephination (cranial surgery) or other ancient medical practices are indicative of an ancient origin.

Radiocarbon (including "bomb curve") dating techniques may also assist in the determination of whether remains are recent. Analysis of radiocarbon values in bones and teeth can distinguish whether an individual died before or after 1950 thereby assisting in the determination of recent versus nonrecent origin (Fig. 4.16).

While direct examination of questioned material is typically preferable and sometimes necessary, forensic anthropologists can often make the determination of medicolegal significance, especially between human and nonhuman bones, on the basis of high-quality photographs that include a scale. In this manner, anthropologists can provide real-time or expedient answers even if they cannot be present at the scene.

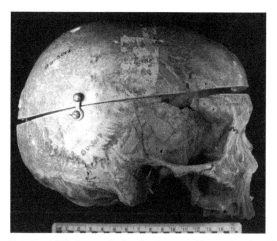

FIG. 4.13   Anatomical teaching specimen. Note the drill holes, sectioning, hardware, writing, and patina. *(Image courtesy of James Pokines.)*

FIG. 4.14   Burial positioning and context (such as the lack of a coffin) suggesting nonrecent mortuary practices. *(Image courtesy of Norman Sauer.)*

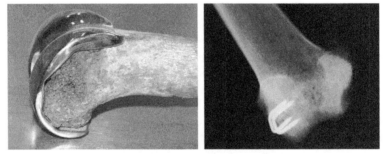

FIG. 4.15   Surgically implanted devices knee replacement (left) and anterior cruciate ligament (ACL) surgery (right). *(From Christensen, A.M., Passalacqua, N.V., Bartelink, E.J., 2014. Forensic Anthropology: Current Methods and Practice. Academic Press.)*

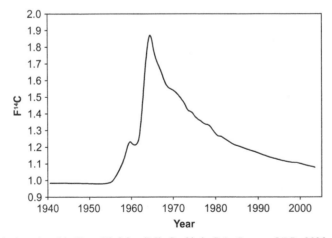

FIG. 4.16   Average annual atmospheric carbon-14. *(From Ubelaker, D.H., Buchholz, B.A., Stewart, J.E.B., 2006. Analysis of artificial radiocarbon in different skeletal and dental tissue types to evaluate date of death. J. Forensic Sci. 51(3), 484–488.)*

EXERCISE 4.1   Skeletal Versus Nonskeletal—Elemental Analysis

Materials needed:
- Images provided in this exercise

Note to instructor: This exercise can also be carried out using XRF spectra obtained from casework or other reference material, if available.

Case scenario: A woman was suspected of killing her husband and burning his remains along with other household trash in a pit behind the couple's house. While searching the contents of the fire pit, investigators located the material pictured below which they suspect to be bone fragments belonging to the husband. A visual examination was inconclusive, and before proceeding to a destructive analysis you decide to use XRF to determine whether the material is skeletal in origin. You test one of the fragments which results in XRF spectrum A; another fragment yields spectrum B.

(Image courtesy of Eric Bartelink.)

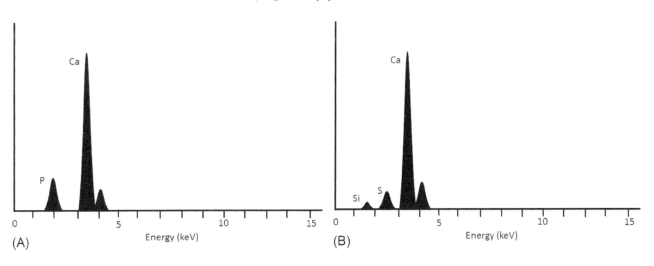

What can you conclude about the material represented by spectrum A? It is likely skeletal or nonskeletal in origin?

_____

Are there other materials that could be represented by spectrum A? Explain.

_____

_____

What does spectrum A tell us about the possible species of the sample?

_____

What can you conclude about the material represented by spectrum B? It is likely skeletal or nonskeletal in origin?

_____

How might you be able to determine what material is represented by spectrum B?

_____

_____

_____

EXERCISE 4.2   Skeletal Versus Nonskeletal—Elemental Analysis

Materials needed:
- X-ray fluorescence spectrometer (and trained operator)
- Bone samples (real, human or nonhuman)
- Nonskeletal materials (e.g., floral, mineral)
- NIST hydroxyapatite reference standard (optional)

Note to instructor: This exercise can be prepared by assembling a small collection of skeletal and nonskeletal material. Since human and nonhuman skeletal material will have essentially the same elemental profile, human bone is not required for this exercise. If possible, obtain a hydroxyapatite standard, which is available from the National Institute of Standards and Technology (NIST). This can be used as a reference for the expected profile of skeletal tissue on your particular instrument.

Case scenario: While executing a search warrant of a suspect's home related to a multiple homicide investigation, police find a strange trinket box filled small suspicious objects. Curious whether the objects may be parts of bones or teeth from victims, they bring them to you for analysis.

Instructions/Procedure:
- First, analyze the hydroxyapatite standard (if available).
- Next, analyze various samples of skeletal tissues (including bones and teeth) and nonskeletal materials.
- Below, list the materials you analyzed and discuss your results. What can you interpret from your results?

Material:_____

Results:

_____

_____

_____

Material:_____

Results:

_____

_____

_____

Material:_____

Results:

_____

_____

_____

EXERCISE 4.3   Skeletal Versus Nonskeletal—Fluorescence

Materials needed:
- Images teprovided in this exercise

Note to instructors: This exercise can be replaced or supplemented with ALS images from casework or reference collections if available.

Case scenario: While searching for a drowning victim in a lake, forensic divers recovered a number of items that they believed could be skeletal material. They are in need of an immediate investigative lead in order to determine whether to send the divers back into the water before departing the scene. The divers are not trained in osteology but recall from a training course that bones will fluoresce, and they have an ALS in their deployment kit. Using a 450-nm light and an orange filter, the divers see the following:

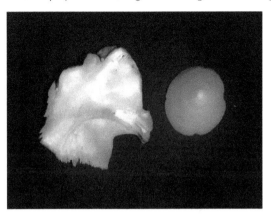

What can the divers conclude about what they see using the ALS? Is the item on the left likely skeletal in origin? What about the item on the right?

_____

_____

Is it possible that the item on the right is skeletal in origin? If so, what might account for the fact that it does not appear to fluoresce?

_____

_____

What can be concluded about the human or nonhuman origin of the items based on fluorescence?

_____

_____

_____

EXERCISE 4.4   Skeletal or Nonskeletal—Fluorescence

Materials needed:
- Alternate light source (ALS) and appropriate filters
- Skeletal material (human or nonhuman)
- Nonskeletal material (e.g., floral, mineral, etc.)

Note to instructor: This exercise can be prepared by assembling a small collection of skeletal and nonskeletal material. Since human and nonhuman skeletal material will both fluoresce, human bone is not required for this exercise. ALS performs best when there is no ambient light, so the exercise is ideally performed in a darkened room.

Case scenario: For the case described in Exercise 4.2, one option for identifying possible skeletal material is using an ALS, so before employing more sophisticated approaches, you decide to use an ALS to see if any of the items fluoresce.

Instructions/Procedure:
- Using the ALS in a darkened room, observe the items through an appropriate filter.

Describe what you saw when observing the items using ALS:

_____

_____

_____

Did you locate materials that you believe could be skeletal in origin based on their fluorescence? If not, did you know there to be skeletal remains present? What might account for the lack of fluorescence?

_____

_____

_____

EXERCISE 4.5   Human Versus Nonhuman—Morphology

Materials needed:

• Images provided in this exercise

Note to instructor: If real bones are available, this exercise can be modified to use real samples instead of (or in addition to) the images below.

Case scenario: While serving a jail sentence for a stolen car, an inmate bragged to a cellmate about having killed several women in the 1990s and dumping their bodies in a wooded area outside of town. The cellmate snitched to guards who notified the police department. The police conducted a search of the wooded area and located numerous bones which they brought to you for examination.

Instructions/Procedure:

• Based on a visual assessment of morphology, indicate whether each bone pictured below is human or nonhuman in origin.

• A response of "undetermined" is also acceptable in cases where the origin cannot be determined based on the features observable in the image.

Human or nonhuman?_____   Human or nonhuman?_____

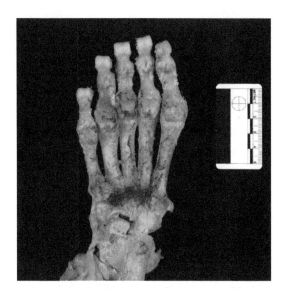

Human or nonhuman?_____   Human or nonhuman?_____

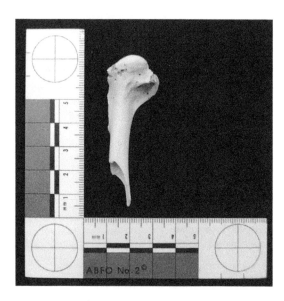

Human or nonhuman?_____ Human or nonhuman?_____

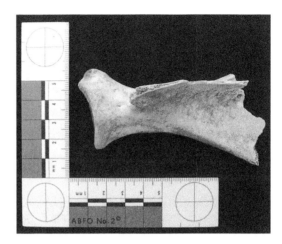

Human or nonhuman?_____ Human or nonhuman?_____

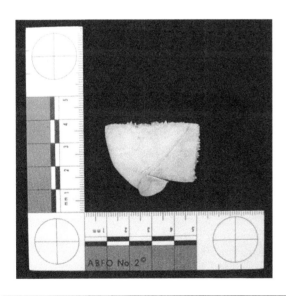

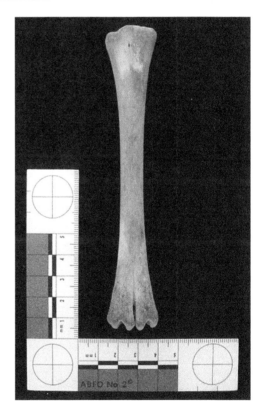

EXERCISE 4.6 Human Versus Nonhuman From Photos

Materials needed:
- Images provided in this exercise

Note to instructor: This exercise can be supplemented with your own cell phone images of human or nonhuman bones.

Case scenario: During a weekend camping trip, some college students discovered several bones scattered along a hiking trail. They believe authorities should be notified, but there is no cell service in the area. They decide to leave the bones in place, note the nearest trail marker, and take some pictures of the bones with their cell phones. When they return to cell phone range, they email the photos to the local sheriff, who forwards them to you, requesting a determination of human or nonhuman origin, and guidance on whether a crime scene unit should be deployed to recover the bones and possibly search for others.

Instructions/Procedure:
- Based on the photographs you received, indicate whether each bone is human or nonhuman in origin.
- Remember that a conclusion of "undetermined" may also be appropriate.

*Human or nonhuman?*_____ *Human or nonhuman?*_____

Human or nonhuman?_____ Human or nonhuman?_____

How confident are you in your conclusions? Explain.

_____
_____

Discuss some of the helpful and challenging features of the photos you received.

_____
_____
_____

Based on your findings, do you think a search of the area is warranted? Why or why not?

_____
_____

What suggestions would you give regarding taking/sending photos for analysis in the future?

_____
_____

If the photos in this case all depicted bones determined to be nonhuman in origin, would you issue the sheriff an official report? Why or why not?

_____
_____
_____

EXERCISE 4.7 Human Versus Nonhuman From Photos

Materials needed:
- Cell phone with camera
- Real or replica human or nonhuman bones

Note to instructor: A small selection of real or replica bones or bone fragments is ideal, but any items can be photographed to demonstrate the principles of this exercise.

Case scenario: Assume/imagine that you were one of the campers in the above scenario.

Instructions/Procedure:
- Using your own cell phone and real or replica bones of human and nonhuman origin, take a series of pictures that would be appropriate to send to a forensic anthropologist for analysis.
- Keep in mind factors such as scale, lighting, and focus
- Exchange photos with a classmate

Are you able to make a determination of human or nonhuman origin from the photos you received? Why or why not? If not, how may the photos be improved?

_____
_____
_____

Describe why the use of a scale is important in these types of analyses.

_____
_____

Discuss any issues that may be associated with using your cell phone to document evidence.

_____
_____
_____
_____

EXERCISE 4.8 Human Versus Nonhuman—Morphology

Materials needed:
- Images provided in this exercise

Note to instructor: If available, real or replica human or nonhuman bones can also be used to replace or supplement the images below.

Case scenario: A deer hunter discovered the long bone fragment pictured below in the woods while out on a weekend hunting trip. Having recently heard a news story about a local missing teenage girl, he wondered whether the bone could belong to her. He collected the bone and notified the local sheriff who then brought the bone to your laboratory to determine whether it is human or nonhuman, and whether it could belong to the missing teen.

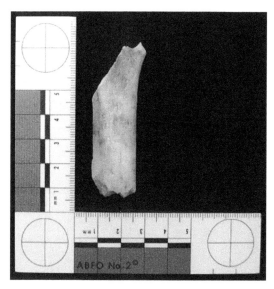
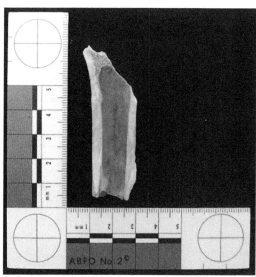

Keeping in mind that your examination should proceed from least to most destructive, how would you proceed with your examination? What would you look for first?

_____
_____
_____

Are the visible landmarks and features consistent with human origin? Why or why not?

_____
_____

If you cannot determine the origin of this bone based on visual assessment of morphology, how might you proceed? Are there any precautions you might take, or permission you might request before you begin other types of analyses?

_____
_____

EXERCISE 4.9 Human Versus Nonhuman—Histology

Materials needed:
- Image provided in this exercise

Note to instructor: If available, histological slides of human or nonhuman bone may be used to replace or supplement the image below.

Case scenario: Based on visual and radiologic analysis of the bone from Exercise 4.8, the origin of the bone remains undetermined. After receiving consent from the sheriff to perform destructive analysis of the bone, you decide to perform a histological examination. You first make a thin section using a wafering saw, grind the section to approximately 50 μm, and mount the section onto a glass microscope slide. When you examine the section with your microscope at 100×, you see the following:

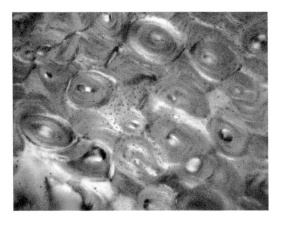

What can you conclude about the origin of bone? Is it likely human or nonhuman in origin?

_____

On what basis did you make your conclusion?

_____
_____

Could there be any alternatives to the conclusion you provide? Why or why not?

_____
_____

EXERCISE 4.10   Human Versus Nonhuman—Histology

Materials needed:
- Bone histology slides
- Microscope (preferably with polarized light)

Note to instructors: Bone histology slides are available from various anatomical supply sources. If the equipment and someone with appropriate training and experience are available, the exercise can also be modified to include learning to prepare a histological slide of bone (from a human or nonhuman bone fragment), including sectioning, grinding/polishing, and mounting the bone sample.

Case scenario: Several suspected bone fragments were turned over to the medical examiner's office to see if they were human in origin. The fragments are very small, and it is not possible to determine origin based on morphology. The ME's technician was able to prepare histological slides but is not an osteologist. They have asked you to examine the slides to make a determination.

Instructions/Procedure:
* Examine the bone histology slides using a microscope at 100×
* Describe the findings for the slides you examined. Were you able to make a determination of human or nonhuman origin? Discuss why or why not

Sample:_____

Findings:

_____
_____

Sample:_____

Findings:

_____
_____

Sample:_____

Findings:

_____
_____

EXERCISE 4.11   Recent Versus Nonrecent

Materials needed:
* Image provided in this exercise

Note to instructor: If available, real or replica human bones of recent and nonrecent origin can be used to supplement or replace the image below.

Case scenario: While preparing for an estate sale at the home of a recently deceased great-grandmother, family members found the item pictured below in a hat box in the attic. They called the police who contacted you to help identify this possible murder victim.

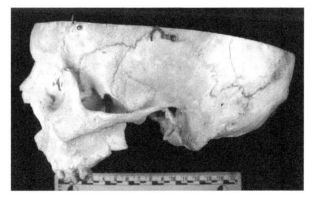

(Image courtesy of James Pokines.)

Do you believe these remains to be of a murder victim? Why or why not?

_____
_____
_____

Are these remains likely of medicolegal significance? Why or why not?

_____

_____

_____

What would you suggest investigators do with the remains?

_____

_____

_____

Chapter 5

Forensic Taphonomy

OBJECTIVES

Knowledge of taphonomic changes can help in interpreting the circumstances surrounding the death event, understanding processes occurring since the death event, and estimating the time since death. It is also important to understand and be able to differentiate taphonomic changes from other causes of skeletal alterations such as trauma. This chapter includes exercises that will guide you through identifying general stages of soft tissue decomposition and skeletal diagenesis, differentiating alterations created by different scavengers, and estimating the postmortem interval based on a scoring system and temperature.

PRINCIPLES OF FORENSIC TAPHONOMY

Forensic taphonomy is the study of postmortem processes which affect the preservation and recovery of human remains. Understanding taphonomic processes can facilitate the reconstruction of events that occurred between the deposition of the remains and their recovery, and in differentiating taphonomic events from antemortem and perimortem events (such as trauma), and can be used for estimating the postmortem interval (PMI) or time since death. In addition, a thorough understanding of taphonomic processes in local environments (including the terrain and scavenger species present) can aid in searches for human remains and the context of their discovery.

DECOMPOSITION AND POSTMORTEM SOFT TISSUE CHANGE

Decomposition is the process by which organic material is broken down into simpler forms. It occurs systematically in all biological organisms with the cessation of normal life functions and results in many physical and biochemical changes that can be observed macroscopically and microscopically. Decomposition occurs through two primary chemical processes: *autolysis* (the destruction of cells through the action of their own enzymes) and *putrefaction* (the microbial deterioration of tissues caused by the proliferation of bacteria). Visible changes associated with decomposition include soft tissue color changes (including marbling), bloating of the body due to gas production, and skin slippage (Fig. 5.1). In some cases, conditions may prevent or significantly delay the complete decomposition of remains resulting in mummification or saponification.

POSTMORTEM SKELETAL CHANGES

Once the soft tissues have decomposed, the skeleton is also subject to modification and decomposition due to a number of factors that are largely dependent on the depositional environment. *Diagenesis* refers to physical and chemical changes to sediments and geological materials but is sometimes also used to describe postmortem changes to bones and teeth. These changes are often the result of interaction with ground water and sediment, soil pH, transport by natural or physical forces, plant growth through bones, and microbes. Weathering is form of diagenesis involving postmortem modification of hard tissues as a response to natural agents in their immediate environment over time. Weathering of bones and teeth can appear as bleaching from exposure to sun, cracking, flaking, warping, and erosion. While a number of factors are involved in this complex process, sun exposure, wet/dry cycles, and freeze/thaw cycles are primarily responsible for physical changes to skeletal material. Other factors that play a role in the progression of bone weathering include microenvironment, weather extremes, bone density, and taxon. The degree and condition of weathering can be documented through detailed descriptions and is often described using stages such as those in Table 5.1. Movement of bones due to recovery, bioturbation, or transport can lead to breakage or abrasion. Bones will also become discolored and stained by their immediate environment, including sediments transported via groundwater into the pore spaces of bone. Soil is commonly responsible for bone

A Laboratory Manual for Forensic Anthropology. https://doi.org/10.1016/B978-0-12-812201-3.00005-0

FIG. 5.1 Bloating, skin slippage, and discoloration on decomposing remains.*(Image courtesy of Robyn Capobianco.)*

TABLE 5.1 Stages of Bone Weathering

Stage	Description
0	Bone surface shows no sign of cracking or flaking due to weathering
1	Bone shows cracking, normally parallel to the fiber structure (e.g., longitudinal in long bones), particular surfaces may show mosaic cracking of covering tissue as well as in the bone itself
2	Outermost concentric thin layers of bone show flaking, usually associated with cracks
3	Bone surface is characterized by patches of rough, homogeneously weathered compact bone, resulting in a fibrous structure, all lamellar bone is absent from these patches
4	The bone surface is coarsely fibrous and rough in texture
5	Bone is falling apart in situ
(From Behrensmeyer, A.K., 1978. Taphonomic and ecological information from bone weathering. Paleobiology 4, 150–162.)	

staining, but it can also result from prolonged contact with decomposition fluids, leaves, algae, or metal objects such as zippers or buttons. Bodies deposited (especially buried) in areas with trees and plants may also be affected by roots, which can adhere to and even etch and degrade the bone surface.

SCAVENGING

Scavenging refers to the consumption and associated modification of remains by other animals. Scavengers of human remains are many, but the most prominent are insects (Fig. 5.2), carnivores (Fig. 5.3 and Table 5.2), and rodents (Fig. 5.4), and it is not uncommon for there to be evidence of multiple scavenger types. The damage to the bone, the pattern of damage, and the environmental context can all help identify which scavenger may be responsible (Table 5.3). In aquatic environments, the scavenging populations are significantly different and may include sharks, fishes, crustaceans, gastropod mollusks, and echinoderms. Some species may also scrape algae or microbes from bone surfaces or adhere to bones as a substrate.

ESTIMATING THE POSTMORTEM INTERVAL

The estimation of the postmortem interval (PMI) is important because it can narrow the pool of potential decedents thus facilitating identification, confirm or refute reports from potential perpetrators, and in some cases can shed light on the circumstances of death. Estimating PMI generally involves determining the probable rate of postmortem changes to the body and working backward. The primary determinant of soft tissue decomposition rate is temperature; other factors that affect the rate of decomposition include humidity, moisture, pH, the presence of clothing, the depositional environment (e.g., burial vs. surface), the presence and extent of animal modification, the presence and extent of perimortem trauma, body weight, and the presence and extent of chemicals including those involved in funerary practices.

FIG. 5.2 Insect development on a corpse. (A) Flies arriving at a corpse, (B) eggs, (C) newly hatched instars, (D) maggots feeding on remains, (E) pupa cases, and (F) adult calliphoridae fly. *(Images courtesy of Rebecca Hurst; From Christensen, A.M., Passalacqua, N.V., Bartelink, E.J. 2014. Forensic Anthropology: Current Methods and Practice. Academic Press.)*

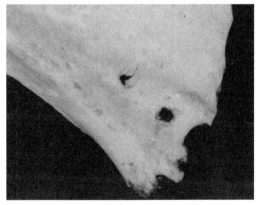

FIG. 5.3 Carnivore scavenging on a scapula. *(From Christensen, A.M., Passalacqua, N.V., Bartelink, E.J. 2014. Forensic Anthropology: Current Methods and Practice. Academic Press.)*

TABLE 5.2 Stages of Carnivore Scavenging

Stage	Condition of Remains
0	Early scavenging of soft tissue with no body unit removal
1	Destruction of the ventral thorax accompanied by evisceration and removal of one or both upper extremities including scapulae and partial or complete clavicles
2	Lower extremities fully or partially removed
3	All skeletal elements disarticulated except for segments of the vertebral column
4	Total disarticulation with only cranium and other assorted skeletal elements or fragments recovered

(Adapted from Haglund, W.D., 1997. Dogs and coyotes: postmortem involvement with human remains. In: Haglund, W.D., Sorg, M.H. (Eds.), Forensic Taphonomy: The Postmortem Fate of Human Remains. CRC Press, Boca Raton, pp. 367–382.)

FIG. 5.4 Rodent scavenging on a cranium. *(Image courtesy of James Pokines.)*

TABLE 5.3 Scavengers and Patterns

Scavenger	Activity	Pattern on Bone	Misc. Info
• Flies/maggots	• Soft tissue consumption	• N/A	• Can be used to estimate PMI • Almost always first scavengers to arrive
• Beetles	• Consume dried soft tissue	• N/A	• Can be used for skeletal processing
• Carnivores (wolves coyotes, foxes, domestic dogs, cats) • Some omnivores (bears, pigs)	• Consume, disarticulate, disperse soft, and skeletal tissue	• Punctures, pits, scoring, furrows • Ends of long bones and sternal rib ends often consumed	
• Bears	• Exploit axial skeleton	• Damage to vertebral column, ribs, sternum	
• Birds (vultures)	• Consume and alter remains	• Shallow linear scratches • Damage to small bones of the face such as orbits	• Can skeletonize a body in 3–24 hours
• Rodents	• Modify and accumulate remains	• Parallel striations • Tend to modify ends or surfaces where one jaw can lock	• May take remains to nests/burrows
• Fishes and sharks	• Tear open skin • Gnaw facial soft tissues	• Unpatterned serrated cuts	• Pieces of shark teeth may break off in bone
• Crustaceans	• Tear through muscle		
• Gastropod mollusks	• Feed on decaying flesh and adipocere	• Scrape algae and microbes from bone surfaces	
• Echinoderms	• May use humans as food source	• May use as substrate to adhere	

The most accurate and reliable methods of PMI estimation based on decomposition are those utilizing scoring systems that assess and quantify the progression of decomposition (e.g., Megyesi et al., 2005). These approaches result in formulae that can be used to calculate an estimate of PMI, which depend primarily on the temperature of the depositional environment. Because of the variation in decomposition rates between regions, methods specific to a particular area or similar physical or depositional environment should be utilized when available.

Because temperature is the primary factor influencing the rate of decomposition, the level of decomposition can be calculated with reference to the accumulated degree days (or ADD). The ADD represents the sum of the average daily temperatures (in °C) for a given number of days, typically with reference to a particular temperature threshold. In the case of decomposing remains, the temperature below which decomposition processes cease is not actually known, but 0°C has been utilized as a threshold in decomposition studies because freezing temperatures severely inhibit bacterial growth. In these calculations of ADD and estimation of PMI, any temperature below the 0°C threshold would be treated as 0.

Decomposition can be quantified by scoring features such as discoloration, bloating, purging, and the amount of soft tissue remaining, which can then be used to estimate PMI (Appendix H: Decomposition Scoring and PMI Estimation). In some approaches (e.g., Megyesi et al., 2005), different scoring systems are applied to different areas of the body (e.g., the trunk, head, and limbs), resulting in a summed score called a total body score (TBS). This score is then used to estimate the accumulated degree days using the following formula (including the standard error of the regression):

$$ADD = 10^{(0.002\,TBS+1.81)} \pm 388.16$$

For example, a set of remains with a TBS of 15 would be calculated as:

$$ADD = 10^{(0.002*15*15+1.81)} \pm 388.16$$

$$ADD = 181.97 \pm 388.16$$

The resulting number represents the accumulated degree days that would be required for the individual to reach the stage of decomposition represented by the TBS. To estimate the PMI, this result needs to be compared to local average daily temperatures (in °C) where the individual was discovered (usually based on the closest weather station data). Working backward from the day that the remains were scored, the daily average temperatures are summed until the calculated ADD is reached. The number of days required to reach the ADD represents the interval since death, in days. The implications of this research are that these nonhuman models are not adequate replacements for studying human decomposition or estimating the postmortem interval in human forensic cases. Little research has addressed the timing of postmortem changes to the skeletal tissues, and there are currently no widely accepted PMI estimation methods based on solely on skeletonized remains.

EXERCISE 5.1   Bone Weathering

Materials needed:
- Images provided in this exercise
- Table 5.1 from this chapter

Note to instructor: This exercise can be supplemented or replaced with human or nonhuman skeletal material from casework or reference collections if available.

Case scenario: The bones below were found during a search of a suspected human remains dump site in a case where a farmer and several of his animals have gone missing. Investigators have requested your assistance to determine whether the condition of the recovered bones is consistent with the time frame of the farmer's disappearance.

Instructions/Procedure:
- For each of the bones depicted later, describe the taphonomic changes you see and indicate the stage of bone weathering using Table 5.1.

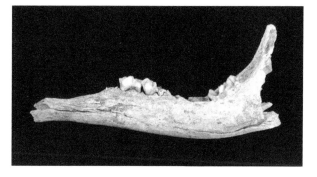

Taphonomic changes:

_____

_____

Weathering stage: _____

Taphonomic changes:

_____

_____

Weathering stage: _____

Taphonomic changes:

_____

_____

Weathering stage: _____

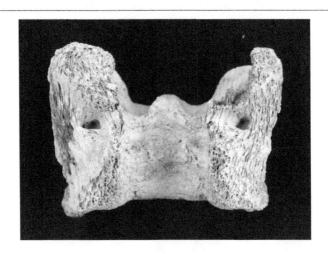

Taphonomic changes:

_____

_____

Weathering stage: _____

What can you interpret about the postmortem interval based on weathering?

_____

_____

What features or other changes might be obscured by bone weathering? How could this impact a forensic investigation?

_____

_____

_____

EXERCISE 5.2   Bone Taphonomy

Materials needed:
- Images provided in this exercise

Note to instructor: This exercise can be supplemented or replaced with human or nonhuman skeletal material from casework or reference collections if available.

Case scenario: The following bones were found in the same depositional environment. You have been asked to provide information regarding how and when the bones came to be at this site. The first image shows two long bones that were found next to each other in the same location. The second image shows two views (lateral and medial) of the same mandible.

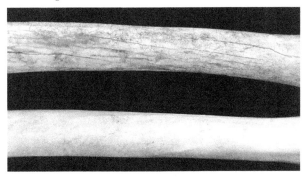

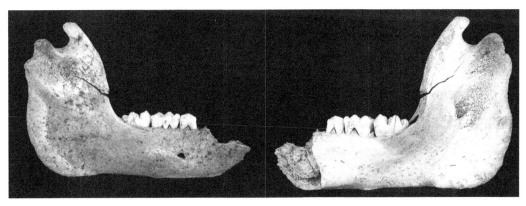

For the long bones, describe the weathering or other taphonomic changes to these two bones. What can you say about the relative PMI or weathering stage of the two bones?

_____

_____

_____

For the mandible, describe the weathering or other taphonomic changes to the bone. What can you say about how the bone was likely positioned in the depositional environment?

_____

_____

_____

EXERCISE 5.3   Scavenging Patterns on Bone

Materials needed:
- Images provided in this exercise
- Table 5.3 from this chapter

Note to instructor: This exercise can be supplemented or replaced with human or nonhuman skeletal material from casework or reference collections if available.

Case scenario: A recent human remains search yielded only a partial skeleton. Investigators believe that parts of the remains may have been consumed and/or moved by scavengers.

Instructions/Procedure:
- For each of the images below, indicate what type of scavenger you believe was responsible for the bone alterations and what features or evidence led you to that conclusion.

Scavenger and supporting features/evidence:

_____

_____

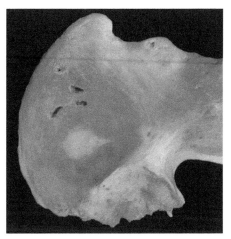

(Image courtesy of Eric Bartelink.)

Scavenger and supporting features/evidence:

_____

_____

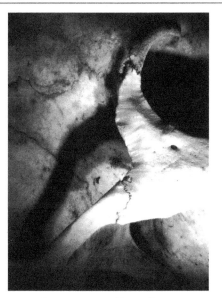

(Image courtesy of Steven Symes.)

Scavenger and supporting features/evidence:

_____

_____

EXERCISE 5.4   Estimating PMI

Materials needed:
- Images provided in this exercise
- Appendix H (Decomposition Scoring and PMI Estimation)
- Internet access
- Calculator and/or paper and writing utensil

Note to instructor: This exercise can be supplemented or replaced with images or cases of decomposing human or nonhuman remains from casework or reference collections if available.

Case scenario: Decomposing human remains were discovered under a bridge near your university's campus. Police suspect that the remains may belong to a man who wandered away from a nearby nursing home and was last seen alive two weeks ago. Police took the photo below and have asked you to assist them in estimating the PMI.

(Image courtesy of Robyn Capobianco.)

Where can you find daily temperature data for the area around your university? Locate this information and have it handy (you will need it later).

_____

Using Appendix H, calculate the total body score (TBS) for the remains. Compare answers with your classmates. Did everyone arrive at the same TBS? Why or why not?

_____

_____

Using the equation provided in Appendix H, calculate how many accumulated degree days (ADD) would be required to reach the TBS you calculated.

_____

Assuming that the body was discovered today, and using the daily temperature data for your area, what is the postmortem interval?

_____

Based on your estimated PMI and when the missing man was last seen, could the remains belong to him?

_____

EXERCISE 5.5   Estimating PMI

Materials needed:
- Images provided in this exercise
- Appendix H (Decomposition Scoring and PMI Estimation)
- Internet access
- Calculator and/or paper and writing utensil

Note to instructor: This exercise can be supplemented or replaced with images or cases of decomposing human or nonhuman remains from casework or reference collections if available.

Case scenario: Decomposing human remains were discovered in a wooded area near Fredericksburg, Virginia. Authorities believe the remains may belong to a man whose carjacking was captured on surveillance video two months prior to the discovery of the remains and who has not been seen since. The following pictures were provided to you to assist in estimating the postmortem interval.

(Images courtesy of Robyn Capobianco.)

Where can you find daily temperature data for Fredericksburg, VA? Locate this information and have it handy (you will need it later).

_____

Using Appendix H, calculate the total body score (TBS) for the remains. Compare answers with your classmates. Did everyone arrive at the same TBS? Why or why not?

_____

_____

How many accumulated degree days would be required to reach the TBS you calculated?

_____

Assuming that the body was discovered 60 days ago, and using the daily temperature data for Fredericksburg, VA, what is the postmortem interval?

_____

Based on your estimated PMI, when the remains were discovered, and when the missing man was last seen, could the remains belong to him?

_____

EXERCISE 5.6   Estimating PMI

Materials needed:
- Image provided in this exercise
- Appendix H (Decomposition Scoring and PMI Estimation)
- Internet access
- Calculator and/or paper and writing utensil

Note to instructor: This exercise can be supplemented or replaced with images or cases of decomposing human or nonhuman remains from casework or reference collections if available.

Case scenario: Nearly skeletonized remains were discovered in a mountainous area west of Denver, Colorado, on August 15 of last year. Because snowfall was expected soon which would complicate the recovery prior to the spring thaw, and because there seemed to be minimal scattering of the remains, the recovery was performed quickly by local authorities (without the assistance of an anthropologist) and taken to the medical examiner's office. You were not at the scene, but were provided with the image below, and informed that the GPS coordinates and latitude/longitude of the scene datum are: 39.664178, −105.704662, 39°39′51.0″N 105°42′16.8″W.

Using Appendix H, calculate the total body score (TBS) for the remains. Compare answers with your classmates. Did everyone arrive at the same TBS? Why or why not?

_____

_____

Using the equation provided in Appendix H, calculate how many accumulated degree days (ADD) would be required to reach the TBS you calculated.

_____

Besides temperature, what other variables might affect decomposition rate? Consider factors related to the body itself as well as the depositional environment. How might these variables affect the accuracy of PMI estimation?

_____

_____

_____

EXERCISE 5.7 Taphonomic Modification

Materials needed:
- Images provided in this exercise

Note to instructor: This exercise can be supplemented or replaced with human or nonhuman skeletal material from casework or reference collections if available.

Case scenario: The skull pictured below was brought into the medical examiner's office with no contextual information. You have been asked to assist in providing any probative information based on an anthropological analysis.

Instructions/Procedure:
- Describe any taphonomic modifications on the remains pictured below and use this information to reconstruct as much information as you can about the likely context of these remains.

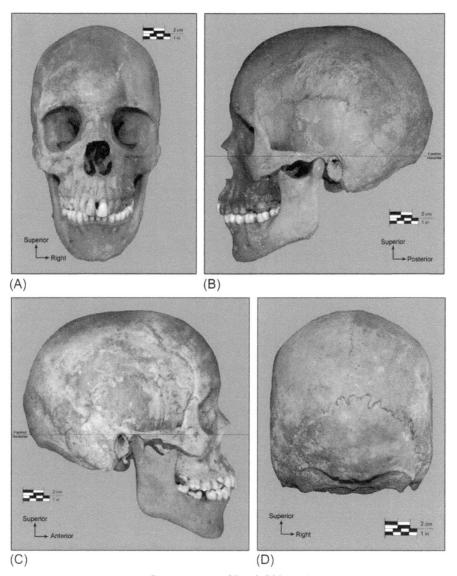

(Images courtesy of Dennis Dirkmaat.)

Describe taphonomic changes to the skull:

_____
_____
_____

What can you say about the likely context and/or PMI of these remains?

_____
_____
_____

Chapter 6

Forensic Archaeology and Scene Processing

OBJECTIVES

Forensic archaeology is the application of archaeological theory and methods to medicolegal cases, including searching for, locating, surveying, sampling, recording, and interpreting evidence, as well as the recovery and documentation of human remains and associated evidence. Exercises in this chapter will guide you through the processes of performing searches for remains, documenting a recovery scene, and properly collecting and packaging evidentiary items, including skeletal remains and other evidence.

PRINCIPLES OF FORENSIC ARCHAEOLOGY

Forensic archaeology is the application of archaeological theory and methods to the resolution of medicolegal and humanitarian issues. It may include methods involved in searching for, locating, surveying, sampling, recording, and interpreting evidence, as well as the recovery and documentation of human remains and associated evidence. Proper implementation of forensic archaeological techniques provides a scientific basis for interpreting the context in which remains and associated evidence are found.

Human remains can be discovered in and recovered from a wide variety of scene types, including indoor and outdoor, confined, or dispersed. The location where human remains are found is called a scene or recovery scene (the term *crime scene*, though often applied to recovery scenes, may not always be appropriate). Outdoor scenes may involve remains that are on the surface, buried, submerged, or involved in fires (which are technically specialized surface scenes, having factors that make recovery approaches somewhat more challenging).

DETECTION METHODS

Forensic archaeological methods are typically applied to the outdoor location and recovery of remains including surface remains and burials, usually when substantial decomposition or fragmentation has occurred. Forensic archaeological principles, however, can also be applied to indoor scenes, as well as underwater and fire scenes. One important feature of archaeological methods is that the processes are inherently and unavoidably destructive. When remains and evidence are collected and removed from the scene, the context is permanently altered and the spatial relationships between evidence and the scene are lost. Thorough documentation and careful preservation of the material and contextual information are therefore very important.

The detection of a scene involves the search for and location of remains. The selection of the methods used in the detection or identification of a recovery scene and its boundaries is dependent on the type and scale of the case as well as aspects of the terrain itself. In many cases, the type of scene may not yet be known when the search begins, and detection methods may need to be modified depending on initial findings. Several common detection methods are described in Table 6.1 and Figs. 6.1 and 6.2, and some indicators of buried bodes are described in Table 6.2 and Fig. 6.3.

RECOVERY METHODS

Recovery methods are aimed at removing the evidence from a scene in a systematic manner while maintaining context. Any overburden such as leaf litter or loose topsoil should be screened for small bones or other evidentiary items that may not have been detected in the initial search. Screens are typically constructed of wire mesh (commonly ¼ inch, but smaller

A Laboratory Manual for Forensic Anthropology. https://doi.org/10.1016/B978-0-12-812201-3.00006-2

TABLE 6.1 Common Scene Detection Methods

Method	Scene Type(s)	Approach	Additional Information
Line search (standing or hands and knees)	• Surface, subsurface submerged	• Form line at one end of search area • Walk search area on foot, observing surroundings at a slow steady pace • Mark possible evidence with flags • Move back and forth if area exceeds length of line	• Line leader should keep pace • Be sure to look up and lateral as well as down • Anthropologist should follow search line, evaluating potential skeletal evidence
Probing	• Subsurface	• Soil probe is inserted into the ground surface using light pressure at regular intervals • Areas exhibiting less-compact soil are investigated further	• Simplest, least invasive ways to detect subsurface disturbances • Soil cores work similarly but are more invasive than probes since they remove soil
Geophysical	• Subsurface	• GPR • Magnetometry	• Very limited utility • Skilled operator required
Cadaver dogs	• Surface, subsurface, submerged	• Dogs and handlers systematically work the scene searching for decomposition odor	• Skilled handler and dog required • Dogs must only have been trained using human remains • Use caution with dogs that have been trained to detect more than one substance (bombs, drugs, remains, etc.)
Construction equipment	• Subsurface	• Backhoe • Bulldozer	• Potential to significantly damage remains • Smooth-edged bucket preferred • One remains located, excavation should proceed using other methods
Sonar/ROV	• Submerged	• May be performed by public safety diver underwater, or from a boat above	• Very limited utility • Skilled operator required

FIG. 6.1 Standing line search. *(From Christensen, A.M., Passalacqua, N.V., Bartelink, E.J., 2014. Forensic Anthropology: Current Methods and Practice, Academic Press.)*

FIG. 6.2   Subsurface coring (left) and soil probing (right). *(Image courtesy of Dennis C. Dirkmaat.)*

TABLE 6.2 Buried Body Indicators

Indicator	Features
Soil disturbances	• Color • Cracks • Mixing • Backdirt
Surface disturbances	• Backdirt • Abnormal piles of branches/debris • Disturbed areas of ingress/egress
Vegetation disturbances	• Excessive vegetation growth • Disturbed/lack of vegetation from ground surface disturbances • Disturbed areas from ingress/egress
Other	• Abnormal accumulation of debris • Burned areas • Broken shovels/tools

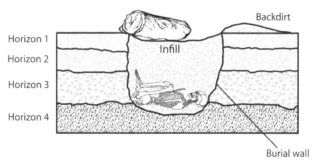

FIG. 6.3   Features of burial site. *(From Christensen, A.M., Passalacqua, N.V., Bartelink, E.J., 2014. Forensic Anthropology: Current Methods and Practice, Academic Press.)*

sizes may be needed) attached to a wooden or metal frame and often suspended by moveable legs so that the screen can be shaken (Fig. 6.4). This configuration facilitates the movement of material through the screen so that skeletal elements or evidentiary items can be located and removed. Depending on factors such as soil quality and available resources, material may be screened dry or wet screened.

The recovery of buried remains typically involves excavation, or the exposure and recovery of the remains through a slow and careful digging process. This usually involves small hand tools including trowels and brushes (Fig. 6.5). When

FIG. 6.4 Screening. *(Image courtesy of Dennis C. Dirkmaat.)*

recovering buried remains, it is important to excavate and recover not only details of the remains themselves but also those of the burial feature in which they are interred. The burial feature may contain evidence such as tool marks from the burial implement (such as a shovel) which may be present along the walls of the pit, shoe prints which may be found in the back-dirt pile or in the bottom of the burial, or disturbed vegetation may be mixed with the infill which could be examined by a forensic botanist to determine when the pit was dug.

Once the outline of the burial feature has been identified and defined, string held by stakes or chaining pins can be used to bisect the feature. Excavation of the infill of one-half of the burial feature should then proceed slowly from the bisection line toward the grave wall using hand trowels. This approach allows for the preservation of possible tool marks in the walls of the burial as the less compact infill will generally be easily removed from the undisturbed grave walls. Exposing half of the remains also allows for documentation of the position of the body and the body's relationship to evidentiary material encountered and the burial feature itself. The interpretation of soil horizons and stratigraphy is also important in an excavation because it can help to differentiate between undisturbed (sterile) soil and disturbed soil. After excavating one-half of the grave feature, the exposed wall should be mapped, creating a profile of the soil and remains, similar to that seen in Fig. 6.3; the other half of the burial can then be excavated. When potential evidence is encountered during a forensic excavation, it should be carefully exposed, photographed, mapped, and then removed.

The excavation of a burial feature should result in an open grave resembling the feature as it was originally dug. Once the remains have been removed from the grave, a metal detector should be used on the grave floor to search for additional evidence such as bullets, coins, or jewelry still obscured by soil. Careful excavation of the bottom of a grave may also reveal shoe or tool impressions.

In recovery scenes (including surface deposited and buried remains), all skeletal and other evidentiary materials should ideally be recovered in situ (in its original, undisturbed position). In some cases, however, bone fragments or other pieces of evidence (e.g., clothing items, bullets) may be small or difficult to see due to their small size or adhering soil and may accidentally be recovered among leaf litter or excavated along with the soil and removed from the grave. Excavated soil and other small debris removed from a scene should therefore always be screened for small bones and teeth or other associated evidence. If something of evidentiary value is recovered in a screen, it is helpful to track and document where in the feature or scene the soil came from (such as a grid quadrant) in order to maintain as much context as possible.

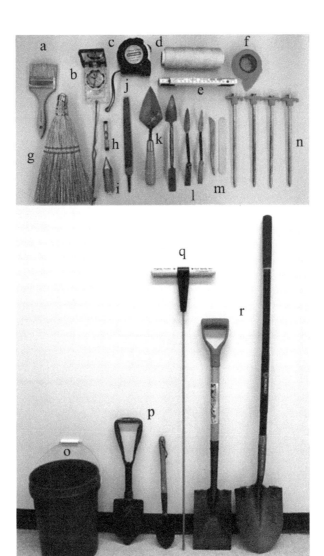

FIG. 6.5 Archaeological tools: (a) Small brush, (b) sighting compass, (c) metric tape measure, (d) string, (e) folding tape measure, (f) flagging tape, (g) whisk broom, (h) line-level, (i) plumb-bob, (j) file (for trowel sharpening), (k) trowel, (l) small leaf trowels, (m) wooden carving tool, (n) stakes, (o) bucket, (p) small shovels, (q) probe, and (r) large shovels. *(From Christensen, A.M., Passalacqua, N.V., Bartelink, E.J., 2014. Forensic Anthropology: Current Methods and Practice, Academic Press.)*

SCENE DOCUMENTATION

Scene documentation should include a detailed scene map or sketch and ample photographs of the overall scene, midrange views, and close-ups of the material recovered (see Appendix I: Scene Mapping and Documentation and Appendix J: Photograph Log). Videography or laser scanning (e.g., Lidar) may also provide good overviews of the scene and the approaches used. It is most important to document the context and provenience of the evidentiary material recovered for later interpretation. The best way to accomplish this is by generating a map, which should document the spatial distribution of all remains and associated materials recovered. Mapping is best conducted after performing a thorough search, denuding the area, and exposing the remains and any associated evidence. Different types of recovery scenes are better documented using certain methods, and several approaches are discussed later.

Prior to scene mapping, a datum is established, from which all evidence in the scene can be mapped. The datum is the primary reference point used for mapping and should be placed in a location that can easily be relocated if necessary. In cases where there may be multiple layers of evidentiary material (e.g., a fire scene), the datum may need to be established prior to denuding so that evidence can be mapped, recorded, and moved to access the next layer beneath.

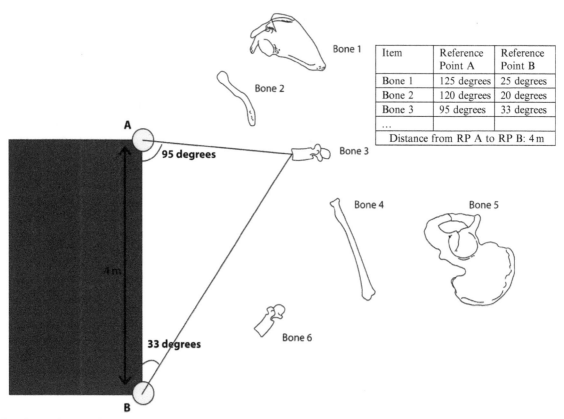

Item	Reference Point A	Reference Point B
Bone 1	125 degrees	25 degrees
Bone 2	120 degrees	20 degrees
Bone 3	95 degrees	33 degrees
...		
Distance from RP A to RP B: 4 m		

FIG. 6.6 Triangulation mapping. *(From Christensen, A.M., Passalacqua, N.V., Bartelink, E.J., 2014. Forensic Anthropology: Current Methods and Practice, Academic Press.)*

Maps can be created in two or three dimensions depending on type and scale of the scene and may range from hand-drawn sketches to electronic maps generated by mapping instruments. Maps should be as accurate as possible and at a minimum should include a north (N) arrow; indicate scale (a not-to-scale map is also referred to as a sketch); and include the author's name, date, and the location of the datum. Mapping a scene can be accomplished using various methods including triangulation (Fig. 6.6), trilateration (Fig. 6.7), azimuth (Fig. 6.8), baseline (Fig. 6.9), or grid mapping (Fig. 6.10). The selection of the mapping approach to be used depends on the extent and terrain of the scene, as well as the proficiencies or preferences of the recovery personnel. For any of these approaches it is important to keep the measurement tapes level to avoid adding measurement error. It is also strongly recommended to use a plumb-bob to keep vertical measurements straight. As a rule, measurements should be taken using metric units, which can later be converted to other units, if necessary.

FINDING RIGHT ANGLES

When measuring evidence from a baseline, it is important that the measurement is taken at a right angle from the baseline (Fig. 6.11). This can be accomplished in several ways. A *square*, which is a triangular-shaped tool used to measure right angles (commonly used in construction), can be used to ensure that the tapes are placed at right angles. Another approach that is useful in the field can be applied quickly and accurately to find a right angle to the baseline. Place the end (the "zero") of the tape measure at the evidence item. Next, move/swing the free end of the tape along the baseline. Wherever the free end of the tape makes the *shortest* distance to the baseline is a right angle.

When establishing a grid, there are a several approaches that can be used to determine a right angle for the axes and the smaller grids within them. One way is to use a construction square. If not readily available, however, other field methods can be used to quickly and accurately find a right angle. These approaches use the Pythagorean Theorem which describes the relationship between the lengths of the sides of any right-angled triangle. For lengths a, b, and c, the theorem states that: $a^2 + b^2 = c^2$, where c is the hypotenuse, and a and b are the other two sides.

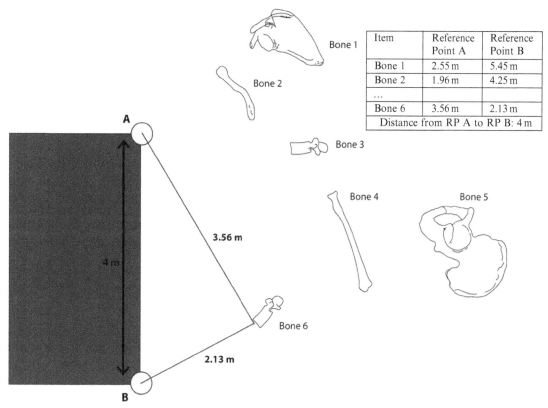

Item	Reference Point A	Reference Point B
Bone 1	2.55 m	5.45 m
Bone 2	1.96 m	4.25 m
...		
Bone 6	3.56 m	2.13 m
Distance from RP A to RP B: 4 m		

FIG. 6.7 Trilateration mapping. *(From Christensen, A.M., Passalacqua, N.V., Bartelink, E.J., 2014. Forensic Anthropology: Current Methods and Practice, Academic Press.)*

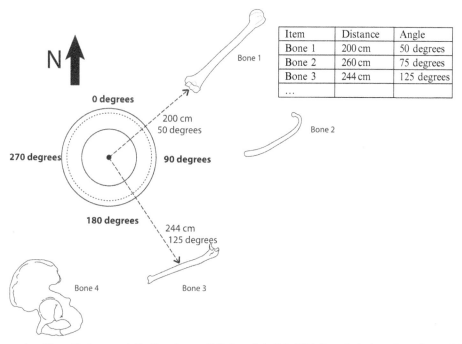

Item	Distance	Angle
Bone 1	200 cm	50 degrees
Bone 2	260 cm	75 degrees
Bone 3	244 cm	125 degrees
...		

FIG. 6.8 Azimuth mapping. *(From Christensen, A.M., Passalacqua, N.V., Bartelink, E.J., 2014. Forensic Anthropology: Current Methods and Practice, Academic Press.)*

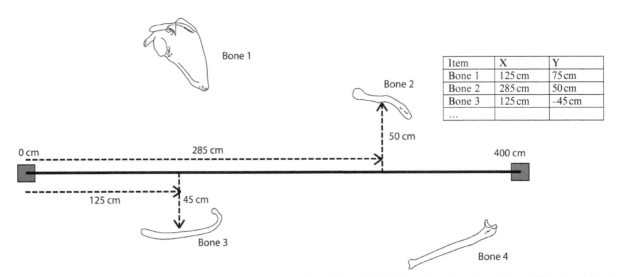

Item	X	Y
Bone 1	125 cm	75 cm
Bone 2	285 cm	50 cm
Bone 3	125 cm	–45 cm
...		

FIG. 6.9 Baseline mapping. *(From Christensen, A.M., Passalacqua, N.V., Bartelink, E.J., 2014. Forensic Anthropology: Current Methods and Practice, Academic Press.)*

One approach is to make a 3-4-5 triangle (Fig. 6.12). For a triangle that has sides of length 3, 4, and 5 in any units (or multiples of 3, 4, and 5 such as 6, 8, and 10), the angle between the 3- and 4-unit sides will form a right angle ($3^2 + 4^2 = 5^2$). From the datum point, simply measure 3 and 4 units away at approximate right angles using two tape measures. Using a third tape measure (which forms the hypotenuse), bring the two ends of the 3 and 4 unit tapes together until they measure 5 units apart. This approach can be used to establish the right angle, regardless of the units that will be used to map the site.

Another approach is to use standard unit sizes with known hypotenuse values and using these measures to find a right angle in the same manner as the 3-4-5 triangle (Table 6.3). Finally, another approach is to calculate what the hypotenuse should be based on the lengths of the two sides of the grid using the derivative of the Pythagorean Theorem: $c = \sqrt{(a^2 + b^2)}$.

COLLECTION OF SKELETAL EVIDENCE

Once evidence has been documented and photographed, it can be removed from the location where it was found and collected. The individual(s) collecting and packaging the evidence will depend on who is in charge of the recovery scene (often law enforcement). If you are assisting law enforcement with a search/recovery, be sure to follow their specific protocols for evidence collection.

Generally, bones should be individually packaged in brown paper bags or other breathable material. Packaging bones separately helps protect them by preventing them from pressing or rubbing against one another causing damage, and the use of breathable material helps prevent the growth of mold that can occur if bones are packaged in airtight packaging such as plastic. The packaging should be sealed in a manner that is tamper-evident, usually by closing the container with evidence tape and initialing across the seal and the packaging. The package should be labeled with the items listed in Table 6.4.

Other considerations may be needed for remains that are not skeletonized and dry or that are taphonomically compromised. For example, remains that are still mostly complete will likely be packaged in a large container such as a body bag (sometimes called a human remains pouch). For remains that are decomposed and may still retain some soft tissue or have large articulated segments, larger plastic or Tyvek packaging may be more appropriate than paper bags. In cases where remains are placed into plastic, the amount of time in the packaging should be limited. For burned remains, wrapping fragile bones individually in foil wrap offers additional protection and also helps maintain relative anatomical positions of fragment in the event of additional breakage in transit (Fig. 6.13). Severely burned or cremated remains may need to be placed into a container such as a plastic tub.

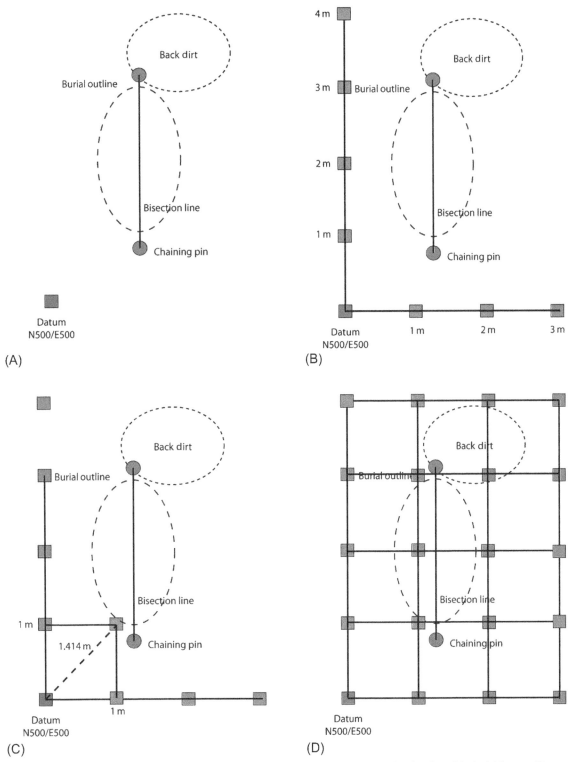

FIG. 6.10 Grid mapping. Steps to setting up a burial feature excavation: (A) Establish datum and bisection line of the burial feature; (B) set up major grid axes; (C) triangulate hypotenuse to make sure grid stakes are placed correctly; and (D) emplace additional grid stakes as needed. *(From Christensen, A.M., Passalacqua, N.V., Bartelink, E.J., 2014. Forensic Anthropology: Current Methods and Practice, Academic Press.)*

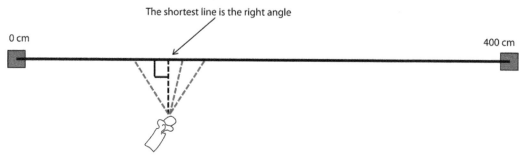

FIG. 6.11 Finding a right angle to a baseline. *(From Christensen, A.M., Passalacqua, N.V., Bartelink, E.J., 2014. Forensic Anthropology: Current Methods and Practice, Academic Press.)*

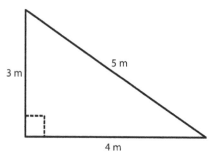

FIG. 6.12 3-4-5 Triangle with right angle. *(From Christensen, A.M., Passalacqua, N.V., Bartelink, E.J., 2014. Forensic Anthropology: Current Methods and Practice, Academic Press.)*

TABLE 6.3 Hypotenuse Values Given a Grid Unit Size

Unit Size (m)	Hypotenuse (cm)
1×1	141
1×2	223
2×2	283
4×2	447
4×4	566
5×5	707
10×10	1414

TABLE 6.4 Evidence Package Labeling

1. Agency
2. Case number
3. Item number
4. Item description
5. Date found
6. Location found
7. Name/initials of person recovering

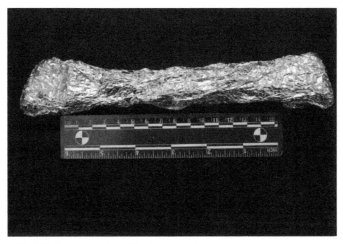

FIG. 6.13 Burned humerus packaged in foil. *(Image courtesy of Lyniece Lewis.)*

EXERCISE 6.1 Line Search

Materials needed:
- Search area
- Evidentiary items (ideally real or replica human or nonhuman skeletal material, and/or other evidentiary items such as clothing and tools)
- Pin flags

Note to instructor: This exercise can be prepared in advance by distributing evidentiary items in the search area. Although ideally conducted in an outdoor setting, a scene could also be prepared in a large indoor area.

Case scenario: The local sheriff's office has good investigative leads on the approximate location of where a body was deposited by a murder suspect three years ago. They have requested your assistance in performing a line search of the area to locate any surface-deposited skeletal remains.

Instructions/Procedure:
- Identify the search area. Along with your classmates, form a line at one side of the scene and proceed across the scene searching the ground and surrounding area for possible evidence
- Make sure to designate a "line leader" on one side of the line who keeps the pace and direction of the search
- If possible evidentiary items are located, place a flag next to the item or feature to be investigated further after completion of the search.

What challenges (if any) did you encounter in your search?

_____
_____
_____

Would you do things differently in future searches? If so, how?

_____
_____

EXERCISE 6.2 Search Using ALS

Materials needed:
- Portable alternate light source (ALS) and appropriate filters
- Outdoor search area
- Real skeletal material (human or nonhuman)
- Nonskeletal material (e.g., floral, mineral, etc.)

Note to instructor: This exercise can be prepared in advance by distributing a selection of bones in the search area. ALS performs best when there is no ambient light, so the exercise is ideally performed at night. Appropriate safety precautions should be considered. If a darkened outdoor search area is not an option, the ALS can be used in a darkened room to sort a selection of skeletal versus nonskeletal material.

Case scenario: A woman is suspected of animal abuse and neglect, and a neighbor told authorities that she may have been depositing dead animals on her large wooded property. A warrant was obtained to search the property but expires at midnight. It is currently 7 p.m. and already getting dark, but if any skeletal remains can be located, it may be enough to obtain another warrant. You decide to conduct an ALS search to see if any skeletal remains can be found.

Instructions/Procedure:

• Using a systematic approach, search your scene for skeletal remains using the ALS.

Describe the procedure you used to search your scene:

_____

_____

_____

Did you locate remains during your search? If not, did you know there to be skeletal remains present? What might account for the inability to locate them?

_____

_____

_____

EXERCISE 6.3 Soil Probing

Materials needed:

• Outdoor search area with disturbed and undisturbed soil
• Soil probe

Note to instructor: This exercise requires the use of an outdoor setting where the soil can be disturbed. A "burial" location can be prepared by digging a hole approximately 6'×3' and then refilling the hole with the soil. For the purpose of this exercise, it is not necessary to put anything (such as a body or evidence) into the burial location (the probe is identifying disturbed soil, not remains, so the objective can be met with only disturbed soil). Probes can be purchased inexpensively from a hardware store.

Case scenario: In a scenario similar to the Exercise 6.1, it is believed that the remains were buried by the suspect rather than deposited on the surface. You determine that a soil probe is a good option for locating the possible burial.

Instructions/Procedure:

• At a far end of the search scene (i.e., not directly in the suspected burial location), probe the soil several times. Do this by *gently* inserting the probe into the ground to assess the level of resistance.
• Working your way toward the suspected burial location, probe every 6–12 inches until you have located the soil disturbance.
• Continue to probe in the area of the disturbance until the outline of the disturbance is identified

Why is it important to first assess the resistance of undisturbed soil in the region of the search area?

_____

_____

_____

Did you find that it was easy to identify when disturbed soil was encountered? Why or why not?

_____

_____

_____

EXERCISE 6.4 Mapping Coordinates

Materials needed:

• Coordinates provided in this exercise
• Appendix I: Scene Mapping and Documentation, or graph paper
• Writing utensil (pen or pencil) and accessories (eraser, compass, etc.)

Note to instructor: For additional practice, you can create other lists of coordinates or have students create them for each other.

Case scenario: The following coordinates were recorded during the mapping of the perimeter of a skeletal remains recovery scene. You would like to visualize the areas where the remains were recovered, but no photos were taken, and no map was created at the time of recovery.

Instructions/Procedure:
- Map the coordinates below on Appendix I or graph paper
- Units are not important for this exercise; it is suggested that each grid square represents one unit.

X	Y
3	1
3	2
3	3
3	4
3	5
4	1
4	5
4	7
5	1
5	5
6	1
6	5
7	1
7	2
7	3
7	5

Do you suspect there may be any errors in the recorded data for this scene perimeter? If so, can you identify the specific error?

_____
_____
_____

Why is it important to create your map while you are in the field, rather than simply recording points and plotting them later, back in your laboratory?

_____
_____
_____

EXERCISE 6.5 Baseline Mapping

Materials needed:
- Surface scatter area (scene)
- Evidentiary items (e.g., real or replica human or nonhuman bones, clothing, tools, etc.)
- Tape measure
- Wooden stakes/chaining pins are optional but preferred
- Appendix I: Scene Mapping and Documentation, or graph paper
- Writing utensil (pen or pencil) and accessories (eraser, straight edge)

Note to instructor: This exercise can be prepared by distributing the evidentiary material over a relatively small area. This exercise can be performed either indoors or outdoors. Optionally, the scene can also be mapped using triangulation and/or azimuth methods.

Case scenario: In the case described in Exercise 6.1, scattered skeletal remains were discovered during the line search. The search phase is now complete, and the evidence needs to be mapped prior to collection. Based on the terrain and distribution of the remains, you have determined that a baseline would be a good mapping option.

Instructions/Procedure:
- Establish a baseline by placing a tape measure along the length of the scene. Depending on the size and nature of the scene, the baseline may transect the scene or may be at one side of it
- Map the evidentiary items using the baseline method
- Make sure to include a scale and indicate magnetic north on your map
- Identify a right angle from the baseline using the "shortest distance" method outlined in Fig. 6.11.

Discuss any challenges or complications that you encountered while mapping the scene.

_____
_____
_____

EXERCISE 6.6   Establishing a Grid

Materials needed:
- Scene (indoor or outdoor)
- Three tape measures
- String
- Line levels
- Hammer/mallet
- Wooden stakes/chaining pins
- Appendix I: Scene Mapping and Documentation, or graph paper
- Writing utensil (pen or pencil) and accessories (eraser, straight edge)

Note to instructor: This exercise can be performed in an outdoor burial site location (and used in conjunction with the next exercise) or can be performed in an indoor setting (with tape measures lying flat on the floor).
Case scenario: In the search described in Exercise 6.2, a likely burial location was located using the soil probe, and the approximate outline of the grave has been identified.
Instructions/Procedure:
- Establish a grid around the burial scene using the grid method
- Square the corners of the grid using the 3-4-5 triangle method described in Fig. 6.12

EXERCISE 6.7   Excavation and Grid Mapping

Materials needed:
- Burial area (scene)
- Evidentiary items (e.g., real or replica human or nonhuman bones, clothing, tools, etc.)
- Tape measures (two are needed)
- String
- Line levels
- Hammer/mallet
- Wooden stakes/chaining pins
- Appendix I: Scene Mapping and Documentation, or graph paper
- Writing utensil (pen or pencil) and accessories (eraser, straight edge)

Note to instructor: This exercise can be prepared in advance by digging a hole, placing some evidence (ideally replica human skeletal material or nonhuman skeletal material, but any items will do) and refilling the hole. Excavating and mapping a burial scene can be a very time-consuming exercise. Depending on class length, this may require a whole class period or even two classes.
Case scenario: Now that you have created your grid, you are ready to excavate and map the burial.
Instructions/Procedure:
- Excavate the burial
- Map the evidence

What challenges did you encounter during your excavation?

_____
_____
_____

Were you able to locate any toolmarks on the grave outline?

_____

_____

_____

EXERCISE 6.8   GPS Mapping

Materials needed:
- GPS receiver or cellular phone with GPS capabilities (most smartphones have built-in GPS receivers). If using a cellular phone, the phone must have a GPS application on it. There are many different apps available for purchase or free.
- Outdoor scene

Note to instructors: This exercise can be carried out in conjunction with any of the other mapping exercises or can be done on its own. This exercise should be performed in an outdoor setting in order to receive a signal for GPS points.

Case scenario: You have completed mapping either a surface scattered or buried remains scene and you decide to record GPS points in order to tie your hand-drawn map into a global context.

Instructions/Procedure:
- Take three or more GPS points from your scene
- For additional practice, consider using your GPS to locate local geocaches (see www.geocache.com)

Which points did you decide to record using your GPS and why?

_____

_____

_____

What types of factors affect the accuracy of using a GPS?

_____

_____

_____

EXERCISE 6.9   Evidence Packaging and Labeling

Materials needed:
- Evidentiary items (real or replica bones, other items of evidence)
- Packaging materials (e.g., brown paper bags, envelopes)
- Evidence tape
- Writing utensil (pen)

Note to instructors: Real human bones are not required for this exercise; any items or materials will suffice.

Case scenario: After you complete the mapping of either the surface scattered or buried remains, the evidence needs to be collected and packaged in preparation for transport to the laboratory.

Instructions/Procedure:
- Collect, package, and label the evidence you discovered. Seal the evidence packing using evidence tape. Sign your initials so that they cross over the evidence tape and the packaging
- Label the evidence package with the appropriate information

What type of evidence did you find and collect (e.g., bones, insects, soil, artifacts)?

_____

What is the most appropriate type of packaging for each type of evidence?

_____

_____

Why is selecting the proper evidence packaging important?

_____

_____

What information should be included on the evidence packaging?

_____

What is the purpose of signing your initials so that they cross over the packaging and the evidence tape?

_____

_____

Chapter 7

Processing and Preparing Remains

OBJECTIVES

Not all skeletal remains cases are presented in a state that is appropriate or ready for a skeletal analysis. In some cases, remains first need to be cleaned, reconstructed, or sorted. In this chapter, you will identify and/or apply appropriate methods for removing soft tissue from bones, reconstructing fragmented skeletal material using temporary and more permanent methods, resolving commingling, and preserving skeletal evidence.

PRINCIPLES OF SKELETAL PROCESSING AND PREPARATION

Most forensic anthropological analyses involve the direct observation and analysis of the outer surfaces (and sometimes internal properties) of bones and teeth. It is not uncommon, however, for forensic anthropological cases to be discovered with soft tissue or other adhering material (such as soil) obscuring the skeletal remains. This adhering material can be removed and the bone surfaces cleaned using a combination of approaches called processing, allowing for gross visual analysis of the surface. It is also fairly common for material to be fractured or fragmented due to scavenging or trauma, which can present certain challenges to anthropological analyses. The careful reconstruction of fragments can help clarify trauma patterns and restore original bone dimensions for metric analyses. Most often, skeletal remains brought to the forensic anthropologist are those of a single person, but sometimes the remains may represent more than one individual. If the remains could represent more than one individual, they should be assessed to resolve commingling and the number of individuals represented by the skeletal material should be determined.

Sampling of skeletal material for DNA may be necessary, and anthropologists may be responsible for selecting an appropriate tissue sample (e.g., bone, tooth, soft tissue) for analysis as well as taking precautions to either acquire a DNA sample before processing or avoid using processing methods which will degrade DNA. Consideration should also be given to the duration and conditions under which the skeletal material will be retained. In some cases, skeletal material may be sent directly back to investigators, while in other cases the remains may need to be curated in the forensic anthropology laboratory or medical examiner's office for relatively long periods of time (or indefinitely). The following sections describe how skeletal material can be processed and prepared for subsequent analyses and long-term storage.

PROCESSING METHODS

Often, material adhering to skeletal remains will be associated with soft tissue that is decomposed, mummified, saponified, or "fixed" through intentional preservation processes such as the use of formalin by medical examiners or embalming chemicals by morticians. Other adhering material may include sediment, concrete, plant debris, or other materials either from the depositional environment or intentionally placed by perpetrators of a crime (Fig. 7.1).

To preserve as much evidence and information as possible, remains should always be documented using both notes and photography in the condition in which they are first received and observed. Radiologic imaging can also be useful in visualizing and locating additional material evidence that may be associated with the remains but which may not be immediately visible. If clothing, personal effects, or evidence (e.g., a ligature around the neck, or a projectile within the cranium) is present, these should be carefully documented prior to removal, and they should always be retained for analysis by other forensic specialists.

There are three generally recognized methods of skeletal processing: maceration, carrion insects, and chemical approaches (Table 7.1). The selection of a processing method may depend on the type of analysis being conducted as well as any long-term storage or curation plans. Material that is removed during processing which may benefit from further analysis by another specialist (e.g., soft tissue, hairs, soil, insect larvae) should be carefully removed and preserved for

A Laboratory Manual for Forensic Anthropology. https://doi.org/10.1016/B978-0-12-812201-3.00007-4

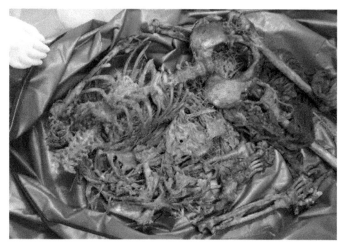

FIG. 7.1 Skeletal material with adhering tissue and other debris. *(From Christensen, A.M., Passalacqua, N.V., Bartelink, E.J., 2014. Forensic Anthropology: Current Methods and Practice. Academic Press.)*

TABLE 7.1 Processing Methods

Processing Method	Procedure	Considerations
Documentation/preservation	• Photography • Radiology • Tissue samples • Personal effects • Evidence	• Thorough documentation of evidence "as received" should always be performed first
Initial assessment	• Careful assessment of remains using visual, microscopic, and/or radiological approaches • Determine best processing approach	• Be sure to assess and skeletal evidence that may be destroyed during processing (e.g., trauma)
Mechanical	• Dissection • Bulk tissue removal • Disarticulation	• Consider removal and preservation of soft tissue sample • Consider biohazard and safety concerns regarding the usage of scalpels and other sharp cutting tools • Care must be taken not to leave marks on the remains
Maceration	• Simmer remains in a (subboiling) hot water bath • Can be performed using a crockpot, hotplate/pots, or incubator	• Water must not be allowed to escape in significant amounts • Allowing pots to cook unchecked can result in damage to, or total destruction of, remains
Carrion insects	• Remains are placed into insect habit for consumption	• Carrion insect will need to continue to be fed to support their colony when forensic cases are unavailable
Chemicals	• Addition of bleaching agents, antiformin, sodium hypochlorite, or papain • Can process remains very quickly	• Can damage bone • Can be hazardous to practitioner • May degrade DNA • Not recommended for forensic casework
Rinse	• Following processing method, rinse with water and clean using a nylon bristled brush (such as a toothbrush)	• A screen, sieve, or cheesecloth should be used in order to catch any small material so that it does not get lost down the drain

further examination. In addition, any alterations caused by the processing approach including the methods and/or instruments used should be documented. Processing approaches should involve consideration for avoiding or minimizing alterations to bone dimensions, deterioration, production of postmortem damage to the bone, changes in bone structure, and commingling.

When processing remains, measures should be taken to ensure physical and biohazard safety. Gloves, eye protection, mask, and a lab coat or apron should be worn when processing remains in any state of decomposition. Care must be taken when manually removing soft tissue using sharp instruments such as scalpels in order to avoid injury. Broken bones or other sharp debris may be present within the body and obscured by tissues and can also present physical and biological hazards.

If a significant amount of soft tissue or other material is adhering to the skeletal remains, this may need to be removed by mechanical methods (Fig. 7.2). As much of the adhering material as possible should be removed without the use of any tools or chemicals. In some cases, bones may be attached by tough connective tissue, and sharp tools such as scalpels, knives, or scissors may be required to separate or disarticulate them. If tools must be used, for example to scrape tough cartilage from a bone surface, it is preferable to use tools that are less likely to damage or leave marks on the bone, such as those made of wood or plastic (versus metal). If any metal tools are used, care should be taken to avoid making any marks on the bones, and any incidental alterations should be noted in the case documentation. If it has not already been done (e.g., by a medical examiner), a sample of the soft tissue should be removed and preserved for possible DNA analysis. In cases where the remains are nearly complete, approaches similar to anatomical dissection may be used and performed carefully with a scalpel.

One of the most common methods used to remove remaining tissue, soil, or other debris is maceration, or softening of the tissues by soaking the remains in water. Various approaches can be used involving different temperatures, times, and the addition of enzymatic detergents and ammonia. Cold (or room temperature) maceration involves simply placing the material into a sealed container with water and allowing the soft tissues to decompose slowly through bacterial action. This method is time consuming (typically on the order of weeks or months) and has a strong associated odor. Cold water maceration does have the advantages of producing excellent preservation of skeletal details and being safe for the material and practitioner (because it involves no heat or chemicals). It is recommended when processing fetal and infant remains or otherwise very small or fragile remains. Lengthy processing in water, however, has been associated with a loss in DNA yield (Steadman et al., 2006) and is impractical in many forensic scenarios.

Warm water maceration is the most common approach used by forensic anthropologists (Fig. 7.3). For best results, the water temperature should be maintained near, yet below, boiling, which can be accomplished through the use of pots and hot plates, incubators, crock-pots, or microwave ovens. These temperatures promote rapid breakdown of the tissues without bacterial action, and the tissues soften, degrade, and separate from the bone. Depending on the amount of remaining soft tissue, this procedure may be repeated several times, changing the water solution to dispose of the excess tissues and fats. At this time, rinsing and some manual removal of remaining tissue (e.g., using tweezers or nylon brushes) may further facilitate processing.

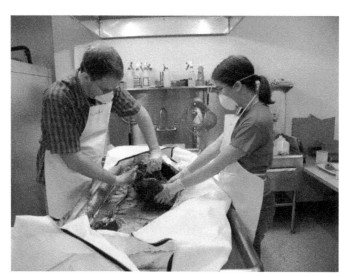

FIG. 7.2 Mechanical disarticulation of remains. *(From Christensen, A.M., Passalacqua, N.V., Bartelink, E.J., 2014. Forensic Anthropology: Current Methods and Practice. Academic Press.)*

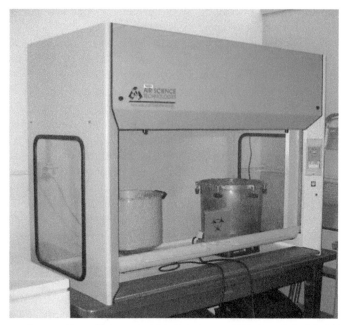

FIG. 7.3 Warm water maceration equipment. *(From Christensen, A.M., Passalacqua, N.V., Bartelink, E.J., 2014. Forensic Anthropology: Current Methods and Practice. Academic Press.)*

Another approach to soft tissue removal involves the use of carrion insects that consume soft tissue, particularly mealworms and dermestid beetles (see Fig. 7.4). Dermestid beetle larvae will consume soft tissue in any stage of decay (although they tend to prefer soft tissue that is at least somewhat desiccated) but do not consume or damage the bones. Processing human remains using dermestid beetles can take up to several weeks, depending on the size of the colony, the amount of soft tissue present, and the condition of the remains. Beetle colonies can be maintained expressly for this purpose, kept in a sealed container such as an aquarium or metal box with a fastened lid. The creation and maintenance of beetle colonies, however, is often time consuming, and the colony needs to be kept approximately at room temperature and in darkness. Dermestid colonies can be more effectively maintained if nonhuman animal carcasses are available to process in between

FIG. 7.4 Dermestid beetle processing. *(From Christensen, A.M., Passalacqua, N.V., Bartelink, E.J., 2014. Forensic Anthropology: Current Methods and Practice. Academic Press.)*

partially fleshed cases, as dermestids require a continuous food supply to maintain a healthy colony. Occasionally, invasive insects (e.g., fly larvae, red-legged ham beetles) are inadvertently introduced, which can affect the overall health and productivity of the colony.

Chemical processing and preparation methods can be employed, including those involving bleaching agents (such as bleach, hydrogen peroxide, or commercial chemicals), antiformin, sodium hypochlorite, and papain. While chemical processing can be quick (sometimes rendering remains in just a few hours), these approaches can degrade the bone, are hazardous to practitioners, are more expensive, and require special handling and storage of the chemicals. Moreover, methods that involve bleach and acids have been shown to reduce DNA yield. These methods are therefore not recommended in most forensic cases. In rare cases, however, the use of chemicals may be required to remove adhering tissue. This may include cases where the remains have been preserved using chemicals, such as formalin used by forensic pathologists or embalming chemicals used by morticians. When chemical processing is performed, the material must be carefully monitored to prevent overprocessing and disintegration of the bone.

Once the bones have been cleaned by one of the above processing methods, the remains can be carefully rinsed and cleaned using water and a soft nylon brush such as a toothbrush. Screens or cheesecloth can be used during the cleaning process to prevent the loss of small bone fragments or teeth down a drain, and to ensure that fractured bone pieces remain together. The disposal of soft tissue removed should follow appropriate protocols regarding biohazard waste (and following universal precautions). The skeletal material can then be allowed to air-dry on wire racks or towels prior to analysis. The use of moving air will facilitate faster drying but may also lead to a greater probability of drying artifacts such as linear cracks along the grain of the remains, particularly the long bones. Heat should not be applied to speed up drying.

SKELETAL RECONSTRUCTION

If skeletal remains are fractured due to trauma or postmortem damage, it is often informative to reassemble or refit them into their original anatomical locations to the extent possible (Fig. 7.5). This can be useful for restoring the bones to their original dimensions to allow for metric analyses and can help visualize and clarify fractures and trauma patterns to facilitate interpretation of their cause.

It may not always be necessary to physically affix or adhere fragments together; as a rule, fragments should only be affixed when additional information may be gained. In some cases, it may only be necessary to hold fragments in place

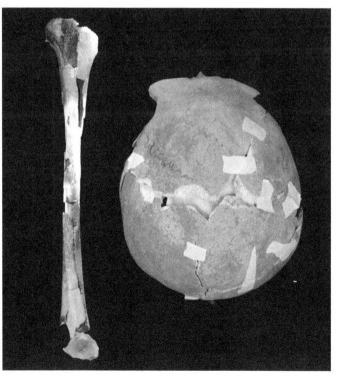

FIG. 7.5 Reconstructed tibia (left) and cranium (right). *(From Christensen, A.M., Passalacqua, N.V., Bartelink, E.J., 2014. Forensic Anthropology: Current Methods and Practice. Academic Press.)*

temporarily using tape, wax, or clay. If fragments need to be more permanently reconstructed, this is typically accomplished using glue or adhesive. Reconstruction should only be performed once the bones are clean and completely dry, and the reconstruction methods should be reversible (e.g., adhesives such as Paraloid B-72, an acrylic resin; not cellulose nitrate-based adhesives such as Duco cement). It may be necessary to separate fragments after reconstruction for subsequent examination, or due to unintentional errors in reconstruction. By using reversible methods, the fragments can be separated without damaging the remains. Certain adhesives, for example, can be dissolved using water or acetone.

Fragments should only be refitted when the anthropologist is certain that the fragments are correctly associated (the same is true for affixing or securing teeth into alveolar sockets). Care should be taken in refitting fragments, since excessive attempts to refit them can damage the fractured edges to the point that they no longer fit together; the use of a microscope may be helpful in some cases. In confirming whether two fragments are correctly associated, the anatomical and physical properties of the fit should be given greater consideration than other factors such as color or condition, since such differences may be the result of taphonomic processes or may represent evidence of trauma or other alterations.

In cases where there is significant missing bone or where contact points are very small, the application of struts (often wooden) may help stabilize and place bone fragments. This approach can be especially helpful when reconstructing highly fragmented facial bones. If adhesives are used, it is helpful to stabilize the bones during the drying process, which can be accomplished with the use of a small sandbox. Complete reconstruction may not always be possible. Fragments that would join two additional portions may be missing due to taphonomic or intentional events. Warping of bone due to taphonomy or trauma may also prevent complete reconstruction, causing fragments that would normally conjoin to fail to do so. This can be especially apparent on the skull. Reconstructions should never be forced in order to correct for warping of the bone since this can lead to further damage. Also be aware that skeletal reconstruction requires patience. Depending on the condition of the remains and the level of fragmentation, the process of locating and refitting associated fragments, affixing struts, and allowing adhesives to dry can be a repetitive, tedious, and time-consuming process.

COMMINGLING

Anthropologically, commingling refers to the presence of more than one body or skeleton, or the intermixing of body parts from more than one individual. Sometimes potential commingling is suggested by the context or investigative information, for example, in mass graves or mass fatality incidents. Sometimes, however, there may be no suggestion of commingling and it may be discovered in the course of an anthropological examination, often during the skeletal inventory. The process of recognizing commingling, segregating the remains into individual sets, and estimating the number of individuals present is referred to as *resolving commingling* (Fig. 7.6). In cases where commingling is detected where it was not previously suspected, this may significantly change the course of the investigation. Whenever possible, all remains should be segregated at the individual level.

During field recovery, documentation of the provenience or location of each set of remains or skeletal element is crucial in preventing or minimizing commingling as well as later interpretations from the recovered material. If elements were articulated when discovered, they should be recovered and maintained together, and their association can be later confirmed in the laboratory.

The skeletal inventory alone may help to identify duplicate elements that can confirm that commingling has occurred. For example, a set of skeletal remains containing two right femora must be commingled (since an individual cannot have two of the same bone from the same side of the body). If commingling is suspected or confirmed, the skeletal elements should be sorted by element and side. It may sometimes be necessary to reconstruct fragments as described above in order to resolve commingling. For example, a distal left tibia and a proximal left tibia may be two fragments of the same bone from a single individual.

Other criteria such as biological parameters may also be used to sort potentially commingled remains. For example, the presence of bones from a skeletally mature adult along with bones from an infant represents commingling, even if individual skeletal elements are not duplicated. Similarly, size and sex indicators may be used to help sort commingled remains.

As additional segregating tools, bones representing the same individual may be associated using visual pair-matching (association of left and right elements based on similarities in morphology and size), articulation (association of congruent elements based on closeness of fit at the joint juncture with another bone), osteometric sorting (association of elements based on statistical evaluation of size and shape relationships), and taphonomy (association of elements based on similarities in preservation such as color and condition). Similarity in these aspects does not mean that it can be concluded with certainty that the elements originated from the same individual. Consideration should also be given to possible pathological conditions that may affect bone size, shape, and articulation. Greater confidence can be given to *exclusionary* conclusions (i.e., incompatibilities that indicate that two elements do *not* originate from the same individual) than those that suggest an

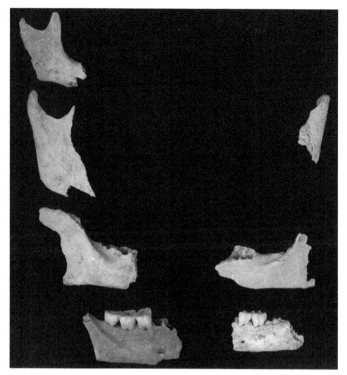

FIG. 7.6 Commingled skeletal remains represented by seven mandibular fragments, three from left sides and four from right sides.

association. Some joint articulations are easy to visualize, such as the hip joint, whereas others are harder to compare, such as a metacarpophalangeal joint.

Once all appropriate recovery and sorting methods have been employed, it may be possible to estimate the number of individuals present among the remains. There are several approaches to this which are dependent on the preservation of the material as well as the scale of the incident. The most common approach is to determine the *minimum number of individuals* present, or MNI. In its simplest form, MNI is calculated by counting the number of repeated elements (or portion thereof) after sorting by element, side, and developmental status (i.e., skeletal maturity) and then taking the highest number as the MNI estimate. For example, if an assemblage contains two left scapulae, one right humerus, two left humeri, three left ulnae, one right femur, and two left tibiae, the MNI would be three (due to the three left ulnae, which is the most repeated element).

When estimating MNI from fragmentary remains, every fragment used to calculate the MNI must share the same specific anatomical landmark to ensure that the portions do not represent the same bone. For example, the proximal and distal tibia portions referenced earlier should not be counted twice if they do not share an anatomical landmark because they could be two portions of the same bone. Three proximal left tibiae that all have a tibial tuberosity present, however, would be counted as three different individuals.

Other approaches can be used to estimate the actual or likely number of individuals present (versus the minimum). The *most likely number of individuals* (MLNI) can be used if preservation is good and skeletal elements can be accurately pair matched (Adams and Konigsberg, 2004). The formula for calculating MLNI is:

$$\text{MLNI} = \left[(L+1)(R+1)/(P+1) \right] - 1$$

where R = right, L = left, and P = pairs.

Resolving commingling becomes increasingly complicated with increasing numbers of individuals, as well as with increasing fragmentation of remains. Extremely fragmentary or poorly preserved remains may not be amenable to meaningful osteological quantification techniques (Fig. 7.7). In some cases, DNA analysis may be useful in resolving commingled fragments.

SKELETAL SAMPLING

Although not necessarily the specific responsibility of the forensic anthropologist, skeletal material and/or associated soft tissue can be sampled (i.e., a small section removed) for DNA analysis. If soft tissue was present on the skeletal material,

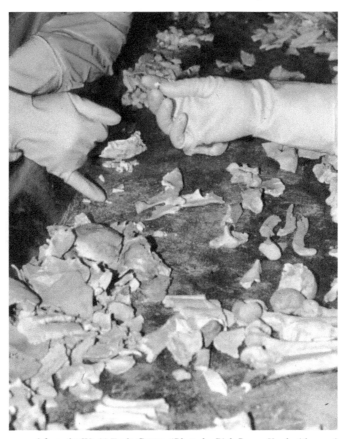

FIG. 7.7 Commingled remains recovered from the World Trade Center. *(Photo by Rich Press; Used with permission of the Office of Chief Medical Examiner—New York City; From Christensen, A.M., Passalacqua, N.V., Bartelink, E.J., 2014. Forensic Anthropology: Current Methods and Practice. Academic Press.)*

samples of various tissue types (such as muscle and brain) should be removed and preserved for possible DNA analysis prior to skeletal processing. Skeletal sampling for DNA analysis typically involves the removal of a small window of bone (see Fig. 7.8) which is subsequently powdered. Due to the fact that DNA sampling is a destructive process, it is very important that anthropological examination (including visual, radiographic, and microscopic analyses) be performed prior to DNA sampling. In addition, sections should not be sampled from areas that have trauma or pathological conditions since these may need to be examined or viewed again later such as in a criminal trial.

Rather than actually cutting the sample, forensic anthropologists are often involved in the selection or recommendation of bones or bone portions for DNA sampling. This may involve assessment of the quality of bone preservation, or

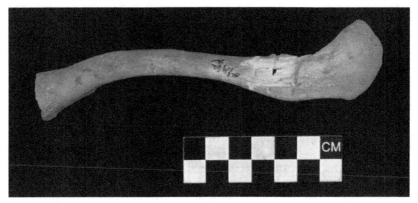

FIG. 7.8 Clavicle sampled for DNA analysis. *(From Christensen, A.M., Passalacqua, N.V., Bartelink, E.J., 2014. Forensic Anthropology: Current Methods and Practice. Academic Press.)*

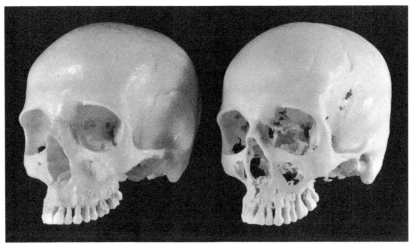

FIG. 7.9 Three-dimensional printing. Cranium (left) and printed replica (right). *(Image courtesy of JPAC-CIL; From Christensen, A.M., Passalacqua, N.V., Bartelink, E.J., 2014. Forensic Anthropology: Current Methods and Practice. Academic Press.)*

the recommendation of bones or areas that lack other important skeletal evidence such as features that may be useful for identification, trauma, or disease.

SKELETAL PRESERVATION

Often, remains are returned directly to investigators or funeral homes following anthropological analyses and other forensic examinations. Sometimes, however, it may be necessary to preserve or replicate portions of the skeleton for future use such as in a trial. One way to preserve the features of skeletal remains is through casting, molds, and other replicas. These methods result in the three-dimensional reproduction of the bone or certain features which can be preserved, examined, studied, or stored in place of the actual skeletal material. Casting methods include plasters, plastics, and epoxies. Latex and silicon can be used to make casts of impressions or tool marks for preservation and examination.

Laser scanning and three-dimensional printing, although more expensive, can also produce high-quality replicas. From digital data collected by computed tomography (CT) scan or laser scanner, 3-D printers can be used to make replicas of bones (Fig. 7.9). These replicas can be used as comparative reference materials similar to pubic symphyseal or sternal rib end casts or be used for courtroom demonstration purposes in cases where the actual skeletal remains will not be available (such as if they will be interred or cremated between the analysis and the trial). Some 3D printers may not produce the resolution needed to replicate fine details of bone morphology.

EXERCISE 7.1 Skeletal Processing

Materials needed:
- Partially decomposed nonhuman remains
- Hot plate
- Cooking pot
- Detergent
- Cheesecloth
- Toothbrush
- PPE (at a minimum, gloves, eye protection, and mask)

Note to instructor: Processing is a skill that most forensic anthropologists will need in their careers, but in which few have practical experience or training as students. This exercise can be carried out using any nonhuman remains accessible. Many campuses have dissection labs which may have nonhuman carcasses available (note, however, that for specimens that have been fixed for dissection using formalin or other preservative chemicals may take considerable time to process). It may also be possible to obtain nonhuman remains from other sources such as animal shelters. After processing, skeletons can be labeled and retained for future teaching and reference material.

Case scenario: The skeletal remains you have just received have significant adhering soft tissue obstructing your ability to thoroughly analyze the bones. The remains will therefore need to be processed to remove the adhering tissue.

Instructions/Procedure:
- If necessary, perform bulk tissue removal or dissection
- Process the remains using the warm water maceration method

What processes or procedures should you consider or perform prior to skeletal processing?

_____

_____

_____

What issues (if any) did you encounter while processing the remains?

_____

_____

_____

EXERCISE 7.2   Resolving Commingling

Materials needed:
- Image provided in this exercise
  Note to instructor:
- This exercise can be supplemented or replaced with a collection of real or replica human skeletal remains from multiple individuals.

Case scenario: Investigators recently recovered a number of skeletal elements from under the porch of an abandoned house, believed to be the victims of a multiple homicide more than 10 years ago. The forensic pathologist is requesting your assistance with the case, specifically with determining how many victims may be present. The pathologist provided you with the below image for your assessment.

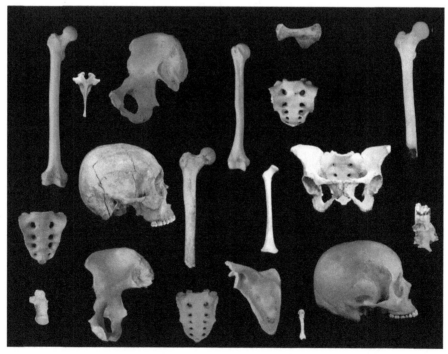

Determine the Minimum Number of Individuals (MNI) present in this assemblage:

_____

What methods did you use to reach your MNI?

_____

_____

_____

Can you estimate MLNI from this assemblage? Can you use pair matching? Osteometric sorting? For each method, discuss why or why not.

_____
_____
_____

EXERCISE 7.3 Skeletal Reconstruction

Materials needed:
- Fractured skeletal material
- Adhesive such as Paraloid or cyanoacrylate
- PPE (at a minimum, gloves, eye protection, and mask)

Note to instructor: Fractured skeletal material can be prepared from nonhuman remains, for example, by placing one or two bones into a bag and applying blunt force with a tool such as a hammer. Cyanoacrylate adhesive (aka "superglue") can be purchased inexpensively from hardware, craft, or drugstores. PPE should be worn when working with adhesives.

Case scenario: After macerating the remains of an apparent hit-and-run victim, you discover that there was trauma to the tibia resulting in a severely comminuted fracture (i.e., resulting in many small bone fragments). In order to help clarify the trauma pattern, you need to reconstruct the fragments into their original anatomic locations.

Instructions/Procedure:
- Reconstruct the assemblage of bone fragments into the original bone(s) by looking for associated fragments and affixing them with adhesive

Upon which features did you primarily rely for locating associated fragments (e.g., anatomy, color, etc.)?

_____
_____
_____

How confident do you feel that you correctly reconstructed the fragments?

_____
_____

How do you think reconstruction may affect metric analysis of skeletal remains?

_____
_____
_____

How might taphonomic processes (such as weathering and warping) affect the ability to correctly reconstruct fragments?

_____
_____
_____

Are there any long-term considerations based on the type of adhesive used to reconstruct the material?

_____
_____
_____

EXERCISE 7.4 Casting

Materials needed:
- Bones with saw marks
- Silicon casting material
- Microscope

Note to instructor: Human bones are not necessary for this exercise; nonhuman bones will suffice. Nonskeletal materials such as wood or plastic could even be used if necessary. Saw marks can be created on the bones in advance of the exercise. Casting materials can be procured inexpensively through various vendors.

Case scenario: You have completed your analysis and need to return skeletal remains to the medical examiner but would like to create a replica of some saw marks you noted on the bones in the event that the case later goes to trial. You decide to make a cast of the tool impressions which could later be used to make a replica.

Instructions/Procedure:
- Following the procedures specific to the casting material used, make a cast of the saw makes on the bone
- Examine the cast and the bone using a microscope

Are you able to see the saw marks in the casting material?

_____

Are there any differences between what you see on the cast and what you see on the real bone?

_____
_____

Can you think of other applications of casting in the analysis or preservation of features of skeletal material?

_____
_____
_____

EXERCISE 7.5   3D Printing

Materials needed:
- Scan of a bone (surface scan or CT scan)
- 3D printer and associated materials

Note to instructor: Surface scans can be created using laser scanners including desktop scanners. Bones with alterations such as trauma may be more instructive. Human bones are not necessary; nonhuman bones could also be used. CT scans can be created for this exercise or may be able to be obtained from clinical or medicolegal settings, or from online repositories. Some models of 3D printers may be affordable to obtain for your institution if possible, or working relationships may be established with institutions known to have one. Even if students are unable to scan or print bones for this exercise, encourage them to consider some of the questions below.

Case scenario: You have just analyzed a case that is likely to go to trial, and you would like to create a 3D print of the bone to preserve it for possible future use.

Instructions/Procedure:
- If appropriate, create surface scan or CT scan of the bone
- Print the bone using a 3D printer

If you created the bone scan, what type of scanner did you use and how was the scan created?

_____
_____
_____

What type of 3D printer was used? Describe the 3D printing process and materials used for that particular device.

_____
_____
_____

Visually compare the 3D printed bone and the original real bone. How detailed is the 3D printed version in your opinion? Does it capture sufficient detail that you would feel comfortable using it as a substitute in a courtroom?

_____
_____
_____

What advantages are there to using replicated materials in court? What objections do you think could be raised to regarding using 3D printed bones in court?

_____
_____

Can you think of other methods of replicating skeletal material for preservation or use in a trial?

_____
_____
_____

Chapter 8

Sex Estimation

OBJECTIVES

It is possible to differentiate between male and female skeletons because humans are sexually dimorphic, that is, females and males differ in size and shape. Sex differences in the skeleton are related primarily to the functions of parturition and locomotion, as well as overall size. These differences can be assessed using macroscopic, metric, and other methods. In this chapter you will examine and assess differences between male and female skeletons through observations of pelvic and other macroscopic approaches, and using metric analyses.

PRINCIPLES OF SEX ESTIMATION

Estimating sex from skeletal remains involves the identification and evaluation of characteristics that tend to show differences between female and male skeletons, which are variably expressed throughout the skeleton. These differences are primarily related to size and architecture which result from different biomechanical functions of joints for efficiency in locomotion (movement, usually walking) and parturition (childbirth). In the analysis and identification of human skeletal remains, the correct determination of sex effectively eliminates approximately 50% of the population from further consideration, thus substantially assisting in the search of missing persons records and databases. In addition, many other analyses such as stature and age estimation are sex specific, making sex estimation an important part of the biological profile, especially in the preliminary stages of an investigation.

On average, adult human males are larger and more robustly built than females, exceeding them in height, weight, and breadth. Their bones tend to be longer, thicker, and have more prominent muscle attachments (males tend to have greater muscle mass, which requires greater surface area for attachment to the bone). However, because human sexual dimorphism is not extreme, there tends to be considerable overlap between smaller males and larger females, meaning that sometimes males can be misclassified as females and vice versa (see Fig. 8.1 for an example of male and female height). When referring to biological phenotypes, the term "sex" is used, while "gender" refers to cultural expressions of feminine and masculine attributes. Estimating sex in subadults is generally considered unadvisable because most sexual differences in the skeleton do not appear until puberty (around age 14), and there is limited juvenile skeletal material of known sex available to study. Although not typically within the purview of forensic anthropologists, it is often possible to determine the sex of skeletal remains using molecular methods (DNA).

Methods of sex estimation from skeletal remains generally fall into one of two categories: macroscopic and metric analysis. Each utilizes certain bones or overall patterns depending on the degree and quality of sexual dimorphism in that bone or anatomical region. Metric methods are generally considered to be more objective, but in the case of sex estimation, visual assessment of the pelvis is the most accurate method. Methods involving dimensions of various long bones of the postcranial skeleton are typically the next most accurate, followed by methods involving the skull.

MORPHOSCOPIC (NONMETRIC) ANALYSIS

Morphoscopic analysis in sex estimation involves a visual, qualitative assessment of skeletal features that tend to vary between males and females. These assessments involve observations of the degree of expression of certain traits, or a determination of the presence or absence of a particular feature. Owing to the functions of childbirth, the pelvis is the most sexually dimorphic region of the human skeleton, displaying the most sexually dimorphic variation in architecture. Assessment of the pelvis is therefore the most accurate method for estimating sex from skeletal material. In general, the pelvis is shorter and broader in females than in males, with a more widely configured pelvic inlet and a wider subpubic angle (Fig. 8.2). The obturator foramen in females tends to be more triangular, while it is more oval in males. Some of the more varied morphological differences that are commonly utilized in sex estimation are described in Table 8.1.

A Laboratory Manual for Forensic Anthropology. https://doi.org/10.1016/B978-0-12-812201-3.00008-6

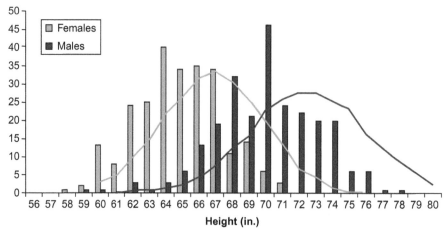

FIG. 8.1 Distribution of female and male height. The peaks are distinct and separate at around 67″ for females and 72″ for males, but there is considerable overlap in the middle. *(From Christensen, A.M., Passalacqua, N.V., Bartelink, E.J., 2014. Forensic Anthropology: Current Methods and Practice. Academic Press, Oxford.)*

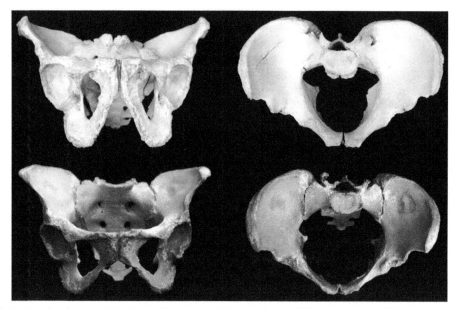

FIG. 8.2 Female (bottom) and male (top) pelvis. *(From Christensen, A.M., Passalacqua, N.V., Bartelink, E.J., 2014. Forensic Anthropology: Current Methods and Practice. Academic Press, Oxford.)*

MORPHOSCOPIC SEX ESTIMATION FROM THE INNOMINATE

One morphoscopic method involves the evaluation of three traits of the pubic region of the innominate (or the pubis) and has a reported accuracy of around 96% (Phenice, 1969). It is one of the most commonly used methods of estimating sex from the pelvis when the pubic region is available for study. The three traits (also shown in Fig. 8.3) are:

(1) The *ventral arc* which is typically present in females and absent in males
(2) The *subpubic concavity* of the ischiopubic ramus which is typically present in females and absent in males
(3) The *medial aspect of the ischiopubic ramus* which is sharp and narrow in females and dull and wide in males

While the assessment of pubic traits has been shown to be highly accurate, it does not allow a practitioner to determine the statistical probability of being male or female. A recent study (Klales et al., 2012) reexamined these three traits, assigning them each five character states (Appendix K, Sex Estimation Using Scoring of Pubic Traits). An ordinal logistic regression equation was then developed based on the character states of the three traits, which provides probabilities for

TABLE 8.1 Traits of the Female and Male Pelvis

Pelvic Feature	Female Pelvis	Male Pelvis
Ilium	Low, wide, flared	High and vertical
Pelvic inlet	Oval	Heart-shaped
Ventral arc	Present	Absent
Subpubic concavity	Present	Absent
Medial ischiopubic ramus	Narrow and sharp	Wide and dull
Obturator foramen	Small and triangular	Large and ovoid
Subpubic angle	Larger	Smaller
Greater sciatic notch	Larger	Smaller
Preauricular sulcus	Present	Absent
Sacral shape	Short, wide, straight	Long, narrow, curved
Auricular surface (sacroiliac articulation)	Elevated	Flush with ilium
Pubic bone shape	Rectangular	Triangular
Acetabulum	Smaller	Larger
Sacral dimensions	Alae wider than promontory	Alae narrower than promontory

both female and male estimates. The method performs with a 94.5% correct classification with high agreement between observers for the various traits and character states. To use the scoring method, each of the three traits is assigned a score from 1 to 5 based on the character state (or degree of expression of each trait). The scores are then used in an equation to calculate a total score, and this score is used to calculate the probability of being female or male (Appendix K).

In addition to the traits of the pubic region, sexual dimorphism has also been noted in the shape and width of the sciatic notch, with females having a wider notch and males having a narrower notch (Fig. 8.4). Studies of documented collections have found that males sometimes have a wide notch, whereas females rarely show evidence of a narrow notch. Due to overlap in the intermediate expressions of the sciatic notch, it is not recommended to estimate sex based solely on this feature.

Morphoscopic sex estimation based on the skull involves analysis of overall shape and relative size of certain cranial and mandibular features (Figs. 8.5 and 8.6). In general, the skulls of males are larger and more rugged and robust than those of females which tend to be smaller and smoother (see Table 8.2). Although relatively high accuracy can be achieved using certain features, interobserver error rates for morphoscopic sex estimation from the skull can be high. The most reliable features tend to be mastoid size, supraorbital ridge size, general size and architecture, rugosity of the suprameatal and supramastoid crest, size and shape of the nasal aperture, and gonial angle. Methods have also been developed to apply statistical tools such as regression models to these visual assessments (Appendix L: Sex Estimation Using Cranial Features).

Various other bones and features have also been shown to display some degree of sexual dimorphism and to have some utility in sex estimation. The pattern of costal cartilage calcification (observed either directly or radiographically) shows sex differences, with females exhibiting a more central ossification pattern while the male pattern is more marginal (Fig. 8.7). The accuracy of this method is age dependent and may vary between populations. Other sexually dimorphic traits include features of the clavicle, scapula, and distal humerus (Fig. 8.8).

METRIC ANALYSIS

Metric analysis in sex estimation involves measuring maximum or minimum dimensions or taking measurements based on osteological landmarks to quantitatively evaluate size and shape differences between females and males. Some metric methods involve the evaluation of a single measurement or index of two measurements, while other more complex multivariate methods may combine numerous measurements into a single analysis (e.g., discriminant function analysis).

Among the most reliable metric methods for estimating sex are those involving dimensions of the long bones of the postcranial skeleton, largely based on the fact that males exceed females in size, especially in more weight-bearing joint areas

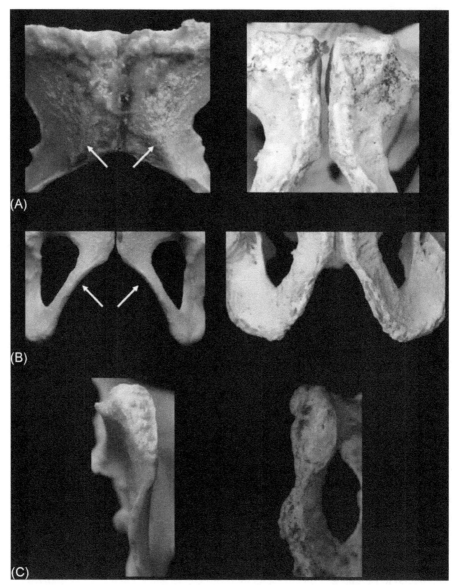

FIG. 8.3 Sex estimation traits of the pubis in the female (left) and male (right). (A) Ventral arc—present in females, absent in males; (B) subpubic concavity—present in females, absent in males; and (C) medial ischiopubic ramus—sharp and narrow in females, wide and blunt in males. *(From Christensen, A.M., Passalacqua, N.V., Bartelink, E.J., 2014. Forensic Anthropology: Current Methods and Practice. Academic Press, Oxford.)*

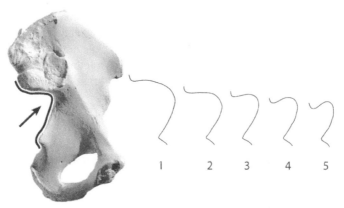

FIG. 8.4 Variation in the sciatic notch. 1 represents a more female expression, while 5 represents a more male expression. *(From Buikstra, J.E., Ubelaker, D.H., 1994. Standards for Data Collection From Human Skeletal Remains. Archaeological Survey Research Seminar Series, vol. 44. Archaeological Survey Fayetteville, AR.)*

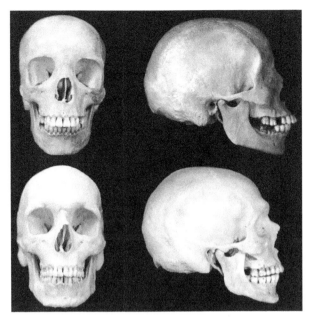

FIG. 8.5 Female (top) and male (bottom) skull. *(From Christensen, A.M., Passalacqua, N.V., Bartelink, E.J., 2014. Forensic Anthropology: Current Methods and Practice. Academic Press, Oxford.)*

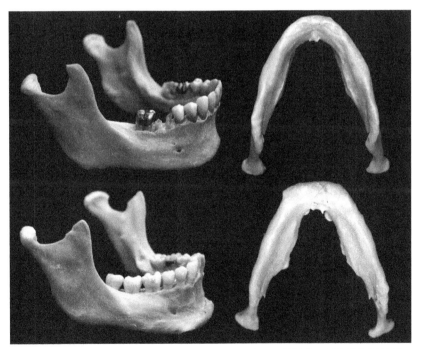

FIG. 8.6 Female (top) and male (bottom) mandible. *(From Christensen, A.M., Passalacqua, N.V., Bartelink, E.J., 2014. Forensic Anthropology: Current Methods and Practice. Academic Press, Oxford.)*

(Fig. 8.9). One comprehensive study (Spradley and Jantz, 2011) provides sectioning points and correct classification rates for sex estimation of American Whites and Blacks based on a series of standard postcranial measurements. Measurements with correct classification rates of 80% or greater for American Blacks and Whites are provided in Appendix L. Metric methods for sex estimation from the skull are generally considered less reliable than those based on the postcranial skeleton but are still widely applied and useful in cases where no postcranial elements are available for analysis. Fordisc can also be used to estimate sex from cranial and/or postcranial measurements.

TABLE 8.2 Traits of the Female and Male Skull

Skull Feature	Female Skull	Male Skull
Nuchal crest	Small	Large
Mastoid process	Small	Large
Supraorbital margin	Sharp	Blunt
Superciliary arch/glabella	Small/absent	Large
Chin shape	Round	Square
Mental eminence	Less pronounced	More pronounced
Frontals and parietals	More bossed	Less bossed
Gonial eversion	Less	Greater
Teeth	Smaller	Larger
Muscle attachments	Smaller	Larger
Palate depth	Shallow	Deep

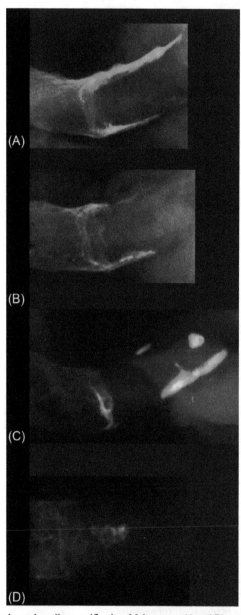

FIG. 8.7 Male trad female patterns of marginal costal cartilage ossification. Male pattern (A and B), and female pattern (C and D). *(From Christensen, A.M., Passalacqua, N.V., Bartelink, E.J., 2014. Forensic Anthropology: Current Methods and Practice. Academic Press, Oxford.)*

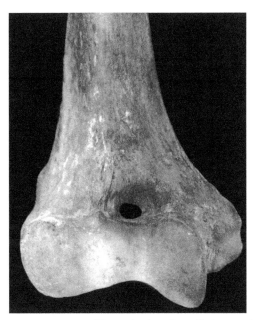

FIG. 8.8 Septal aperture in a female humerus. *(Image courtesy of Karen Gardner; From Christensen, A.M., Passalacqua, N.V., Bartelink, E.J., 2014. Forensic Anthropology: Current Methods and Practice. Academic Press, Oxford.)*

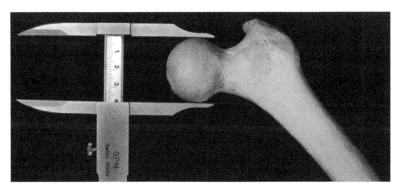

FIG. 8.9 Measurement of maximum femoral head diameter. *(From Christensen, A.M., Passalacqua, N.V., Bartelink, E.J., 2014. Forensic Anthropology: Current Methods and Practice. Academic Press, Oxford.)*

EXERCISE 8.1   Sex Estimation Using Pubic Traits

Materials needed:
- Images provided in this exercise
- Fig. 8.3 from this chapter

Note to instructor: This exercise can be supplemented or replaced with images or materials from a forensic case or skeletal reference collection.

Case scenario: While on a hunting trip in a wooded area, a hunter came across an isolated human innominate on the ground surface. Authorities have searched the area but found no additional remains. Prior to contacting you, the remains were examined by a death investigator who said that the remains must belong to a male based on their size; however there are no males listed as missing persons in this area. Law enforcement officials know of a female that went missing around 6 months ago and are asking you to estimate sex based on the following images.

Instructions/Procedure:
- Using Fig. 8.3, assess the human innominate pictured below and determine the states of the three pubic traits

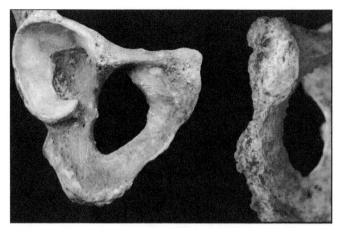

(Images courtesy of Eric Bartelink.)

Trait	State	Sex Indicated (Male or Female)
Ventral arc	Present/absent	
Subpubic concavity	Present/absent	
Medial aspect of the ischopubic ramus	Sharp and narrow/dull and wide	

What is your overall estimate of sex for this specimen?

_____

How confident are you in your assessment?

_____

EXERCISE 8.2 Sex Estimation by Scoring of Pubic Traits

Materials needed:
- Images provided in Exercise 8.1
- Appendix K: Sex Estimation Using Scoring of Pubic Traits

Note to instructor: This exercise can be supplemented or replaced with images or materials from a forensic case or skeletal reference collection.

Case scenario: In Exercise 8.1, you estimated the sex of a human innominate based on three pubic traits. However, the medical examiner would like to know whether you can provide statistical support for your confidence in your analytical conclusion.

Instructions/Procedure:
- Using Appendix K, score the traits of the innominate pictured in Exercise 8.1
- Using the Total Score Equation provided in Appendix K, calculate the total score
- Using the Sex Probability Equations provided in Appendix K, calculate the probability of being female and the probability of being male

Trait	Score
Subpubic concavity (SPC)	
Medial aspect (MA)	
Ventral arc (VA)	
Total score	

Probability of female (P_f) = _____
Probability of male (P_m) = _____
What does the result of the scoring method indicate in terms of confidence for your analysis?

_____
_____
_____

What advantages does the scoring method have over strictly visual methods in forensic anthropology casework?

_____
_____
_____

EXERCISE 8.3   Sex Estimation Using Cranial Morphology

Materials needed:
- Images provided in this exercise
- Appendix L: Sex Estimation Using Cranial Features

Note to instructors: This exercise can be supplemented or replaced with real or replica human skeletal material.

Case scenario: A nearly complete but decomposed adult human body was recovered from the trunk of an abandoned car. You have already processed the remains, preserving some of the adhering soft tissue for DNA analysis. You have decided that prior to taking measurements, you will see if cranial morphology provides any clues to whether the individual is male or female.

Instructions/Procedure:
- Using Appendix L, assess the degree of expression of each of the cranial morphology traits shown in the images below and calculate an estimate of sex

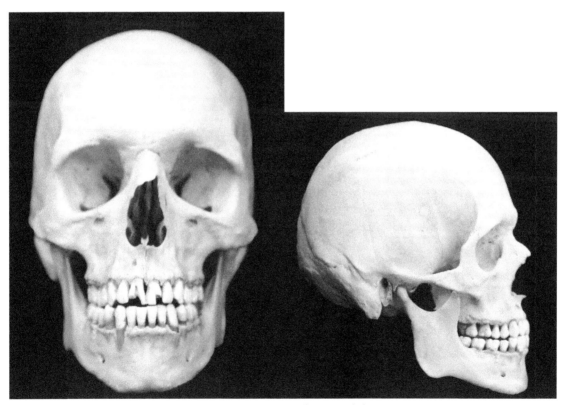

(Images courtesy of Eric Bartelink.)

Trait	Score
Nuchal crest	
Mastoid process	
Supraorbital margin	
Supraorbital ridge	
Mental eminence	

What is your assessment of whether the skull is female or male? Why?

_____

_____

How confident are you in your assessment?

_____

_____

EXERCISE 8.4 Sex Estimation Using Other Skeletal Traits

Materials needed:
• Image provided in this exercise
Note to instructors: This exercise can be supplemented or replaced with real or replica human skeletal material.
Case scenario: The skeleton described in Exercise 8.3 displays some other features that may suggest female or male sex including ossified costal cartilage.

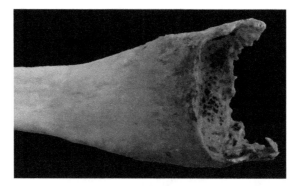

Based on the pattern of costal cartilage ossification pictured above, do you think this rib belongs to a female or male? Why?

_____

_____

How confident are you in your assessment of sex based on this feature?

_____

_____

Why might it be problematic to estimate sex based on this single feature (or any single feature)?

_____

_____

EXERCISE 8.5 Sex Estimation Using Postcranial Measurement Sectioning Points

Materials needed:
• Measurements provided in this exercise
• Appendix M: Sex Estimation from Postcranial Measurement Sectioning Points

Note to instructors: This exercise can be supplemented or replaced with measurements from a forensic case or skeletal reference collection if available.

Case scenario: Six months have passed since the isolated innominate from Exercise 8.1 was recovered. A group of campers near that same area stumbled across two human bones that have been partially consumed by scavengers. The bones have been identified as a distal humerus and a proximal femur that may or may not be related to the isolated innominate. While it was not possible to take all the standard measurements due to the condition of the remains, the following measurements were taken:

Humerus epicondylar breath	56 mm
Maximum femoral head diameter	40 mm
Femoral AP subtrochanteric diameter	27 mm

Instructions/Procedure:
- Using Appendix M, determine the sectioning point, sex assessment, and correct classification rate for each of the above measurements
- Since ancestry is unknown, do this for both American Whites and American Blacks

Assuming American White ancestry:

Measurement	Sectioning Point	Sex Assessment (Female or Male)	Correct Classification Rate
Distal humeral breath			
Maximum femoral head diameter			
Femoral AP subtrochanteric diameter			

Assuming American Black ancestry:

Measurement	Sectioning Point	Sex Assessment (Female or Male)	Correct Classification Rate
Distal humeral breath			
Maximum femoral head diameter			
Femoral AP subtrochanteric diameter			

Overall, what do you estimate to be the sex of the bones based on your assessment? Why?

_____

_____

Were you able to use all measurements in all of your assessments? Why or why not?

_____

_____

Which of the three measurements has the highest classification rate for sex estimation using the sectioning points?

_____

Based on your sex estimate, could these remains belong to the same individual as the innominate from Exercises 8.1 and 8.2? Explain why or why not.

_____

EXERCISE 8.6   Sex Estimation Using Fordisc

Materials needed:
- Fordisc output provided in this exercise

Note to instructors: This exercise can be supplemented or replaced with Fordisc analyses from a forensic case or skeletal reference collection.

Case scenario: For the skeleton in Exercise 8.3, you have now taken the standard set of cranial and postcranial measurements and analyzed the measurements using Fordisc. Below are both the cranial and postcranial outputs from Fordisc based on your measurements.

Cranial results:

Group	Classified into	Distance from	Probabilities			
			Posterior	Typ F	Typ Chi	Typ R
WF	**WF**	0.7	0.925	1.000	1.000	0.994 (1/172)
HF		7.3	0.034	0.998	0.997	0.973 (1/37)
BF		7.7	0.027	0.997	0.996	0.985 (1/68)
WM		9.4	0.012	0.987	0.985	0.976 (7/288)
HM		12.4	0.003	0.937	0.928	0.918 (15/182)
BM		17.0	0.000	0.743	0.710	0.794 (21/102)

Postcranial results:

Group	Classified into	Distance from	Probabilities			
			Posterior	Typ F	Typ Chi	Typ R
WF	**WF**	23.9	0.902	0.193	0.160	0.180 (132/161)
BF		28.3	0.098	0.096	0.058	0.200 (20/25)
WM		47.2	0.000	0.000	0.000	**0.016 (380/386)**
BM		57.5	0.000	0.000	0.000	**0.014 (72/73)**

What is your assessment of sex based on the two analyses?

_____

_____

Did you rely more on the cranial or postcranial output? Why?

_____

_____

How did the posterior probability and typicalities affect your sex estimate?

_____

_____

_____

_____

EXERCISE 8.7 Sex Estimation Using Fordisc and Sectioning Points

Materials needed:
- Measurements provided in this exercise
- Fordisc
- Appendix M: Sex Estimation from Postcranial Measurement Sectioning Points

Note to instructors: This exercise can be supplemented or replaced with measurements from a forensic case or skeletal reference collection. This exercise requires the use of Fordisc but not measurement instruments. Optionally, you can also have students take their own measurements on reference skeletal material if available. Keep in mind that some landmarks may be difficult to identify on replica skeletal material.

Case scenario: Unidentified partial skeletal remains have been brought to you for analysis. As part of your assessment of sex, you have taken the measurements below.

------------------------------ CRANIAL MEASUREMENTS ------------------------------

			left	right
1. MAXIMUM CRANIAL LENGTH (g-op):	185	15. NASAL BREADTH:	23	
2. NASIO-OCCIPITAL LENGTH (n-op):	_____	16. ORBITAL BREADTH (d-ec):	40	41
3. MAXIMUM CRANIAL BREADTH (eu-eu)	136	17. ORBITAL HEIGHT:	30	30
4. BIZYGOMATIC BREADTH (zy-zy):	122	18. BIORBITAL BREADTH (ec-ec):	87	
5. BASION-BREGMA HEIGHT (ba-b):	136	19. INTERORBITAL BREADTH (d-d):	17	
6. CRANIAL BASE LENGTH (ba-n):	99	20. FRONTAL CHORD (n-b):	109	
7. BASION-PROSTHION LENGTH (ba-pr):	90	21. PARIETAL CHORD (b-l):	124	
8. MAXILLO-ALVEOLAR BREADTH (ecm-ecm):	60	22. OCCIPITAL CHORD (l-o):	113	
9. MAXILLO-ALVEOLAR LENGTH (pr-alv):	45	23. FORAMEN MAGNUM LENGTH:	38	
10. BIAURICULAR BREADTH (ra-ra):	129	24. FORAMEN MAGNUM BR.:	32	
11. NASION-PROSTHION HEIGHT (n-pr):	66	25. MASTOID HEIGHT (po-ms):	27	28
12. MINIMUM FRONTAL BREADTH (ft-ft):	94	26. BIASTERIONIC BR. (ast-ast):	_____	
13. UPPER FACIAL BREADTH (fmt-fmt):	102	27. ZYGOMAXILLARY BR. (zym-zym):	_____	
14. NASAL HEIGHT:	49	28. ZYGOORBITALE BR. (zo-zo):	_____	

------------------------------ MANDIBULAR MEASUREMENTS ------------------------------

	left	right		left	right
29. CHIN. HEIGHT (id-gn):		30	34. MAX. RAMUS HEIGHT:	_____	_____
30. MANDIBULAR BODY HEIGHT:	29	30	35. *MAX. RAMUS HEIGHT:	_____	
31. MANDIBULAR BODY BREADTH:	10	11	36. *MAND. LENGTH:	_____	
32. BIGONIAL BREADTH (go-go):		90	37. *MAND. ANGLE:	_____	
33. BICONDYLAR BR. (cdl-cdl):		119			

*Record only if mandibulometer is used

------------------------------ POSTCRANIAL MEASUREMENTS ------------------------------

	left	right		left	right
CLAVICLE:			INNOMINATE:		
38. MAXIMUM LENGTH:	143	_____	64. MAXIMUM HEIGHT:	_____	_____
39. MAX. MIDSHAFT DIAM:	15	_____	65. MAX. ILIAC BREADTH:	_____	_____
40. MIN. MIDSHAFT DIAM:	11	_____	66. MIN. ILIAC BREADTH:	_____	_____
			67. MAX. PUBIS LENGTH:	_____	_____
SCAPULA:			68. MIN. PUBIS LENGTH:	_____	_____
41. HEIGHT:	_____	_____	69. ISCHIAL LENGTH:	_____	_____
42. BREADTH:	_____	_____	70. MIN. ISCHIAL LENGTH:	_____	_____
43. GLENOID CAVITY BREADTH:	_____	_____	71. MAX. ISCHIOPUB RAM L.:	_____	_____
44. GLENOID CAVITY HEIGHT:	_____	_____	72. ASIS – SYMPHYSION:	_____	_____
			73. MAX. PSIS – SYMPHYSION:	_____	_____
HUMERUS:			74. MIN. APEX – SYMPHYSION:	_____	_____
45. MAXIMUM LENGTH:	326	_____			
46. EPICONDYLAR BREADTH:	62	_____	FEMUR:		
47. MAX. VERT. HEAD DIAM.:	47	_____	75. MAXIMUM LENGTH:	_____	_____
48. MAX. MIDSHAFT DIAM.:	24	_____	76. BICONDYLAR LENGTH:	_____	_____
49. MIN. MIDSHAFT DIAM.:	17	_____	77. EPICONDYLAR BREADTH:	_____	_____
			78. MAX. HEAD DIAMETER:	_____	_____
RADIUS:			79. TRANS. SUBTROCH DIAM:	_____	_____
50. MAXIMUM LENGTH:	_____	_____	80. A-P SUBTROCH DIAM:	_____	_____
51. MAX. MIDSHAFT DIAM.:	_____	_____	81. MAX. MIDSHAFT DIAM.	_____	_____
52. MIN. MIDSHAFT DIAM.:	_____	_____	82. MIN. MIDSHAFT DIAM.	_____	_____
53. MAX. HEAD DIAMETER:	_____	_____	83. MIDSHAFT CIRCUM.	_____	_____
			84. MAX AP L. LAT. CONDYLE:	_____	_____
ULNA:			85. MAX AP L. MED. CONDYLE:	_____	_____
54. MAXIMUM LENGTH:	_____	_____			
55. MAX. MIDSHAFT DIAM.:	_____	_____	TIBIA:		
56. MIN. MIDSHAFT DIAM.:	_____	_____	86. CONDYLO-MALLEOLAR L.:	_____	_____
57. PHYSIOLOGICAL LENGTH:	_____	_____	87. MAX. PROX. EPIP. BR.:	_____	_____
58. MIN. CIRCUMFERENCE:	_____	_____	88. DISTAL EPIP. BREADTH:	_____	45
59. OLECRANON BREADTH:	_____	_____	89. MAX. MIDSHAFT DIAM.:	_____	_____
			90. MIN. MIDSHAFT DIAM.:	_____	_____
SACRUM:			91. MIDSHAFT CIRCUM.:	_____	_____
60. ANTERIOR HEIGHT:	_____				
61. ANTERIOR BREADTH:	_____		FIBULA:		
62. TRANSVERSE DIAM. S1:	_____		92. MAXIMUM LENGTH:	_____	_____
63. A-P DIAMETER S1:	_____		93. MAX. MIDSHAFT DIAM.:	_____	_____
			CALCANEUS:		
			94. MAXIMUM LENGTH:	_____	_____
			95. MIDDLE BREADTH:	_____	_____

Instructions/Procedure:
- Enter the cranial and postcranial measurements into the appropriate Fordisc tab page, selecting all male and female groups for comparison
- Follow the recommended procedure for eliminating groups until an appropriate number of groups remain
- Identify any measurements that are also present in Appendix M

Provide an interpretation for your Fordisc results, including discussion of the "Distance from," "Posterior Probabilities," and "Typ F Probabilities."

_____
_____
_____

Did you get the same results using cranial and postcranial data? Explain any differences.

_____
_____
_____

What is your sex estimate based on sectioning points? How the classification probabilities compare to your Fordisc result?

_____
_____
_____

Discuss some advantages and limitations of using multiple measurements versus single measurements to estimate sex.

_____
_____
_____

Chapter 9

Ancestry Estimation

OBJECTIVES

Ancestral differences in the skeleton can be assessed using metric and morphoscopic characteristics which are the result of evolutionary processes. The estimation of ancestry from human remains requires an understanding of human biological variation and cultural context. In this chapter you will apply various methods to estimate ancestry from skeletal remains including cranial morphoscopic analysis, craniometrics analysis using Fordisc, and dental metric analysis.

PRINCIPLES OF ANCESTRY ESTIMATION

Ancestry refers to an individual's geographic region of ancestral origin. The estimation of ancestry from human skeletal remains is possible due to geographically patterned human variation. Moreover, because ancestry has both biological and social aspects (particularly in terms of how individuals self-identify and how they are identified by others), the estimation of ancestry also often involves interpreting skeletal variation within the context of social labels and geopolitical histories. Ancestry, like the other components of the biological profile, is estimated in order to facilitate the identification of an unknown individual by helping to narrow the pool of possible matches with missing persons. In addition, other aspects of the biological profile may depend on the correct estimation of ancestry because sexual dimorphism, limb proportions, and growth rates tend to vary between different ancestral groups.

Ancestry estimation in forensic anthropology involves the study of morphoscopic traits and skeletal measurements that correspond to geographically patterned genetic variation (Fig. 9.1). Because of the range of variation in modern humans and different population histories, the estimation of ancestry is not always straightforward. Forensic anthropologists recognize that differences can be identified between groups by focusing on the morphoscopic and metric traits that show a moderate to high level of heritability. Within the United States, forensic anthropologists are typically concerned with estimating ancestry of individuals of European, Africa, Asian, Hispanic, and Native American origin. In some cases, however, it may be possibly and relevant to estimate ancestry on a more geographically or temporally specific level, such as Southeast Asian, Southwest Hispanic, or 18th century European. Many of the skeletal characteristics associated with ancestry are underdeveloped until around puberty; it is therefore difficult and generally unadvisable to estimate ancestry from subadult skeletons.

An individual who is a product of parents from two different ancestral backgrounds is an example of gene flow and is considered to be "admixed" although these individuals may more strongly identify or be associated with one particular group socially. Morphological traits more frequently found in a particular population may be expressed differently in admixed individuals due to differential gene expression, environmental factors, and other factors that contribute to human variation. Since the frequency distributions of particular character states in admixed groups are not well understood, it is generally not advisable to automatically conclude that an individual is of mixed ancestry; it is better to simply identify the ancestry group that the remains most closely resemble and include other possibilities. Despite the known biological basis for many geographically varying morphological traits, ancestry estimation remains one of the most challenging assessments for most modern forensic anthropology practitioners.

CRANIAL MORPHOSCOPIC ANALYSIS

Morphoscopic traits are quasicontinuous morphological features that show varying forms, degrees of expression, or frequencies in presence or absence. There are a number of morphoscopic traits that show variation associated with ancestry, and these traits can be identified and scored using statistically valid methods to estimate ancestry such as Optimized Summed Scoring Attributes (OSSA) and Decision Tree Modeling (Hefner and Ousley, 2014).

A Laboratory Manual for Forensic Anthropology. https://doi.org/10.1016/B978-0-12-812201-3.00009-8

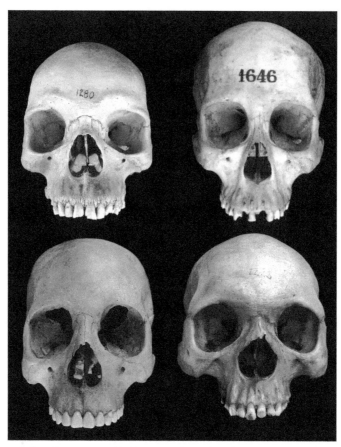

FIG. 9.1 Differences in cranial morphology due to geographically patterned genetic variation. *(Image courtesy of Joseph Hefner; From Christensen, A.M., Passalacqua, N.V., Bartelink, E.J., 2014. Forensic Anthropology: Current Methods and Practice, Academic Press.)*

OSSA uses the frequency of morphoscopic traits and their character states to estimate ancestry as either American White or American Black. The traits assessed in the OSSA method include Anterior Nasal Spine (ANS), Inferior Nasal Aperture (INA), Interorbital Breadth (IOB), Nasal Aperture Width (NAW), Nasal Bone Structure (NBS), and PostBregmatic Depression (PBD). Each character state is scored on the basis of shape, presence or absence, or degree of expression (Appendix N: Ancestry Estimation Using Optimized Summed Scored Attributes). Scores are then transformed into binary (0,1) variables (Appendix N); scores more common in American Blacks are optimized to a score of 0, while those more common in American Whites are optimized to a score of 1.

Once all traits have been transformed to their binary scores, the character state scores are summed. Summed scores of 0–3 are classified as American Black while scores of 4 or greater are classified as American White (Fig. 9.2). OSSA estimates ancestry correctly at a rate of ~86% (Hefner and Ousley, 2014). OSSA does make the assumption that the individual is of either European or African ancestry and will always classify an individual into one of these two groups (even if they are actually from a different group). Moreover, all traits must be present and scorable in order to use the OSSA method. Score-transformation, summing, and classification can be carried out using the guide in Appendix N.

A more robust approach to cranial morphoscopic ancestry estimation uses a decision tree, or classification tree (Hefner and Ousley, 2014). Decision trees are regression-based models that use sequential rules to determine group membership through a series of nodes. These nodes separate the group into two or more subgroups in order to achieve the most accurate classification possible for each individual based on known group memberships. Morphoscopic traits are scored and used to classify an unknown individual into one of three groups: White, Black, or Hispanic. Following this approach, morphoscopic traits, ANS, INA, IOB NAW, and NBS (several of the same traits used in the OSSA method) are scored. Beginning at the top of the decision tree, the splitting nodes are followed using the character state score for each trait until the final (terminal) node is reached (see Appendix O: Ancestry Estimation Using a Decision Tree of Morphoscopic Traits). Classification of an unknown individual to an ancestry is based on the ancestry group in the terminal node that has the greatest amount of individuals present in that node. This decision tree approach has been shown to correctly classify individuals into the appropriate ancestry group ~80% of the time (Hefner and Ousley, 2014).

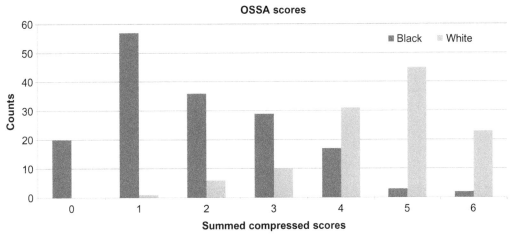

FIG. 9.2 Distribution of American Black and White individuals based on OSSA score. *(From Hefner, J.T., Ousley, S.D., 2014. Statistical classification methods for estimating ancestry using morphoscopic traits. J. Forensic Sci. 59 (4), 883–890.)*

CRANIOMETRIC ANALYSIS

Craniometric analysis involves measuring the dimensions of the skull. In some cases, analyses may involve one or two measurements or a ratio of two measurements, but the most accepted approach is the use of discriminant functions, typically using the program Fordisc. When using Fordisc in ambiguous cases or those in which only a skull is available, all measurements and all groups can be selected for inclusion in the analysis. Ancestry estimation is often more accurate and straightforward, however, when sex can be assessed by other methods. Once sex has been estimated, analyses in Fordisc can then be limited to include only the groups of that sex, providing a more accurate estimate of ancestry and eliminating the effects of size differences associated with sex. Two examples of Fordisc results and interpretations of likely ancestry classification are shown in Figs. 9.3 and 9.4. Craniometric data can also be collected using digitizers, which record the locations of particular points (such as skeletal landmarks) in three dimensions. Software programs such as ThreeSkull (Ousley, 2010) can then be used to transfer 3D landmark data into databases which can then be extracted into other statistical programs such as Fordisc.

Ancestry can also be estimated as African, Asian, or European using discriminant function analysis of tooth crown measurements (Pilloud et al., 2014). This approach uses equations from 28 measurements representing both buccolingual and mesiodistal crown measurements from all teeth except the third molars (Appendix P: Ancestry Estimation Using Dental Metric Analysis), with different equations for females and males. A first set of equations classifies individuals as either African/Asian or European, and a second equation (if needed) classifies individuals as African or Asian (Appendix P). This approach correctly classifies 88.1% of females and 71.9% of males (Pilloud et al., 2014).

Multigroup Classification of Current Case

Group	Classified into	Distance from	Probabilities Posterior	Typ F	Typ Chi	Typ R	
HF	**HF**	5.1	0.791	0.723	0.651	0.702	(15/47)
AF		9.2	0.099	0.419	0.236	0.207	(24/29)
BF		9.3	0.097	0.300	0.234	0.268	(53/71)
WF		13.4	0.013	0.078	0.064	0.077	(168/181)
JF		31.2	0.000	0.001	0.000	**0.017**	**(59/59)**

Current Case is closest to HFs

FIG. 9.3 Fordisc example 1. The associated postcranial remains in this case were estimated to be female using morphological indicators of the pelvis; thus only females were included in the analysis of cranial measurements. The measurements of the unknown individual are most similar to the Hispanic females in the reference database. In this case, an ancestry estimate of *Hispanic* is most appropriate. *(From Christensen, A.M., Passalacqua, N.V., Bartelink, E.J., 2014. Forensic Anthropology: Current Methods and Practice, Academic Press.)*

Group	Classified into	Distance from	Probabilities Posterior	Typ F	Typ Chi	Typ R	
CHM	**CHM**	11.2	0.337	0.866	0.742	0.586	(30/70)
VM		12.2	0.202	0.872	0.665	0.510	(25/49)
GTM		12.3	0.192	0.815	0.658	0.600	(29/70)
JM		12.6	0.160	0.770	0.630	0.624	(33/85)
HM		14.5	0.064	0.567	0.490	0.503	(97/193)
AM		16.4	0.024	0.669	0.353	0.481	(28/52)
HF		18.7	0.008	0.597	0.228	0.298	(34/47)
JF		19.2	0.006	0.490	0.205	0.169	(50/59)
BM		20.0	0.004	0.318	0.173	0.291	(74/103)
AF		20.8	0.003	0.767	0.144	0.138	(26/29)

FIG. 9.4 Fordisc example 2. In this case, the results for a cranium where the groups with typicality levels below 0.05 have already been removed. The measurements of the unknown cranium are most similar to those of Chinese males (CHM), but the Mahalanobis distances to Vietnamese males (VM), Guatemalan males (GTM), and Japanese males (JM) are all very similar. In this case, an ancestry estimate of *Asian* is most appropriate. *(From Christensen, A.M., Passalacqua, N.V., Bartelink, E.J., 2014. Forensic Anthropology: Current Methods and Practice, Academic Press.)*

POSTCRANIAL METHODS

Compared to the skull, the postcranial skeleton has received relatively little attention for ancestry estimation. This is due to the fact that ancestry variation in the postcranial skeleton is poorly understood, more difficult to visualize, and also possibly that geographic adaptations are simply less strongly correlated with postcranial morphology. Fordisc can be utilized to estimate ancestry based on postcranial measurements although reference samples are currently limited to Black and White female and male groups. Assuming that the individual is from one of these groups, however, Fordisc likely represents the most accurate approach to ancestry estimation from postcranial material. Applying Fordisc to postcranial measurements is the same process as for cranial analyses, but the measurements are entered onto the "Postcranial Measurements" page. When estimating ancestry from postcranial remains using Fordisc, particular caution must be taken with individuals who may possibly be Hispanic as well as other groups due to population differences in sexual dimorphism.

EXERCISE 9.1 Ancestry Estimation Using OSSA

Materials needed:
- Appendix N: Ancestry Estimation Using Optimized Summed Scored Attributes
- OSSA scores provided in this exercise

Note to instructor: This exercise can also be supplemented or replaced with OSSA scores from a forensic case or reference material.

Case scenario: You are developing a biological profile for unidentified skeletal remains. While you also plan to perform metric analysis, the cranium is complete and in good condition, so an assessment of ancestry using OSSA is also appropriate. Based on your assessment, you recorded the OSSA scores below.

Instructions/Procedure:
- Using the OSSA scores below, estimate ancestry using Appendix N
- First translate the character state scores to OSSA scores
- Then, sum the scores using the guidance in Appendix N

OSSA Trait	Character State/Score	OSSA Score
ANS	1	
INA	3	
IOB	2	
NAW	3	
NBS	1	
PBD	1	
Sum		

What ancestry is indicated by your OSSA assessment?

_____
_____

Modify several of the character trait scores provided. How do they affect the ancestry estimate?

_____
_____
_____

EXERCISE 9.2 Ancestry Estimation Using OSSA

Materials needed:
- Appendix N: Ancestry Estimation using Optimized Summed Scored Attributes
- Images provided in this exercise

Note to instructor: This exercise can also be supplemented or replaced with real or replica human skeletal material.

Case scenario: A cranium was found in an evidence storage area of a police department. The officer now assigned to the case is unable to locate any associated records, and she is unsure the context of the remains. Hoping that you might be able to provide an estimation of the biological profile, she brought the cranium to your laboratory for analysis.

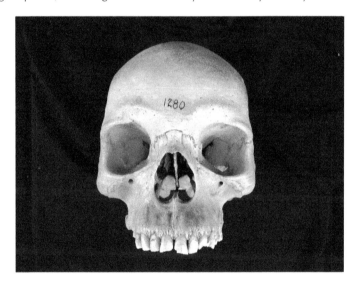

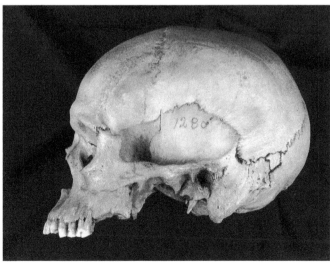

(Images courtesy of Joseph Hefner.)

Instructions/Procedure:
- Using Appendix N, score the character states of the six OSSA traits pictured in the above skull
- Next, use Appendix N to translate and then sum the scores

OSSA Trait	Character State/Score	OSSA Score
ANS		
INA		
IOB		
NAW		
NBS		
PBD		
Sum		

Compare your scores with your classmates' scores. Did you all arrive at the same score for each character state? If not, why?

_____
_____
_____

What ancestry is indicated by your scores? For any differences in character states between you and your classmates, did they affect the outcome of ancestry estimation using OSSA?

_____
_____
_____

EXERCISE 9.3   Ancestry Estimation Using the Ancestry Estimation Decision Tree

Materials needed:
- Appendix O: Ancestry Estimation using a Decision Tree of Morphoscopic Traits
- OSSA scores from Exercise 9.2

Note to instructor: This exercise can be supplemented or replaced with real or replica human skeletal material.

Case scenario: Based on a missing person's report from the area, it is suspected that the cranium from the previous exercise may be Hispanic in origin, so you have determined that a decision tree analysis for ancestry estimation is more appropriate.

Instructions/Procedure:
- Using the character state scores from the previous exercises, use the decision tree in Appendix O to estimate ancestry
- Start at the top node (the score for INA) and continue to follow the splits in the tree until you reach a terminal node. Note that the ancestry classification for each terminal node is based on the group with the highest number of individuals in that node.

What ancestry is indicated by your analysis? For any differences in character states between you and your classmates, did they affect the outcome of ancestry estimation using the decision tree?

_____
_____
_____

Was your ancestry estimate different using this method than OSSA? If so, what traits are responsible and what are the implications of a different ancestry estimate?

_____
_____
_____

EXERCISE 9.4 Ancestry Estimation Using Fordisc

Materials needed:
- Fordisc output provided in this exercise

Note to instructors: This output can be supplemented or replaced with Fordisc results from a forensic case or skeletal reference collection.

Case scenario: While cleaning out their attic, home owners discovered a human skull in a box. They do not recognize the box and believe it may have been there since before they purchased the home. They contacted the authorities who then contacted you hoping that you can estimate the ancestry of this individual and provide a lead for their case. You took measurements and analyzed them using Fordisc, with the following results.

Multigroup Classification of Current Case

Group	Classified into	Distance from	Posterior	Typ F	Typ Chi	Typ R	
WM	**WM**	15.5	0.574	0.525	0.491	0.536	(173/373)
BM		16.9	0.279	0.436	0.391	0.495	(48/95)
BF		18.4	0.131	0.350	0.299	0.197	(49/61)
AF		22.5	0.017	0.180	0.126	0.074	(25/27)

Explain what "Distance from" means and how it relates to each "Group" in this case:

Provide an interpretation of the "Posterior Probabilities" in this case:

Provide an interpretation for the "Typ F Probabilities" in this case:

How would you report ancestry for this case and how confident are you in your conclusion?

EXERCISE 9.5 Ancestry Estimation Using Fordisc

Materials needed:
- Fordisc output provided in this exercise

Note to instructors: This output can be supplemented or replaced with Fordisc results from a forensic case or skeletal reference collection.

Case scenario: In the same scenario as Exercise 9.4, your Fordisc analysis instead appears as below.

Multigroup Classification of current case

Group	Classified into	Distance from	Posterior	Typ F	Typ Chi	Typ R	
BM	**BM**	29.6	0.930	0.135	0.100	0.324	(69/102)
WM		34.8	0.070	**0.045**	**0.030**	0.056	(272/288)
BF		49.1	0.000	0.001	0.000	**0.015**	**(67/68)**
WF		52.4	0.000	0.000	0.000	0.006	(171/172)

Explain what "Distance from" means and how it relates to each "Group" in this case:

_____
_____
_____

Provide an interpretation of the "Posterior Probabilities" in this case:

_____
_____
_____

Provide an interpretation for the "Typ F Probabilities" in this case:

_____
_____
_____

How would you report ancestry for this case and how confident are you in your conclusion?

_____
_____
_____

EXERCISE 9.6   Ancestry Estimation Using Fordisc

Materials needed:
- Measurements provided in this exercise
- Fordisc

Note to instructor: These measurements can be supplemented or replaced with measurements from a forensic case or skeletal reference collection. Optionally, you can also have students take their own measurements on reference skeletal material if available. Keep in mind that some landmarks may be difficult to identify on replica skeletal material.

Case scenario: In the case scenario in Exercise 9.2, you would like to supplement your OSSA assessment with a cranometric assessment. You took the measurements listed below.

Instructions/Procedure:
- Enter the measurements (all of which are in mm) below into Fordisc and select all male and female groups for comparison
- Follow the recommended procedure for eliminating group until 4 groups remain

Maximum length	175	Nasal height	48
Maximum breadth	132	Nasal breadth	25
Bizygomatic breadth	122	Orbital breadth	39
Basion-Bregma height	132	Orbital height	34
Basion-Nasion length	99	Biorbital breadth	100
Basion-Prosthion length	99	Interorbital breadth	22
Maximum alveolar breadth	62	Frontal chord	108
Maximum alveolar length	58	Parietal chord	113
Biauricular breadth	116	Occipital chord	97
Upper facial height	67	Foramen magnum length	39
Minimum frontal breadth	93	Foramen magnum breadth	35
Upper facial breadth	100	Mastoid length	20

Provide an interpretation for your results, including discussion of the "Distance from," "Posterior Probabilities," and "Typ F Probabilities."

_____
_____
_____

Repeat the analysis comparing the measurements only to female groups. Discuss any differences in your procedure and your results.
_____
_____
_____

EXERCISE 9.7   Ancestry Estimation Using Dental Metric Analysis

Materials needed:
* Measurements provided in this exercise
* Appendix P: Ancestry Estimation Using Dental Metric Analysis

Note to instructors: This exercise can also be supplemented or replaced with real or replica human skeletal material.

Case scenario: Based on the maxilla and mandible of the skull pictured below, you have determined that sufficient dental metric data are available to estimate ancestry based on dental measurements and you took the dental measurements in the table below. A DNA examination has determined that the remains are female.

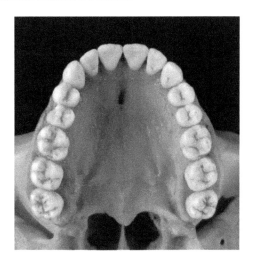

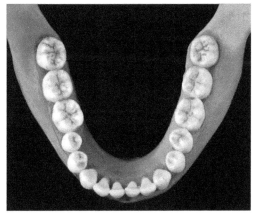

Tooth (Upper)	MD	BL	Tooth (Lower)	MD	BL
UI1	9.20	7.40	LI1	5.51	5.50
UI2	7.24	6.70	LI2	6.20	6.12
UC	7.90	8.45	LC	7.15	7.50
UP3	7.50	9.65	LP3	7.42	8.20
UP4	7.10	9.60	LP4	7.55	8.54
UM1	11.01	11.60	LM1	11.75	10.75
UM2	10.38	11.75	LM2	11.03	10.41

Instructions/Procedure:
- Using the measurements provided and the appropriate discriminant function equation in Appendix P, assess whether this individual is African/Asian versus European
- If necessary, use the appropriate discriminant function equation in Appendix P to assess whether this individual is African or Asian

What is your ancestry assessment and how confident are you in your conclusion?

_____

_____

_____

What if sex had been unknown? Based on the measurements provided, what would the ancestry estimate be if these remains were male? Is the conclusion different?

_____

_____

_____

Chapter 10

Age Estimation

OBJECTIVES

Age estimation from the skeleton is typically part of the biological profile not only used to narrow the list of potential missing persons in the case of unidentified remains but can also be applied to living individuals for other legal reasons. In this chapter, you will estimate age from subadult remains using the degree of dental development, dental eruption, long bone growth, and epiphyseal union. Adult age estimation will be performed using changes in the pubic symphysis, the morphology of the auricular surface, sternal rib ends, and bone histology.

PRINCIPLES OF AGE ESTIMATION

Estimation of age from the skeleton is possible through a comprehensive understanding of the nature, sequence, and timing of skeletal changes across the lifespan and understanding the relationship between these processes and chronological measures. Skeletal age estimation therefore involves correlating biological age (or physiological age) with chronological age (the length of time a person has been alive). Traits or processes useful as age indicators should change unidirectionally with age, correlate with chronological age, and change consistently across individuals. Reported age intervals often encompass decades for adults; an estimated age interval should be as narrow as possible but should take into account all possible variation in biological age.

In some cases, age estimation may be facilitated by knowledge of other biological parameters first. For example, development in females occurs earlier than in males, and growth trajectories show variation between populations. Any evidence for sex or ancestry should therefore be considered when estimating age, and when possible, standards for age estimation should be used that are based on the population of the skeletal material examined. When population-specific standards are not available, standards that are more inclusive and which have wider age intervals should be used.

AGE CATEGORIES

In childhood, the skeleton changes as a function of growth and development—structures mineralize, increase in size, and model their shape to achieve their mature adult form. These changes are influenced largely by genetic and other intrinsic factors. In adulthood, the skeleton begins to show degenerative changes. These changes are influenced largely by extrinsic factors such as biomechanical loading, diet, and health status. Because age estimation approaches are fundamentally different for the growth and development and degenerative phases of the lifespan, skeletal age can be considered to be in one of two broad categories: subadult, those ages during the growth and development process including the embryonic, fetal, infant, child, and adolescent periods, and adult, those ages occurring during the mature, degenerative stage of skeletal change. The growth and development of the skeleton is considered complete when all permanent teeth have erupted and all epiphyses have fused. The skeletal age category (subadult or adult) should be assessed early in the examination process because the ability to estimate other biological parameters such as sex, ancestry, and stature may depend on whether an individual is a subadult or adult. There are several texts on skeletal aging that cover different periods of the human lifespan (Black et al., 2010; Fazekas and Kosa, 1978; Iscan, 1989; Latham and Finnegan, 2010; Scheuer and Black, 2000).

SUBADULT AGE ESTIMATION

Dental Methods

In general, dental development is more highly correlated with chronological age than bone development, and therefore dental methods are typically more accurate and are preferable when possible. Dental development begins around the sixth fetal week and is completed in early adulthood (Fig. 10.1), making it a very useful means of estimating age during virtually

A Laboratory Manual for Forensic Anthropology. https://doi.org/10.1016/B978-0-12-812201-3.00010-4

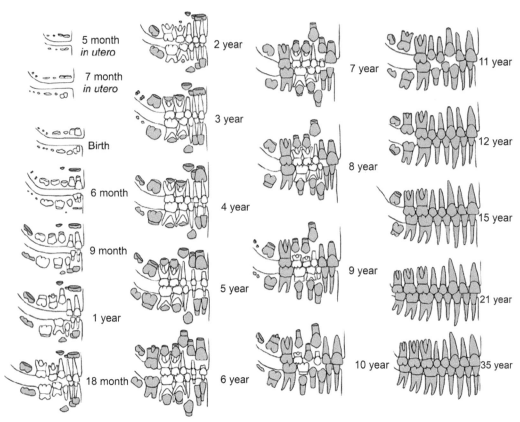

FIG. 10.1 General sequence and approximate ages of primary and secondary dental development and eruption. *(From Ubelaker, D.H., 1989. Human Skeletal Remains: Excavation, Analysis, Interpretation, second ed. Taraxacum, Washington, DC.)*

the entire subadult period. Because dental enamel is the hardest and most radiopaque substance in the body, radiologic examination of the developing dentition is very easy and often necessary, allowing visualization of root apices and unerupted teeth not visible to the naked eye (Fig. 10.2). Tooth eruption is the process whereby a tooth advances from the alveolar crypt where it develops to its functional occlusal position (i.e., the occlusal plane) in the oral cavity and also follows a particular pattern that is correlated with age.

One method of subadult age estimation is the assessment of dental development stages. The method involves determining the developmental stage of each available tooth, including the development of the crown and root, by reference to

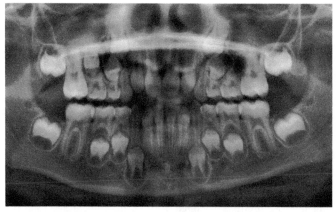

FIG. 10.2 Radiograph of developing dentition in a 7-year old. *(Image courtesy of Mikylee Vaughan; From Christensen, A.M., Passalacqua, N.V., Bartelink, E.J., 2014. Forensic Anthropology: Current Methods and Practice, Academic Press.)*

illustrated developmental stages (see Appendix Q: Age Estimation Using Dental Development). Although development follows the same sequence for each tooth (progressing from the crown cusp(s) to the root apex/apices), the timing is different for each tooth position. Once the degree of development is assessed, skeletal age is estimated by referencing calculated mean ages for achieving that developmental stage for each tooth (see Appendix Q). Females tend to be more advanced in their dental development compared to males during most of the growth and development period. Tooth calcification rates also vary between populations. Because sex and ancestry are often not known for juvenile skeletal remains, these issues can pose some limitations. Most methods are based on specific teeth (e.g., the mandibular dentition) and are therefore not applicable to other teeth. Several methods specific to third molar development are often used to determine the probability that an individual is at least 18 years old (Appendix Q).

Osteological Methods

Another method of estimating subadult age is by assessing diaphyseal growth. There is a strong linear relationship between diaphyseal length and age, especially during fetal development, and there is little variation between the sexes or different populations. This method is useful until the epiphyses begin to fuse with the diaphysis, typically around age 10. The method is particularly useful for aging fetal skeletal material because dental development may be minimal. Forensic anthropologists are sometimes involved in estimating fetal age in cases where the viability of the infant is in question, which may be relevant to the manner of death. Diaphyseal lengths for fetal (12–40 weeks) and subadult (2–12 years) bones can be found in Appendix R: Age Estimation Using Long Bone Diaphyseal Length.

The appearance and fusion of certain primary ossification centers can also be useful in the estimation of juvenile age because of their correlation with age. Among these are the bones of the cranium, whose union results in the closure of the fontanelles and metopic suture (Fig. 10.3 and Table 10.1). The sphenoid and mastoid fontanelles close soon after birth and the occipital during the first year. During the second year, the frontal fontanelle, left and right mandible halves, and left and right frontal halves close. The squamous and lateral portions of the occipital close in the fifth year, and the lateral and basilar portions close in the sixth year.

Many bones, including the long bones of the limbs; bones of the hands and feet; ribs; vertebrae; clavicle; and scapula, form from a primary ossification center (Fig. 10.4) and several (usually at least two) secondary ossification centers (Fig. 10.5). The primary and secondary ossification centers unite in a process referred to as epiphyseal union. The sequence

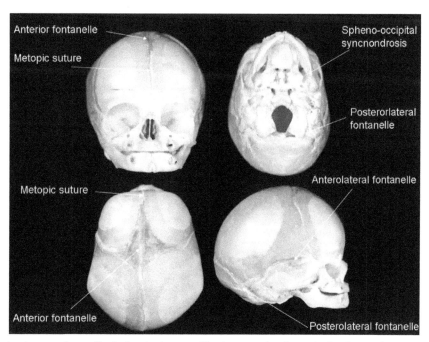

FIG. 10.3 Fetal skull, showing open fontanelles (unfused primary ossification centers) and open (unfused) metopic suture. *(From Christensen, A.M., Passalacqua, N.V., Bartelink, E.J., 2014. Forensic Anthropology: Current Methods and Practice, Academic Press.)*

TABLE 10.1 Fusion of Primary Ossification Centers of the Skull

Bone/Feature	Age of Closure
Sphenoid, mastoid, and occipital fontanelle	Birth—1 year
Left and right mandible halves	Birth—1 year
Frontal fontanelle	1–2 years
Occipital squamous and lateral portions	1–3 years
Left and right frontal halves (metopic suture)	2–4 years
Occipital lateral and basilar portions	5–7 years
Spheno-occipital synchondrosis	11–18 years

Modified from Stewart, T.D., 1979. Essentials of Forensic Anthropology, Charles C. Thomas, Springfield, IL; Scheuer, L., Black, S., 2000. Developmental Juvenile Osteology, Academic Press, San Diego, CA.

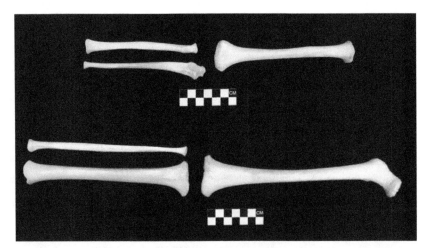

FIG. 10.4   Long bone diaphyses (primary ossification centers) of the arm (top) and leg (bottom) in a juvenile (~7 years of age). *(From Christensen, A.M., Passalacqua, N.V., Bartelink, E.J., 2014. Forensic Anthropology: Current Methods and Practice, Academic Press.)*

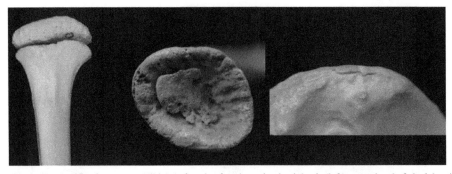

FIG. 10.5   Primary and secondary ossification centers. Tibial shaft and unfused proximal epiphysis (left), sternal end of clavicle with developing epiphysis (middle), and iliac crest in the process of fusing (right). *(From Christensen, A.M., Passalacqua, N.V., Bartelink, E.J., 2014. Forensic Anthropology: Current Methods and Practice, Academic Press.)*

of epiphyseal union is consistent and is correlated with chronological age (Fig. 10.6). Most epiphyses unite between the ages of 10 and 25, making epiphyseal union a reliable method for estimating age from adolescent and young adult remains (Appendix S: Age Estimation Using Ossification and Epiphyseal Union). Because epiphyseal union occurs as a process rather than an event, it is often necessary to assess the degree of union on a scale from commencement to completion. Early in union, a distinct line is visible between the two components which tends to obliterate through remodeling with age.

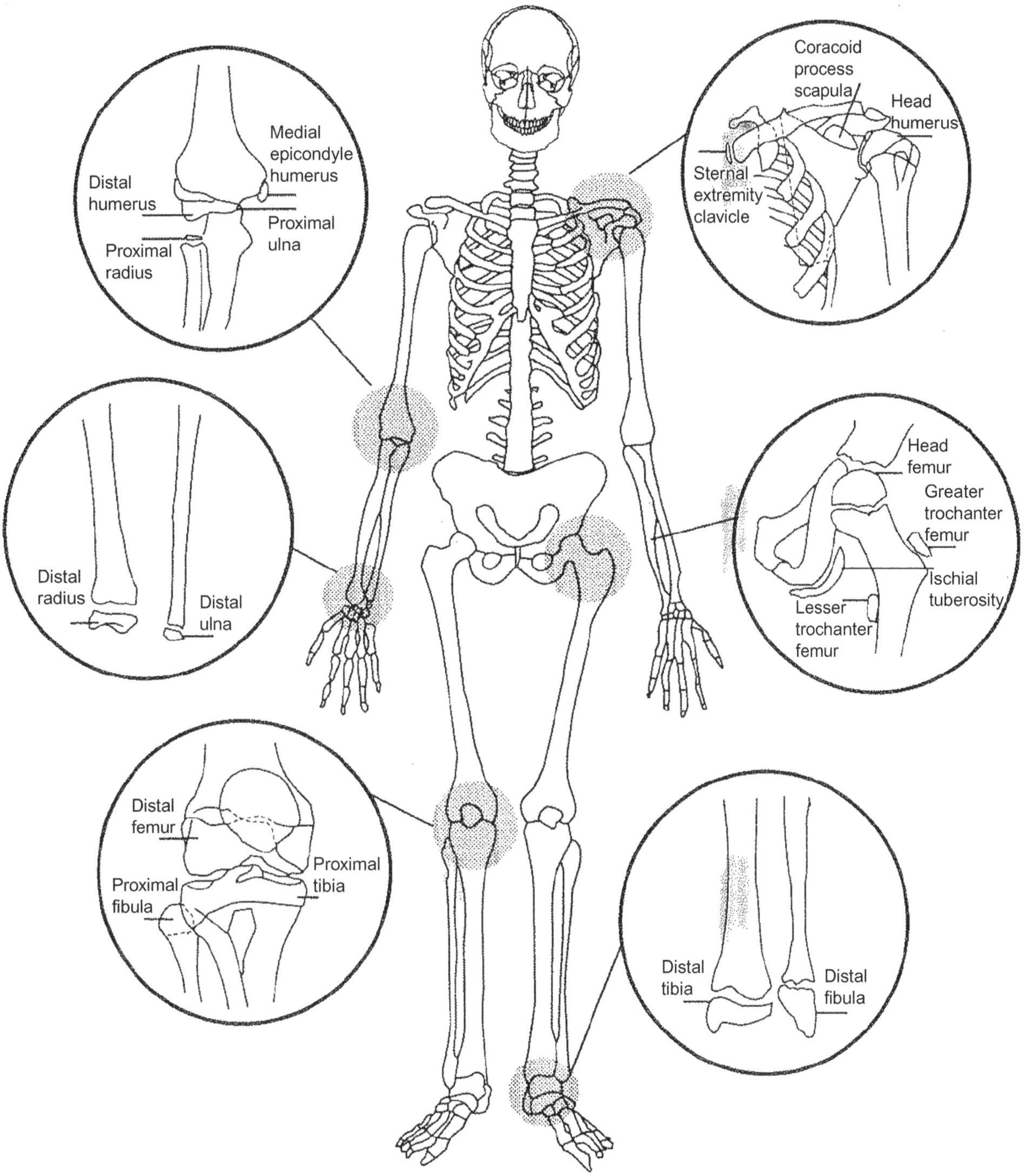

FIG. 10.6 Epiphyseal union locations. *(From Buikstra, J.E., Ubelaker, D.H., 1994. Standards for Data Collection From Human Skeletal Remains. Archaeological Survey Research Seminar Series, vol. 44. Archaeological Survey, Fayetteville, AR.)*

The process of initial union to final epiphyseal closure may take several years. The iliac crest of the innominate and the sternal end of the clavicle (Fig. 10.5) are the last epiphyses to fuse, which can occur as late as the mid-20s to early 30s.

For intact bodies or living individuals, assessment of the appearance and union of the ossification centers can be accomplished using radiology. The appearance of ossification centers and stages of epiphyseal union, however, can appear somewhat differently in visual assessments as compared to assessments of radiographs. These differences should be taken into consideration when the assessment approach varies from that described in the method.

ADULT AGE ESTIMATION

Pubic Symphysis

Age estimation based on the pubic symphysis focuses on the changing features found on and surrounding the face of the pubic symphysis. In young individuals, the pubic symphyseal face is characterized by a series of horizontally oriented ridges and furrows (also referred to as billowing) (Figs. 10.7 and 10.8). In younger individuals, the symphyseal face lacks a distinctive border, meaning there is no defined edge where the symphyseal face is separated from the ischial and pubic rami. With increasing age, the billows disappear as new bone is deposited on the symphyseal face. An ossific nodule, similar to a small epiphysis, fuses to the upper portion of the symphyseal surface, and the face becomes smooth and defined with a distinct rim. In the last stages of aging, the symphyseal surface becomes roughened and porous in appearance and the symphyseal rim shows evidence of osteophytic lipping (bony projections extending from the joint margin). Appendix T: Age Estimation using Pubic Symphyseal Morphology provides descriptions and age estimates for features of pubic symphyseal morphology.

Auricular Surface

The auricular surface of the ilium, as well as the area just posterior to this surface, also goes through age-related changes, characterized by remodeling of the auricular joint surface, the development of a rim around the surface, an increase in auricular surface cortical bone porosity, and the growth of bony spicules in the area posterior to the auricular surface (Fig. 10.9). Like the pubic symphysis, the young auricular surface initially has horizontally distributed billows which

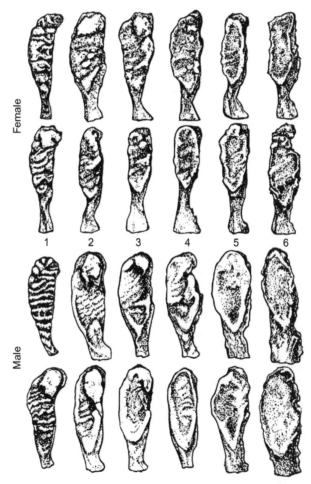

FIG. 10.7   Changes in the pubic symphysis based on the six-phase Suchey-Brooks (Brooks and Suchey, 1990) system, where 1=younger, 6=older, and the above rows for each sex reflect younger expressions and the lower rows reflect older expressions of the same phase. *(From Buikstra, J.E., Ubelaker, D.H., 1994. Standards for Data Collection From Human Skeletal Remains. Archaeological Survey Research Seminar Series, vol. 44. Archaeological Survey, Fayetteville, AR.)*

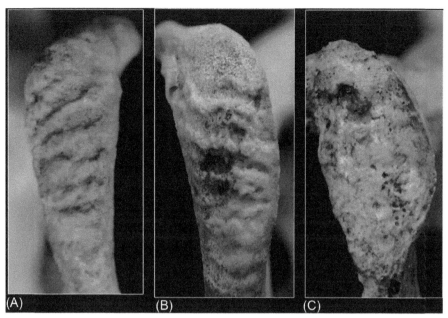

FIG. 10.8   Young (A), middle (B), and older (C) adult pubic symphysis. *(From Christensen, A.M., Passalacqua, N.V., Bartelink, E.J., 2014. Forensic Anthropology: Current Methods and Practice, Academic Press.)*

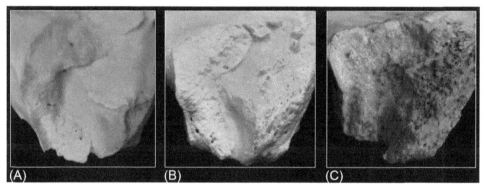

FIG. 10.9   Young (A), middle (B), and older (C) adult auricular surface. *(From Christensen, A.M., Passalacqua, N.V., Bartelink, E.J., 2014. Forensic Anthropology: Current Methods and Practice, Academic Press.)*

are reduced to faint striae over time, and eventually the surface becomes smooth. The texture of the auricular surface changes from finely grained to coarsely grained (having a sandpaper-like texture) to smooth, dense (remodeled) bone. The apex, located at the intersection of the arcuate line and auricular surface, is smooth and rounded in younger individuals and becomes progressively sharp and irregular with age, often showing osteophytic lipping among older individuals. Also associated with increasing age is the appearance and proliferation of porosity of the auricular surface, which can be characterized as microporosity (very small holes) or macroporosity (larger-sized holes). Osteophytic lipping of the rim occurs with advancing age and is most obvious on the inferior margin of the auricular surface, often projecting inferiorly. The retroauricular area is located on the ilium posterior to the auricular surface. As a muscle attachment site, changes that occur are related to the ossification of ligaments, resulting in increasing rugosity and the formation of bony spicules. Appendix U: Age Estimation Using Auricular Surface Morphology provides descriptions and age estimates for features of auricular surface morphology.

One advantage of auricular surface aging is that due to its more protected location and greater bone density, this area is often better preserved than other adult aging features such as the pubic symphysis or sternal rib ends. The morphological changes to this area, however, are much more subtle, and thus auricular surface methods can be more difficult to apply. Methods typically involve phase analysis similar to those applied to the pubic symphysis and have become increasingly refined through simplification of phasing criteria, more refined statistics, and larger, more diverse samples.

Sternal Rib Ends

The sternal ends of the ribs (where the bone connects to the costal cartilage) also undergo systematic, age-related changes. Much work has focused on the fourth rib because it is easily accessible at autopsy, but most ribs undergo similar changes, and ribs 3–9 can be used interchangeably for age estimation if the fourth is not available (Yoder et al., 2001). The estimation of age from this region focuses on changes in the shape of the rib as well as the overall quality of the bone. Generally, the sternal ends of the ribs go from a billowy, flat appearance when young, to a cupped, flared shape when middle aged, to a wide shape with irregular sharp margins in advanced age (Fig. 10.10). Along with these changes in shape, the overall quality of the rib tends to decrease with age, becoming lighter, more fragile, and more porous. Appendix V: Age Estimation Using Sternal Rib End Morphology provides age-related morphological changes of the right fourth sternal rib.

Other Age-Related Changes

Histomorphometry can also be used to estimate skeletal age. The basis of bone histomorphometric methods of adult age estimation is bone remodeling and the accumulation of intact and fragmentary osteons; the bone is continually remodeled through osteoclastic and osteoblastic activity. Over an individual's lifetime, lamellar bone is reorganized and maintained through the remodeling process. This is achieved through individual remodeling units called Bone Structural Units or BSUs, known as secondary osteons (Fig. 10.11). Age estimation using histomorphometry is most useful when applied to fragmentary skeletons where other morphological methods cannot be reliably applied but requires partial bone destruction in addition to specialized equipment and additional training. Histological age estimation can also be used to collect additional age indicators for the construction of the age interval in nonfragmentary remains.

Bone histomorphometric age estimation is performed by using a reticule (a counting tool placed into the eyepiece of the microscope, see Fig. 10.12) superimposed on a bone thin section (Fig. 10.13). Which features to count and how to count

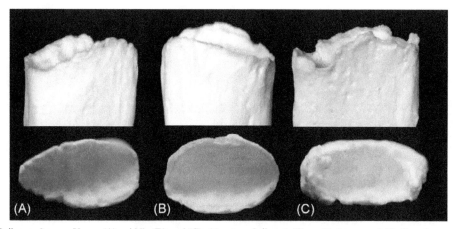

FIG. 10.10 Sternal rib age changes. Young (A), middle (B), and (C) older sternal rib end. *(From Christensen, A.M., Passalacqua, N.V., Bartelink, E.J., 2014. Forensic Anthropology: Current Methods and Practice, Academic Press.)*

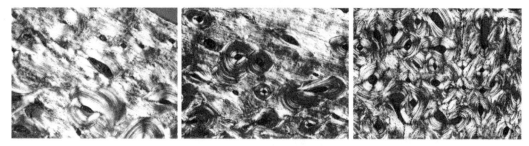

FIG. 10.11 Histological changes in bone with age. Left: Young adult anterior femur showing unremodeled bone, primary osteons (nonHaversian systems), and low secondary osteon population density. Middle: Middle-aged adult anterior femur showing increase in secondary osteon population density and sparse areas of unremodeled bone. Right: Old-aged adult anterior femur showing high-secondary osteon population density and no areas of unremodeled bone. *(100×, polarized light, Images courtesy of Christian Crowder and Amy Beresheim; From Christensen, A.M., Passalacqua, N.V., Bartelink, E.J., 2014. Forensic Anthropology: Current Methods and Practice, Academic Press.)*

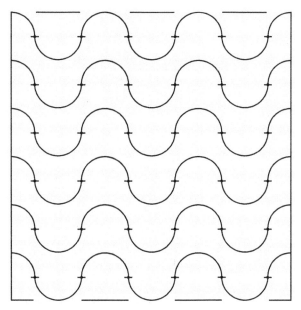

FIG. 10.12   Merz 36-point (hit) counting reticule.

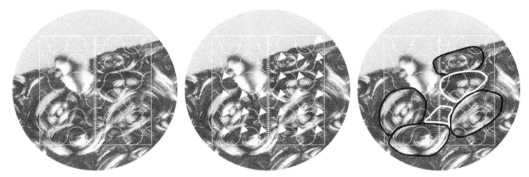

FIG. 10.13   Merz reticule superimposed on a rib thin section and used to collect data for age estimation (left). For this pictured field, the total number of hits is 26 (middle, *white arrows*), the number of intact osteons is 4 (right, highlighted in *black*), and the total number of fragmentary osteons is 2 (right, highlighted in *white*). (*Modified from Crowder, C., Heinrich, J., Stout, S.D., 2012. Rib histomorphometry for adult age estimation. In: Lynne, S. Bell, L.S. (Eds.), Forensic Microscopy for Skeletal Tissues: Methods and Protocols, Methods in Molecular Biology, vol. 915, pp. 109–127.*)

them is determined by the specific method used. Following one method for age estimation using ribs (Crowder et al., 2012), using the reticule and combined with details of the microscope magnification, the area of bone evaluated is calculated and the number of intact and fragmentary osteons is counted (Fig. 10.13). From these variables, population-specific regression formulae are used to calculate estimated age (Appendix W).

Several other skeletal changes generally reflect advanced age with little correlation to a particular age. These methods are typically used when other areas like the pubic symphysis and sternal rib ends are unavailable or unsuitable for examination and provide only a general estimate of adult skeletal age such as younger or older adult. Examples include cranial suture closure, osteoarthritis, and osteoporosis. Teeth also undergo age-related changes including attrition, changes in root transparency, and addition of cementum. When examining the skeleton for specific or general age-related changes, it is important to be attentive to pathological conditions that might have an effect on traits used for aging, especially degenerative changes.

MULTIFACTORIAL AGE ESTIMATION

Since in many cases there may be multiple skeletal regions available for estimating age, statistical approaches may be used to combine information from multiple regions, in an approach often referred to as multifactorial age estimation. One multifactorial age estimation method involves using transition analysis (a Bayesian approach that relies on estimating the mean age of the transition from one phase or state to the next) of age-related data from cranial sutures, the pubic symphysis, and/or the auricular surface (Boldsen et al., 2002). The data are analyzed using a freely available computer program called ADBOU, which provides probability-based age estimates. The benefits of ADBOU are that it allows for missing data as well as any combination of variables when generating an age estimate. However, while ADBOU is statistically robust, this approach has been found to perform about as well as single method age estimates and other multifactorial regression approaches. Another multifactorial aging method combines the pubic symphysis and auricular surface data in "look-up" tables, and this method has been demonstrated to perform better than the individual methods from which it is based (Samworth and Gowland, 2007; Passalacqua, 2010).

EXERCISE 10.1 Subadult Age Estimation Using Dental Development

Materials needed:
- Image provided in this exercise
- Appendix Q: Age Estimation Using Dental Development

Note to instructor: This exercise can be replaced or supplemented with real or replica human skeletal material from forensic cases or reference collections.

Case scenario: A partial skeleton including a mandible was discovered in an unmarked box in a medical examiner's office. You have identified the remains as being subadult in age based on the fact that the dentition is still developing. Unfortunately your x-ray machine is undergoing required maintenance this week, but you are able to remove the permanent first molar from the mandible and directly observe its stage of development.

Mandible: Developing permanent M1:

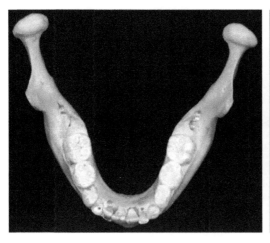 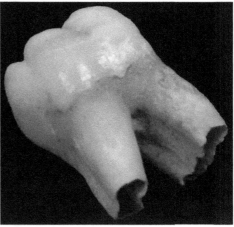

Instructions/Procedure:
- Using Appendix Q, determine the developmental stage of the depicted tooth
- Based on the development stage, determine the approximate age of the individual (in years). The sex is unknown at this point, so provide estimates for males and females.

	Females	Males
Development stage		
Estimated age (years)		

How confident are you in your age assessment based on a single tooth?

_____
_____
_____

EXERCISE 10.2   Subadult Age Estimation Using Dental Development

Materials needed:
- Image provided in this exercise
- Appendix Q: Age Estimation Using Dental Development

Note to instructor: This image can be supplemented or replaced by radiographs of subadult dentition from casework or reference materials. Additional radiographic images may also be located using an Internet search.

Case scenario: A mandible was found washed up on a river shore by fishermen who notified the local police. The jaw is pretty small, and they suspect it may belong to a missing 2-year-old girl and have brought it to you to see if the age of the jaw is consistent with the missing child. You are able to have a dentist colleague take a panorex (a radiographic image that captures the whole jaw) of the mandible. DNA tests have confirmed that the remains are female.

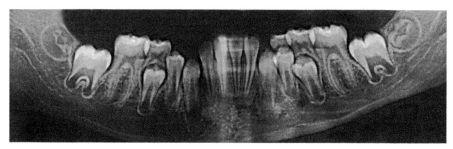

(Image courtesy of Mikylee Vaughan.)

Instructions/Procedure:
- Using Appendix Q, determine the developmental stage of all applicable teeth visible in the radiograph. (Note: This will also require you to identify deciduous and permanent teeth.)

Tooth	Development Stage	Age Estimate

Are all of the teeth in the radiograph in the same developmental stage? Explain.

_____
_____
_____

What is your overall age estimate for this individual? How confident are you in your estimate?

_____

_____

Can this mandible belong to the missing 2-year-old child? Why or why not?

_____

_____

_____

Do you think that knowing the age of missing child to which authorities believed this mandible belonged could have introduced bias into your analysis? Why or why not? Discuss the advantages and disadvantages of having detailed case information prior to conducting your analysis.

_____

_____

_____

_____

EXERCISE 10.3   Fetal Age Estimation Using Diaphyseal Length

Materials needed:
- Appendix R: Age Estimation Using Long Bone Diaphyseal Length
- Measurements provided in this exercise

Note to instructor: This exercise can be supplemented or replaced with measurements from cases or reference collections.

Case scenario: Skeletal remains were inadvertently discovered during construction of a new highway. Although it is possible that the remains are Native American and therefore not medicolegally significant, authorities have requested your assistance with some of the analysis. In particular, there is one bone they suspected was nonhuman in origin. You confirm that the bone is actually fetal human humerus, with a diaphyseal length of 60 mm.

(Image courtesy of Eric Bartelink.)

Based on your measurement of the humerus and using data from Appendix R, what is the likely age of this individual?

_____

_____

Given that the remains may not be modern in origin, would this have any influence on your estimate?

_____

_____

_____

EXERCISE 10.4   Subadult Age Estimation Using Epiphyseal Union

Materials needed:
- Image provided in this exercise
- Appendix S: Age Estimation Using Ossification and Epiphyseal Union

Note to instructor: This exercise can be replaced or supplemented with real or replica human skeletal material from forensic cases or reference collections.

Case scenario: Backpackers discovered a collection of skeletal remains in a cave in a remote area. Several years ago, a family disappeared during a camping trip near this area and were never found, including two adults (female and male), their 8-year-old son, and a 19-year-old nephew. All of the remains recovered appear to be from subadults. Authorities have requested your assistance in determining whether the remains could belong to one or more of the campers.

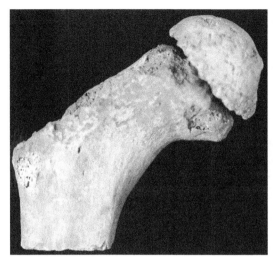
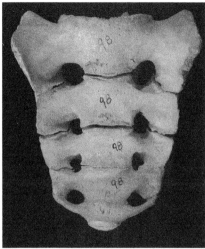

Instructions/Procedure:
- Using Appendix S, estimate the likely age associated with each of these bones

What is the approximate age of the individual represented by the femur?

_____

What is the approximate age of the individual represented by the sacrum?

_____
_____

Based on your age estimation, is it possible that the remains represent the same individual, or do they belong to different individuals?

_____

Could either or both of the bones belong to the missing 19-year old? The 8-year old? Explain.

_____
_____
_____

EXERCISE 10.5   Adult Age Estimation Using Pubic Symphysis

Materials needed:
- Images provided in this exercise
- Appendix T: Age Estimation Using Pubic Symphyseal Morphology

Note to instructor: This exercise can be supplemented or replaced with forensic or reference skeletal materials. Note that the data provided in Appendix S are from Hartnett (2010a,b) using the modified (and recommended) 7-phase system. If you have the Suchey-Books pubic symphysis casts using the 6-phase system, they can still be used for this exercise, which primarily examines relative age differences in pubic symphyseal morphology, though students should be made aware of this adaptation.

Case scenario: Investigators responded to a car fire and discovered two victims, one in the driver's seat and one in the passenger's seat. They suspect the decedents may be the 51-year-old owner of the car and his 23-year-old son, and they are trying to determine which victim was the driver and which was the passenger. Due to the thermal alterations to the remains, the identities have not yet been confirmed, but the pelvis regions were preserved and are available for assessment. You advised investigators that you may be able to assess the relative ages of the pubic symphyses and determine where the older and younger individuals were seated at the time of the accident.

Passenger: Driver:

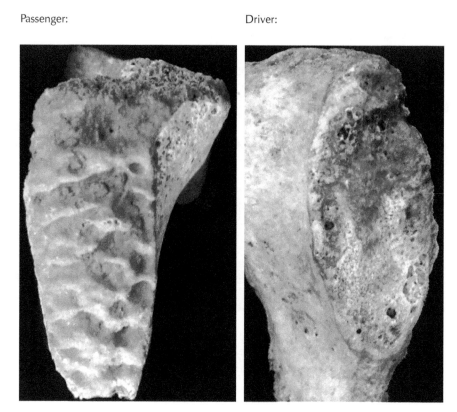

Instructions/Procedure:
- Using Appendix T, assess the stage and age interval for each pubic symphysis pictured above.

Individual	Stage	Age Interval
Passenger		
Driver		

Which pubic symphysis is consistent with being the older individual and which with the younger?

_____

_____

_____

Are the pubic symphyseal ages consistent with being the ages of the alleged victims?

_____

_____

_____

Discuss which features of the pubic symphysis you found to be easiest and most challenging to assess.

_____

_____

_____

_____

EXERCISE 10.6   Adult Age Estimation Using Auricular Surface

Materials needed:
- Image provided in this exercise
- Appendix U: Age Estimation Using Auricular Surface Morphology

Note to instructor: This exercise can be supplemented or replaced with forensic or reference skeletal materials.

Case scenario: Partial skeletal remains were founded in a remote wooded area. The remains appear to represent a skeletally mature adult, but most of the remains have been highly scavenged by carnivores, including the pubic region and anterior ribs. The back of the pelvis, however, including the auricular surface region, remained well preserved, and you can therefore use it to assess age.

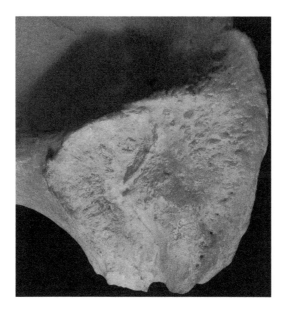

Instructions/Procedure:
- Using Appendix U, assess the phase of the pictured auricular surface

Phase	Age Interval

What do you estimate to be the age of this individual and how confident are you in your assessment?

_____
_____
_____

For the phase that you selected, explain the relationship between *n, mean, SD*, and *95% interval*.

_____
_____
_____

Did you find these features easier or more challenging to assess than those of the pubic symphysis? Explain.

_____
_____
_____

EXERCISE 10.7   Adult Age Estimation Using Ribs

Materials needed:
- Images provided in this exercise
- Appendix V: Age Estimation Using Sternal Rib End Morphology

Note to instructor: This exercise can be supplemented or replaced with forensic or reference skeletal materials. Note that the data provided in Appendix U are from Hartnett (2010a,b) using the modified (and recommended) rib phase descriptions. If you have and would like to use the Iscan rib end casts, they may be used for this exercise together with the descriptions from Appendix U, though students should be made aware of this adaptation.

Case scenario: The medical examiner has performed an autopsy on an unidentified male. There is moderate decomposition, so he is unable to estimate age based on visual indicators. He removed the fourth ribs and requested your assistance to estimation age.

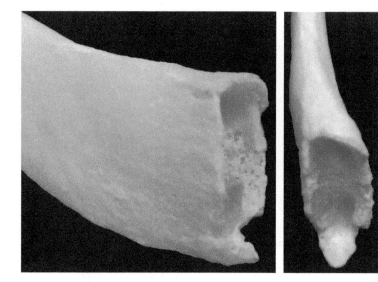

Instructions/Procedure:
• Using Appendix V, assess the phase of the pictured sternal rib end

Phase	Age Interval

What do you estimate to be the age of this individual and how confident are you in your assessment?

_____
_____
_____

What if the fourth rib was not available due to carnivore scavenging?

_____
_____
_____

EXERCISE 10.8   Age Estimation Based on Third Molar Development

Materials needed:
• Image provided in this exercise
• Appendix Q: Age Estimation Using Dental Development

Note to instructor: This exercise can be supplemented or replaced with radiographs or CT scans from forensic or reference skeletal materials, or even using students' own dental records if they can access them.

Case scenario: A suspect in an assault investigation is about to stand trial, and prosecutors need to determine whether he can be tried as an adult, the legal threshold for which is 18 years of age. The suspect does not have any legal identification or birth certificate that can be located, but he suffered a head injury during the altercation which resulted in his arrest, and a CT scan was taken at the hospital. A copy of the CT scan was obtained, and the roots of the maxillary right third molar are visible. The suspect is a white male.

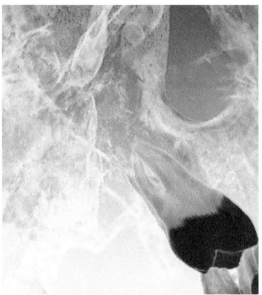

(From Christensen, A.M., Smith, M.A., Cunningham, D., Wescott, D., Glieber, D., 2018. The use of industrial X-ray computed tomography technologies in forensic anthropology. Forensic Anthropology (in press).)

Instructions/Procedure:
- Using Appendix Q, determine the developmental stage of the pictured third molar

Which stage of development is the molar?

_____

What is the probability that the suspect is at least 18 years of age? Should he be tried as a juvenile or an adult?

_____
_____
_____

EXERCISE 10.9   Age Estimation Using Histomorphometry

Materials needed:
- Image provided in this exercise
- Appendix W: Age Estimation Using Rib Histomorphometry

Note to instructor: This exercise can be supplemented or replaced with the use of histological slides of human ribs, if available, following the procedure outlined in Crowder et al. (2012).

Case scenario: For the same highly scavenged skeletal remains described in Exercise 10.6, you have determined that histomorphometric analysis of the ribs is also possible and may help clarify your overall age estimate. Investigators have approved destructive analysis of a rib for your examination. Although the postcranial skeleton is extensively modified, the skull is relatively complete and craniometric data strongly suggest African ancestry.

Instructions/Procedure:
- Using the image below, which depicts Field #5 of your assessment, complete the data collection table provided, including the total reticle hits, the number of intact osteons, and number of fragmentary osteons
- Use the data from the completed table, along with the equations provided in Appendix W, to calculate an estimate. A 36-hit grid is being used at 200× (20× objective X 10× eye piece), and the area of one hit is 0.0064 mm^2.
- Mean osteonal cross sectional area (On.Ar.), cortical area (Ct.Ar.), and total area (Tt.Ar.) have been provided.

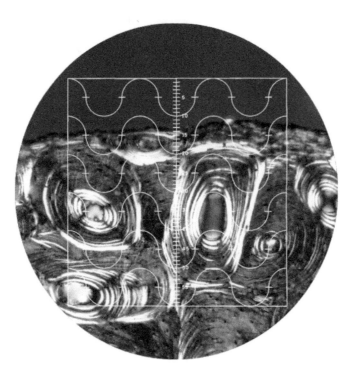

(Image courtesy of Christian Crowder.)

Sa.Ar. (total number of hits overlaying cortical bone for each field, multiplied by the area represented by one hit in the reticle):

_____

OPD (Sum of intact osteons and fragmentary osteons divided by Sa.Ar.):

_____

On.Ar.	0.023 mm^2
Ct.Ar.	19.1 mm^2
Tt.Ar.	50.5 mm^2

Relative Cortical Area (Ct.Ar. divided by Tt.Ar.): _____
What is your age estimate for this individuals based on rib histomorphometry?

_____

Why is it important to evaluate at least 50% of the rib section, or in some cases multiple sections?

_____
_____
_____

What if the skull suggested European ancestry? Does this significantly change the estimated age?

_____
_____
_____

How does this method compare to the other adult age at death estimation methods discussed in this chapter? Do you prefer this method or the others? Why?

_____
_____
_____

Chapter 11

Stature Estimation

OBJECTIVES

Stature estimation from skeletal remains is possible because there is a relationship between bone lengths and height. Stature is most accurately measured using full skeleton methods, which utilize measurements of all bones that contribute to stature. Stature is most often estimated using regression methods, which utilize the mathematical relationship (correlation) between bone lengths and stature using regression formulae. In this chapter you will estimate stature using various mathematical approaches and assess issues related to antemortem stature data.

PRINCIPLES OF STATURE ESTIMATION

The estimation of living stature from the skeleton is possible because there is a relationship between an individual's skeletal dimensions and his or her height. The selected stature estimation method depends on the skeletal elements present as well as the condition of these elements, and stature estimates are most accurate when the majority of the skeletal material is present and in good condition. It is important to keep in mind the source of stature reference data, both for the antemortem information for the deceased and for the population upon which the stature estimated data are based. Stature data for method development, for example, can be obtained by measuring antemortem/living stature, or by measuring cadaver length. Comparison data from the deceased is often obtained from a reported source such as driver's license, sometimes referred to as "forensic stature."

Full skeleton methods are generally considered the most reliable. As the name suggests, however, a mostly complete skeleton is necessary, and therefore these methods are not as frequently used. The most commonly utilized methods of estimating stature are regression methods, which are based on a mathematical relationship between bone dimensions and stature.

FULL SKELETON METHODS

Full skeleton methods, or anatomical methods, involve estimating stature based on the sum of the vertical measurements of all bones that contribute to stature. Bones typically measured in these methods are the height of the skull, the heights of the vertebrae, the lengths of the femur and tibia, and the height of the ankle (Table 11.1 and Fig. 11.1). The skeletal element sum is used in a formulae that adjusts the stature estimate for anatomical components such as soft tissue (i.e., intervertebral disks, heel, etc.) as well as vertebral column curvature and other corrections (Table 11.2). If age is known, an equation can be applied that corrects for age-related decrease in stature. These methods therefore require that the skeleton is relatively complete. An advantage of full skeleton methods is that they can be applied regardless of the sex or ancestry of the individual (this differs from regression methods, which ideally employ population-specific formulae).

REGRESSION METHODS

Regression methods, also known as mathematical methods, are the most commonly utilized methods for estimating stature. These methods are based on the correlation between height and body segments (i.e., taller people tend to have longer body segments than shorter people). For skeletal remains, these segments are represented by the lengths of single or multiple long bones, typically the maximum length of long bones of the legs and arms (Fig. 11.2).

Methods that use the dimensions of complete limb bones (versus incomplete bones or nonlimb bones) are the most accurate. In general, the femur is the most accurate because it contributes the most to stature, followed by lower leg bones and arm bones. Stature estimates that combine multiple bone measurements are typically more accurate than estimates based solely on a single skeletal element. If regression methods are employed, it is common to report a point estimate along with

A Laboratory Manual for Forensic Anthropology. https://doi.org/10.1016/B978-0-12-812201-3.00011-6

TABLE 11.1 Measurements for Full Skeleton Stature Estimation

- Basion-bregma height of the cranium

- Maximum body heights of vertebra C2 to L5

- Anterior height of the first sacral segment

- Oblique (physiological) length of the femur

- Maximum length of the tibia (minus the spine, including the malleolus)

- Articulated maximum height of the talus and calcaneus

Modified from Fully, G., 1956. Un Nouvelle Methode de determination de la taille. Annales de Medecine Legale 35, 266–273; Raxter, M.H., Auerbach, B.M., Ruff, C.B., 2006. Revision of the Fully technique for estimating statures. Am. J. Phys. Anthropol. 130, 374–384.

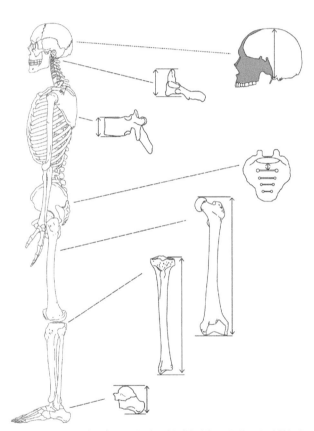

FIG. 11.1 Measurements used in full skeleton stature estimation methods. *(Modified from Willey, P., 2009. Stature estimation. In: Blau, S., Ubelaker, D.H. (Eds.), Handbook of Forensic Anthropology and Archaeology. Left Coast Press, Walnut Creek, pp. 236–245.)*

TABLE 11.2 Stature Estimation Equations Based on Skeletal Element Sum (All in cm)

Age	Equation	r	SEE
Unknown	Stature = (0.996*Skeletal Height) + 11.7	0.952	2.31
Known	Stature = (1.009*Skeletal Height) − (0.0426*Age) + 12.1	0.956	2.22

Modified from Raxter, M.H., Auerbach, B.M., Ruff, C.B., 2006. Revision of the Fully technique for estimating statures. Am. J. Phys. Anthropol. 130, 374–384.

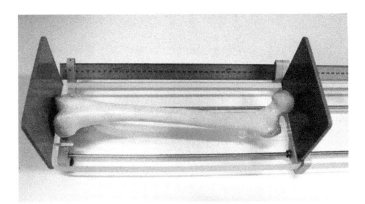

FIG. 11.2   Maximum length of the femur measured using an osteometric board. *(From Christensen, A.M., Passalacqua, N.V., Bartelink, E.J., 2014. Forensic Anthropology: Current Methods and Practice, Academic Press.)*

a 95% prediction interval. The relationship between stature and individual bones varies between different geographic and temporal groups, and therefore population-specific regression formulae will produce the most accurate estimates. Examples of stature estimation formulae for females and males of European and African ancestry derived from one study are shown in Table 11.3. Stature estimates based on lengths of the bones of the lower limb are more accurate than those based on bones of the upper limb, and those based on multiple bones are more accurate than those based on a single bone. This is usually seen in the standard errors of the estimates. Notice in Table 11.3, for example, that the standard error is always lowest for the femur and always greatest for the humerus.

Stature estimates using regression formulae may be carried out manually (Fig. 11.3) or can be performed using software packages such as Fordisc. If using Fordisc, available skeletal measurement data are entered, and the most appropriate reference sample can be selected by the user. Fordisc can then carry out an automated calculation of stature including selected prediction intervals (e.g., 90%, 95%, and 99%) and graphic representation of the results (Table 11.4 and Fig. 11.4). For cases where ancestry cannot be estimated, there is an option to select formulae that will use the entire reference sample to derive the estimate; however, this will result in larger standard errors than population-specific formulae.

TABLE 11.3 Regression Formulae for Different Sex and Ancestral Groups for the Femur, Fibula, and Humerus (All Measurements in cm)

	Stature Equation	Standard Error
European males	$2.38 \times$ (femur length) $+ 61.41$	± 3.27
	$2.68 \times$ (fibula length) $+ 71.78$	± 3.29
	$2.89 \times$ (humerus length) $+ 78.10$	± 4.57
African males	$2.11 \times$ (femur length) $+ 70.35$	± 3.94
	$2.19 \times$ (fibula length) $+ 85.65$	± 4.08
	$2.88 \times$ (humerus length) $+ 75.48$	± 4.23
European females	$2.47 \times$ (femur length) $+ 54.10$	± 3.72
	$2.93 \times$ (fibula length) $+ 59.61$	± 3.57
	$3.36 \times$ (humerus length) $+ 57.97$	± 4.45
African females	$2.28 \times$ (femur length) $+ 59.76$	± 3.41
	$2.49 \times$ (fibula length) $+ 70.90$	± 3.80
	$3.08 \times$ (humerus length) $+ 64.67$	± 4.25

Modified from Trotter, M., Gleser, G.C., 1952. Estimation of stature from long bones of American Whites and Negroes. Am. J. Phys. Anthropol. 10, 463–514.

Using the formula from Table 11.2 for calculation of stature of European males from the length of the femur:

$$2.38 \text{ (femur length)} + 61.41 \pm 3.27,$$

for a femur length of 500 mm (50 cm), the calculation would be carried out as follows:

$$(2.38) \times (50 \text{ cm}) + (61.41) \pm (3.27)$$

$$= 180.41 \pm 3.27 \text{ cm}$$

$$= 177.14 \text{ cm to } 183.68 \text{ cm}$$

$$= 69.74'' \text{ to } 72.31''$$

or about 5'10'' to 6'2'' tall

FIG. 11.3 Manual calculation of stature from regression formulae. *(From Christensen, A.M., Passalacqua, N.V., Bartelink, E.J., 2014. Forensic Anthropology: Current Methods and Practice, Academic Press.)*

TABLE 11.4 Example Stature Results and Equations From Fordisc With 95% Prediction Interval

Stature	SE	P.I.	Regression Formulae
67.1″ ±	4.0″	63.2–71.1″	0.050* FEMXLN +TIBXLN (826 mm) +26.11″
67.1″ ±	4.0″	63.2–71.1″	0.051* FEMXLN +FIBXLN (821 mm) +25.63″
67.2″ ±	4.0″	63.2–71.1″	0.034* FEMXLN +FIBXLN +TIBXLN (1194 mm) +26.79″
67.2″ ±	4.0″	63.2–71.2″	0.040* FEMXLN +FIBXLN +ULNXLN (1084 mm) +23.50″
67.2″ ±	4.0″	63.2–71.2″	0.040* FEMXLN +RADXLN +TIBXLN (1072 mm) +24.70″
67.2″ ±	4.0″	63.2–71.2″	0.040* FEMXLN +TIBXLN +ULNXLN (1089 mm) +23.85″
67.2″ ±	4.0″	63.2–71.2″	0.040* FEMXLN +FIBXLN +RADXLN (1067 mm) +24.52″
67.5″ ±	4.0″	63.5–71.5″	0.037* FEMXLN +HUMXLN +TIBXLN (1158 mm) +24.63″
67.5″ ±	4.0″	63.5–71.5″	0.037* FEMXLN +FIBXLN +HUMXLN (1153 mm) +24.42″
67.6″ ±	4.0″	63.5–71.6″	0.037* FIBXLN +HUMXLN +TIBXLN (1073 mm) +27.68″

OTHER CONSIDERATIONS IN STATURE ESTIMATION

Estimating stature of subadults is usually of limited utility because children grow very quickly and therefore reported statures are quickly out of date; stature or body size of children is typically used to estimate age rather that height. Stature tends to decrease with advancing adult age, usually a result of loss or compression of cartilage (especially the intervertebral discs), or fractures of the vertebral centra. Methods for adjusting (reducing) stature estimates based on advanced adult age have been proposed, but their application is problematic for various reasons, including a lack of validation.

An individual's stature can also vary depending on how it is measured (e.g., with or without shoes) and when (including different times of the day). Pathological conditions and other skeletal anomalies may also affect stature estimates, either by directly affecting the length of the bone(s) of interest or by affecting the relationship between bones and total stature (such as those that might affect body proportions).

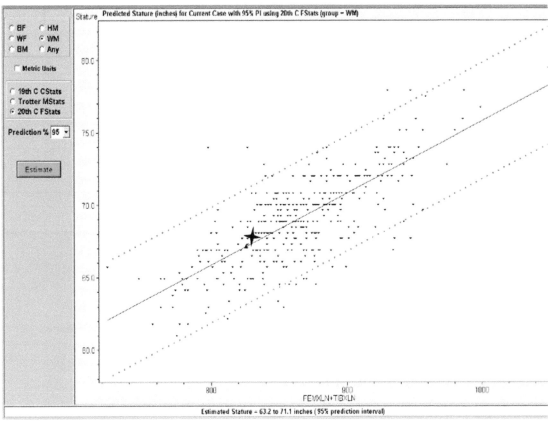

FIG. 11.4   Graphic representation of Fordisc stature results. *(From Christensen, A.M., Passalacqua, N.V., Bartelink, E.J., 2014. Forensic Anthropology: Current Methods and Practice, Academic Press.)*

EXERCISE 11.1   Stature Estimation Using the Full Skeleton Method

Materials needed:
- Measurements provided in this exercise
- Table 11.2 from this chapter
- Calculator or paper and writing utensil

Note to instructor: This exercise can also be completed using measurements from a forensic case or reference collection if available.

Case scenario: You have been asked to estimate stature from mostly complete unidentified human skeletal remains. You took the following measurements (in mm):

Cranial height	129	Height of T4	17	Height of L2	25
Height of C2	33	Height of T5	17	Height of L3	26
Height of C3	11	Height of T6	18	Height of L4	27
Height of C4	11	Height of T7	18	Height of L5	25
Height of C5	12	Height of T8	19	Height of sacral segment 1	29
Height of C6	12	Height of T9	20		
Height of C7	12	Height of T10	21	Length of femur	392
Height of T1	16	Height of T11	22	Length of tibia	311
Height of T2	16	Height of T12	23	Height of talus/ calcaneus	70
Height of T3	17	Height of L1	24		

What is the sum of the measurements (skeletal element sum)?

_____

Using the equations provided in Table 11.2, and assuming age is unknown, what is your estimate of stature?

_____

What sources of error may there be in this estimate?

_____

Based on the skeletal element sum you calculated and the equations provided in Table 11.2, estimate stature assuming an age of 35 years, and assuming 80 years. Discuss how and why your estimates differ.

_____
_____
_____

EXERCISE 11.2   Stature Estimation Using Regression Method (Manual)

Materials needed:
- Measurements provided in this exercise
- Table 11.3 from this chapter
- Calculator or paper and writing utensil

Note to instructor: This exercise can also be completed using measurements from a forensic case or reference collection if available.

Case scenario: You have been asked to estimate stature from incomplete unidentified human skeletal remains. You took the following measurements:

Femur length: 447 mm

Fibula length: 365 mm

Humerus length: 309 mm

Assuming that the individual is a European Male, what is the estimated stature based on the following measurements using Table 11.3? Be sure to include the point estimate and standard error.
Femur length: _____
Fibula length: _____
Humerus length: _____

Assuming that the individual is an African Female, what is the estimated stature based on the following measurements using Table 11.3? Be sure to include the point estimate and standard error.
Femur length: _____
Fibula length: _____
Humerus length: _____

If you were going to provide investigators just one of these estimates, which one would you provide and why?

_____
_____

What might account for the different stature estimates from different bones?

_____
_____

What might account for the different regression formula for different sexes and ancestral groups?

_____
_____

EXERCISE 11.3   Stature Estimation—Interpreting Fordisc

Materials needed:
- Data provided in this exercise

Note to instructor: This exercise can also be completed using Fordisc results from a forensic case or reference collection if available.
Case scenario: From a series of measurements you took on a partial set of skeletal remains, you decide to estimate stature using Fordisc. Because the sex and ancestry of the remains were undetermined, you estimated stature using various parameters and got the following Fordisc results:

Run 1:

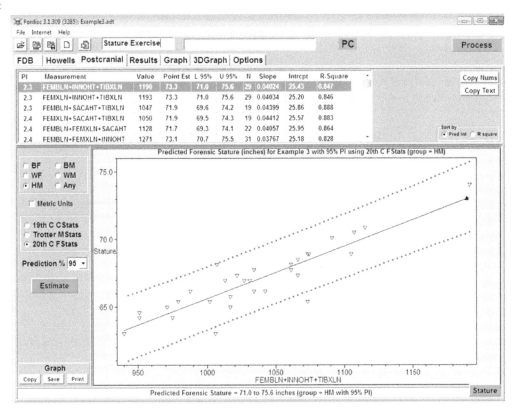

Run 2:

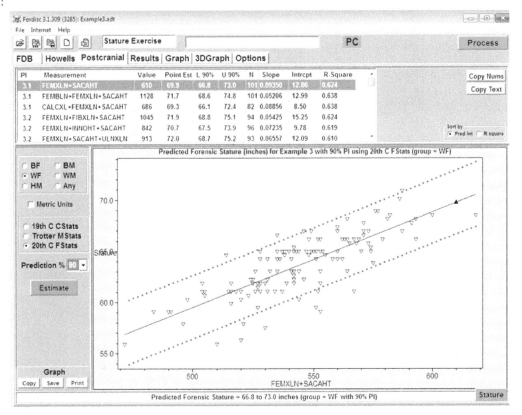

For Run 1, what reference population and prediction interval were used for the stature estimation?

Which bone (or combination of bones) resulted in the most accurate stature estimation formula? (Hint: look at the standard errors)

For the stature estimation formula in the previous question, what is the point estimate for stature? What is the prediction interval?

For Run 2, what reference population and prediction interval were used for the stature estimation?

How did these changes affect the results of the stature estimate in terms of the point estimate, predicted stature, formula, and standard error? Why?

EXERCISE 11.4   Stature Estimation Using Fordisc

Materials needed:
- Measurements provided in this exercise
- Fordisc
- PC computer

Note to instructor: This exercise can also be completed using measurements from a forensic case or reference collection if available.

Case scenario: You have been asked to estimate stature from incomplete unidentified human skeletal remains. Your assessment of the innominate has led you to the conclusion that the remains are most likely female, and Fordisc analysis of cranial measurements suggests African (Black) ancestry. You also took the following postcranial measurements:

Clavicle max length	145 mm
Humerus max length	310 mm
Ulna max length	258 mm
Radius max length	241 mm
Femur epicondylar breadth	75 mm
Femur max length	450 mm
Femur bicondylar length	445 mm
Fibula max length	370 mm

Instructions/Procedure:
- Input your measurements into the "Postcranial" tab screen in Fordisc
- Select "Stature"
- Select the appropriate reference population and estimate stature

Which measurement(s) has the lowest standard error for the stature estimate?

What is the point estimate for stature using the measurement(s) with the lowest standard error?

For the stature estimate with the lowest standard error, what is the 95% prediction interval? The 90% prediction interval? What do these intervals mean?

For the stature estimate with the lowest standard error, what is regression equation that Fordisc used?

_____

Select a different (ancestral and/or temporal) reference group. How does this change your stature estimate? Why?

_____
_____
_____

EXERCISE 11.5   Antemortem Stature Data

Materials needed:
- Tape measure
- Straight edge (such as a ruler)
- Writing utensil
- Driver's license

Note to instructor: This exercise can be carried out in pairs or small groups.

Case scenario: Aware that stature can vary depending on how and when it is measured, you decide to investigate how your own stature might vary with different conditions.

Instructions/Procedure:
- Standing with your back against a wall, use a straight edge and a writing utensil to mark your height
- Measure your height from the floor to the marking using a tape measure
- Repeat the height measurement with your shoes off
- Repeat the height measurement early in the morning, and at night

What is your stature measured with shoes on? With shoes off?

_____

What is your stature in the morning? In the evening? If these measurements are different, what might account for this difference?

_____

What height is reported on your driver's license, and where did this height come from? Is this height the same as any of your measured heights?

_____

Given that you have demonstrated that antemortem stature can vary depending on how and when it is measured, what implications do you think this may have for stature estimation in forensic contexts?

_____
_____
_____

Chapter 12

Individual Skeletal Variation

OBJECTIVES

Individual skeletal variation can be useful for personal identification, and it is important to be familiar with possible skeletal variants so that they are not confused with trauma or taphonomic damage. In this chapter you will learn to describe and identify different types of skeletal variants including normal variants, anomalies, and pathologies.

PRINCIPLES OF SKELETAL VARIATION

Individual skeletal variants may be congenital, developmental, degenerative or may result from disease processes or trauma. Skeletal variants can reveal features of an individual's health, lifestyle, or life history, thereby helping to further narrow the pool of potential matches, or may be useful in identification comparisons. Certain skeletal variants or conditions, such as diseases or injuries that may have been fatal, may also provide information relevant to circumstances surrounding death. It is also important that skeletal morphological variants are not confused with trauma or taphonomic alterations.

Individual skeletal variations typically fall into one of four categories:

(1) Normal anatomical variation.
(2) Skeletal anomalies.
(3) Pathological conditions.
(4) Skeletal changes related to repetitive mechanical stress.

The identification of a variant or condition present on skeletal remains is ideally achieved through a process called differential diagnosis, a deductive process of elimination used to narrow down and identify a likely condition or a small number of possibilities that cannot be excluded (Fig. 12.1). A differential diagnosis begins with a description of the skeletal variant including its location (i.e., the name of the bone or bones involved), distribution (i.e., how much and which part or parts of the bone or bones are affected) and which types of abnormal activity are present (abnormal bone formation, abnormal bone loss, abnormal bone shape, abnormal bone size).

The diagnosis then proceeds by ruling out conditions that are inconsistent with the observations. This may involve comparison with published clinical and research literature (e.g., Ortner, 2003; Barnes, 1994, 2012) or exemplars such as photographs, casts, or documented pathological specimens. If the condition is present on a paired bone or tooth, the suspected variant can also be compared to its normal antimere (the same bone or tooth from the other side) as a reference, which may help in confirming the presence or extent of the condition. In many cases, specialized methods such as radiology, microscopy, and histology may be useful. Differential diagnosis of a particular skeletal variant or condition is not always possible. The analysis of skeletal variants should be amply supplemented with notes, diagrams, photos, radiographs, etc., and all reasonable interpretations should be presented.

NORMAL SKELETAL VARIATION

Normal skeletal variation refers to the range of morphological expression commonly observed in the skeleton. Examples of normal variation include differences in paranasal sinus shape (Fig. 12.2) and cranial suture pattern (Fig. 12.3). These features and characteristics are all present in normal bone anatomy but show small but significant differences between different people. Because these features are present in almost everyone and because they tend to show so much individual variation, they are often studied for their potential to facilitate personal identification.

A Laboratory Manual for Forensic Anthropology. https://doi.org/10.1016/B978-0-12-812201-3.00012-8

Variant type
- Normal variation
- Skeletal anomaly
- Pathological condition
- Repetitive activity
- Cultural practice

Extent
- Single versus multiple bones
- Unilateral or bilateral
- Diffuse or localized
- Type of bone tissue and region
  - Cortical
  - Trabecular
  - Medullary cavity
  - Periosteum
  - Endosteum

Location
- Bones affected
- Bone region affected
  - Diaphysis (shaft)
  - Epiphysis
  - Metaphysis (growth plate)

Lesion type
- Lytic (osteoclastic, bone loss)
- Proliferative (osteoblastic, bone formation)
- Deformative (change in shape) multiple processes involved

Anomaly type
- Supernumerary (extra) bones or teeth
- Supernumerary (extra) foramina
- Nonunion (fusion anomaly)

Quality of bone
- Loosely organized, woven
- Dense, remodeled
- Porous
- Spiculate
- Sclerotic
- Diffuse or well-defined edge

Disease class
- Congenital (birth defects, genetic anomalies)
- Traumatic (fractures)
- Degenerative (age or overuse related)
- Infectious (bacterial, viral, fungal)
- Circulatory (related to blood formation or circulation)
- Metabolic (lack of nutrients)
- Endocrine (hormonal)
- Neoplastic (cancerous)

Radiologic appearance
- Radiodense
- Radiolucent

FIG. 12.1   Differential diagnosis.

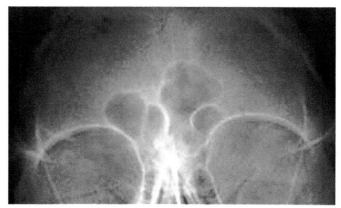

FIG. 12.2   Frontal sinus configuration as seen in posterior-anterior radiograph. *(From Christensen, A.M., 2003. An Empirical Examination of Frontal Sinus Outline Variability Using Elliptic Fourier Analysis: Implications for Identification, Standardization, and Legal Admissibility (PhD dissertation). The University of Tennessee, Knoxville, TN.)*

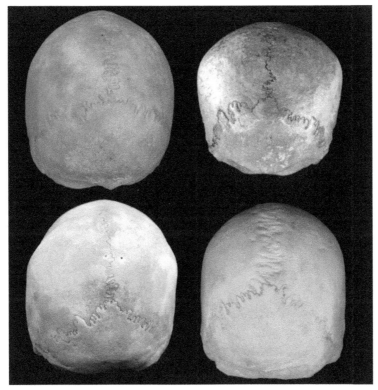

FIG. 12.3   Differences in cranial suture patterns. *(From Christensen, A.M., Passalacqua, N.V., Bartelink, E.J., 2014. Forensic Anthropolgy: Current Methods and Practice, Academic Press.)*

ANOMALIES

Anomalies are characteristics that are considered deviations from normal skeletal anatomy. Depending on their nature, these variants are sometimes called nonmetric or epigenetic variants. Examples of skeletal anomalies include accessory or supernumerary bones or teeth (Figs. 12.4–12.6), accessory foramina (Figs. 12.7 and 12.8), and nonfusion anomalies (Figs. 12.9–12.12).

PATHOLOGICAL CONDITIONS

Pathology refers to the study of disease, and a pathological condition is the abnormal anatomy which is the manifestation of a disease process. These disease processes may be the result of infection, injury, or a disorder. Not all diseases affect the skeleton, but when they do, they may manifest as localized bony alterations that are called lesions. All abnormal bone formation is the result of osteoblastic activity, and all abnormal bone loss is the result of osteoclastic activity. In a healthy body, osteoblasts and osteoclasts work together to remodel bone. Various pathological processes may disrupt of these cells and result in abnormal bone.

Pathological lesions on bone may be proliferative, lytic, or deformative. Proliferative (or osteoproliferative) lesions are those that are characterized by excess deposition of bone due to abnormal osteoblastic activity (Figs. 12.13–12.16). Lytic (or osteolytic) lesions involve a loss of bone due to abnormal osteoclastic activity (Figs. 12.17–12.19). The relative rate of bone loss can be assessed by examining the margins of the lesion; sharp bone margins result from rapid bone loss, while smooth or rounded lesion margins result from slower bone loss. Deformative lesions involve changes in overall bone shape (Figs. 12.20–12.23). Abnormal bone shape and/or size are typically associated with developmental disorders. Examples of abnormal bone shape include bowing of leg bones due to vitamin D deficiency, or rickets (Fig. 12.21), and cranial synostosis (Fig. 12.22). Examples of abnormal bone size include a variety of dysplasias, such as achondroplasia (i.e., dwarfism). Fractures/trauma also result in lesions which may be proliferative, lytic, deformative, or some combination (Fig. 12.24).

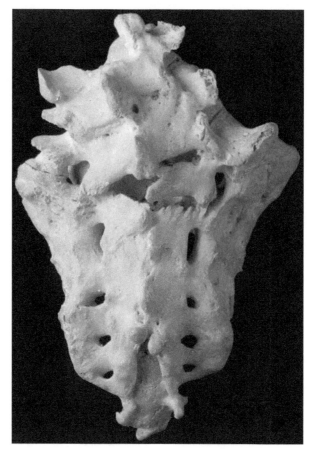

FIG. 12.4 Hemivertebrae in the lumbar region. *(Photo by Rebecca Meeusen; Specimen courtesy of the National Museum of Natural History; From Christensen, A.M., Passalacqua, N.V., Bartelink, E.J., 2014. Forensic Anthropology: Current Methods and Practice, Academic Press.)*

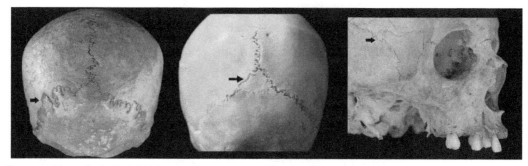

FIG. 12.5 Extrasutural bones in the lambdoidal suture, also known as a Wormian bone (left), at lambda, or Inca bone (center), and at the landmark pterion, also known as an epipteric bone (right). *(From Christensen, A.M., Passalacqua, N.V., Bartelink, E.J., 2014. Forensic Anthropology: Current Methods and Practice, Academic Press.)*

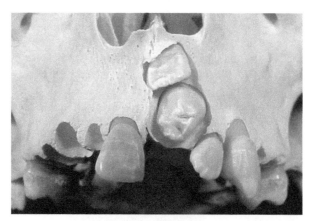

FIG. 12.6 Supernumerary teeth. *(From Christensen, A.M., Anderson, B.E., 2013. Personal identification. In: Tersigni-Tarrant, M.T., Shirley, N. (Eds.), Forensic Anthropology: An Introduction, CRC Press, Boca Raton, FL, pp. 397–420.)*

FIG. 12.7 Septal aperture in a distal humerus. *(Photo by Rebecca Meeusen; Specimen courtesy of the National Museum of Natural History; From Christensen, A.M., Passalacqua, N.V., Bartelink, E.J., 2014. Forensic Anthropology: Current Methods and Practice, Academic Press.)*

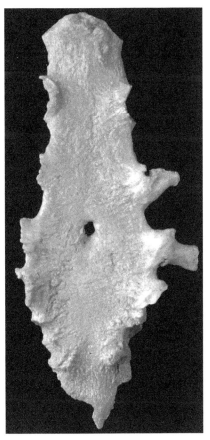

FIG. 12.8 Sternal foramen. *(Photo by Rebecca Meeusen; Specimen courtesy of the National Museum of Natural History; From Christensen, A.M., Passalacqua, N.V., Bartelink, E.J., 2014. Forensic Anthropology: Current Methods and Practice, Academic Press.)*

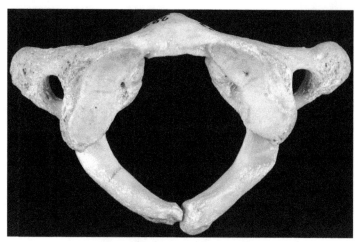

FIG. 12.9 Cleft neural arch of C1. *(Image courtesy of the National Museum of Health and Medicine; From Christensen, A.M., Passalacqua, N.V., Bartelink, E.J., 2014. Forensic Anthropology: Current Methods and Practice, Academic Press.)*

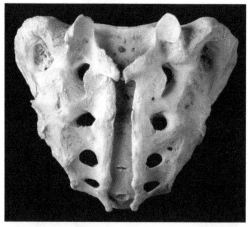

FIG. 12.10 Spina bifida occulta. *(Photo by Rebecca Meeusen; Specimen courtesy of the National Museum of Natural History; From Christensen, A.M., Passalacqua, N.V., Bartelink, E.J., 2014. Forensic Anthropology: Current Methods and Practice, Academic Press.)*

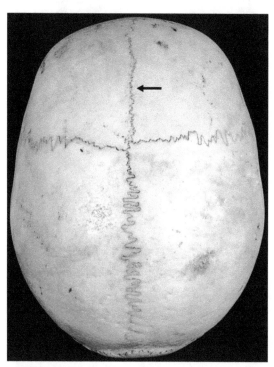

FIG. 12.11 Metopic suture. *(Image courtesy of the National Museum of Health and Medicine; From Christensen, A.M., Passalacqua, N.V., Bartelink, E.J., 2014. Forensic Anthropology: Current Methods and Practice, Academic Press.)*

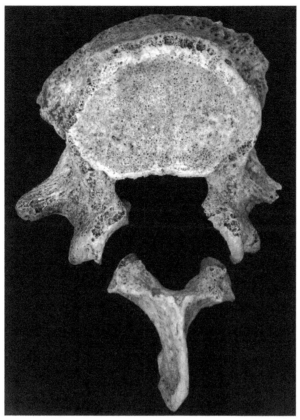

FIG. 12.12 Spondylolysis of L5 with nonunion. *(From Christensen, A.M., Passalacqua, N.V., Bartelink, E.J., 2014. Forensic Anthropology: Current Methods and Practice, Academic Press.)*

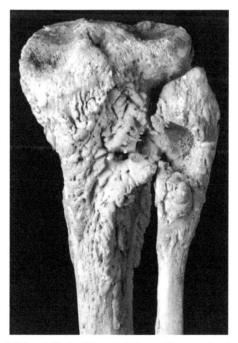

FIG. 12.13 Proliferative lesion of the proximal tibia and fibula. *(Photo by Rebecca Meeusen; Specimen courtesy of the National Museum of Natural History; From Christensen, A.M., Passalacqua, N.V., Bartelink, E.J., 2014. Forensic Anthropology: Current Methods and Practice, Academic Press.)*

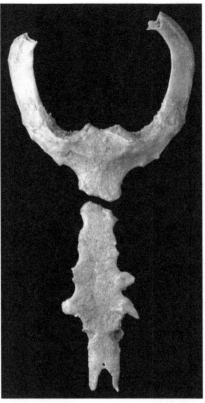

FIG. 12.14 Ossification of costal cartilage with fusion of first ribs to sternum. *(Photo by Rebecca Meeusen; Specimen courtesy of the National Museum of Natural History; From Christensen, A.M., Passalacqua, N.V., Bartelink, E.J., 2014. Forensic Anthropology: Current Methods and Practice, Academic Press.)*

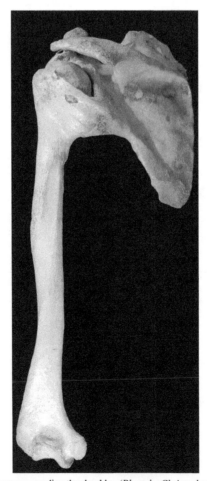

FIG. 12.15 Heterotopic ossification of the tissues surrounding the shoulder. *(Photo by Christopher Rainwater; Specimen courtesy of the Cleveland Museum of Natural History; From Christensen, A.M., Passalacqua, N.V., Bartelink, E.J., 2014. Forensic Anthropology: Current Methods and Practice, Academic Press.)*

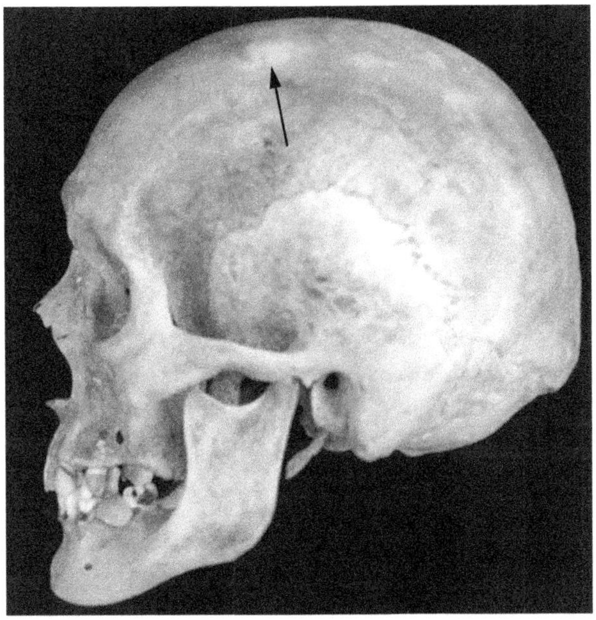

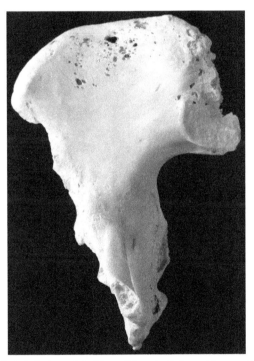

FIG. 12.16   Button osteoma. *(From Christensen, A.M., Passalacqua, N.V., Bartelink, E.J., 2014. Forensic Anthropology: Current Methods and Practice, Academic Press.)*

FIG. 12.17   Metastatic carcinoma resulting in lytic lesions of the ilium. *(Photo by Rebecca Meeusen; Specimen courtesy of the National Museum of Natural History; From Christensen, A.M., Passalacqua, N.V., Bartelink, E.J., 2014. Forensic Anthropology: Current Methods and Practice, Academic Press.)*

REPETITIVE MECHANICAL STRESS

Repeated mechanical stresses on the skeleton, sometimes resulting from cultural activities, can cause the bones to adapt their morphology in response to these stresses. Examples include cradle boarding, dental wear, and other cultural activities performed repetitively. Other (not necessarily cultural) repetitive activities can also result in skeletal modifications including hyperdevelopment of muscle attachments from weight lifting, or asymmetry in the size or shape of paired bones due to handedness.

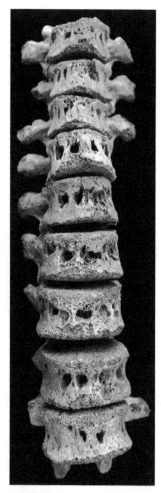

FIG. 12.18 Brucellosis lesions of the spine. *(Image courtesy of Todd Fenton; From Christensen, A.M., Passalacqua, N.V., Bartelink, E.J., 2014. Forensic Anthropology: Current Methods and Practice, Academic Press.)*

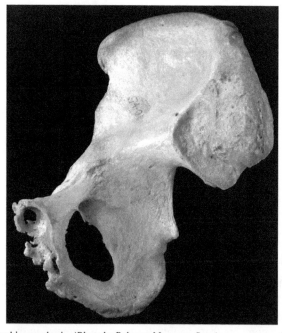

FIG. 12.19 Tuberculosis lesions of the pubic symphysis. *(Photo by Rebecca Meeusen; Specimen courtesy of the National Museum of Natural History; From Christensen, A.M., Passalacqua, N.V., Bartelink, E.J., 2014. Forensic Anthropology: Current Methods and Practice, Academic Press.)*

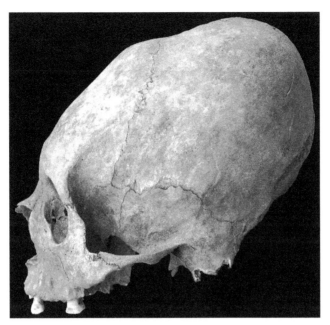

FIG. 12.20   Artificial cranial deformation. *(Photo courtesy of Diana Messer and Valarie Andrushko; From Christensen, A.M., Passalacqua, N.V., Bartelink, E.J., 2014. Forensic Anthropology: Current Methods and Practice, Academic Press.)*

FIG. 12.21   Rickets in a tibia and fibula. *(Photo by Christopher Rainwater; Specimen courtesy of the Cleveland Museum of Natural History; From Christensen, A.M., Passalacqua, N.V., Bartelink, E.J., 2014. Forensic Anthropology: Current Methods and Practice, Academic Press.)*

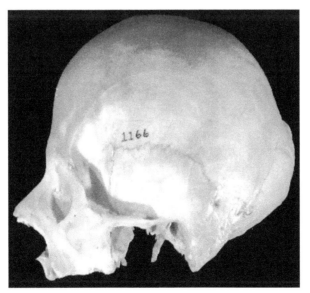

FIG. 12.22   Craniostenosis. *(Photo by Christopher Rainwater; Specimen courtesy of the Cleveland Museum of Natural History; From Christensen, A.M., Passalacqua, N.V., Bartelink, E.J., 2014. Forensic Anthropology: Current Methods and Practice, Academic Press.)*

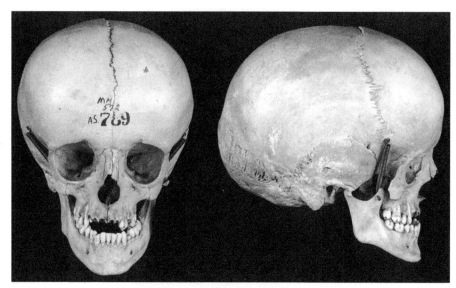

FIG. 12.23 Hydrocephalic skull. *(Image courtesy of the National Museum of Health and Medicine; From Christensen, A.M., Passalacqua, N.V., Bartelink, E.J., 2014. Forensic Anthropology: Current Methods and Practice, Academic Press.)*

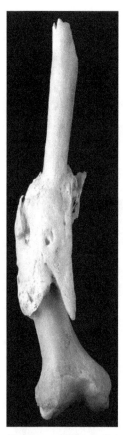

FIG. 12.24 Proliferative bone and deformation associated with fracture. *(Photo by Rebecca Meeusen; Specimen courtesy of the National Museum of Natural History; From Christensen, A.M., Passalacqua, N.V., Bartelink, E.J., 2014. Forensic Anthropology: Current Methods and Practice, Academic Press.)*

EXERCISE 12.1   Types of Skeletal Variation

Materials needed:

* Images provided in this exercise

Note to instructor: This exercise can be supplemented or replaced with skeletal material from a forensic case or skeletal collection if available.

Case scenario: A skeleton brought to you for analysis appears to have a number of different skeletal variants. Describing these variants may assist in narrowing the pool of potential matches as well as suggesting types of antemortem information that may be most useful for an identification comparison (e.g., cranial radiographs).

Instructions/Procedure:

* For each of the following skeletal variants, identify whether the arrow is indicating a *normal* skeletal variant, a skeletal *anomaly*, a skeletal *pathology*, or the result of *repetitive mechanical stress*.
* Provide a thorough description of the variant's anatomical location and extent.

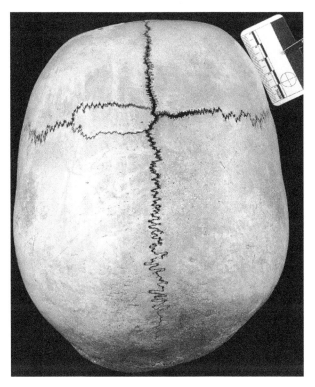

(Image courtesy of National Museum of Health and Medicine.)

Variant type: _____

Description: _____

_____

_____

(Photo by Christopher Rainwater; Specimen courtesy of the Cleveland Museum of Natural History.)

Variant type: _____

Description: _____

_____

_____

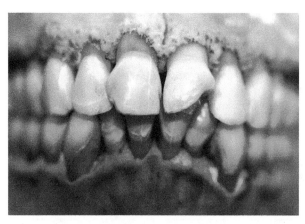

(Image courtesy of Eric Bartelink.)

Variant type:_____

Description: _____

_____

_____

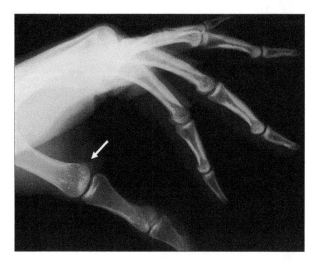

Variant type: _____

Description: _____

_____

_____

In the images above, did you notice any other skeletal variants not indicated by the arrows? If so, what and where are they?

_____

_____

_____

EXERCISE 12.2 Types of Pathological Conditions

Materials needed:
- Images provided in this exercise

Note to instructor: This exercise could be supplemented or replaced with skeletal material from a forensic case or skeletal collection if available.

Case scenario: You have been requested to assist in the analysis of skeleton material recovered from a plane crash, and you note that several bones appear to have types of pathologic lesions. The medicolegal authority has asked you to provide some initial information about the types of lesions present in order to begin the process of differential diagnosis for each individual.

Instructions/Procedure:
- For each of the following skeletal lesions, identify whether it is *proliferative*, *lytic*, or *deformative*

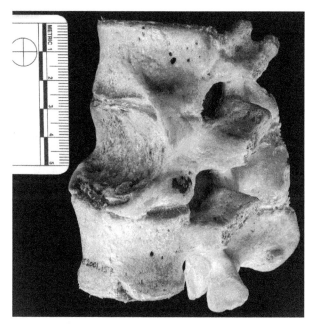

(Image courtesy of National Museum of Health and Medicine.)

Lesion type:_____

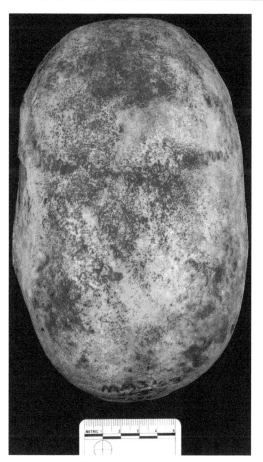

(Image courtesy of National Museum of Health and Medicine.)

Lesion type:_____

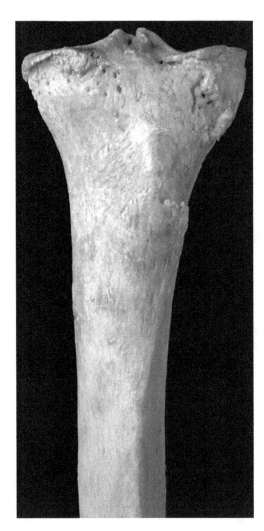

(Image courtesy of Eric Bartelink.)

Lesion type:_____

EXERCISE 12.3   Differential Diagnosis

Materials needed:
- Image provided in this exercise
- Internet access (or other medical/anthropological/osteological reference literature)

Note to instructor: This exercise could be supplemented or replaced with skeletal material from a forensic case or skeletal collection if available.

Case scenario: A skeleton brought to you for analysis has the feature pictured below. Knowing that such variants may be useful in identifying the remains, you would like to include information about this variant in your report.

Instructions/Procedure:
- Using the process of differential diagnosis, identify or narrow down the likely skeletal variant.

(Image courtesy of Eric Bartelink.)

Describe the variant/feature in terms of its location and distribution:

_____
_____
_____

Do you think the variant/feature is the result of normal skeletal variation, an anomaly, a pathology, or the result of habitual activity? Why?

_____
_____
_____

Using information from this chapter and/or the internet and/or medical/anthropological/osteological reference material, see if you can diagnose this skeletal variant:

_____
_____
_____

How confident are you in your final diagnosis?

_____
_____
_____

EXERCISE 12.4   Differential Diagnosis

Materials needed:
- Image provided in this exercise
- Internet access (or other medical/anthropological/osteological reference literature)

Note to instructor: This exercise could be supplemented or replaced with skeletal material from a forensic case or skeletal collection if available.

Case scenario: A skeleton brought to you for analysis has the feature pictured below. Knowing that such variants may be useful in identifying the remains, you would like to include information about this variant in your report.

Instructions/Procedure:
- Using the process of differential diagnosis, identify or narrow down the likely skeletal variant

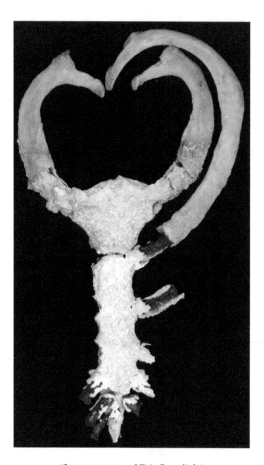

(Image courtesy of Eric Bartelink.)

Describe the variant/feature in terms of its location and distribution:

_____

_____

_____

Do you think the variant/feature is the result of normal skeletal variation, an anomaly, a pathology, or the result of habitual activity? Why?

_____

_____

_____

Using information from this chapter and/or the internet and/or medical/anthropological/osteological reference material, see if you can diagnose this skeletal variant:

_____

_____

How confident are you in your final diagnosis?

_____
_____

EXERCISE 12.5   Differential Diagnosis

Materials needed:
*   Image provided in this exercise
*   Internet access (or other medical/anthropological/osteological reference literature)

Note to instructor: This exercise could be supplemented or replaced with skeletal material from a forensic case or skeletal collection if available.

Case scenario: A skeleton brought to you for analysis has the feature pictured below. Knowing that such variants may be useful in identifying the remains, you would like to include information about this variant in your report.

Instructions/Procedure:
*   Using the process of differential diagnosis, identify or narrow down the likely skeletal variant.

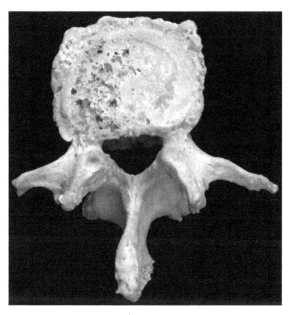

(Image courtesy of Eric Bartelink.)

Describe the variant/feature in terms of its location and distribution:

_____
_____
_____

Do you think the variant/feature is the result of normal skeletal variation, an anomaly, a pathology, or the result of habitual activity? Why?

_____
_____
_____

Using information from this chapter and/or the internet and/or medical/anthropological/osteological reference material, see if you can diagnose this skeletal variant:

_____
_____

How confident are you in your final diagnosis?

_____
_____

EXERCISE 12.6   Differential Diagnosis

Materials needed:
- Image provided in this exercise
- Internet access (or other medical/anthropological/osteological reference literature)

Note to instructor: This exercise could be supplemented or replaced with skeletal material from a forensic case or skeletal collection if available.

Case scenario: A skeleton brought to you for analysis has the feature pictured below. Knowing that such variants may be useful in identifying the remains, you would like to include information about this variant in your report.

Instructions/Procedure:
- Using the process of differential diagnosis, identify or narrow down the likely skeletal variant

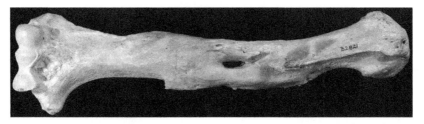

(Photo by Christopher Rainwater; Specimen courtesy of the Cleveland Museum of Natural History.)

Describe the variant/feature in terms of its location and distribution:

_____
_____
_____

Do you think the variant/feature is the result of normal skeletal variation, an anomaly, a pathology, or the result of habitual activity? Why?

_____
_____
_____

Using information from this chapter and/or the internet and/or medical/anthropological/osteological reference material, see if you can diagnose this skeletal variant:

_____
_____

How confident are you in your final diagnosis?

_____
_____

Chapter 13

Analysis of Skeletal Trauma

OBJECTIVES

Skeletal trauma can be characterized by its timing in relation to the death event as well as the mechanism that caused the trauma. In this chapter you will learn features that can differentiate antemortem, perimortem, and postmortem trauma, as well as features that indicate the type of force that may have caused the trauma, including blunt, sharp, high-velocity projectile, and thermal.

PRINCIPLES OF TRAUMA ANALYSIS

The analysis of trauma and other alterations to the skeleton by forensic anthropologists can help answer important questions, including those that might be related to the circumstances of death or could facilitate personal identification. An *alteration* is any change to the physical properties of a bone, while *trauma* refers to the physical disruption of living tissues by outside forces. The conclusions reached from the analysis of skeletal trauma typically include the *timing* of the trauma relative to the death event, and the *mechanism* or type of force that caused the trauma. Trauma timing can be categorized as antemortem (occurring before death) or perimortem (occurring around the time of death). Postmortem alterations are not considered trauma (because by definition they do not disrupt *living* tissue) but will also be addressed to some degree in this chapter (postmortem taphonomic changes are primarily addressed in Chapter 5). Trauma mechanism is usually categorized as blunt, high-velocity projectile, sharp, thermal, or some combination of these categories.

Trauma analysis involves careful observation, thorough documentation, and cautious interpretation. When analyzing trauma on skeletonized remains, definitive conclusions are not always possible, and in some cases it is best to simply describe what is observed. Interpreting traumatic alterations to the bone requires knowledge and application of a variety of scientific principles, including those relating to physics, biomechanics, and engineering. While anthropologists may assist in examining alterations that may be related to the death event, cause and manner of death are legal determinations made by a medicolegal authority (such as a medical examiner or coroner), not a forensic anthropologist.

TRAUMA TIMING

Trauma timing can be categorized according to when it occurred relative to the death event. Antemortem trauma is an alteration produced before death, typically unrelated to the death event. The primary evidence of antemortem trauma is osteogenic reaction (or the formation of new bone) since such responses will only occur if an individual is still alive. Osteogenic reaction is usually in the form of fracture healing (Table 13.1) or infectious response. Fracture healing may be evidenced by rounded fracture margins or a fracture callus (Fig. 13.1). Infectious response may be evidenced by proliferative or lytic lesions. Similarly, antemortem fractures of teeth are characterized by a rounding of the fractured enamel through dental wear.

Other antemortem alterations in which bone remodeling processes are observed include healing from surgical procedures (Fig. 13.2) as well as the resorption or filling in of the vacant alveolar space when teeth are lost or extracted (Fig. 13.3). Although the identification of antemortem trauma typically eliminates that injury from being directly related to the death event, certain antemortem trauma patterns can indicate a particular injury history (such as a major accident, a history of abuse, or human rights violations) which may provide clues regarding possible causes of death or may have indirectly contributed to the death. In addition, the presence of antemortem trauma in unidentified skeletal remains serves as information that can be useful in the identification process.

Perimortem trauma refers to an injury that occurred relatively near the time of death, typically directly related to the death event. Perimortem trauma to the bone is best defined as those injuries that occur when the bone is in a biomechanically fresh state; that is, when it retains components and properties that make it fracture in the same mechanical manner as viable bone but lacks any indications of bony healing. This means that the perimortem interval for forensic anthropological

A Laboratory Manual for Forensic Anthropology. https://doi.org/10.1016/B978-0-12-812201-3.00013-X

TABLE 13.1 Stages of Fracture Repair

Stage	Repair Processes
1. Reactive or inflammation stage	• Bleeding and blood pooling (hematoma) • Inflammation due to increase in plasma and white blood cells • Osteoclasts resorb dead bone • Fracture margin becomes blurred • Osteoid formation to bridge broken surfaces (first few days)
2. Reparative stage	• Soft fracture callus of fibrous bone (first few weeks) • Hard callus formation (6–12 weeks) • Calluses visible on gross or radiologic examination
3. Remodeling stage	• Remodeling of callus (months to years)

FIG. 13.1 Healed fracture (antemortem trauma) on a femur. *(Photo by Rebecca Meeusen; Specimen courtesy of the National Museum of Natural History; From Christensen, A.M., Passalacqua, N.V., Bartelink, E.J., 2014. Forensic Anthropology: Current Methods and Practice, Academic Press.)*

assessments could be quite long and extend relatively far (e.g., months) into the postmortem period, as long as the bone is still in a fresh state when the fracture occurred.

Evidence of perimortem trauma to the bone includes plastic deformation (Fig. 13.4) and staining on the bone associated with a hematoma. By comparison to antemortem fractures, perimortem fractures will lack evidence of osteogenic reaction. Compared to postmortem fractures, fresh bone fractures are often smooth and straight whereas dry bone fractures tend to have a more sharp and jagged appearance. Another indicator of perimortem trauma is an overall fracture pattern that is characteristic of a terminal event such as a gunshot trauma or fall from a great height.

Postmortem damage refers to taphonomic alterations to the bone that are produced after death and are unassociated with the death event. In some cases, postmortem damage may be *related* to the death event (e.g., mutilation or dismemberment inflicted by a perpetrator after a homicide), but in most cases, postmortem bone alterations are considered taphonomic. Postmortem damage can sometimes be distinguished from perimortem trauma by differential staining, such as where perimortem fracture edges are stained by hemorrhage, decomposition fluids, soil, or other materials. The fracture edges

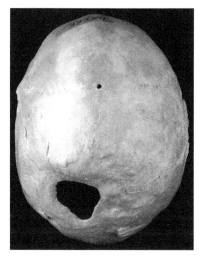

FIG. 13.2   Trephination. *(Photo by Rebecca Meeusen; Specimen courtesy of the National Museum of Natural History; From Christensen, A.M., Passalacqua, N.V., Bartelink, E.J., 2014. Forensic Anthropology: Current Methods and Practice, Academic Press.)*

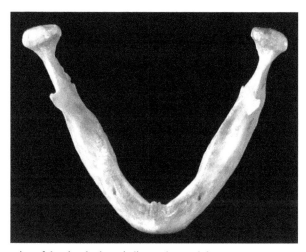

FIG. 13.3   Edentulous mandible. Resorption of the alveolar bone indicates that tooth loss was an antemortem process. *(Photo by Rebecca Meeusen; Specimen courtesy of the National Museum of Natural History; From Christensen, A.M., Passalacqua, N.V., Bartelink, E.J., 2014. Forensic Anthropology: Current Methods and Practice, Academic Press.)*

of bones damaged postmortem will often be lighter than the surrounding bone because these surfaces are exposed to the environment at a later time (Fig. 13.5). Like perimortem trauma, postmortem damage will not show evidence of healing. An overall pattern of damage consistent with known postmortem causes such as animal scavenging patterns can also differentiate the damage from perimortem trauma. In long bones, postmortem breaks will tend to occur at right angles to the long axis of the bone and postmortem fractures often follow the grain of the bone. Although assessment of fractures can yield clues that can differentiate postmortem damage from perimortem trauma, several factors can complicate this differentiation including abrasive modification that can round fracture edges, sun exposure and bleaching of perimortem fractures which can alter previous coloration differences, and other destructive postmortem alterations such as scavenging that can obscure or destroy the perimortem trauma.

TRAUMA MECHANISM

Trauma mechanism refers to the way force was applied to the bone, resulting in the alteration. Trauma mechanism is typically classified as being blunt, high-velocity projectile, sharp, thermal, or some combination and is usually determined by examination of the overall pattern of alteration. Although these categories can be descriptive and helpful, the mechanisms that produce skeletal trauma occur along a continuum and not in discrete categories. For example, the difference between

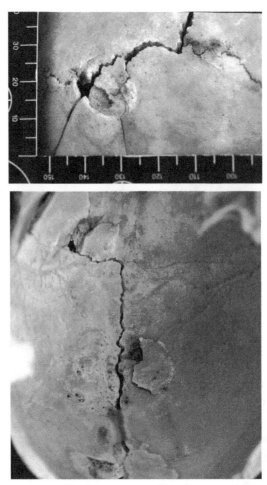

FIG. 13.4 Cranial perimortem trauma—ectocranial view (top) and endocranial view (bottom). *(Images courtesy of Eric Bartelink.)*

FIG. 13.5 Postmortem damage. Note the lighter color of recently exposed (and therefore unstained) fracture surfaces.

blunt trauma and some types of sharp trauma is the area of impact, with sharp trauma resulting from a force applied by a tool with very small surface area (i.e., a knife blade). The difference between blunt trauma and high velocity projectile trauma is the rate at which the force is applied, with high-velocity projectile trauma resulting from a force applied by an object moving at a very high rate of speed and impacting a small surface area. At their extremes, trauma mechanisms are often more apparent, but they can sometimes be difficult to discern. Reconstruction of fractured bone fragments is frequently necessary in order to observe the overall pattern of trauma, especially in cases with a large amount of fragmentation. It is also possible that there may be multiple mechanisms of trauma occurring on a single bone.

BLUNT TRAUMA

Blunt trauma results from (relatively) slow load application to the bone over a (relatively) large surface area (Fig. 13.6). Such traumas may result from a blow from an object (such as a club, hammer, or fist) but also include deceleration injuries such as transportation accidents and falls from heights. Blunt traumas are usually interpreted by their fracture patterns. Fractures from blunt trauma will follow the path of least resistance, propagating until the energy has dissipated. In the cranium, fractures will often terminate into one of the cranial sutures which dissipate the fracture energy; greater amounts of force are typically involved in fractures that continue through sutures.

In blunt trauma to the cranial vault, the bone typically bends internally, creating tensile stress on the inner table. This internal tensile stress causes fractures which start at the inner table but often continue through to the outer table and radiate outward from the impact site, creating a pattern of radiating fractures. If the object continues inward on the skull, concentric fractures (which are collapsing the bone inwardly) may also form, circumscribing the impact site (Fig. 13.7).

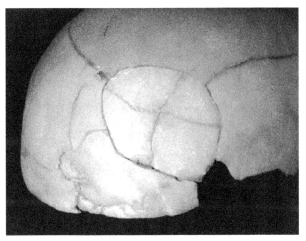

FIG. 13.6   Blunt trauma to the cranium. *(Image courtesy of Steven A. Symes.)*

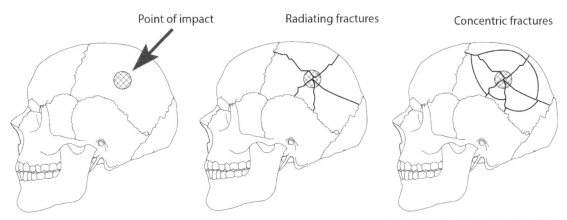

FIG. 13.7   Blunt trauma with radiating and concentric fractures. *(From Christensen, A.M., Passalacqua, N.V., Bartelink, E.J., 2014. Forensic Anthropology: Current Methods and Practice, Academic Press.)*

Characteristics of blunt trauma include plastic deformation, cortical bone delamination, and tool marks or impressions in the bone surface (Fig. 13.8). Because of the slow-loading nature of blunt trauma, there is time for the bone to bend, which results in a permanent deformation of the material. When an implement or tool is used to inflict blunt trauma, the size and shape of the alteration or impressions from tool features may give clues about the tool class and direction of impact.

In cases of multiple blunt impacts, it may be possible to determine the sequence in which the impacts occurred. Fractures from an impact will propagate until the energy has dissipated or until they encounter a discontinuity in the bone through which the energy is dissipated. This means that fractures from subsequent impacts will terminate into fractures from pre-existing impacts. In Fig. 13.9, for example, the fractures originating from impact "A" do not terminate into any of the other fractures. The fractures from impact "B" terminate into fractures from impacts "A" and "C." Fractures from impact "C" terminate into fractures from impact "A." The sequence of the impacts is therefore A, then C, and then B.

Another form of blunt trauma is the slow application of force through compression of the neck as is seen in cases of strangulation (either manual or using a ligature) or hanging (which may be related to a suicide, homicide, or judicial hangings).

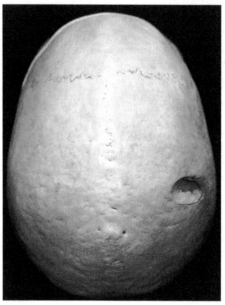

FIG. 13.8 Blunt trauma with tool (hammer) impression. *(From Christensen, A.M., Passalacqua, N.V., Bartelink, E.J., 2014. Forensic Anthropology: Current Methods and Practice, Academic Press.)*

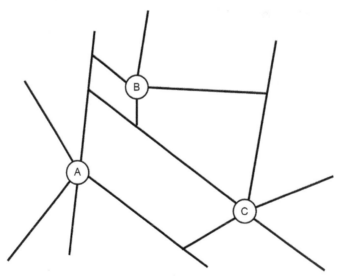

FIG. 13.9 Determination of sequence of trauma events. The impacts occurred in the following sequence: A-C-B. *(From Christensen, A.M., Passalacqua, N.V., Bartelink, E.J., 2014. Forensic Anthropology: Current Methods and Practice, Academic Press.)*

Perimortem hyoid fractures have been noted to indicate manual strangulation although other forms of neck trauma cannot be excluded without further investigation. Apparent hyoid fractures should be examined carefully, however, because unfused or incompletely ossified hyoids can easily be mistaken for traumatic separation, and manual strangulation can occur without fracturing the hyoid bone.

HIGH-VELOCITY PROJECTILE TRAUMA

High-velocity projectile trauma is characterized by a very rapid application of force over a (relatively) small surface area. Typically these traumas are produced by bullets from firearms (which travel at speeds of ~1100–4000 ft/s) but may also result from shrapnel from a blast or any other very fast-moving small object. Other projectiles, such as thrown javelins or arrows (which travel at ~300 ft/s), are not considered high-velocity projectiles; rather the resulting alterations from these types of projectile produce defects consistent with blunt trauma because they are moving at relatively slow speeds. High-velocity projectile trauma can usually be recognized by the fracture characteristics, shape and size of the defect/s, and associated beveling.

Most high-velocity projectile alterations are relatively round, but they may also be oval, keyhole shaped, or irregularly shaped. Round defects are commonly seen in cases where the impact of the projectile is roughly perpendicular to the surface of the bone (Fig. 13.10). When the projectile trajectory is not perpendicular, the defects are more likely to be oval or keyhole shaped. The more extreme the angle (i.e., the more tangential the trajectory), the more likely a keyhole-shaped defect is to occur (Fig. 13.10).

The size of the projectile defect is related to various factors, including characteristics of the projectile (e.g., its size, how it is constructed, and how fast it is moving) and characteristics of the bone (e.g., whether it is a flat or tubular bone). While the size of a projectile (such as the *caliber* or size of a bullet) is often roughly correlated with the size of the defect, the bone deforms when force is applied, and the defect may not be a true representation of the projectile size. It is therefore generally not possible to determine the size of the projectile based on the size of the defect.

One characteristic of high-velocity projectile trauma is beveling, or angling of the alteration in the direction of the projectile, especially on flat bones such as those of the cranial vault. Beveling is the result of plug-and-spall fractures caused by fast-moving objects (Fig. 13.11). As a high-velocity projectile passes through the bone, a plug of bone in the projectile's path is displaced. Spall refers to small flakes of the bone that are broken off when the projectile penetrates the other side of the bone. The result is that the side of the bone where the projectile exits has a greater extent of missing bone than the side where the projectile enters. Entrance defects are therefore typically internally beveled, while exit defects are externally beveled (Fig. 13.12). The direction and path of a projectile can often be deduced from beveling characteristics.

Similar to blunt trauma, high-velocity projectile trauma occurring on the cranial vault often results in two common types of fractures, radiating and concentric (Fig. 13.13). Radiating fractures are linear fractures that radiate out from the impact site, and concentric fractures are curved or circular lines that surround the impact site. In contrast to the collapsing concentric fractures produced in blunt trauma, which tend to be internally beveled, the concentric fractures associated with high-velocity projectile trauma tend to be externally beveled because they are heaving outward from intracranial pressure caused by the bullet passing through the cranium. Little or no plastic deformation is associated with high-velocity projectile trauma because the force is applied so rapidly that the bone does not have time to bend and deform before it fractures.

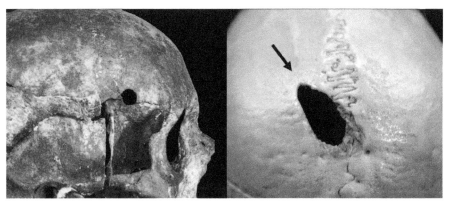

FIG. 13.10 Round defect from a perpendicular high-velocity projectile entrance (left), and keyhole-shaped entry from a tangential entrance (right). *(From Christensen, A.M., Passalacqua, N.V., Bartelink, E.J., 2014. Forensic Anthropology: Current Methods and Practice, Academic Press.)*

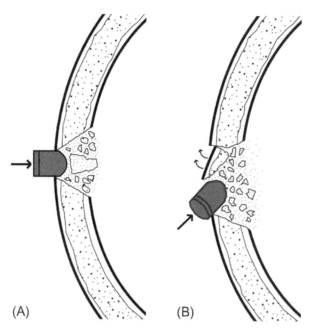

FIG. 13.11 Beveling from plug-and-spall; (A) represents a roughly perpendicular entrance, while (B) represents a tangential, or "keyhole" entrance; *arrow* indicates direction of projectile.

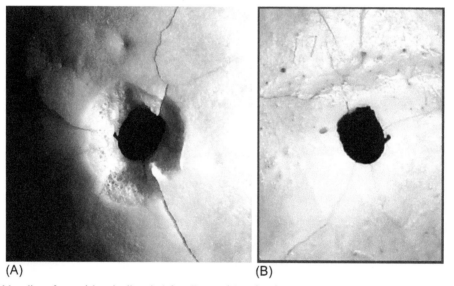

FIG. 13.12 External beveling of a cranial projectile exit defect. Ectocranial surface is shown left, and endocranial surface is shown right. *(Images courtesy of Steven A Symes.)*

Additionally, because of the magnitude of the force, high-velocity projectile traumas also tend to result in a greater degree of fracturing and fragmentation than other traumas.

Even in the absence of a recognizable injury pattern, the involvement of a projectile may be evident from remnants of the projectile left behind which are often visible radiologically (Fig. 13.14). Projectiles are typically constructed of metals which are more radiodense than the bone and will appear distinct from the bone radiographically. In some cases, fragments of the projectile may be present within the bone, and sometimes even if the projectile has passed all the way through the bone, small remnants of the projectile may have been deposited on the bone as they made contact (often called "lead wipe") which will also be visible in radiographs. Pellets from shotgun traumas usually do not have enough remaining force to exit the body and can often be located using radiology either within soft tissues or embedded in the bone.

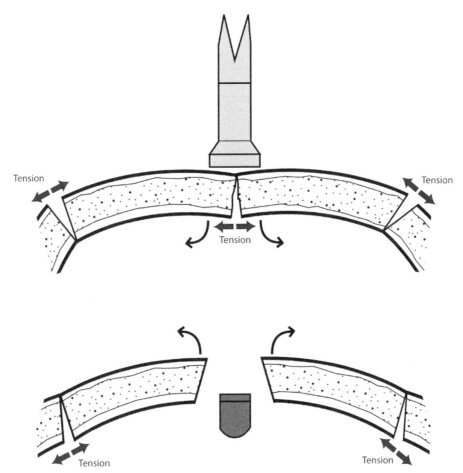

FIG. 13.13 Comparison of concentric cranial fractures in blunt (top) and high-velocity projectile (bottom) traumas. Blunt fractures cave the bone in, while high-velocity projectile fractures push the bone out. *(From Christensen, A.M., Passalacqua, N.V., Bartelink, E.J., 2014. Forensic Anthropology: Current Methods and Practice, Academic Press.)*

Multiple projectile traumas can often be sequenced similar to blunt trauma impacts on the basis of fracture patterns. It is important to note, however, that fractures can travel though the bone at an extremely high speed, and it is common for radiating fractures from an entrance defect to reach the other side of the cranial vault before the projectile exits the cranium.

SHARP TRAUMA

Sharp trauma is characterized as trauma created by a tool with a pointed or beveled edge. Sharp trauma occurs under loading conditions similar to blunt trauma, but using a tool with a very small surface area (e.g., the edge of a knife blade). Sharp traumas often leave distinctive marks (cuts) on the bone. While sharp traumas can be caused by a wide variety of implements, two commonly utilized and heavily researched tools are knives and saws. Functionally, the purpose of a knife is to cut soft material, while a saw is designed to cut hard material and they therefore function rather differently. Knives typically have a narrow beveled edge which comes back to a wide spine. Saws have wide teeth which come back to a relatively narrow spine (Fig. 13.15) so that they will not bind when cutting through hard material.

Knife cuts and stab traumas typically leave alterations such as straight line incisions, punctures, gouges, and clefts. There are two general classes of knives: serrated and nonserrated. Serrated knives have teeth built into the blade, whereas nonserrated knives have smooth blades. The teeth on serrated blades create patterned striations on the bone that are distinctive from nonserrated blades and can be used to determine the class of the knife used. While nonserrated blades may leave striations in the bone or cartilage as they cut the material, it is the patterned nature of striations that indicates that they came from a serrated blade.

Saws consist of teeth which are designed to cut through hard material. As saws progress though material, they create a kerf, or groove (Fig. 13.16). The marks created by saws can be analyzed to determine the class of the saw used.

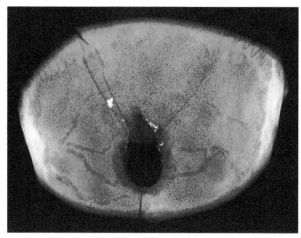

FIG. 13.14 Projectile fragments visible in a radiograph of a cranial fragment. *(Image courtesy of Eric Bartelink.)*

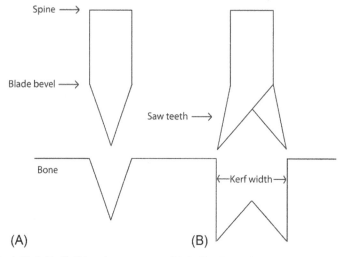

FIG. 13.15 Cross sections of a single bladed knife (A), and a cross-cut saw blade (B). *(From Christensen, A.M., Passalacqua, N.V., Bartelink, E.J., 2014. Forensic Anthropology: Current Methods and Practice, Academic Press.)*

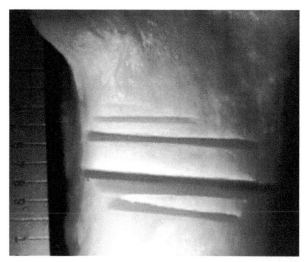

FIG. 13.16 Saw trauma. *(From Christensen, A.M., Passalacqua, N.V., Bartelink, E.J., 2014. Forensic Anthropology: Current Methods and Practice, Academic Press.)*

Class characteristics of saws include such traits as the blade and tooth size and shape, teeth-per-inch, blade and tooth set, cutting action, and saw power (i.e., hand vs mechanical). The direction of the progress (of the saw cut) as well as the direction of the stroke can also be determined by examining the cut for exit chipping and breakaway spurs.

Dismemberment is almost always associated with sharp trauma on the bone. It is not uncommon to find both knife and saw marks on dismembered remains, or to have incomplete knife cuts in bones which are then broken at these weakened areas. Other (though considerably rarer) methods of dismemberment include tools with less typical "blades" such as chainsaws or wood chippers. Dismemberment generally occurs after death which is technically in the postmortem period (in relation to the death event) but is usually performed while bones are still in a biomechanically fresh state; alterations would therefore have the biomechanical properties of perimortem trauma.

THERMAL ALTERATIONS

Thermal alterations result from exposure of the body to fire or other heat sources. Early stages of thermal alteration involve the burning of the fleshed human body. With the continued application of the thermal source to a body, the bones may become exposed and damaged as the organic components become fuel for the continuing exothermic reaction of a fire. Understanding the normal burn pattern (i.e., that seen in an unobstructed body under typical burning conditions) can help with determining whether any unusual circumstances were at play. The soft tissues are altered first, resulting in a loss of moisture which causes the muscles (typically the larger flexors) and ligaments to contract. As this occurs, the position of the body shifts, resulting is what is referred to as the *pugilistic posture* (Fig. 13.17). With continued exposure to heat, the soft tissues will continue to burn. The thickness of the soft tissues plays a large role in the exposure and heat alteration of the bone. Skeletal regions with less overlying soft tissue will typically be exposed first, while those areas with more overlying soft tissue will burn last (Fig. 13.18). Understanding the cause and mechanism of the pugilistic posture and general body soft tissue thicknesses allows for burn patterns to be analyzed and abnormal burn patterns to become apparent, and careful documentation of the fire scene is important in order to fully interpret the burn pattern present on a set of remains.

Once the soft tissues have burned away, the bones become exposed to heat and flames, resulting in thermal alterations to the bone. Heat-altered bone is evident by color changes, shrinkage, fractures, and other physical alterations. Color changes are typically the first to occur in heat-altered bone, with these changes corresponding primarily to changes in the organic component (Fig. 13.19). Normal, unheated bone is a pale yellow color. In the very early stages of heat alteration, occurring in areas that are still covered by soft tissues (such that the bone is exposed to heat but not to direct flame, resulting in loss of moisture and some molecular alteration), altered osseous tissue will first appear as a white color, sometimes referred to as the *heat border*. As thermal exposure continues, the bone becomes darkened in color, eventually becoming black, a condition referred to as charred. Charred bone has been directly exposed to fire and is a result of the carbonization of the organic component of the bone. As the thermal exposure continues, the bone will eventually become calcined. Calcined bone has been thermally altered to the extent that it has lost all organic content and moisture and is usually grey

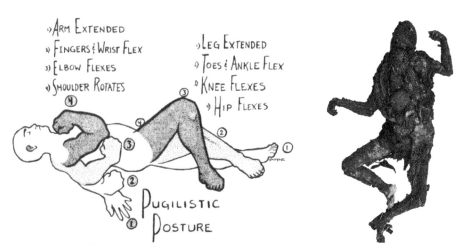

FIG. 13.17 Pugilistic posture with flexion of the fingers, elbows, toes, knees, and hip. *(Images courtesy of Elayne Pope; From Christensen, A.M., Passalacqua, N.V., Bartelink, E.J., 2014. Forensic Anthropology: Current Methods and Practice, Academic Press.)*

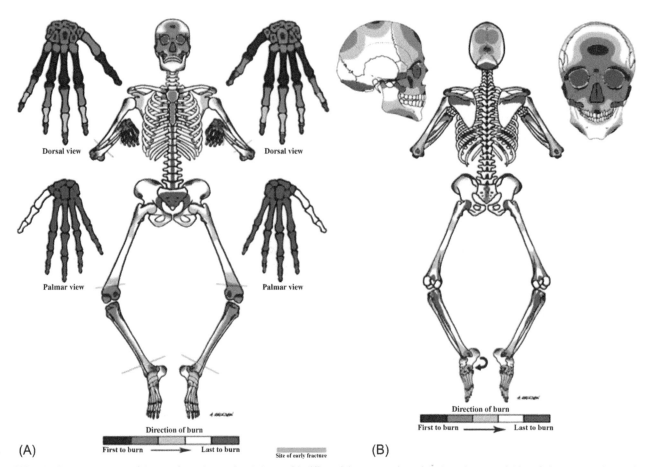

FIG. 13.18 Burn patterns of the anterior and posterior skeleton with differential exposure sites of the bone in areas of thin soft tissue protection, while other surfaces remain protected by muscle. *(From Symes, S.A., Rainwater, C.W., Chapman, E.N., Gipson, D.R., Piper, A.L., 2008. Patterned thermal destruction of human remains in a forensic setting. In: Schmidt, C., Symes, S. (Eds.), The Analysis of Burned Human Remains. Elsevier Ltd, Burlington, pp. 15–54.)*

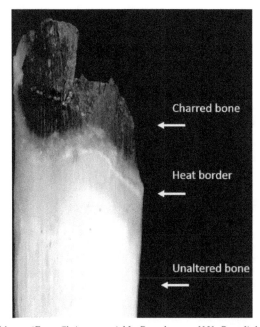

FIG. 13.19 Color changes in heat-altered bone. *(From Christensen, A.M., Passalacqua, N.V., Bartelink, E.J., 2014. Forensic Anthropology: Current Methods and Practice, Academic Press.)*

TABLE 13.2 Heat-Induced Fractures

Fracture Type	Fracture Characteristics
Transverse fracture	Fracture occurring transversely in long bone shafts as a function of the bone structure weakening and failing from heat alteration
Curved transverse fracture	Half-moon-shaped fractures which occur in long bone shafts as the soft tissues shrink and pull back from the bone; these fractures are indicative of direction of fire progression
Step fracture	Fractures extending transversely from a longitudinal fracture across a long bone shaft
Patina	Superficial microfractures which often have a mesh or spider-web appearance

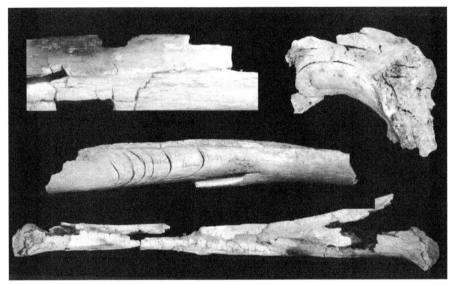

FIG. 13.20 Heat-induced bone fractures. *(From Christensen, A.M., Passalacqua, N.V., Bartelink, E.J., 2014. Forensic Anthropology: Current Methods and Practice, Academic Press.)*

to white in color. At the calcined stage, the remains are simply a framework of the inorganic components of the bone (i.e., hydroxyapatite) and are very fragile.

Thermally altered bone also decreases in dimension or shrinks. This shrinkage is a function of the combustion of the organic components of the bone and evaporation of water, causing the bone to decrease in overall size. Shrinkage may also be associated with heat-related warping and deformation. These changes in dimensions and overall shape should be considered in laboratory analysis since they could affect metric analyses such as those used to estimate sex and stature.

Another effect of heat on the bone (as well as teeth) is fractures. Burned bone fractures share many characteristics with other postmortem dry bone fractures in that they have sharp (rather than smooth) margins and they often occur along the grain of the bone (longitudinally). Burned bone also fractures in response to soft tissue shrinkage and the direction of fire progression, resulting in fractures that are specific to heat-altered bone. Heat-induced fractures include transverse, curved transverse (thumbnail), step, and patina (Table 13.2 and Fig. 13.20). On the cranium, there is often delamination of the outer cortical bone layer (Fig. 13.21).

Cremation is an extreme form of thermal alteration where the body is reduced to the bone that is completely calcined and disintegrates to ash (Fig. 13.22). Cremation can occur as a part of funerary practices, it may be performed intentionally as a criminal act to dispose of a body, or it may be accidental such as in a structure fire. In modern commercial cremation, remains are placed into a furnace called a retort where they are burned at high temperatures until they are calcined. The remains are then placed into mechanical pulverizers that reduce the remains to ashes. Whether funerary, accidental, or criminal, the analysis of cremated remains (often referred to as *cremains*) can be complex because there are typically few if any bones that retain any morphological features of value. In some cases, elemental analysis to determine the presence of bone may be the furthest extent of possible examinations.

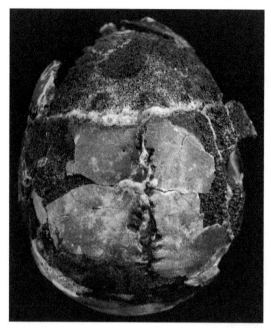

FIG. 13.21 Delamination in a charred skull. *(From Christensen, A.M., Passalacqua, N.V., Bartelink, E.J., 2014. Forensic Anthropology: Current Methods and Practice, Academic Press.)*

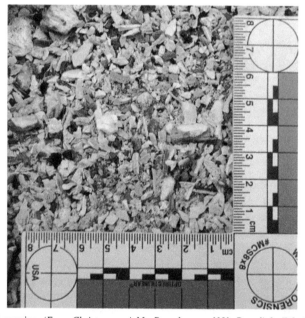

FIG. 13.22 Commercially cremated remains. *(From Christensen, A.M., Passalacqua, N.V., Bartelink, E.J., 2014. Forensic Anthropology: Current Methods and Practice, Academic Press.)*

EXERCISE 13.1   Assessment of Trauma Timing

Materials needed:
- Images provided in this exercise

Note to instructors: This exercise can be supplemented or replaced with forensic cases or reference specimens.

Case scenario: Skeletonized human remains were discovered in a remote field. The individual has not yet been identified, and the cause of death has not been determined. Your assistance was requested, particularly to analyze several suspected alterations to the skeleton, which may help with identification, and reconstruction of events around (or after) the time of death.

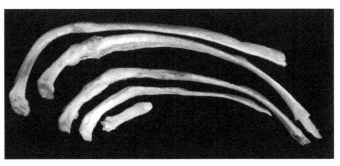

(Image courtesy of Eric Bartelink.)

(Image courtesy of Eric Bartelink.)

Provide a written description (not an interpretation) of the alterations visible in these images. Include any observations of missing bone, fractures, etc., using appropriate anatomical and reference terminology.

_____
_____
_____
_____

What is your interpretation of the timing of the alterations to the ribs? Explain your answer.

_____
_____
_____

What is your interpretation of the timing of the alterations to the tibia? Explain your answer.

_____
_____
_____

EXERCISE 13.2   Trauma Description and Interpretation

Materials needed:
- Image provided in this chapter

Note to instructors: This exercise can be supplemented or replaced with forensic cases or reference specimens.

Case scenario: The medical examiner is performing an autopsy on remains of a possible homicide victim. She believes there was blunt trauma to the cranium involving multiple impacts and has requested your assistance in interpreting the sequence of the impacts. Her examination and report are not yet complete, but she provided you with her sketch of the fracture pattern.

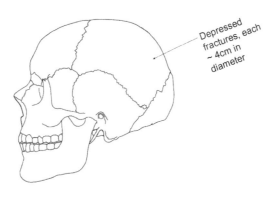

Depressed fractures, each ~4cm in diameter

Provide a written description (not an interpretation) of the alterations visible in this image. Include any observations of missing bone, fractures, etc., using appropriate anatomical and reference terminology.

_____

_____

_____

What type of force/mechanism most likely caused the alterations seen in this skull? Explain.

_____

_____

_____

In which order do you think the impacts occurred? Explain your answer.

_____

_____

_____

Are you able to say anything about the possible implement used? Why or why not?

_____

_____

_____

EXERCISE 13.3 Trauma Description and Interpretation

Materials needed:
- Images provided in this exercise

Note to instructors: This exercise can be supplemented or replaced with forensic cases or reference specimens.

Case scenario: During construction of a new highway, workers unearthed a human skull. Although the area is known to be near possible Native American burial grounds, the damage to the skull lead investigators to believe that this is a more recent specimen. They have brought it to you for analysis. Due to the fragmentation, you first reconstructed the cranium to see if it would clarify any trauma patterns.

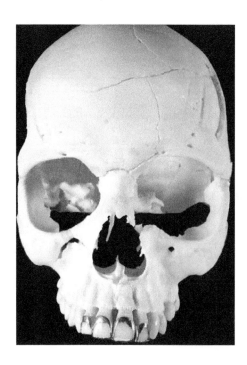

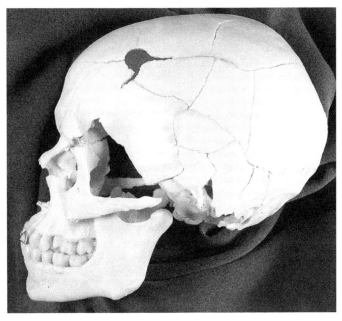

(Images courtesy of Steven A. Symes.)

Provide a written description (not an interpretation) of the alterations visible in these images. Include observations of missing bone, fractures, etc., using appropriate anatomical and reference terminology.

_____
_____
_____

_____

What type of force/mechanism most likely caused the alterations seen in this skull? Explain.

_____
_____

_____

From these images, are you able to determine the direction of the force/trauma? Explain.

_____
_____
_____

EXERCISE 13.4   Trauma Description and Interpretation

Materials needed:
- Image provided in this exercise

Note to instructors: This exercise can be supplemented or replaced with forensic cases or reference specimens.

Case scenario: A suspected drowning victim was recovered from a nearby lake. The decedent was apparently partying and drinking with friends at a house on the lake two nights before, and at some point in the evening, friends noticed he was missing. Although none of the usual indicators of drowning were noted at autopsy, the medical examiner noticed the below fractures on the hyoid during her examination.

Provide a written description (not an interpretation) of the alterations visible in this image. Include any observations of missing bone, fractures, etc., using appropriate anatomical and reference terminology.

_____
_____
_____
_____

What type of force/mechanism most likely caused the alterations seen? Explain.

_____
_____
_____

Are there any alternative explanations for the trauma observed? Explain.

_____
_____
_____

EXERCISE 13.5 Trauma Description and Interpretation

Materials needed:
- Images provided in this exercise

Note to instructors: This exercise can be supplemented or replaced with forensic cases or reference specimens.

Case scenario: A man was brought to the hospital unconscious with lacerations of the face and cranium and later died of these and other internal injuries. Witnesses questioned about events of that night claim that the victim was drinking and fell down a flight of stairs. An autopsy and assessment by a forensic anthropologist revealed the alterations seen below.

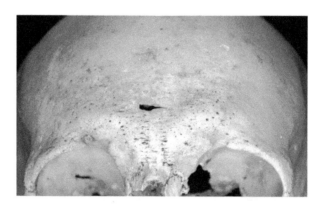

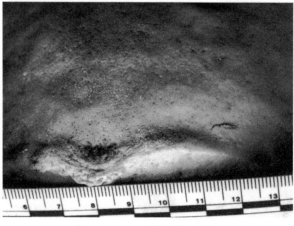

(Images courtesy of Eric Bartelink.)

Provide a written description (not an interpretation) of the alterations visible in these images. Include any observations of missing bone, fractures, etc., using appropriate anatomical and reference terminology.

_____
_____
_____
_____

What type of force/mechanism most likely caused the alterations seen? Explain.

_____
_____
_____

Are the alterations consistent with the witnesses' accounts? Are there any alternative explanations for the trauma observed? Explain.

_____
_____
_____

EXERCISE 13.6   Trauma Description and Interpretation

Materials needed:
- Image provided in this exercise

Note to instructors: This exercise can be supplemented or replaced with forensic cases or reference specimens.

Case scenario: A partial skeleton was discovered in a wooded area. Investigators believe they have identified the decedent based on DNA obtained from the teeth, but the cause of death is still unknown so they have requested your assistance in a trauma analysis. Your visual examination revealed a few fractures and missing bone on several vertebrae and ribs of undetermined origin. You then X-ray the remains including one of the vertebrae pictured below.

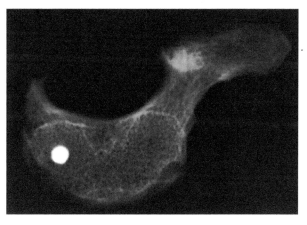

(Image courtesy of Eric Bartelink.)

Provide a written description (not an interpretation) of the alterations visible in this image. Include any observations of missing bone, fractures, etc., using appropriate anatomical and reference terminology.

_____
_____
_____
_____

What type of force/mechanism most likely caused the alterations seen? Explain.

_____
_____
_____

How might this finding explain or relate to the other alterations observed?

_____
_____
_____

What other types of forensic examination(s) might you suggest for this specimen? Explain.

_____
_____
_____

EXERCISE 13.7 Trauma Description and Interpretation

Materials needed:
- Images provided in this exercise

Note to instructors: This exercise can be supplemented or replaced with forensic cases or reference specimens.

Case scenario: While executing a search warrant in relation to a missing person whose wife is a suspect in the husband's disappearance, a wood-burning stove in the basement was found to contain apparent bones. The wife claims that she used the stove to cremate the remains of her recently deceased German shepherd. The picture below was provided to you by investigators at the scene. You advised that a closer examination would be needed to confirm the origin of the pictured material. When you examine the stove contents visually, some of the material is of undetermined origin but may be the bone, some materials clearly consists of bone fragments but you cannot determine whether they are human. You also locate the two fragments pictured below and are able to reconstruct several fragments of a third bone.

Photo from scene:

(Image courtesy of Eric Bartelink.)

Items found in your examination:

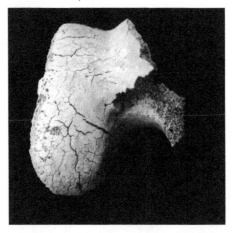

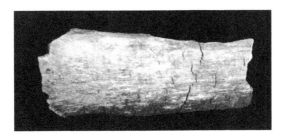

(Images courtesy of Eric Bartelink.)

Bone reconstructed from several fragments:

(Image courtesy of Eric Bartelink.)

Which bones (or portions) are pictured?

_____

_____

_____

Provide a description (not an interpretation) of the alterations to the bones. Include a discussion of missing bone, fractures, color, etc.

_____

_____

_____

For the material for which you are unable to determine the (skeletal or nonskeletal) origin based on a visual examination, what other technique(s) might you use to make this determination?

_____

_____

_____

For the bones for which you are unable to determine the (human or nonhuman) origin based on a visual examination, what other technique(s) might you use to make this determination?

_____

_____

Chapter 14

Personal Identification

OBJECTIVES

Forensic anthropologists assist in the identification process by comparing antemortem and postmortem skeletal information. Quantitative approaches incorporate information such as the frequency of skeletal features in the overall population to provide statistical support to an identification. Forensic anthropologists may also be involved in the process of creating facial approximations. In the exercises in this chapter, you will use anthropological identification techniques to compare antemortem and postmortem skeletal information, calculate likelihood ratios, use online databases and repositories, and create a facial approximation.

PRINCIPLES OF PERSONAL IDENTIFICATION

Although the ultimate confirmation of identity lies with the medicolegal authority, usually a medical examiner or coroner, if remains are skeletonized, forensic anthropologists are often involved in the identification process, the extent to which may vary based on jurisdiction, condition of the remains, and the availability of antemortem information about the possible decedent. Typically forensic anthropologists are involved in narrowing the pool of potential matches and identification comparisons.

NARROWING THE POOL OF POTENTIAL MATCHES

An anthropological analysis may be used to assess biological information about the individual including age, sex, ancestry, stature, or other skeletal conditions such as anomalies, pathologies, and previous traumas. This assessment, of course, is not itself an identification but is very useful in narrowing the pool of potential candidates in the search for identity. Missing persons' records or repositories can be searched for individuals who share the biological profile of the remains and could therefore be included and further investigated as potential matches to the skeletal remains. NamUs, for example, is a national repository of missing persons and unidentified decedent records. It is a free online system that can be accessed and searched by anyone (www.namus.gov) and consists of two primary portals: The Missing Persons Database and the Unidentified Persons Database. Missing persons' information can be entered into the Missing Persons Database by anyone (pending verification). Medical examiners and coroners can enter unidentified deceased information into the Unidentified Persons Database. The estimation of the postmortem interval can also be very useful in narrowing the pool of potential matches. For example, skeletal remains determined to have a time since death of 5–10 years could not have originated from an individual who was last seen several weeks ago.

IDENTIFICATION COMPARISONS

Once a potential match has been located, an identification comparison can be made. In an identification comparison, antemortem and postmortem information or records are examined, looking for consistencies and inconsistencies that may confirm or exclude the skeletal remains as belonging to the person. Antemortem information is required for comparison, which is usually obtained by law enforcement officials or medicolegal investigators through the next of kin or medical and dental facilities. The comparison will typically result in one of several conclusions, which vary depending on the comparison approach used as well as the reporting requirements of the forensic anthropology laboratory (Table 14.1).

It is important to understand when differences or inconsistencies between the antemortem and postmortem information are explainable versus unexplainable. For example, a hip replacement that appears in the postmortem record but not in an antemortem record can be explained (the hip replacement could have occurred sometime after the antemortem record was made); these two records could still have originated from the same individual. A hip replacement that is present in the antemortem record but absent in the postmortem record, however, would be an unexplainable difference, and the person from whom the antemortem data was collected can be excluded as the source of the skeletal remains.

A Laboratory Manual for Forensic Anthropology. https://doi.org/10.1016/B978-0-12-812201-3.00014-1

TABLE 14.1 Example Conclusions Form Radiologic Comparisons

Conclusion	Description
Consistent with or cannot exclude	The two sets of information are consistent with originating from the same individual with no unexplainable differences (and therefore the presumed decedent should continue to be *included* as a possible source of the remains).
Exclusion	The two sets of information are inconsistent with originating from the same individual (and therefore the presumed decedent can be *excluded* as the source of the remains).
Inconclusive	There is insufficient information to include or exclude the presumed decedent as the source of the remains.

The most common identification comparison technique used by forensic anthropologists is radiologic comparison or radiologic identification, sometimes called "RADid" (Hatch et al., 2014), which involves the comparison of antemortem (clinical) radiologic images with postmortem images. These may include 2-D radiographs, digital radiographs, or computed tomography (CT) scans. The two images are typically compared by direct side-by-side visual inspection (Fig. 14.1). Depending on whether the image is on film or in an electronic format, the comparison may be performed using a light box or computer screen. Although features such as injuries and skeletal anomalies may be useful, the extent of normal anatomical detail revealed in radiographs of the skeleton can be equally if not more important in identification comparisons. Such details may include general bone morphology, trabecular patterns, skull features such as the paranasal sinuses, and cranial sutures, as well as dental features such as tooth morphology, pathological conditions, and antemortem tooth loss.

To make a postmortem record for comparison to the antemortem, an image of the skeletal remains is taken with a similar scope, orientation, and magnification as the antemortem image so that the images being compared are truly comparable. If both records are CT scans, standardization approaches can be employed to ensure direct comparisons (Fig. 14.2). Not all forensic anthropologists have training in radiology and radiography, and those who do not have sufficient experience should consult with a radiologist.

Forensic anthropologists who are experienced in osteology and odontology and in assessing radiographic images may also compare bone and tooth morphology in antemortem and postmortem radiographic dental records (Fig. 14.3). Descriptions and comparisons involving the identification and analysis of dental treatments such as restorations and implants (also seen in Fig. 14.3) should be examined by a forensic odontologist when possible. Examinations by both experts will strengthen the probability of a correct identification or exclusion.

SURGICAL DEVICES

Sometimes skeletal remains have associated surgical implants or orthopedic devices. These implants (also called surgical implements, artifacts, or appliances) typically have a lot number, serial number, or insignia of the manufacturer stamped into them (Fig. 14.4). Local or national registries or the manufacturer may be contacted for information associated with that device. In some cases it may be possible to link the device to a specific individual; in other cases, the devices may only be useful in narrowing the search, since not all devices have a unique serial number and registries may not necessarily provide

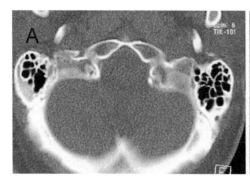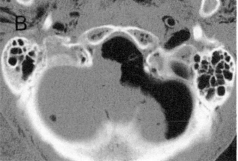

FIG. 14.1 Identification comparison using mastoid air cells in CT (antemortem shown left, postmortem right). *(From Hatch, G.M., Dedouit, F., Christensen, A.M., Thali, M.J., Ruder, T.D., 2014. RADid: a pictorial review of radiologic identification using postmortem CT. J. Forensic Radiol. Imaging 2, 52–59.)*

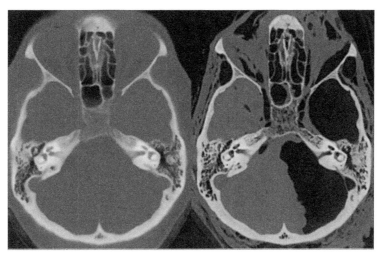

FIG. 14.2 Antemortem (left) and postmortem (right) CT scans aligned using a standardization approach. *(From Ruder T., Brun, C., Christensen, A.M., Thali, M., Gascho, D., Schweitzer, W., Hatch, G.M., 2016. Comparative radiologic identification with CT images of paranasal sinuses—development of a standardized approach. J. Forensic Radiol. Imaging 7, 1–9.)*

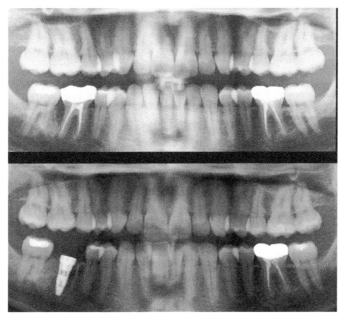

FIG. 14.3 Comparison of two Panorex images from the same individual. Similarities can be seen in the contours of the teeth as well as the trabecular pattern of the alveolar bone. Several dental restorations can also be observed. This case also represents an example of explainable differences that can sometimes be observed in radiologic comparisons—between the time of the top image and bottom image, the bottom right M1 with a root canal was extracted and replaced with a post, and cadaver bone was transplanted distal to the implant. These differences would therefore not form the basis for an exclusion. *(Images courtesy of Megan Gilpin.)*

FIG. 14.4 Surgically implanted device with visible imprinted manufacturer information. *(Image courtesy of Bruce Anderson; From Christensen, A.M., Passalacqua, N.V., Bartelink, E.J., 2014. Forensic Anthropology: Current Methods and Practice. Academic Press.)*

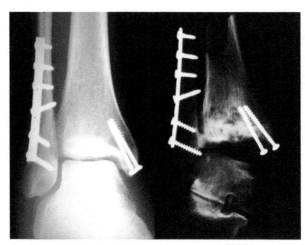

FIG. 14.5 Radiographic comparison of ankle region including surgical devices—antemortem (left) and postmortem (right). *(From Christensen, A.M., Anderson, B.E., 2013. Personal identification. In: Tersigni-Tarrant, M.T., Shirley, N. (Eds.), Forensic Anthropology: An Introduction. CRC Press, Boca Raton, pp. 397–420.)*

adequate information to associate the device with a particular individual. Because they typically are more radiodense than bone, they also appear rather distinctly on radiologic images (Fig. 14.5).

QUANTITATIVE APPROACHES

Most identification comparisons result in a largely unquantified opinion as to whether the antemortem and postmortem information agree in sufficient detail to conclude that they originated from the same person. In order to provide more objective and quantitative conclusions, the results of identification comparisons can also be expressed quantitatively, for example, as likelihood ratios. In anthropological identification comparisons, a likelihood ratio would be expressed as the probability of finding shared skeletal features in the antemortem and postmortem records given that the identification is correct, over the probability of finding shared skeletal features given that the identification is incorrect. This ratio is effectively a function of how common the particular shared feature is in the population.

For example, in comparing a postmortem radiograph of a knee to an antemortem radiograph of a presumed match, both radiographs show a feature known to occur in 1% of the general population. For the numerator, the probability that the skeletal features match given that the identification is correct would be 1; for the denominator, the probability that you would get a match of that feature with someone else (an incorrect identification) is 1 in 100 (or 1/100 or 0.01). The likelihood ratio would be 1/0.01 or 100; it is therefore 100 times more likely that the skeletal information would match if the identification is correct than if it is incorrect. Moreover, for a likelihood ratio involving more than on feature, rates can be multiplied via the product rule (assuming the traits are independent). A likelihood ratio greater than 1 is evidence in favor of the hypothesis that the two sets of data are from the same individual, while a likelihood ratio less than 1 is evidence against it, with exactly 1 being neutral (the two hypotheses are equally likely). The further from 1 the likelihood ratio is, the greater the probative value of the evidence.

Although preferable, quantitative approaches are not always straightforward because trait frequency data do not exist for many features that forensic anthropologists use in identification comparisons. A recently developed repository (the RADid Resource, 2016), however, contains documented population frequencies for numerous skeletal traits that can be used in identification (Christensen and Hatch, 2016). These frequencies reflect how often certain skeletal features are seen in particular populations and can be used to quantify the strength of a comparison where these features are shared. Odontosearch (Aschheim and Adams, 2015) provides an objective approach to assessing the frequency of the occurrence of dental patterns including missing, filled, and unrestored teeth.

FACIAL APPROXIMATION

Facial approximation is the practice of artistic recreation of possible facial features based on the underlying skeletal structures (Fig. 14.6). This approach is typically used when all scientific leads have been exhausted, with the goal of capturing public attention and seeing if anyone recognizes the approximation as possibly belonging to someone they know.

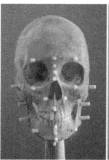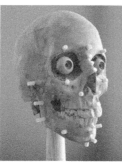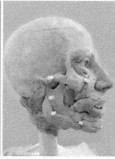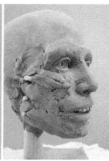

FIG. 14.6 Process of facial approximation using clay sculpture. *(Image courtesy of Lisa Bailey.)*

In addition to knowledge of cranial and soft tissue anatomy, artistic ability is also naturally required for making successful facial approximations, and thus the best practice is a joint effort between anthropologists and anatomical or forensic artists. While there are certain cranial structures that may be reliably reflected in the facial features (such as the breadth of the nose, the projection of the cheekbones, and the shape of the chin), there are many other features which necessarily require some artistic interpretation (such as the shapes of the ears and the style of the hair). The ultimate goal of a facial approximation is for it to be publicized in order to potentially generate identification leads. If a visual recognition by a relative, friend, or acquaintance is made, the identification process must then proceed to comparative methods (such as DNA, dental records, and medical radiographs).

Recent DNA-based methods have also been developed for predicting facial morphology, in an approach referred to as *phenotyping*. This approach uses DNA to determine sex and genomic ancestry, as well as predict the architecture of facial morphology and other traits such as eye and hair color (Claes et al., 2014). Although these methods are DNA-based, such approximations are not exact replicas of an individual's appearance (similar to facial approximation methods based on skull features) and cannot predict or account for extrinsic factors such as dietary habits, lifestyles, or injuries that may affect facial features. Moreover, this technology is still new, has only been used in a handful of forensic investigations, and requires additional validation.

EXERCISE 14.1   Narrowing the Match Pool With the Biological Profile

Materials needed:
- Missing person data provided in this exercise

Note to instructor: This exercise can be modified or supplemented with information from forensic cases.

Case scenario: You analyzed skeletal remains which you estimated to be a European female aged 25–40 years who was 5′7″ ± 2″ tall. The sex estimation was based on a complete pelvis which indicated a 94% probability of female sex based on scoring pubic traits. Ancestry estimation was based on several cranial measurements even though there was some apparent perimortem trauma. Age estimation was based on pubic symphyseal morphology that you scored a Hartnett phase 3. Stature was calculated using Fordisc based on measurements of the femur and tibia. You further estimated based on significant adhering soft tissue and recent weather conditions that the postmortem interval was approximately 3–12 months. Investigators searched missing person records and found that five people have been reported missing in the area:
- Missing Person #1: A 33-year-old Black male, 6′1″ tall, last seen 4 months ago
- Missing Person #2: A 42 year old White female, 5/4″ tall, last seen 18 months years ago
- Missing Person #3: A 19-year-old White male, 5′6″ tall, last seen 1 week ago
- Missing Person #4: A 40-year old Black female, 5′6″ tall, last seen, 6 months ago
- Missing Person #5: A 70-year-old Hispanic female, 5′7″ tall, last seen 6 years ago

Instructions/Procedure:
- For each Missing Person (MP), indicate whether you think they should be included or excluded from further consideration and why.

MP1: Include/Exclude Why?

_____

_____

MP2: Include/Exclude Why?

_____

_____

MP3: Include/Exclude Why?

_____

_____

MP4: Include/Exclude Why?

_____

_____

MP5: Include/Exclude Why?

_____

_____

For those missing persons that you think should still be considered, how would you proceed?

_____

_____

_____

EXERCISE 14.2   NamUs Search

Materials needed:
- Internet access

Note to instructor: This exercise can be performed individually (either in class or as a take-home exercise), as well as in small groups, or as a whole-class/demonstration exercise led by the instructor. If you have used NamUs before, discuss your experience with students.

Case scenario: After all of the local possible matches from Exercise 14.1 were excluded based on DNA comparisons, you decide to search NamUs to see if there might be a possible match with a missing person from another area.

Instructions/Procedure:
- Visit the NamUs website at www.namus.gov and review the contents of the home page
- Navigate to the "Unidentified Persons" page by clicking the icon on the left side of the webpage
- Review the content of this page, including watching the video "NamUs behind the Scenes: How It Works, Why It Matters"
- Using the dropdown menu on the right side of the page, review the "State Case Breakdown" for your state
- Perform a search of the missing persons' records against your unidentified person by going to "Search" and entering the appropriate biological profile and last known alive data under the "Case Information" tab

How many records match this profile? (If none, perform a revised search by either omitting or changing your search parameters until the search provides results).

_____

Scroll through your search results. How well do they fit the data you entered?

_____

_____

How might you proceed if you do not locate a possible match?

_____

_____

_____

EXERCISE 14.3   Radiologic Comparison

Materials needed:
- Images provided in this exercise

Note to instructor: This exercise can be modified or supplemented with your own case-related radiologic images or those of reference material if available.

Case scenario: After you issued your report which included an estimated biological profile and postmortem interval, investigators have located a potential match to a local missing person who had a clinical cranial radiograph taken several years ago. Investigators brought you a copy of the radiograph which was taken in an anterior-posterior orientation. You simulated this position and took a postmortem radiograph for comparison.

Antemortem:

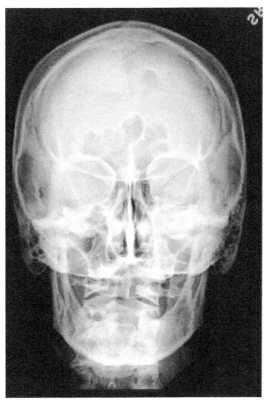

(Image courtesy of Gary Hatch.)

Postmortem:

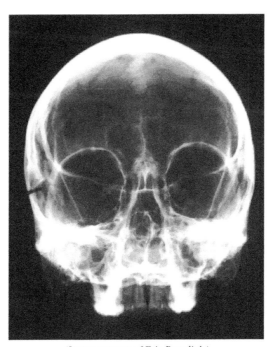

(Image courtesy of Eric Bartelink.)

How well did you approximate the antemortem orientation? Do you feel that these are comparable and suitable for comparison?

_____

_____

_____

What skeletal features are you able to identify in both images?

_____

_____

_____

Do you believe these radiographs are from the same person? Why or why not?

_____

_____

_____

EXERCISE 14.4   Radiologic Comparison

Materials needed:

• Images provided in this exercise

Note to instructor: This exercise can be modified or supplemented with your own case-related radiologic images if available.

Case scenario: Following receipt of your report on decomposed remains that you estimated to be from a 60+-year old African ancestry male, police believe they have narrowed possible matches to two individuals. During your examination, you took a CT scan as well as a posterior-anterior radiograph of the cranium.

A section of your postmortem CT scan:

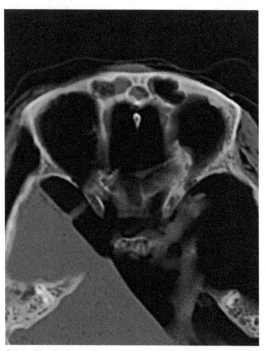

(Image courtesy of Gary Hatch; From Christensen, A.M., Passalacqua, N.V., Bartelink, E.J., 2014. Forensic Anthropology: Current Methods and Practice. Academic Press.)

Cranial radiograph:

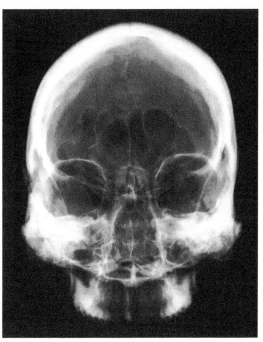

(Image courtesy of Eric Bartelink; From Christensen, A.M., Passalacqua, N.V., Bartelink, E.J., 2014.
Forensic Anthropology: Current Methods and Practice. Academic Press.)

One of the possible matches had an antemortem CT scan at a local hospital, the other had a cranial radiograph:
CT scan of Missing Person 1:

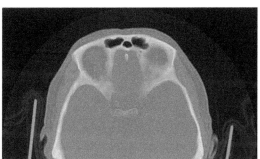

(Image courtesy of Gary Hatch; From Christensen, A.M., Passalacqua, N.V., Bartelink, E.J., 2014.
Forensic Anthropology: Current Methods and Practice. Academic Press.)

Radiograph of Missing Person 2:

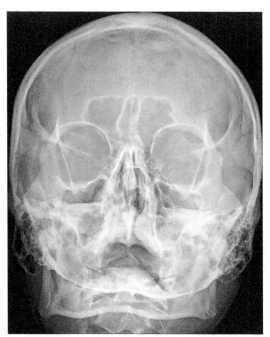

(Image courtesy of Gary Hatch; From Christensen, A.M., Passalacqua, N.V., Bartelink, E.J., 2014. Forensic Anthropology: Current Methods and Practice. Academic Press.)

Can either of these Missing Persons be the source of the remains? Why or why not?

_____
_____
_____

How confident are you in your inclusion or exclusion?

_____
_____
_____

EXERCISE 14.5 Quantitative Identification—Likelihood Ratio Calculation

Materials needed:
- Data and formulae provided in this exercise

Note to instructors: This exercise can be carried out individually or in small groups. For additional practice calculating LRs, you can also provide students a series of other (real or fictional) population frequencies.

Case scenario: You recently made an identification comparison of an antemortem hand radiograph of a missing Black female, and a postmortem radiographs you took of a skeleton that you believe to be a Black female, and concluded that the records could originate from the same person. The case is now going to trial, and the prosecutor would like to know the probability that the identification is correct. The primary matching feature on which you made your conclusion was a triquetral-lunate fusion, which has been documented to occur in 1.98% (or 1.98/100 or 0.0198) of Black females.

Instructions/Procedure:
- Using the equation provided below, determine the likelihood ratio based on the two records sharing a triquetral-lunate fusion

$$\frac{Probability\ of\ matching\ feature\ given\ the\ correct\ identification}{Probabiltiy\ of\ matching\ feature\ given\ incorrect\ identification}$$

Or

$$\frac{P(match)correct\ ID}{P(match)incorrect\ ID}$$

Or

$$\frac{1}{population\ frequency}$$

What likelihood ratio did you calculate?

_____

Would you consider this likelihood ratio to be convincing evidence of a correct identification? Why or why not?

_____
_____
_____

Why might it be important to use population-specific frequency data in quantitative identification comparisons?

_____
_____
_____

EXERCISE 14.6   Quantitative Identification—Odontosearch

Materials needed:
* Internet access
* Completed form provided in this exercise

Note to instructor: This exercise can also be supplemented with charted dental remains from skeletal reference material or forensic cases if available, or by having students complete Appendix X based on reference or skeletal material.

Case scenario: In comparing dental remains from an unidentified individual to known dental records, you notice that the dental coding charts appear the same. You wonder how common this dental pattern might be in the population and decide to check Odontosearch.

Instructions/Procedure:
* Visit the website of Odontosearch (www.odontosearch.com)
* Select "Click Here to Begin Using Odontosearch"
* Review the page and codes/instructions
* Select "Universal" tooth numbering, "Detail" coding, "All" Gender, "All" Race, and "14–90" Age
* Based on the completed Appendix X: OdondoSearch Dental Coding Form below, enter the Detail dental codes into the Odontosearch input fields. Select "Combined Data All Detailed," and click "Search."

Tooth	Code (Detail)	Code (Generic)	Tooth	Code (Detail)	Code (Generic)
1	X	X	17	X	X
2	O	R	18	O	R
3	OD	R	19	V	V
4	V	V	20	OM	R
5	OL	R	21	V	V
6	V	V	22	V	V
7	V	V	23	V	V
8	V	V	24	V	V
9	V	V	25	V	V
10	V	V	26	V	V
11	V	V	27	V	V
12	V	V	28	MODFL	R
13	OMD	R	29	X	X
14	V	V	30	O	R
15	O		31	O	R
16	X	X	32	X	X

How many patterns matched the pattern you entered? In what percent of the target population does this pattern occur?

_____
_____

Repeat the search using the Generic Codes. Describe and explain any differences in the result.

_____
_____
_____

Code the dentition from Exercise 9.7. In what percent of the target population does this pattern occur?

_____
_____

In what percent of the target population does your own dental pattern occur? (This will require you to chart and code your own dentition using Appendix X.)

_____
_____

EXERCISE 14.7   Quantitative Identification—RADid Resource

Materials needed:
• Internet access

Note to instructor: This exercise can also be supplemented with features/data from a forensic case if available.

Case scenario: In comparing antemortem and postmortem radiographs, you note that both records show a dorsal patellar defect and an *os inca*. You want to provide statistical evidence to support the likelihood that the records originated from the same person. You decide to check the RADid Resource for population frequency data for these traits and calculate the likelihood ratio for this comparison.

Instructions/Procedure:
• Visit the website of the RADid Resource (http://cfi.unm.edu/rad-id-index.html)
• Explore the available data by selecting body/tissue regions and specific anatomy

What is the population frequency of a dorsal patellar defect? (*Hint*: this trait occurs on the patella, which is in the lower extremity.)

_____

What sample population was used in the dorsal patellar defect study and what was the sample size?

_____

What is the likelihood ratio for a match between and antemortem and postmortem radiographs that both have a dorsal patellar defect (see the equation in Exercise 14.5)?

_____

What is the population frequency of an *os inca*? (*Hint*: this trait occurs on the occipital bone of the cranium.)

_____

What is the likelihood ratio for a match between antemortem and postmortem radiographs that both have a dorsal patellar defect AND an *os inca*?

_____

Discuss some of the challenges and limitations of using quantitative radiologic identification approaches in a given forensic case.

_____
_____
_____

EXERCISE 14.8   Facial Approximation

Materials needed:
• Skull replica
• Modeling clay
• Sculpting tools
• Tissue depth markers (e.g., erasers, drink stirrers)

- Ruler
- Adhesive
- Blade or cutting tool
- Access to the website and/or book: Ask a Forensic Artist (Bailey, 2014)

Note to instructor: If possible, use a replica skull for which you have a photograph of the individual while alive (so that students can compare their results to the individual's actual appearance). Note that this exercise will be very time-consuming and probably require multiple class periods and/or take-home work. While many of the instructions/guidance can be found at the Ask a Forensic Artist website, it would be helpful to have a couple of copies of the book as well (available from Amazon.com for ~$10).

Case scenario: Despite extensive efforts (including checks of missing persons records and NamUs), police have been unable to identify skeletal remains found in an abandoned warehouse. You previously examined the remains and estimated a biological profile, but no missing persons matching the profile had been reported. A facial approximation has been requested, which authorities would like to use at a press conference to see if any viewers recognize the approximation as belonging to someone they know.

Instructions/Procedure:

- Using a replica skull (and associated biological profile), and following the guidance and data provided by Bailey (2014), sculpt a facial approximation using modeling clay
- Using the tissue depth guide, cut markers to the appropriate lengths and affix them to the skull using adhesive
- Sculpt and position eyes within the orbits
- Apply clay of appropriate depth and sculpt facial features

When you first receive a real skull for facial approximation how should you proceed?

_____

_____

What did you find to be most challenging about creating the facial approximation?

_____

_____

_____

_____

Chapter 15

Other Issues in Modern Forensic Anthropology and Final Case Study

OBJECTIVES

In addition to the primary areas discussed in the previous chapters, knowledge of additional topics related to evidence, documentation, research methods, and other areas is often essential to forensic anthropology practitioners. In this chapter, you will review the role of forensic anthropology within broader contexts including the legal system, the media, research, and evidence analysis. This chapter also includes a final comprehensive exercise.

FORENSIC ANTHROPOLOGY IN THE MEDIA

Many forensic disciplines, including forensic anthropology, have enjoyed significant media attention in recent years including documentaries, TV dramas, and news stories. While they have had a positive impact on educating the public to some degree about the role of forensic anthropology in crimes and legal cases, there is also significant artistic license taken in the interest of entertainment. As a result, many in the public have a narrow and often inaccurate knowledge of the science behind forensic investigations. For example, TV crimes are often solved quickly, using flashy, fictitious, or misrepresented techniques and technologies.

The field of forensic anthropology specifically was launched into the public spotlight with the FOX TV series *Bones* which premiered in 2005. Featuring Dr. Temperance Brennan as a forensic anthropologist at the fictitious "Jeffersonian Institute," the show is based on the fictional writings of board certified forensic anthropologist Dr. Kathleen Reichs. As in many other crime shows, Dr. Brennan solves bone-related mysteries in short order (often while still on scene) with the help of her FBI agent sidekick (and later, her husband). Her high-tech toys are largely science-fiction and are not found even in the most sophisticated forensic anthropology laboratories in existence today. While most students of forensic science and forensic anthropology can separate the real science from the drama, this is likely much more challenging for the nonscientific public and this should be kept in mind when interacting with the media and the public in situations such as court testimony.

From such popular interest in fictional programming, many in the general public have developed unrealistic perceptions regarding how forensic science functions and what results can be expected. This is commonly referred to as *The CSI Effect* and is believed to cause many jurors to expect more forensic evidence in trials. Moreover, criminals may be adjusting their behavior based on popular crime TV shows in order to destroy evidence of their association to the crime. This can pose challenges to forensic anthropologists in terms of both the quantity and quality of evidence they receive, as well as when testifying in court.

CASE DOCUMENTATION AND REPORT WRITING

The culmination of a forensic anthropological analysis is typically a final written report. This report, however, does not represent the only form of documentation in a case and should be based on analytical notes and other primary forms of documentation that are maintained throughout the analysis. Case documentation generally includes any materials that formed the basis for analysis or analytical conclusions that are contained in the report. This may include documentation of tests, such as notes (laboratory or field notes), inventories, observations, diagrams, and charts, as well as photographs, radiographs, computer print-outs (such as Fordisc results), and antemortem records (such as medical or dental records used in a comparison). Documentation/notes should include all steps of an analysis and any modification of the remains that occurred while they were in the analyst's custody. They should contain sufficient detail and information to facilitate traceability and replication of the work and ensure transparency of the scientific process. Analytical notes should be recorded at

A Laboratory Manual for Forensic Anthropology. https://doi.org/10.1016/B978-0-12-812201-3.00015-3

the time they are made, and each page of case documentation/notes should include the case number, the date(s) that the observations were recorded, and the signature or initials of the anthropologist. Notes can be structured (such as the examples provided in Appendix Y: Case Notes Forms) or can be more free-form. Especially for documentation made in the field, a photograph log is often maintained (see Appendix J: Photograph Log) in addition to field notes and scene maps (Appendix I: Scene Mapping and Documentation).

While it is recognized that forensic anthropologists may have varying needs and constraints based on the laboratory in which they work, as well as different writing and reporting styles, an anthropological report should always contain certain basic components such as the name and address of the laboratory where the work was performed, a case identification number, and the name and signature of the person who performed the work. The report should contain the examination results in an organized and clearly stated fashion, keeping the audience (often law enforcement) in mind. Reports should also contain information regarding the strength of conclusions or possible limitations where applicable. For example, if a significance level or a confidence interval can be calculated (such as with Fordisc results or regression methods for stature estimation), these should be included in the report. If a comparison is made (such as between an antemortem and postmortem record), the strength of the agreement between the two records should also be communicated in the report. In some cases, this may be quantitative, while in other cases it may be more qualitative. If appropriate, the report should also note whether results were inconclusive. Examples of case reports can be found in Appendix AA.

Chain of custody refers to the documentation of the physical (or sometimes electronic) transfer of evidence from one individual/institution to another and from the time it is determined to be evidence until its final disposition. This documentation verifies who had custody/control over the evidence at any given time and can be very important in legal proceedings. An example of a chain of custody form is shown in Appendix Z: Chain of Custody Form.

FORENSIC ANTHROPOLOGY IN THE LEGAL SYSTEM

In many cases, there may be no criminal investigation at all because no crime is suspected to have been committed. In these instances, the forensic anthropologist may simply be trying to assist in the identification process, and there may be no involvement beyond writing the report. In other cases, however, the results of a forensic anthropological examination may have bearing on whether a suspect is determined to be innocent or guilty of a crime. The results of a forensic anthropological examination may facilitate legal determinations such as identity and cause and manner of death, or have relevance in terrorist, conflict, or humanitarian rights investigations. In these cases, it is much more likely that the anthropologist will receive a subpoena to testify in a trial in addition to issuing his or her report. Expert witness testimony is an important way in which forensic anthropologists' knowledge is utilized in the legal system, and testifying as an expert witness has become an important role of the forensic anthropologist.

Testifying is relatively rare for most forensic anthropologists, particularly those who are primarily employed by higher learning institutions and only occasionally consult on cases. The infrequency of testifying is also due in part to the fact that many forensic anthropological reports consist of biological profiles that provide lead information for investigators, and such information is rarely if ever the subject of a trial. Most courtroom testimony by forensic anthropologists focuses on trauma, recovery and scene investigation, and estimation of the postmortem interval (Murray and Anderson, 2007). Court testimony will be based on the findings and wording used in the final forensic anthropology report. Written reports should therefore clearly communicate the methods used, the conclusions reached, and the significance and limitations of those conclusions. Speculation or claims which cannot be justified by the evidence should be avoided.

Those testifying in court should also be aware of evidence admissibility and other laws and rulings relevant to the jurisdiction in which they are testifying. Evidence admissibility standards, for example, vary depending on whether the trial is in federal or state court (and which state). The first ruling regarding the admissibility of scientific evidence was issued in Frye v. United States (1923). In this case, the admissibility of the results of a "lie detector" test was challenged, and the Court's opinion stated that:

> [w]hile courts will go a long way in admitting expert testimony deduced from a well-recognized scientific principle or discovery, the thing from which the deduction is made must be sufficiently established to have gained general acceptance in the particular field in which it belongs.

Frye v. United States (1923)

This general acceptance test, known as the "*Frye* Rule," became the standard for determining the admissibility of scientific evidence in the majority of courts. Over time, however, many courts and legal commentators began to modify or ignore the *Frye* standard. One of the primary concerns was that new scientific techniques, though valid, often failed the *Frye* test.

TABLE 15.1 The *Daubert* Guidelines

1. Has the technique been tested using the scientific method?

2. Has the technique been subjected to peer review, preferably in the form of publication in peer-reviewed literature?

3. What are the known or potential error rates of the technique?

4. Are there applicable professional standards for the technique?

5. Is the technique generally accepted within the relevant scientific community?

In 1975, Congress enacted the first modern and uniform set of evidentiary rules for the trial of civil and criminal cases in US federal courts: *The Federal Rules of Evidence* (1975; 2000). *Rule 702* specifically addressed expert witness testimony, stating that:

If scientific, technical or other specialized knowledge will assist the trier of fact to understand the evidence or to determine a fact in issue, a witness qualified as an expert by knowledge, skill, experience, training or education may testify thereto in the form of an opinion or otherwise.

Fed. R. Evid. 702 (1975)

The *Federal Rules of Evidence*, however, did not eliminate the confusion surrounding the admissibility of scientific evidence but rather led to a mixed use of *Frye*, the *Federal Rules of Evidence*, or some hybrid of the two. Since then, admissibility standards for expert testimony have been established and clarified through several US Supreme Court decisions intended to ensure the reliability and relevance of scientific and technical testimony admitted as evidence in federal courts.

In the case of Daubert v. Merrell Dow Pharmaceuticals, Inc. (1993), the Supreme Court concluded that the *Federal Rules of Evidence* supersede *Frye* and should thus govern admissibility. The Court also interpreted the language of *Rule 702* to set forth the standards of *reliability* and *relevance* for the admissibility of scientific evidence. The reliability standard requires that "scientific knowledge" be grounded in the methods and procedures of science and more than subjective belief or speculation. The relevance standard requires that the information facilitate the fact-finder in reaching a conclusion in the case (i.e., that there is a valid scientific connection to the pertinent inquiry). Furthermore, to assist trial judges, the Court identified several factors intended to assist in determining whether scientific evidence is reliable. These factors are often referred to as the "*Daubert* guidelines" (see Table 15.1).

In addition to providing the guidelines, the decision also instructed judges to be the "gatekeepers" in keeping "junk science" (i.e., nonscientific results, opinion, or speculations) out of the courtroom. It further indicated that judges should be flexible in conducting their inquiry and focus on the principles and the methods used and not the conclusions that they generate. Given this focus on the methods themselves, a separate proceeding, called a "*Daubert* hearing" or "admissibility hearing," is sometimes held before or during the trial in which the expert has been asked to testify.

In 2000, *Federal Rule 702* was amended to include the issues of reliability and relevance:

If scientific, technical or other specialized knowledge will assist the trier of fact to understand the evidence or to determine a fact in issue, a witness qualified as an expert by knowledge, skill, experience, training or education may testify thereto in the form of an opinion or otherwise, if (1) the testimony is based upon sufficient facts or data, (2) the test is the product of reliable principles and methods, and (3) the witness has applied the principles and methods reliably to the facts of the case.

Federal Rules of Evidence (1975; 2000).

EXERCISE 15.1   Rules of Evidence

Materials needed:
- Internet access

Note to instructors: This exercise can be carried out individually or in small groups. If you have ever testified as an expert witness, discuss your experience with students.

Case scenario: You have recently been subpoenaed to testify for the first time. In order to be as prepared as possible, you decide to become familiar with the rules of evidence for the state in which you will testify.

Instructions/Procedure:
- Using an Internet search, locate the laws that govern scientific evidence, expert witness testimony, and evidence admissibility in your state.

For scientific evidence admissibility, does your state follow guidelines similar to *Frye* or *Daubert* or some combination?

_____
_____
_____

Were there any other laws regarding evidence admissibility or expert witness testimony with which you were not previously familiar?

_____
_____
_____

EXERCISE 15.2   Photodocumentation

Materials needed:
- Camera
- Scale
- Evidence
- Appendix J: Photograph Log

Note to instructors: This exercise could also be carried out individually or in small groups. A recovery scene can be prepared in advance and the exercise can be performed in an outdoor setting using real or replica human remains but can also be carried out in a classroom setting using other items as evidentiary material.

Case scenario: When skeletal remains were found in a wooded area, your forensic anthropology team was requested to assist in the search, documentation, and recovery of the remains. You have been designated as the team photographer.

Instructions/Procedure:
- Work in teams of two, with one person taking the photographs and one person maintaining the photo log. Consider switching roles half way through the exercise
- Photograph the overall scene from multiple views and distances
- Photograph each item of evidence from mid-range and close-up, with scale
- Document your photographs on Appendix J

Which role was more challenging—photographer or photo logger?

_____
_____
_____

Why is it important to maintain a photo log at a recovery scene? What legal challenges could result from an improperly or poorly maintained photo log?

_____
_____
_____

EXERCISE 15.3   Chain of Custody

Materials needed:
- Appendix Z: Chain of Custody Form
- Evidence
- Role-players (Police Officer, Evidence Custodian, Examiner/Analyst, etc.)

Note to instructors: Depending on class size, this exercise could also be carried out as a class or in small groups. Real or replica human or nonhuman remains can be used, but any (preferably) packaged item can serve as evidence for this exercise.

Case scenario: Skeletal evidence is being submitted to your laboratory for analysis, and the chain of custody needs to be documented.

Instructions/Procedure:
- Pass the evidentiary items from one student/role-player to another
- Document the transfer of evidence on Appendix Z from the time the Police Officer delivers the evidence to the laboratory, until the evidence is returned to the Officer at the completion of examinations

Why is documentation of chain of custody important? What issues can you foresee if the chain of custody is not properly documented?

_____
_____
_____

EXERCISE 15.4   Mock Court Exercise

Materials needed:
- Forensic anthropology case report
- Classroom set up to mimic a courtroom (a place in the front of the room for the judge and witness, a place to the side for a jury, tables for prosecution and defense team)
- Role-players (e.g., expert witness, prosecuting attorney, defense attorney, defendant, judge, jurors, bailiff, courtroom audience)

Note to instructors: This exercise can be carried out as a class exercise, with students playing different roles. For smaller classes, consider repeating the exercise with each student having an opportunity to be the expert witness. Create (or have the students create) multiple mock case reports that involve a wide variety of conclusions (e.g., human vs. nonhuman, trauma analysis, PMI estimation, personal identification, etc.) and a variety of case scenarios (e.g., homicide, identification, accident, etc.). Alternatively, some forensic anthropology testimonies from real cases are available online and may be viewed and discussed rather than performed by students. If you have ever testified as an expert witness, describe and discuss the experience with your students.

Case scenario: You have been subpoenaed to testify in court about a case in which you analyzed skeletal remains. The case involves a defendant who is accused of homicide. The victim was positively identified using DNA analysis. Your results indicate that there was perimortem blunt trauma to the cranium. (Alternatively, modify scenario to fit the case report created/used.)

Instructions/Procedure:
- Draft a mock report based on the scenario above
- Carry out a mock trial based on this case
- Be sure to follow consistent rules for scientific evidence admissibility

What did you find most challenging about being an expert witness? Did you feel prepared? If not, what would you do prior to your next testimony to be more prepared? What do you think forensic anthropologists could/should do prior to a testimony?

_____
_____
_____

What did you like or dislike about participating in other roles (i.e., prosecuting attorney, defense attorney, judge, juror)?

_____
_____
_____

Have you ever been involved in a trial (e.g., as a jury member or a witness)? If so, consider sharing your experience with classmates. Was scientific testimony involved? What role did it play in the case?

_____
_____
_____

EXERCISE 15.5 Forensic Anthropology in the Media

Materials needed:
- Internet access
- Audio/visual equipment or other visual aids

Note to instructors: This exercise could also be carried out as a written assignment or group project. This exercise is an opportunity to assess students on forensic anthropological knowledge as well as critical thinking and presentation skills. Remind students that presentation skills are important for those considering careers in forensic anthropology or forensic science.

Case scenario: You are aware that forensic anthropology is often portrayed in popular media. Also aware that such portrayals are typically fictional and may exaggerate or misrepresent the science, you decide to review several episodes of TV shows portraying forensic anthropology to see how accurate these portrayals actually are.

Instructions/Procedure:
- Select an episode of a TV show portraying the use of forensic anthropology, such as *Bones* and *CSI*
- While watching the episode, consider and make notes on the questions below
- Give a presentation to your classmates summarizing the episode and your assessment

Were there any procedures that appeared to be inaccurately portrayed or performed? If so, describe them and discuss how these procedures *should* be performed.

_____
_____
_____

Were there any procedures that that appeared to be accurately portrayed or performed? If so, describe them.

_____
_____
_____

Were there any procedures portrayed with which you were not familiar from this course? If so, describe them and see what you can learn about them from an Internet and/or library search.

_____
_____
_____

What do you think are some advantages of popular TV shows about forensic anthropology? Disadvantages?

_____
_____
_____

EXERCISE 15.6 Final Case Exercise

Materials needed:
- Images provided in this exercise
- Other materials to be determined by students

Note to instructors: This exercise is intended to promote synthesis of information presented in the preceding chapters, encouraging the combination of various ideas and examination methods without prompting students to consider a particular approach or analysis. It is suggested that all equipment, instruments, and other resources be made available to students for this exercise. Images are provided here as one example but can be supplemented or replaced with material from a forensic case or reference collection if available. A recovery scene can also be prepared in advance of the exercise if desired.

Case scenario: Law enforcement officials have contacted you to assist in the search, recovery, and analysis of what appear to be multiple skeletal remains discovered in a wooded area. Several months ago, a family of four as well as their pet dog departed for a camping trip and never returned, and authorities believe these could be the family's remains. Two other missing persons have also been reported in the area.

Instructions/Procedure:
- Record/document any relevant observations or information on appropriate analytical note forms
- If there are any examinations/methods you would perform/use but are not possible because of the nature of this exercise (photograph-based) or because the appropriate instruments/equipment are not available to you, note this and describe what you *would* do in your case documentation if you had access to the remains and unlimited resources
- Prepare a written forensic anthropological report based on the missing persons data, and recovery and analysis scenarios provided below

Missing person information:

Missing Person 1 (father missing from camping trip)

- White Male, 56 years old, height of 5′8″
- Suffered several broken right ribs in a fall 2 years ago
- Had a cranial radiograph taken 8 years ago in association with a sinus infection
    - Antemortem radiograph from Missing Person 1:

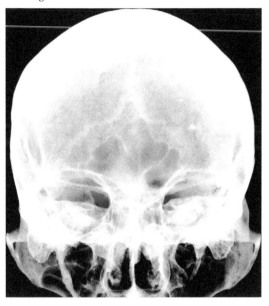

Missing Person 2 (mother missing from camping trip)

- Chinese Female, 42 years old, height of 5′4″
- Broken collar bone at the age of 20, but medical records are in China and could not be located.

Missing Person 3 (child missing from camping trip)

- Male, 3 years old
- Individual was taking medication for anemia

Missing Person 4 (child missing from camping trip)

- Female, 9 months old
- No known anomalies or antemortem medical records

Missing Dog 1 (dog missing from camping trip)

- Golden retriever, female, 2 years old, 65 pounds

Missing Person 5

- Black Male, 16 years old, height of 5′8″
- Reportedly had a broken right humerus at the age of four, no medical records available
- Had a cranial radiograph taken at the age of 15 following a sports-related head injury
    - Antemortem radiograph from Missing Person 5:

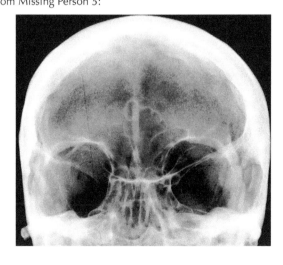

Missing Person 6:
- Hispanic Female, 85 years old, height of 5′3″
- Individual had no reported antemortem trauma but did suffer from Parkinson's

Search/Recovery:

The recovery scene is a wooded area, with a moderate density of deciduous trees and ground cover that includes soil and floral debris (e.g., leaves, sticks, etc.). The terrain is relatively flat (i.e., no large hills/valleys or changes in elevation) and is easy to navigate on foot. The weather is mild with temperatures in the 60s and no forecasted precipitation. You have an available team of six law enforcement personnel and two additional forensic anthropologists.

Skeleton 1 was located first, as pictured below:

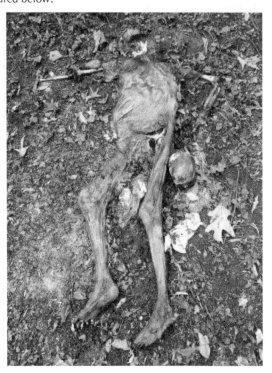

Describe how you would conduct your search of this scene:

_____
_____
_____

In what way(s) would you document the scene?

_____
_____
_____

What mapping method would you use and why? (If a mock scene is used, document the scene using the mapping method selected.)

_____
_____
_____

If remains (or suspected remains) are found, how would you document and recover them?

_____
_____
_____

Analysis:

The search yielded what appear to be three distinct assemblages (sets) of skeletal remains as well as a collection of questioned material that investigators believe may contain skeletal remains. All evidence was collected, packaged, and transported to your laboratory for analysis. Skeleton 1 was processed using warm water maceration. Various photographs for each skeleton and other materials are provided below.

Skeleton 1:

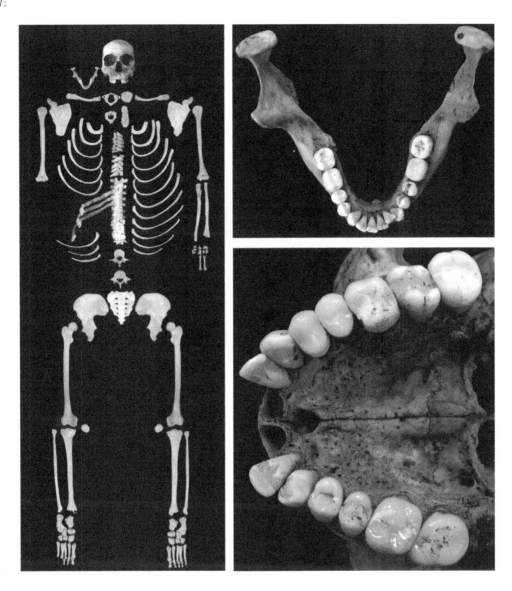

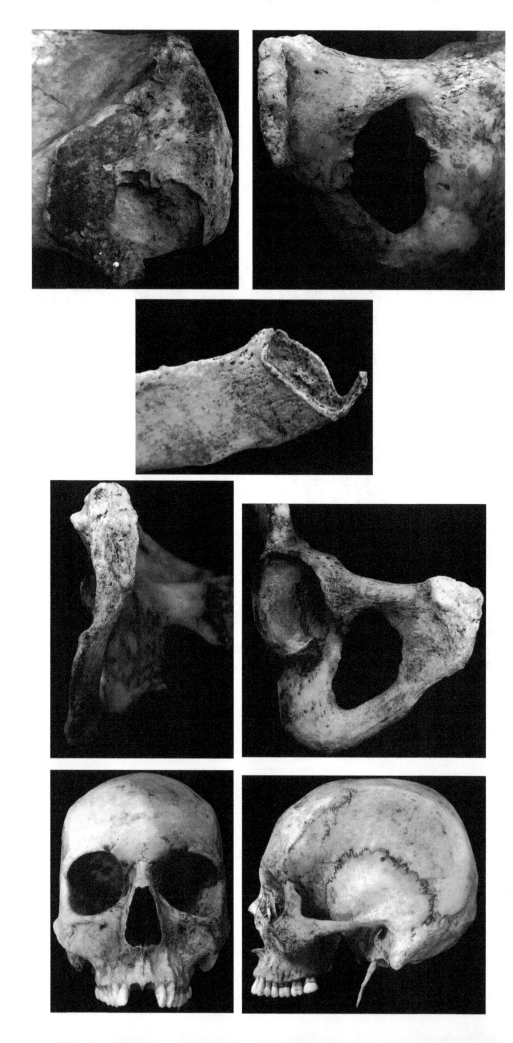

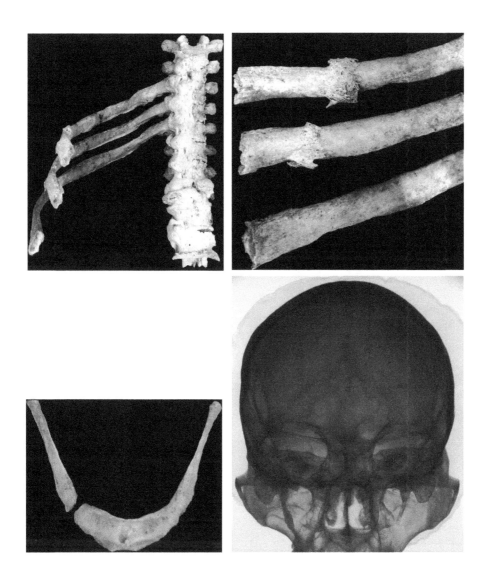

------------------------------ CRANIAL MEASUREMENTS ------------------------------

		left	right
1. MAXIMUM CRANIAL LENGTH (g-op):	177		
2. NASIO-OCCIPITAL LENGTH (n-op):	176		
3. MAXIMUM CRANIAL BREADTH (eu-eu)	138		
4. BIZYGOMATIC BREADTH (zy-zy):	125		
5. BASION-BREGMA HEIGHT (ba-b):	139		
6. CRANIAL BASE LENGTH (ba-n):	105		
7. BASION-PROSTHION LENGTH (ba-pr):	96		
8. MAXILLO-ALVEOLAR BREADTH (ecm-ecm):	62		
9. MAXILLO-ALVEOLAR LENGTH (pr-alv):	55		
10. BIAURICULAR BREADTH (ra-ra):	116		
11. NASION-PROSTHION HEIGHT (n-pr):	72		
12. MINIMUM FRONTAL BREADTH (ft-ft):	98		
13. UPPER FACIAL BREADTH (fmt-fmt):	107		
14. NASAL HEIGHT:	49		
15. NASAL BREADTH:		22	
16. ORBITAL BREADTH (d-ec):		42	41
17. ORBITAL HEIGHT:		35	35
18. BIORBITAL BREADTH (ec-ec):		97	
19. INTERORBITAL BREADTH (d-d):		23	
20. FRONTAL CHORD (n-b):		115	
21. PARIETAL CHORD (b-l):		106	
22. OCCIPITAL CHORD (l-o):		99	
23. FORAMEN MAGNUM LENGTH:		33	
24. FORAMEN MAGNUM BR.:		29	
25. MASTOID HEIGHT (po-ms):		30	
26. BIASTERIONIC BR. (ast-ast):		114	
27. ZYGOMAXILLARY BR. (zym-zym):		90	
28. ZYGOORBITALE BR. (zo-zo):		54	

------------------------------ MANDIBULAR MEASUREMENTS ------------------------------

	left	right		left	right
29. CHIN. HEIGHT (id-gn):		34	34. MIN. RAMUS HEIGHT:	_____	_____
30. MANDIBULAR BODY HEIGHT:	30	29	35. *MAX. RAMUS HEIGHT:		_____
31. MANDIBULAR BODY BREADTH:	11	12	36. *MAND. LENGTH:		_____
32. BIGONIAL BREADTH (go-go):		94	37. *MAND. ANGLE:		_____
33. BICONDYLAR BR. (cdl-cdl):		108	*Record only if mandibulometer is used		

------------------------------ POSTCRANIAL MEASUREMENTS ------------------------------

	left	right		left	right
CLAVICLE:			INNOMINATE:		
38. MAXIMUM LENGTH:	140	140	64. MAXIMUM HEIGHT:	215	216
39. MAX. MIDSHAFT DIAM:	13	13	65. MAX. ILIAC BREADTH:	155	154
40. MIN. MIDSHAFT DIAM:	9	9	66. MIN. ILIAC BREADTH:	62	62
			67. MAX. PUBIS LENGTH:	_____	_____
SCAPULA:			68. MIN. PUBIS LENGTH:	_____	_____
41. HEIGHT:	144	145	69. ISCHIAL LENGTH:	_____	_____
42. BREADTH:	101	101	70. MIN. ISCHIAL LENGTH:	_____	_____
43. GLENOID CAVITY BREADTH:	27	28	71. MAX. ISCHIOPUB RAM L.:	_____	_____
44. GLENOID CAVITY HEIGHT:	38	39	72. ASIS – SYMPHYSION:	_____	_____
			73. MAX. PSIS – SYMPHYSION:	_____	_____
HUMERUS:			74. MIN. APEX – SYMPHYSION:	_____	_____
45. MAXIMUM LENGTH:	319	319			
46. EPICONDYLAR BREADTH:	57	56	FEMUR:		
47. MAX. VERT. HEAD DIAM.:	44	45	75. MAXIMUM LENGTH:	453	453
48. MAX. MIDSHAFT DIAM.:	21	21	76. BICONDYLAR LENGTH:	451	452
49. MIN. MIDSHAFT DIAM.:	17	17	77. EPICONDYLAR BREADTH:	80	81
			78. MAX. HEAD DIAMETER:	43	43
RADIUS:			79. TRANS. SUBTROCH DIAM:	30	30
50. MAXIMUM LENGTH:	240	_____	80. A-P SUBTROCH DIAM:	28	28
51. MAX. MIDSHAFT DIAM.:	15	_____	81. MAX. MIDSHAFT DIAM.	28	28
52. MIN. MIDSHAFT DIAM.:	11	_____	82. MIN. MIDSHAFT DIAM.	25	25
53. MAX. HEAD DIAMETER:	21	_____	83. MIDSHAFT CIRCUM.	84	84
			84. MAX AP L. LAT. CONDYLE:	63	63
ULNA:			85. MAX AP L. MED. CONDYLE:	62	62
54. MAXIMUM LENGTH:	255	_____			
55. MAX. MIDSHAFT DIAM.:	18	_____	TIBIA:		
56. MIN. MIDSHAFT DIAM.:	12	_____	86. CONDYLO-MALLEOLAR L.:	370	369
57. PHYSIOLOGICAL LENGTH:	227	_____	87. MAX. PROX. EPIP. BR.:	71	70
58. MIN. CIRCUMFERENCE:	33	_____	88. DISTAL EPIP. BREADTH:	51	51
59. OLECRANON BREADTH:	25	_____	89. MAX. MIDSHAFT DIAM.:	28	28
			90. MIN. MIDSHAFT DIAM.:	22	22
SACRUM:			91. MIDSHAFT CIRCUM.:	78	77
60. ANTERIOR HEIGHT:	139 (6 segments)				
61. ANTERIOR BREADTH:	114		FIBULA:		
62. TRANSVERSE DIAM. S1:	48		92. MAXIMUM LENGTH:	364	364
63. A-P DIAMETER S1:	35		93. MAX. MIDSHAFT DIAM.:	17	18
			CALCANEUS:		
			94. MAXIMUM LENGTH:	80	80
			95. MIDDLE BREADTH:	38	38

Skeleton 2:

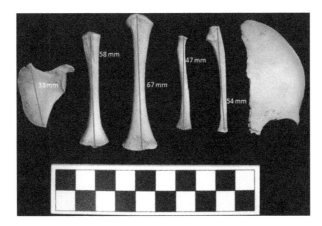

Skeleton 3:

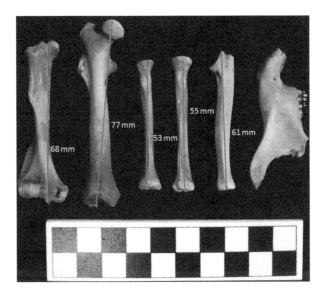

Questioned material:

Provide as much information about the sets of remains and other collected evidence as possible.

Outline how you will conduct your examination. Consider chain of custody, evidence preservation, documentation, and analytical methods you might use, and document/record observations on appropriate analytical notes forms. Think about what types of questions you will be able to address about the remains, and what law enforcement and medicolegal authorities may want to know for their investigations. Prepare analytical notes and a final report based on your examination, considering the context in which the remains were found, and to whom the police think the remains may belong.

How would you document each set of skeletal remains? The questioned material?

_____
_____
_____

What type(s) of information can be estimated/determined from each set of remains/material? Using which methods or techniques?

_____
_____
_____

How would you deal with the questioned material? What methods would you use to determine if any of the material is bone? What if some of the bone is human?

_____
_____
_____

Could any of the remains or material belong to the missing family members? Why or why not?

_____
_____
_____

Are there any other forensic examinations that could/should be performed after your anthropological analysis?

_____
_____
_____

Appendices

APPENDIX A: SKELETAL SIDING AND ORIENTATION GUIDE

General Siding and Orientation Information

- Holding (or imagining) the bone or fragment in anatomical position in relation to your own skeleton is often helpful.
- Siding is often straightforward when bones are complete and becomes more challenging when bones are fragmentary. Bone fragments with few or no features present are often more challenging to side than fragments with more features.
- The use of comparative specimens (such as real or replica human bones of known side) can be helpful, especially for fragments.
- More in-depth siding techniques can be found in human osteology texts such as White et al. (2011) and Bass (2004), including greater siding detail for specialized bones (such as different ribs and vertebrae) as well as bone portions/ fragments.
- For most bones, anatomical siding is presented; for carpals, metacarpals, tarsals, and metatarsals, positional siding is presented.
- There are several bones such as the vomer, inferior nasal conchae, pisiform, and phalanges which are generally considered impractical to side.
- The following guide provides *some* helpful hints for determining the side (left or right) of paired bones, or orientation (in some cases) for unpaired bones. Many other features that are not listed here may also be used to side bones and bone fragments.

Siding and Orienting Bones of the Skull and Axial Skeleton

Frontal	• The coronal suture is posterior and courses anteromedially • The frontal sinus is anterior • The temporal lines are ectocranial and weaken posteriorly
Parietal	• The squamosal suture is inferior and lateral • The lambdoidal suture is posterior and is more complex than the coronal suture which is anterior • The sigmoid sulcus crosses the mastoid angle which is oriented posterior laterally • The meningeal grooves are endocranial, and generally course anteroinferiorly to posterosuperiorly
Temporal	• The mastoid process points inferiorly and angles anteriorly • The squamosal suture is superior • The zygomatic process extends anteriorly
Occipital	• The foramen magnum is inferior and the squama is posterior • The edge of the foramen magnum is medial somewhat posterior to the centers of the condylar bodies
Maxilla	• The alveolar process is inferior and the frontal process is superior • The incisors (or their sockets in the alveolus) are medial and anterior, and the molars (or their sockets in the alveolus) are lateral and posterior • The medial surface of the frontal process (which also comprises the nasal aperture) has vascular markings
Palatine	• The superior surface is smooth and the inferior surface is rough • The posterior edge is nonarticular • The palatine foramina are posterolateral
Ethmoid	• The crist galli and perpendicular plate are on the midline
Lacrimal	• The lacrimal crest is oriented vertically, and the lacrimal groove is anterior to the crest

Siding and Orienting Bones of the Skull and Axial Skeleton—cont'd

Nasal	• The inferior ends are nonarticular • The articulation with the frontal bone is superior, and with the other nasal bone is medial
Zygomatic	• The masseteric origin is inferior, and the frontal process is superior • The orbital rim is blunt and oriented medially
Sphenoid	• The pterygoid fossa faces posteriorly, and the inferior pterygoid plates are nonarticular • The orbital surfaces of the greater wing face anteriorly • The base of the endocranial surface is marked by numerous foramina
Mandible	• The incisors (or their sockets in the alveolus) are medial and anterior, and the molars (or their sockets in the alveolus) are lateral and posterior • The ramus is posterior, with greatest relief on the medial surface
Hyoid	• The superior surface bears the lesser horns • The widest part of the greater horn is anterior and thins as it extends posteriorly
Sternum	• The anterior surface is rougher and more convex than the posterior surface
Vertebrae (generally)	• The spinous process is posterior • The superior articular facets face posteriorly, and the inferior facets face anteriorly • The inferior dimensions of the body are greater than its superior dimension
Sacrum	• The anterior surface is smooth and concave • The size of the sacral vertebrae decrease inferiorly • The auricular surface is lateral
Coccyx	• The size of the vertebral elements decrease inferiorly • The cornua project posteriorly
Ribs (generally)	• The head is toward the midline, and the tubercle is inferior • The costal groove is inferior

(Modified from White, T.D., Black, M.T., Folkens, P.A., 2011. Human Osteology, third ed. Academic Press, San Diego, CA.)

Siding and Orienting Teeth

	Description	Upper vs. Lower	Left vs. Right
Incisor	• Flat and blade-like	• Upper are broad mesiodistally; lower are narrow • Upper have more lingual relief; lower have less • Upper have more circular root cross sections; lower are more mesiodistally compressed	• Distal occlusal corner more rounded than mesial • Root angles distally
Canine	• Conical and tusk-like	• Upper crowns broad relative to height; lower are narrow • Upper have lingual relief; lower have less • Upper have lingual apical wear; lower have labial wear	• Mesial occlusal edge usually shorter than the distal • Root angles distally • Distal root surface more deeply grooved than the mesial
Premolar	• Round crowns usually have two cusps • Usually single-rooted	• Upper crowns have two cusps of nearly equal size; lower have large buccal cusp and smaller lingual • Upper have strong mesiodistal occlusal grooves; lower have weak grooves	• Lingual cusp centered mesially • Root angles distally
Molar	• Large, square, more cusps than other teeth • Usually multiple roots	• Upper usually have 3–4 major cusps; lower usually have 4–5 major cusps • Upper crown outline is rhombus shaped; lower is square, rectangular, or oblong • Upper cusps are asymmetric relative to mesiodistal axis; lower are symmetric about the midline • Upper usually have three variably fused roots; lower usually have 2 or 3 roots	• Upper: buccal cusps more prominent; lower: lingual cusps more prominent • Upper: largest root often compressed buccolingually, while two smaller roots are rounder; lower: two major roots are mesiodistally compressed • Roots angle distally

(Modified from White, T.D., Black, M.T., Folkens, P.A., 2011. Human Osteology, third ed. Academic Press, San Diego, CA.)

Siding and Orienting Bones of the Appendicular Skeleton

Clavicle	• The medial end is round, and the lateral end flattened • The bone curves anteriorly from the medial end, curves posteriorly around midshaft, and then curves toward the anterior at the lateral end • The bone is more rough/irregular on the inferior surface
Scapula	• The glenoid is lateral, and the spine is posterior
Humerus	• The head is medial, and capitulum is lateral • The olecranon fossa is posterior • The intertubercular groove is anterior
Radius	• The ulnar notch, radial tuberosity, and interosseous crest are medial • The dorsal tubercles are posterior • The styloid process is lateral
Ulna	• The olecranon process is proximal and posterior • The radial notch and interosseous crest are lateral
Scaphoid	• With the concave facet toward you and the tubercle up, the tubercle leans toward the side the bone is from
Lunate	• With the flat side on the table and the most concave facet toward you, the remaining facets rise up and toward the side the bone is from
Triquetral	• With the common edge of the two largest facets facing toward you and vertical and the third facet up, the third facet points toward the side the bone is from
Trapezium	• With the tubercle up and the concave facets facing you, the groove near the tubercle is on the side the bone is from
Trapezoid	• With the bottom of the "boot" down and the v-shaped space between the articular facets toward you, the toe of the boot points to the side the bone is from
Capitate	• With the head up and the long narrow articulation facing you, this articulation is on the side the bone is from
Hamate	• With the flat side down and the hook and two adjacent facts away from you, the hook leans toward the side the bone is from
First metacarpal	• From the base with the dorsal side up, the smaller of the portions of the articular surface is on the side the bone is from
Second metacarpal	• From the base with the dorsal side up, the wedge-shaped projection is on the side the bone is from
Third metacarpal	• From the base with the dorsal side up, the styloid process is on the opposite side the bone is from
Fourth metacarpal	• From the base with the dorsal side up, the right-angle articular edge is on the side the bone is from
Fifth metacarpal	• From the base with the dorsal side up, the nonarticular side of the base is the side the bone is from
Innominate	• The pubis is anterior • The iliac crest is superior • The acetabulum is lateral
Femur	• The head is proximal and faces medially • The lesser trochanter and linea aspera are posterior
Patella	• The apex is distal • The lateral articular facet is larger than the medial

Continued

Siding and Orienting Bones of the Appendicular Skeleton—cont'd

Tibia	• The tibial tuberosity is proximal and anterior • The medial malleolus is distal and medial
Fibula	• The articular surfaces are medial, and the rounded head is proximal • The flattened end is distal, and the malleolar fossa is posterior
Talus	• With the saddle-shaped articular facet facing you and the head up, the projecting malleolar surface for the tibia is on the side the bone is from
Calcaneus	• With the tubercle down and the articular surfaces facing you, the shelf projects opposite the side the bone is from
Cuboid	• With the flat nonarticular side facing you, the bone angles/pinches toward the side the bone is from
Navicular	• With the concave articular surface facing you and the tubercle down, the tubercle angles toward the side the bone is from
Medial (1st) cuneiform	• With the large tear-shaped articular surface facing you and the pointy end up, the articular surface wraps toward the side the bone is from
Intermediate (2nd) cuneiform	• With the large triangular articular surface facing you and the pointy end down, the side that is slightly concave is the side the bone is from
Lateral (3rd) cuneiform	• With the Africa-shaped facet away from you and the pointy side down, the longest boundary of the upper surface is on the side the bone is from
First metatarsal	• The basal facet is convex on the opposite side the bone is from, and straight on the side the bone is from
Second metatarsal	• Viewed dorsally, the base angles toward the side the bone is from
Third metatarsal	• Viewed dorsally, the base angles toward the side the bone is from
Fourth metatarsal	• Viewed dorsally, the base angles toward the side the bone is from
Fifth metatarsal	• Viewed dorsally, the base angles toward the side the bone is from

(Modified from White, T.D., Black, M.T., Folkens, P.A., 2011. Human Osteology, third ed. Academic Press, San Diego, CA.)

APPENDIX B: SKELETAL INVENTORY FORM

Codes: 1- Present, complete   2- Present, fragmentary   3- Absent   4- Antemortem loss
Parenthesis can be used to indicate number of bones/fragments

Bone	Code		Bone	Code	
	Left	*Right*		*Left*	*Right*
Cranium			Phalanges, prox.	_____	_____
Frontal	_____		Phalanges, med.	_____	_____
Parietal	_____	_____	Phalanges, dist.	_____	_____
Occipital	_____		Manubrium	_____	
Temporal	_____	_____	Sternal body	_____	
Zygomatic	_____	_____	Ribs	_____	_____
Palate	_____	_____	Cervical 1 (C1)	_____	
Maxilla	_____	_____	Cervical 2 (C2)	_____	
Nasal	_____	_____	Cervical 3-7	_____	
Ethmoid	_____		Thoracic 1-12	_____	
Lacrimal	_____	_____	Lumbar 1-5	_____	
Vomer	_____		Sacrum	_____	
Sphenoid	_____	_____	Coccyx	_____	
Mandible	_____		Innominate		
Hyoid	_____		Femur	_____	_____
Clavicle	_____	_____	Patella	_____	_____
Scapula	_____	_____	Tibia	_____	_____
Humerus	_____	_____	Fibula	_____	_____
Radius	_____	_____	Calcaneus	_____	_____
Ulna	_____	_____	Talus	_____	_____
Scaphoid	_____	_____	Navicular	_____	_____
Lunate	_____	_____	Cuboid	_____	_____
Triquetral	_____	_____	Cuneiform 1	_____	_____
Pisiform	_____	_____	Cuneiform 2	_____	_____
Trapezium	_____	_____	Cuneiform 3	_____	_____
Trapezoid	_____	_____	MT1	_____	_____
Capitate	_____	_____	MT2	_____	_____
Hamate	_____	_____	MT3	_____	_____
MC1	_____	_____	MT4	_____	_____
MC2	_____	_____	MT5	_____	_____
MC3	_____	_____	Phalanges, prox.	_____	_____
MC4	_____	_____	Phalanges, med.	_____	_____
MC5	_____	_____	Phalanges, dist.	_____	_____
Undetermined Fragments	_____		Non-human	_____	
				_____	

Skeletal inventory diagram

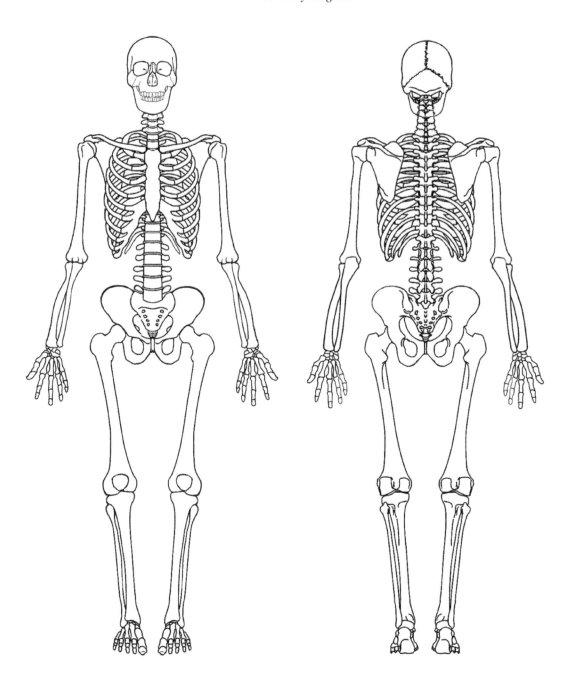

Shaded area represents elements

Present

Absent

APPENDIX C: DENTAL CHARTING FORMS

Adult dentition

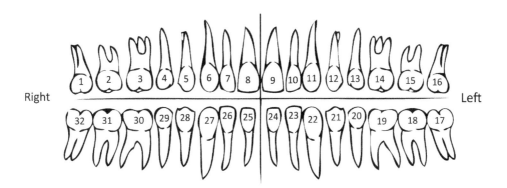

Right   Left

Tooth	Notes	Tooth	Notes
1		17	
2		18	
3		19	
4		20	
5		21	
6		22	
7		23	
8		24	
9		25	
10		26	
11		27	
12		28	
13		29	
14		30	
15		31	
16		32	

Deciduous dentition

Right ——————————————— Left

Tooth	Notes	Tooth	Notes
A		K	
B		L	
C		M	
D		N	
E		O	
F		P	
G		Q	
H		R	
I		S	
J		T	

APPENDIX D: CRANIOMETRIC LANDMARKS

Craniometric Landmarks, Abbreviations, and Definitions

Landmark (and Abbreviation)	Definition
Alare (al)	The most laterally positioned point on the anterior margin of the nasal aperture
Alvelon (alv)	The point where the midline of the palate is intersected by a straight tangent connecting the posterior borders of the alveolar crests
Asterion (ast)	The point where the lambdoidal, pareitomastoid, and occipitomastoid sutures meet
Basion (ba)	The point where the anterior margin of the foramen magnum is intersected by the mid-sagittal plane
Bregma (b)	The point where the sagittal and coronal sutures meet
Condylon (cdl)	The most lateral points of the mandibular condyles
Dacryon (d)	The point on the medial border of the orbit at which the frontal, lacrimal, and maxilla intersect
Ectoconchion (ec)	The intersection of the most anterior surface of the lateral border of the orbit and a line bisecting the orbit along its long axis
Ectomolare (ecm)	The most lateral point on the lateral surface of the alveolar crest
Euryon (eu)	The most laterally positioned point on the side of the braincase
Frontomalare temporale (fmt)	The most laterally positioned point on the frontomalar suture
Frontotemporale (ft)	A point located generally forward and inward on the superior temporal line directly above the zygomatic process of the frontal bone
Glabella (g)	The most forwardly projecting point in the mid-sagittal plane at the lower margin of the frontal bone, which lies above the nasal root and between the superciliary arches
Gnathion (gn)	The lowest point on the inferior margin of the mandibular body in the mid-sagittal plane
Gonion (go)	The point on the mandible where the inferior margin of the mandibular corpus and the posterior margin of the ramus meet
Infradentale (id)	The point between the lower incisor teeth where the anterior margins of the alveolar processes are intersected by the mid-sagittal plane
Lambda (l)	The point where the two branches of the lambdoidal suture meet with the sagittal suture
Mastoidaele (ms)	Point at the most inferior tip of the mastoid
Nasion (n)	The point of intersection of the nasofrontal suture and the mid-sagittal plane
Nasospinale (ns)	The lowest point on the inferior margin of the nasal aperture as projected in the mid-sagittal plane
Opisthocranion (op)	The most posteriorly protruding point on the back of the braincase, located in the mid-sagittal plane
Opisthion (o)	The point at which the mid-sagittal plane intersects the posterior margin of the foramen magnum
Porion (po)	Point at the most superior aspect of the external auditory meatus
Prosthion (pr)	The most anterior point on the alveolar border of the maxilla between the central incisors in the mid-sagittal plane; note that this point is anteriorly located on the alveolar process for measurements 6 and 8, and inferiorly located for measurement 10
Radiculare (ra)	The point on the lateral aspect of the root of the zygomatic process at the deepest incurvature
Zygion (zy)	The most laterally positioned point on the zygomatic arches
Zygomaxillare (zym)	The most inferior point on the zygomaticomaxillary suture
Zygoorbitale (zo)	The intersection of the orbital margin and the zygomaxillary suture

(Modified from Moore-Jansen, P.M., Ousley, S.D., Jantz, R.L., 1994. Data collection procedures for forensic skeletal material. Report of investigations no. 48. Department of Anthropology, University of Tennessee, Knoxville, TN.)

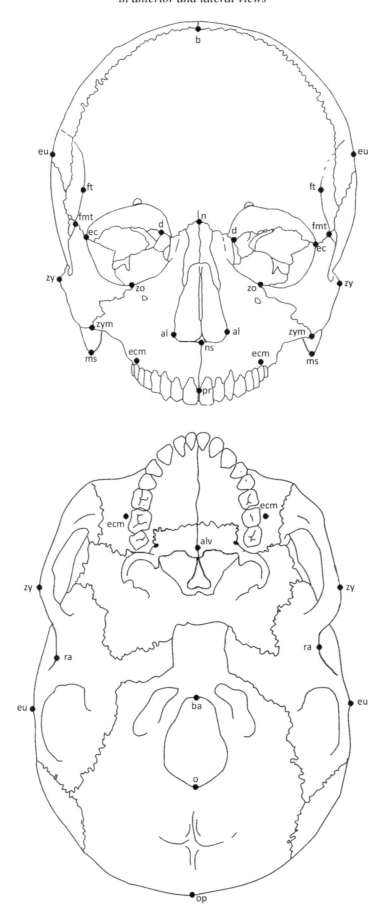

Craniometric landmarks: cranium shown in anterior, lateral, and inferior views; mandible shown in anterior and lateral views

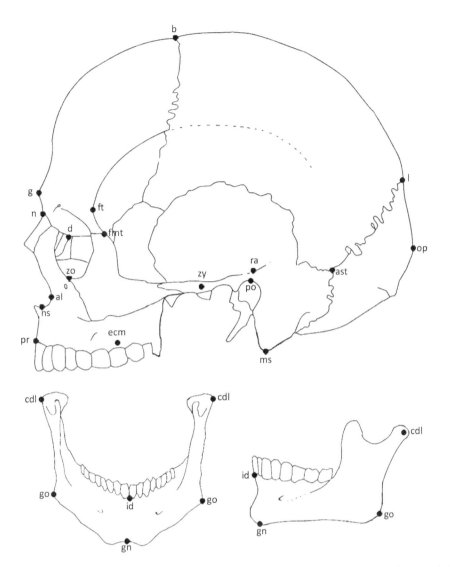

(Modified from Langley, N.R., Jantz, L.M., Ousley, S.D., Jantz, R.L., Milner, G., 2016. Data Collection Procedures for Forensic Skeletal Material 2.0. Department of Anthropology, University of Tennessee; Anatomy Department, Lincoln Memorial University, Knoxville, TN.)

APPENDIX E: SKELETAL MEASUREMENTS

Measurements of the Skull (1–34) and Postcranial Skeleton (35–78)

Measurement (and Abbreviations)	Definition
1. Maximum Cranial Length (g-op, GOL)	The distance of glabella (g) from opisthocranion (op) in the mid-sagittal plane measured in a straight line
2. Nasiooccipital length (n-op, NOL):	Maximum length in the midsagittal plane, measured from nasion (n) to opisthocranion (op)
3. Maximum Cranial Breadth (eu-eu, XCB)	The maximum width of the cranial vault perpendicular to the mid-sagittal plane wherever it is located
4. Bizygomtic Breadth (zy-zy, ZYB)	The maximum breadth across the zygomatic arches, perpendicular to the mid-sagittal plane
5. Basion-Bregma Height (ba-b, BBH)	The direct distance from the lowest point on the anterior margin of the foramen magnum, basion (ba), to bregma
6. Cranial Base Length (ba-n, NL)	The direct distance from nasion (n) to basion (ba)
7. Basion-Prosthion Length (ba-pr, BPL)	The direct distance from basion (ba) to prosthion (pr)
8. Maxillo-Alveolar Breadth (ecm-ecm, MAB)	The maximum breadth across the alveolar borders of the maxilla measured on the lateral surfaces at the location of the second maxillary molars
9. Maxillo-Alveolar Length (pr-avl, MAL)	The direct distance from prosthion to alveolon (alv)
10. Biauricular Breadth (ra-ra, AUB)	The least exterior breadth across the roots of the zygomatic processes, wherever found
11. Upper Facial Height (n-pr, NPH, also called: Nasion-Prosthion Height)	The distance from nasion (n) to prosthion (pr)
12. Minimum Frontal Breadth (ft-ft, WFB)	The direct distance between the left and right frontotemporale
13. Upper Facial Breadth (fmt-fmt)	The direct distance between the two frontomalare temporalia
14. Nasal Height (n-ns, NLH)	The direct distance from nasion (n) to the lowest point on the border of the nasal aperture on either side (ns)
15. Nasal Breadth (al-al, NLB)	The maximum breadth of the nasal aperture
16. Orbital Breadth (d-ec, OBB)	The distance from dacryon (d) to ectoconchion (ec)
17. Orbital Height (OBH)	The direct distance between the superior and inferior orbital margins perpendicular to orbital breadth
18. Biorbital Breadth (ec-ec, EKB)	The distance from left to right ectoconchion (ec)
19. Interorbital Breadth (d-d, DKB)	The direct distance between right and left dacryon
20. Frontal Chord (n-b, FRC)	The distance from nasion (n) to bregma (b) taken in the mid-sagittal plane
21. Parietal Chord (b-l, PAC)	The distance from bregma (b) to lambda (l) taken in the mid-sagittal plane
22. Occipital Chord (l-o, OCC)	The distance from lambda (l) to opisthion (o) taken in the mid-sagittal plane
23. Foramen Magnum Length (ba-o, FOL)	The distance of basion (b) from opisthion (o) taken in the mid-sagittal plane
24. Foramen Magnum Breadth (FOB)	The distance between the lateral margins of the foramen magnum at the point of greatest lateral curvature

Measurements of the Skull (1–34) and Postcranial Skeleton (35–78)—cont'd

Measurement (and Abbreviations)	Definition
25. Mastoid Height (p-m, MDH)	The projection of the mastoid process below, and perpendicular to, the eye-ear plane in the vertical plane
26. Biasterionic Breadth (ast-ast, ASB)	The distance from left asterion to right asterion
27. Zygomaxilary Breadth (also called: bimaxillary breadth) (zym-zym, ZMB)	Breadth across the maxillae, from the left to right zygomaxillare anterior (zym)
28. Zygoorbitale Breadth (zo-zo, ZOB)	The distance between right and left zygoorbitale (zo)
29. Chin Height (id-gn)	The distance from infradentale (id) to gnathion (gn)
30. Height of Mandibular Body	The distance from the alveolar process to the inferior border of the mandible perpendicular to the base at the level of the mental foramen
31. Breadth of Mandibular Body	The maximum breadth measured in the region of the mental foramen perpendicular to the long axis of the mandibular body
32. Bigonial Width (go-go)	The distance between both gonia (go)
33. Bicondylar Breadth (cdl-cdl)	The distance between the most lateral points on the two condyles (cdl)
34. Minimum Ramus Breadth	The minimum breadth of the mandibular ramus measured perpendicular to the height of the ramus
35. Maximum Ramus Height (*mandibulometer needed*)	The distance from the highest point on the mandibular condyle to gonion
36. Mandibular Length (*mandibulometer needed*)	The distance of the anterior margin of the chin from a center point on a projected straight line placed along the posterior border of the two mandibular angles
37. Mandibular Angle (*mandibulometer needed*)	The angle formed by the inferior border of the corpus and the posterior border of the ramus
38. Maximum Length of Clavicle	The maximum distance between the most extreme ends of the clavicle
39. Maximum Diameter of the Clavicle at Midshaft*	The maximum diameter of the bone measured at midshaft. (Note this is a new measurement, which replaces Sagittal Diameter of the Clavicle at Midshaft)
40. Minimum Diameter of the Clavicle at Midshaft*	The minimum diameter of the bone measured at midshaft. (Note this is a new measurement, which replaces Vertical Diameter of the Clavicle at Midshaft)
41. Height of the Scapula	The distance from the most superior point of the cranial angle to the most inferior point on the caudal angle
42. Breadth of the Scapula	The distance from the midpoint on the dorsal border of the glenoid fossa to midway between the two ridges of the scapular spine on the vertebral border
43. Glenoid Cavity Breadth	Maximum distance from the ventral to dorsal margins of the glenoid cavity, taken perpendicular to glenoid cavity height (in cases of severe lipping, this measurement should not be taken)
44. Glenoid Cavity Height	The distance from the most superiorly located point on the margin of the glenoid cavity to the most inferiorly located point on the margin, taken perpendicular to glenoid cavity breadth (in cases of severe lipping, this measurement should not be taken)
45. Maximum Length of the Humerus	The distance from the most superior point on the head of the humerus to the most inferior point on the trochlea

Continued

Measurements of the Skull (1–34) and Postcranial Skeleton (35–78)—cont'd

Measurement (and Abbreviations)	Definition
46. Epicondylar Breadth of the Humerus	The distance of the most laterally protruding point on the lateral epicondyle from the corresponding projection of the medial epicondyle
47. Maximum Vertical Diameter of the Head of the Humerus	The distance between the most superior and inferior points on the border of the articular surface
48. Maximum Diameter of the Humerus at Midshaft	The maximum diameter that can be found at the humeral midshaft
49. Minimum Diameter of the Humerus at Midshaft	The minimum diameter that can be found at the humeral midshaft
50. Maximum Length of the Radius	The distance from the most proximally positioned point on the head of the radius to the tip of the styloid process without regard to the long axis of the bone
51. Maximum Diameter of the Radius at Midshaft*	The maximum diameter of the radial shaft taken at midshaft. (Note this is a new measurement, which replaces Sagittal Diameter of the Radius at Midshaft)
52. Minimum Diameter of the Radius at Midshaft*	The minimum diameter of the radial shaft taken at midshaft. (Note this is a new measurement, which replaces Transverse Diameter of the Radius at Midshaft)
53. Maximum Diameter of the Radial Head	The maximum diameter of the radial head measured on the margin of the head that articulates with the ulna. The bone is rotated until the maximum distance is obtained
54. Maximum Length of the Ulna	The distance between the most proximal point on the olecranon and the most distal point on the styloid process
55. Maximum Diameter of the Ulna*	The maximum diameter of the diaphysis taken at midshaft. (Note this is a new measurement, which replaces Dorso-Volar Diameter of the Ulna)
56. Minimum Diameter of the Ulna*	The minimum diameter of the diaphysis taken at midshaft. (Note this is a new measurement, which replaces Transverse Diameter of the Ulna)
57. Physiological Length of the Ulna	The distance between the deepest point on the surface of the coronoid process and the lowest point on the inferior surface of the distal head of the ulna
58. Minimum Circumference of the Ulna	The least circumference near the distal end of the bone
59. Olecranon Breadth	The maximum breadth of the olecranon process, taken perpendicular to the longitudinal axis of the semilunar notch
60. Anterior Height of the Sacrum	The distance from a point on the promontory in the mid-sagittal plane to a point on the anterior border of the tip of the sacrum measured in the mid-sagittal plane
61. Anterior Breadth of the Sacrum	The maximum transverse breadth of the sacrum at the level of the anterior projection of the auricular surfaces
62. Transverse Diameter of the Sacral Segment 1	The distance between the two most lateral points on the superior articular surface measured perpendicular to the mid-sagittal plane
63. Anterior-Posterior Diameter of Sacral Segment 1	The distance between the anterior and posterior borders of the superior articular surface of S1, taken in the mid-sagittal plane
64. Maximum Innominate Height (also called Innominate Height)	The distance from the most superior point on the iliac crest to the most inferior point on the ischial tuberosity
65. Maximum Iliac Breadth	The distance from the anterior superior iliac spine to the posterior superior iliac spine
66. Minimum Iliac Breadth	The minimum distance measured from the area below the anterior inferior iliac spine to the most inward curvature of the greater sciatic notch (Note this measurement was recently added as a standard measurement and is not currently included in Fordisc)

Measurements of the Skull (1–34) and Postcranial Skeleton (35–78)—cont'd

Measurement (and Abbreviations)	Definition
67. Maximum Pubis Length	The distance between symphysion (the most superior point on the symphyseal face) to the farthest point on the acetabular rim. (Note this measurement was recently added as a standard measurement and is not currently included in Fordisc)
68. Minimum Pubis Length	The distance between symphysion (the most superior point on the symphyseal face) to the closest point on the acetabular rim. (Note this measurement was recently added as a standard measurement and is not currently included in Fordisc)
69. Ischial Length	The distance from the point on the acetabular rim where the iliac blade meets the acetabulum to the most medial point on the epiphysis of the ischial tuberosity. (Note this measurement was recently added as a standard measurement and is not currently included in Fordisc)
70. Minimum Ischial Length	The distance from the most medial point on the epiphysis of the ischial tuberosity to the closest point on the acetabular rim. (Note this measurement was recently added as a standard measurement and is not currently included in Fordisc)
71. Maximum Ischiopubic Ramus Length	The distance from the most inferior point on the symphyseal face to the most distant point on the ischial tuberosity. (Note this measurement was recently added as a standard measurement and is not currently included in Fordisc)
72. Anterior Superior Iliac Spine to Symphysion	Measurement from the apex of the anterior superior iliac spine (most projecting area or point) to symphysion. (Note this measurement was recently added as a standard measurement and is not currently included in Fordisc)
73. Maximum Posterior Superior Iliac Spine to Symphysion	Maximum measurement from the posterior border of the posterior superior iliac spine to symphysion. (Note this measurement was recently added as a standard measurement and is not currently included in Fordisc)
74. Minimum Apical Border to Symphysion	Minimum measurement from symphysion to the apex (anterior border) of the auricular surface. (Note this measurement was recently added as a standard measurement and is not currently included in Fordisc)
75. Maximum Length of the Femur	The distance from the most superior point on the head of the femur to the most inferior point on the distal condyles, located by raising the bone up and down and shifting sideways until the maximum length is obtained
76. Bicondylar Length of the Femur	The distance from the most superior point on the head of the femur to a plane drawn along the inferior surfaces of the distal condyles
77. Epicondylar Breadth of the Femur	The distance between the two most laterally projecting points on the epicondyles
78. Maximum Diameter of the Femoral Head	The maximum diameter of the femur head measured on the border of the articular surface
79. Transverse Subtrochanteric Diameter of the Femur	The transverse diameter of the proximal portion of the diaphysis at the point of its greatest lateral expansion below the base of the lesser trochanter
80. Anterioposterior Subtrochantic Diameter of the Femur	The anterioposterior diameter of the proximal end of the diaphysis measured perpendicular to the transverse diameter at the point of the greatest lateral expansion of the femur below the lesser trochanter
81. Maximum Midshaft Diameter of the Femur	The maximum diameter of the femoral shaft taken at midshaft. (Note this is a new measurement, which replaces Anterioposterior Diameter of the Femur at Midshaft)
82. Minimum Midshaft Diameter of the Femur	The minimum diameter of the femoral shaft taken at midshaft. The distance between the medial and lateral margins of the femur from one another measured perpendicular to and at the same level as the sagittal diameter. (Note this is a new measurement, which replaces Transverse Diameter of the Femur at Midshaft)
83. Circumference of the Femur at Midshaft	The circumference measured at the midshaft at the same level of the sagittal and transverse diameters

Continued

Measurements of the Skull (1–34) and Postcranial Skeleton (35–78)—cont'd

Measurement (and Abbreviations)	Definition
84. Maximum Anteroposterior Length of the Lateral Condyle	The distance between the most anterior and posterior points on the articular surface of the lateral condyle
85. Maximum Anteroposterior Length of the Medial Condyle	The distance between the most anterior and posterior points on the articular surface of the medial condyle
86. Length of the Tibia	The distance from the superior articular surface of the lateral condyle of the tibia to the tip of the medial malleolus
87. Maximum Epiphyseal Breadth of the Proximal Tibia	The maximum distance between the two most laterally projecting points on the medial and lateral condyles of the proximal epiphysis
88. Epiphyseal Breadth of the Distal Tibia	The distance between the most medial point on the medial malleolus and the lateral surface of the distal epiphysis
89. Maximum Midshaft Diameter of the Tibia	The maximum diameter of the tibial shaft taken at midshaft. (Note this is a new measurement, which replaces Maximum Diameter of the Tibia at the Nutrient Foramen)
90. Minimum Midshaft Diameter of the Tibia	The minimum diameter of the tibial shaft taken at midshaft. (Note this is a new measurement, which replaces Transverse Diameter of the Tibia at the Nutrient Foramen)
91. Circumference of the Tibia at the Midshaft	The circumference measured at the level of the midshaft. (Note this is a new measurement, which replaces Circumference of the Tibia at the Nutrient Foramen)
92. Maximum Length of the Fibula	The maximum distance between the most superior point on the fibular head and the most inferior point on the lateral malleolus
93. Maximum Diameter of the Fibula at Midshaft	The maximum diameter at the midshaft
94. Maximum Length of the Calcaneus	The distance between the most posteriorly projecting point on the tuberosity and the most anterior point on the superior margin of the articular facet for the cuboid measured in the sagittal plane and projected onto the underlying surface
95. Middle Breadth of the Calcaneus	The distance between the most laterally projecting point on the dorsal articular facet and the most medial point on the sustentaculum tali

*represents that a new measurement that is similar to, but replacing a previous measurement.

(Modified from Langley, N.R., Jantz, L.M., Ousley, S.D., Jantz, R.L., Milner, G., 2016. Data Collection Procedures for Forensic Skeletal Material 2.0. Department of Anthropology, University of Tennessee; Anatomy Department, Lincoln Memorial University, Knoxville, TN and references therein.)

Measurements of the cranium and mandible

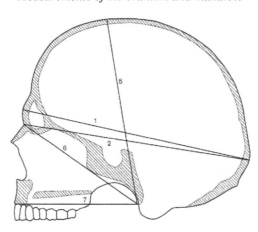

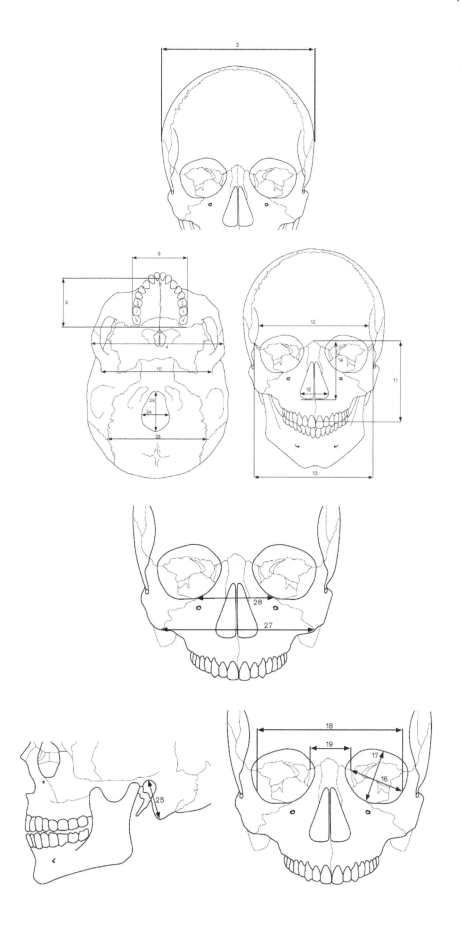

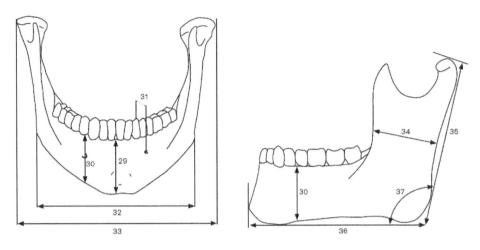

(Modified from Langley, N.R., Jantz, L.M., Ousley, S.D., Jantz, R.L., Milner, G., 2016. Data Collection Procedures for Forensic Skeletal Material 2.0. Department of Anthropology, University of Tennessee; Anatomy Department, Lincoln Memorial University, Knoxville, TN.)

Measurements of the postcranial skeleton

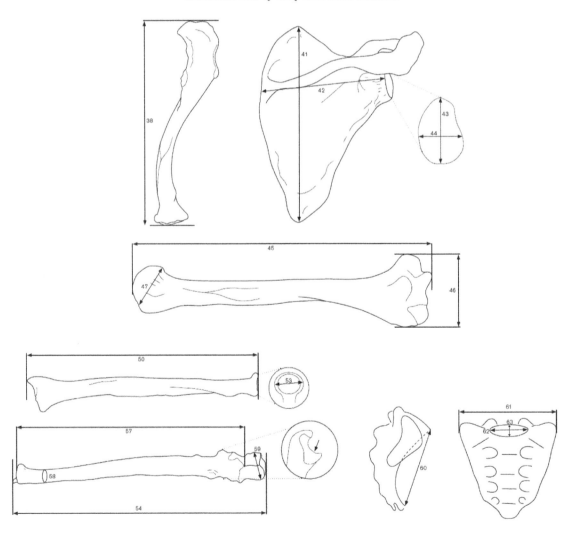

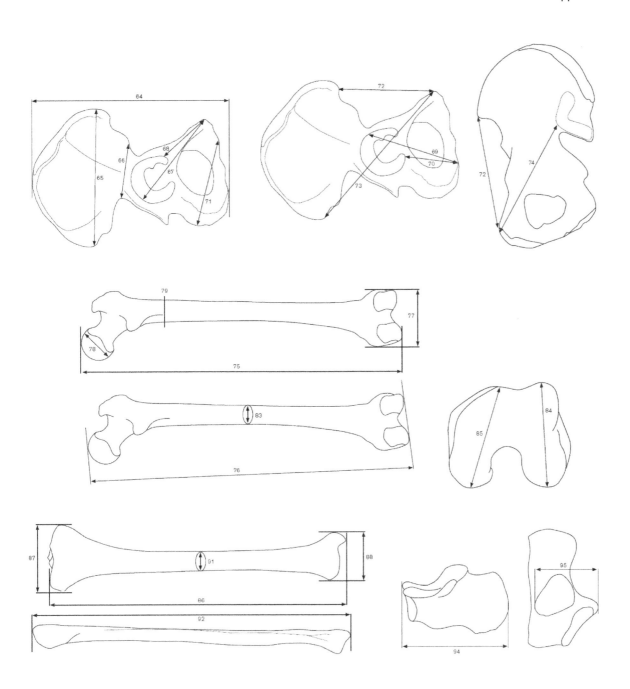

APPENDIX F: SKELETAL MEASUREMENT FORM

Cranial and mandibular measurements (all recorded in mm)

------------------------------ CRANIAL MEASUREMENTS ------------------------------

		left	right
1. MAXIMUM CRANIAL LENGTH (g-op): _____	15. NASAL BREADTH (al-al):	_____	
2. NASIO-OCCIPITAL LENGTH (n-op): _____	16. ORBITAL BREADTH (d-ec):	_____	_____
3. MAXIMUM CRANIAL BREADTH (eu-eu) _____	17. ORBITAL HEIGHT:	_____	_____
4. BIZYGOMATIC BREADTH (zy-zy): _____	18. BIORBITAL BREADTH (ec-ec):	_____	
5. BASION-BREGMA HEIGHT (ba-b): _____	19. INTERORBITAL BREADTH (d-d):	_____	
6. CRANIAL BASE LENGTH (ba-n): _____	20. FRONTAL CHORD (n-b):	_____	
7. BASION-PROSTHION LENGTH (ba-pr): _____	21. PARIETAL CHORD (b-l):	_____	
8. MAXILLO-ALVEOLAR BREADTH (ecm-ecm): _____	22. OCCIPITAL CHORD (l-o):	_____	
9. MAXILLO-ALVEOLAR LENGTH (pr-alv): _____	23. FORAMEN MAGNUM LENGTH (ba-o):	_____	
10. BIAURICULAR BREADTH (ra-ra): _____	24. FORAMEN MAGNUM BR:	_____	
11. NASION-PROSTHION HEIGHT (n-pr): _____	25. MASTOID HEIGHT (po-ms):	_____	
12. MINIMUM FRONTAL BREADTH (ft-ft): _____	26. BIASTERIONIC BR. (ast-ast):	_____	
13. UPPER FACIAL BREADTH (fmt-fmt): _____	27. ZYGOMAXILLARY BR. (zym-zym):	_____	
14. NASAL HEIGHT (n-ns): _____	28. ZYGOORBITALE BR. (zo-zo):	_____	

------------------------------ MANDIBULAR MEASUREMENTS ------------------------------

	left	right		left	right
29. CHIN. HEIGHT (id-gn):		_____	34. MIN. RAMUS HEIGHT:	_____	_____
30. MANDIBULAR BODY HEIGHT:	_____	_____	35. *MAX. RAMUS HEIGHT:	_____	
31. MANDIBULAR BODY BREADTH:	_____	_____	36. *MAND. LENGTH:	_____	
32. BIGONIAL BREADTH (go-go):		_____	37. *MAND. ANGLE:	_____	
33. BICONDYLAR BR. (cdl-cdl):		_____			

*Record only if mandibulometer is used

(Modified from Langley, N.R., Jantz, L.M., Ousley, S.D., Jantz, R.L., Milner, G., 2016. Data Collection Procedures for Forensic Skeletal Material 2.0. Department of Anthropology, University of Tennessee; Anatomy Department, Lincoln Memorial University, Knoxville, TN.)

Postcranial measurements (all recorded in mm)

------------------------------ POSTCRANIAL MEASUREMENTS ------------------------------

	left	right		left	right
CLAVICLE:			**INNOMINATE:**		
38. MAXIMUM LENGTH:	___	___	64. MAXIMUM HEIGHT:	___	___
39. MAX. MIDSHAFT DIAM:	___	___	65. MAX. ILIAC BREADTH:	___	___
40. MIN. MIDSHAFT DIAM:	___	___	66. MIN. ILIAC BREADTH:	___	___
			67. MAX. PUBIS LENGTH:	___	___
SCAPULA:			68. MIN. PUBIS LENGTH:	___	___
41. HEIGHT:	___	___	69. ISCHIAL LENGTH:	___	___
42. BREADTH:	___	___	70. MIN. ISCHIAL LENGTH:	___	___
43. GLENOID CAVITY BREADTH:	___	___	71. MAX. ISCHIOPUB RAM L.:	___	___
44. GLENOID CAVITY HEIGHT:	___	___	72. ASIS – SYMPHYSION:	___	___
			73. MAX. PSIS – SYMPHYSION:	___	___
HUMERUS:			74. MIN. APEX – SYMPHYSION:	___	___
45. MAXIMUM LENGTH:	___	___			
46. EPICONDYLAR BREADTH:	___	___	**FEMUR:**		
47. MAX. VERT. HEAD DIAM.:	___	___	75. MAXIMUM LENGTH:	___	___
48. MAX. MIDSHAFT DIAM.:	___	___	76. BICONDYLAR LENGTH:	___	___
49. MIN. MIDSHAFT DIAM.:	___	___	77. EPICONDYLAR BREADTH:	___	___
			78. MAX. HEAD DIAMETER:	___	___
RADIUS:			79. TRANS. SUBTROCH DIAM:	___	___
50. MAXIMUM LENGTH:	___	___	80. A-P SUBTROCH DIAM:	___	___
51. MAX. MIDSHAFT DIAM.:	___	___	81. MAX. MIDSHAFT DIAM.	___	___
52. MIN. MIDSHAFT DIAM.:	___	___	82. MIN. MIDSHAFT DIAM.	___	___
53. MAX. HEAD DIAMETER:	___	___	83. MIDSHAFT CIRCUM.	___	___
			84. MAX AP L. LAT. CONDYLE:	___	___
ULNA:			85. MAX AP L. MED. CONDYLE:	___	___
54. MAXIMUM LENGTH:	___	___			
55. MAX. MIDSHAFT DIAM.:	___	___	**TIBIA:**		
56. MIN. MIDSHAFT DIAM.:	___	___	86. CONDYLO-MALLEOLAR L.:	___	___
57. PHYSIOLOGICAL LENGTH:	___	___	87. MAX. PROX. EPIP. BR.:	___	___
58. MIN. CIRCUMFERENCE:	___	___	88. DISTAL EPIP. BREADTH:	___	___
59. OLECRANON BREADTH:	___	___	89. MAX. MIDSHAFT DIAM.:	___	___
			90. MIN. MIDSHAFT DIAM.:	___	___
SACRUM:			91. MIDSHAFT CIRCUM.:	___	___
60. ANTERIOR HEIGHT:	___				
61. ANTERIOR BREADTH:	___		**FIBULA:**		
62. TRANSVERSE DIAM. S1:	___		92. MAXIMUM LENGTH:	___	___
63. A-P DIAMETER S1:	___		93. MAX. MIDSHAFT DIAM.:	___	___
			CALCANEUS:		
			94. MAXIMUM LENGTH:	___	___
			95. MIDDLE BREADTH:	___	___

(Modified from Langley, N.R., Jantz, L.M., Ousley, S.D., Jantz, R.L., Milner, G., 2016. Data Collection Procedures for Forensic Skeletal Material 2.0. Department of Anthropology, University of Tennessee; Anatomy Department, Lincoln Memorial University, Knoxville, TN.)

APPENDIX G: FORDISC DFA FLOWCHART

Flowchart for using Fordisc

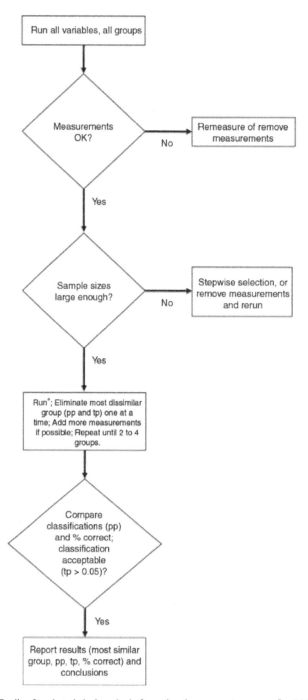

(From Ousley, S.D., Jantz, R.L., 2012. Fordisc 3 and statistical methods for estimating sex and ancestry. In: Dirkmaat, D.C. (Ed.), A Companion to Forensic Anthropology, Wiley-Blackwell, Chichester, pp. 311–329.)

APPENDIX H: DECOMPOSITION SCORING AND PMI ESTIMATION

Scores for Decomposition of the Trunk

Score	Description
1	Fresh, no discoloration
2	Pink-white appearance with skin slippage and marbling present
3	Gray to green discoloration, some flesh relatively fresh
4	Bloating with green discoloration and purging of fluids
5	Release of gases, discoloration changing from green to black
6	Decomposition of tissue producing sagging of flesh
7	Moist tissue with bone exposure over less than one-half of the area being scored
8	Dry tissue with bone exposure over less than one-half of the area being scored
9	Bones with decomposed tissue, fluids, and grease still present
10	Dry tissue, bone exposure over more than one-half of the area being scored
11	Bones largely dry, but retaining some grease
12	Dry bone

(Modified from Megyesi, M.S., Nawrocki, S.P., Haskell, N.H., 2005. Using accumulated degree-days to estimate the postmortem interval from decomposed human remains. J. Forensic Sci. 50(3), 1–9.)

Scores for Decomposition of the Head and Neck

Score	Description
1	Fresh, no discoloration
2	Pink-white appearance with skin slippage and some hair loss
3	Gray to green discoloration, some flesh relatively fresh
4	Brown discoloration, drying of nose, ears, lips
5	Purging of fluids via orifices, some bloating may be present
6	Brown to black discoloration
7	Caving in of flesh and tissues of eyes and throat
8	Moist tissue with bone exposure over less than one-half of the area being scored
9	Dry tissue with bone exposure over less than one-half of the area being scored
10	Greasy tissue with bone exposure over more than one-half of the area being scored
11	Dry tissue and bone exposure over more than one-half of the area being scored
12	Bones largely dry, but retaining some grease
13	Dry bone

(Modified from Megyesi, M.S., Nawrocki, S.P., Haskell, N.H., 2005. Using accumulated degree-days to estimate the postmortem interval from decomposed human remains. J. Forensic Sci. 50(3), 1–9.)

Scores for Decomposition of the Limbs

Score	Description
1	Fresh, no discoloration
2	Pink-white appearance with skin slippage of hands and/or feet
3	Gray to green discoloration, marbling, some flesh relatively fresh
4	Brown discoloration, drying of fingers, toes, projecting extremities
5	Brown to black discoloration, skin having leathery appearance
6	Moist tissue with bone exposure over less than one-half of the area being scored
7	Dry tissue with bone exposure over less than one-half of the area being scored
8	Remaining tissue and fluid, bone exposure over one-half of the area being scored
9	Bones largely dry, but retaining some grease
10	Dry bone

(Modified from Megyesi, M.S., Nawrocki, S.P., Haskell, N.H., 2005. Using accumulated degree-days to estimate the postmortem interval from decomposed human remains. J. Forensic Sci. 50(3), 1–9.)

Total Body Score (TBS) Equation:

$$TBS = (\text{Trunk Score}) + (\text{Head and Neck Score}) + (\text{Limb Score})$$

ADD from TBS Equation:

$$ADD = 10^{0.002*TBS*TBS+1.81} \pm 388.16$$

APPENDIX I: SCENE MAPPING AND DOCUMENTATION

Scene Documentation Form

Date:	Agency:	Location:
Time:	Case Number:	Preparer:

Site Description (rural/forested, suburban, aquatic, etc.):

Environmental Conditions (temperature, weather, etc.):

Remains Description (scattered, buried, clothed, etc.):

Additional Scene Notes (other evidence, sampling, etc.):

Scene Map

| Location: | Preparer: | N |
| Date: | Case Number: | |

APPENDIX J: PHOTOGRAPH LOG

Date:	Agency:	Location:
Time:	Case Number:	Photographer:

Photo Number:	Notes/Description:

Page ____ of ____

APPENDIX K: SEX ESTIMATION USING SCORING OF PUBIC TRAITS

Scoring of pubic traits. Top—subpubic concavity (SPC); middle—medial aspect (MA); bottom—ventral arc (VA)

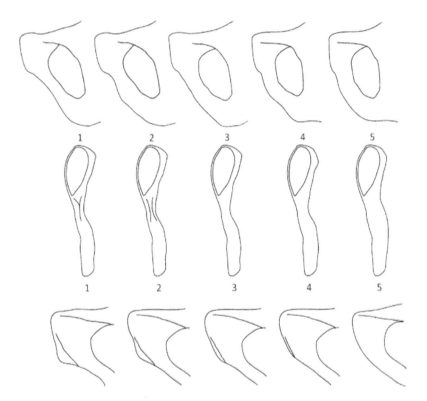

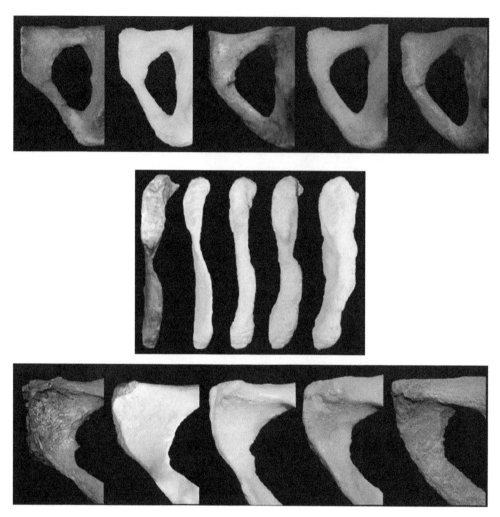

(From Klales, A.R., Ousley, S.D., Vollner, J.M., 2012. A revised method of sexing the human innominate using Phenice's nonmetric traits and statistical methods. Am. J. Phys. Anthropol. 149 (1), 104–114.)

Total Score Equation:

$$\text{Score} = 2.726\left(\text{VA}\right) + 1.214\left(\text{MA}\right) + 1.073\left(\text{SPC}\right) - 16.312$$

Sex Probability Equations:

$$\text{Probability of female}\left(P_{\text{f}}\right) = 1 / \left(1 + e^{\text{score}}\right)$$

$$\text{Probability of male}\left(P_{\text{m}}\right) = 1 - P_{\text{f}}$$

A spreadsheet to facilitate calculations is also available at http://www.morphopasse.com/.

APPENDIX L: SEX ESTIMATION USING CRANIAL TRAITS

Features and scores used for cranial sex estimation

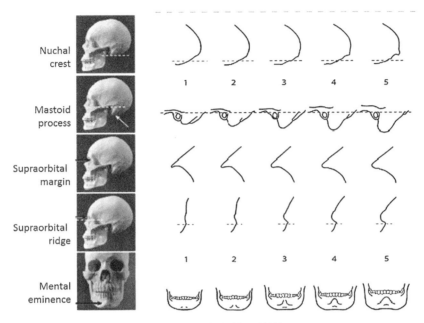

(From Buikstra and Ubelaker, 1994.)

Skull Scoring

Trait	Description/Procedure	Minimal Expression (score = 1)	Maximal Expression (score = 5)
Nuchal crest	View skull laterally and assess the occipital bone, noting the development of bone on the external surface of the occipital associated with the attachment of the nuchal muscles, and ignoring the contour of the underlying bone (e.g., the presence or absence of an occipital bun in scoring this trait)	The external surface of the occipital is smooth with no bony projections visible	A massive nuchal crest that projects considerable distance from the bone and forms a well-defined ledge or hook of bone
Mastoid process	Comparing the mastoid size with that of surrounding structures such as the external auditory meatus and zygomatic process of the temporal bone. Mastoid processes vary considerably in their proportions. The most important variable to consider in scoring this trait is the volume of the mastoid not its length	A very small mastoid process that projects only a small distance below the inferior margins of the external auditory meatus and the digastric groove	A massive mastoid process with lengths and widths several times that of the external auditory meatus
Orbital margin	Hold your finger against the margin of the orbit in the area lateral to the supraorbital foramen. Look at each of the diagrams to determine which diagrams it feels like it matches most closely	Extremely sharp, border feels like the edge of a dull knife	A thick rounded margin with a curvature that approximates that of a pencil
Glabella-supra-orbital ridge	View the cranium laterally and assess the glabellar region	The contour of the frontal is smooth with little or no projection in the glabellar area	The glabella and/or supraorbital ridge are massive and from a rounded loaf-shaped projection
Mental eminence*	Hold the mandible between your thumbs and your index fingers with your thumbs on either side of the mental eminence. Move your thumbs medially so that they delimit the lateral borders of the mental eminence	Area of the mental eminence is smooth. There is little or no projection of the mental eminence above the surrounding bone	A massive mental eminence that occupies most of the anterior portion of the mandible

Trait expressions are scored as minimal (score=1) to maximal (score=5) expressions. Use the descriptions below and compare each feature to the diagram above to determine score.
(Adapted from Walker, P.L., 2008. Sexing skulls using discriminant function analysis of visually assessed traits. Am. J. Phys. Anthropol. 136, 39–50.)

Skull Trait Sex Estimation Equations

Discriminant function equations	% correctly classified	
	Females	Males
Pooled African American, European American, and English ancestry		
$Y = \text{glabella}*-1.375+\text{mastoid}*-1.185+\text{mental}*-1.151+9.128$	86.4	88.4
$Y = \text{glabella}*-1.568+\text{mastoid}*-1.459+7.434$	82.9	85.4
$Y = \text{glabella}*-1.525+\text{mental}*-1.485+7.372$	82.1	86.6
$Y = \text{mental}*-1.629+\text{mastoid}*-1.415+7.382$	83.6	79.9
$Y = \text{orbit}*-1.007+\text{mental}*-1.850+6.018$	77.6	78.1
$Y = \text{nuchal}*-0.700+\text{mastoid}*-1.559+5.329$	82.9	76.8
Ancient Native American ancestry		
$Y = \text{orbit}*-0.499+\text{mental}*-0.606+3.414$	77.9	78.1
$Y = \text{mental}*-0.576+\text{mastoid}*-1.136+4.765$	72.7	74.1
$Y = \text{glabella}*-0.797+\text{mastoid}*-1.085+5.025$	82.9	69.5

(Adapted from Walker, P.L., 2008. Sexing skulls using discriminant function analysis of visually assessed traits. Am. J. Phys. Anthropol. 136, 39–50.)

Skulls with scores of <0 are more likely to be males, while those with scores >0 are likely to be female. The probability of being female or male can be calculated using the following equation(s):

$$\text{Probability of female } (p_f) = 1/(1+e^{-y})$$

$$\text{Probability of male } (p_m) = 1 - p_f$$

APPENDIX M: SEX ESTIMATION USING POSTCRANIAL MEASUREMENT SECTIONING POINTS

Univariate Sectioning Points and Classification Rates for American Blacks

Measurement (in mm)	Female			Male			SP	Class. Rate
	N	Mean	SD	N	Mean	SD		
Fem. Epicondylar Br. (62)	33	72.88	3.86	65	83.35	3.97	78	0.89
Tib. Prox. Epiphyseal. Br. (70)	29	69.14	3.68	60	78.73	5.07	74	0.88
Scapula Height (38)	36	138.61	8.46	64	160.7	8.6	150	0.87
Fem. Max. Head Diam. (63)	39	41.33	2.18	69	47.22	2.47	44	0.86
Humerus Epicondylar Br. (41)	34	55.38	2.66	65	64.14	3.87	60	0.86
Humerus Head Diameter (42)	37	41.03	2.46	68	46.99	2.3	44	0.86
Scapula Breadth (39)	36	95.92	6.52	64	109.55	6.71	103	0.86
Radius Max. Length (45)	37	239.19	12.45	69	267.58	13.68	253	0.85
Clavicle Max. Length (35)	38	142.21	7.77	62	156.81	7.41	150	0.84
Calcaneus Max. Length (77)	20	76.45	4.62	50	85.38	4.74	81	0.83
Fem. AP Subtroch Diam. (64)	37	25.86	2.56	66	28.73	2.28	27	0.83
Ischium Length (59)	30	77.33	4.91	47	89.15	6.23	83	0.83
Ulna Max. Length (48)	33	256.42	15.01	63	285.56	13.89	271	0.83
Ulna Phys. Length (51)	25	226.48	13.38	53	254.51	13.94	240	0.83
Fibula Maximum Length (75)	32	367.09	22.11	65	400.55	22.05	384	0.82
Fem. Bicondylar Length (61)	36	444.94	25.63	65	484.32	25.9	465	0.81
Humerus Max. Length (40)	39	309.46	15.95	76	340.91	17.1	325	0.81
Os Coxa Height (56)	36	191.69	11.78	61	211.59	10.1	202	0.81
Tib. Diameter Nut. For. (72)	30	32.23	2.81	59	37.31	2.85	35	0.8

Numbers in parentheses correspond to measurements in Moore-Jansen et al. (1994).
(From Spradley, M.K., Jantz, R.L., 2011. Sex estimation in forensic anthropology: skull versus postcranial elements. J. Forensic Sci. 56(2), 289–296.)

Univariate Sectioning Points and Classification Rates for American Whites

Measurement (mm)	N	Female Mean	SD	N	Male Mean	SD	SP	Class. Rate
Tib. Prox. Epiphyseal. Br. (70)	113	69.19	3.37	226	79.31	4.1	74	0.9
Scapula Height (38)	127	141.87	9.48	231	163.33	8.95	153	0.89
Fem. Epicondylar Br. (62)	129	74.53	3.8	248	85.27	4.38	80	0.88
Fem. Max. Head Diam. (63)	142	42.05	2.09	261	48.4	2.6	45	0.88
Humerus Epicondylar Br. (41)	136	54.9	3.8	258	64.38	3.64	60	0.87
Radius Max. Length (45)	130	228.22	11.21	251	253.41	12.95	241	0.86
Os Coxa Height (56)	124	201.06	13.71	235	222.94	10.8	212	0.85
Scapula Breadth (39)	127	95.48	5.07	237	108.15	6.33	102	0.84
Ulna Max. Length (48)	127	244.94	11.66	250	271.07	13.49	258	0.84
Humerus Head Diameter (42)	139	42.47	2.44	256	48.81	3.22	46	0.83
Clavicle Max. Length (35)	123	139.79	7.04	224	156.96	9.33	148	0.82
Humerus Max. Length (40)	144	305.75	14.43	263	333.99	17.03	320	0.82
Hum. Min. Diam. MS (44)	139	15.32	1.35	256	18.9	1.79	17	0.82
Ulna Phys. Length (51)	105	217.69	11.71	217	240.17	12.68	229	0.82
Fem. Bicondylar Length (61)	134	431.96	20.87	250	470.75	23.63	451	0.82
Tibia Circum. Nut. For. (74)	106	85.36	6.31	199	97.65	7.16	92	0.81
Fibula Maximum Length (75)	117	351.29	19.65	235	386.49	22.11	369	0.81
Femur Max. Length (60)	151	436.15	20.63	268	474.21	23.23	455	0.8

Numbers in parentheses correspond to measurements in Moore-Jansen et al. (1994).
(From Spradley, M.K., Jantz, R.L., 2011. Sex estimation in forensic anthropology: skull versus postcranial elements. J. Forensic Sci. 56(2), 289–296.)

APPENDIX N: ANCESTRY ESTIMATION USING OPTIMIZED SUMMED SCORED ATTRIBUTES (OSSA)

Character states and scores

(a) Anterior Nasal Spine (ANS)
The ANS is scored from 1 to 3 progressively as slight, intermediate, and marked.

1	2	3
(illustration)	(illustration)	(illustration)
Slight—minimal to no projection of the anterior nasal spine beyond the inferior nasal aperture.	Intermediate—moderate projection of the anterior nasal spine beyond the inferior nasal aperture.	Marked—pronounced projection of the anterior nasal spine beyond the inferior nasal aperture.

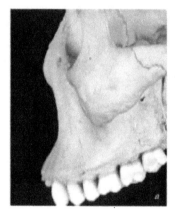
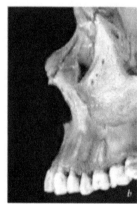

(b) Inferior Nasal Aperture (INA)

INA refers to the inferior border of the nasal aperture just lateral to the anterior nasal spine, which defines the transition from nasal floor to the vertical portion of the maxillae. Bilateral asymmetry may occur. If so, the left side is scored. The morphology of INA ranges from an inferior slope with no delineation of the inferior border (1) to a sharp, vertical ridge of bone, or nasal sill (5).

1	2	3
An inferior sloping of the nasal floor which begins within the nasal cavity and terminates on the vertical surface of the maxilla, producing a smooth transition.	Sloping of the nasal aperture beginning more anteriorly than in INA 1, and with more angulation at the exit of the nasal opening.	The transition from nasal floor to the vertical maxilla is not sloping, nor is there an intervening projection, or sill. Generally, this morphology is a right angle, although a more blunted form may be observed.

4	5	
Any superior incline of the anterior nasal floor, creating a weak (but present) vertical ridge of bone that traverses the inferior nasal border (partial nasal sill).	A pronounced ridge (nasal sill) obstructing the nasal floor-to-maxilla transition.	

(c) Interorbital Breadth (IOB)

IOB is assessed as being narrow (1), medium (2), or broad (3). This assessment is made relative to the facial skeleton.

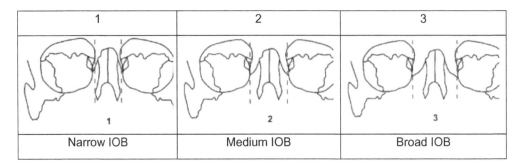

1	2	3
Narrow IOB	Medium IOB	Broad IOB

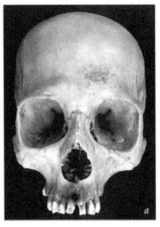
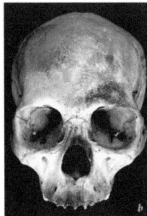
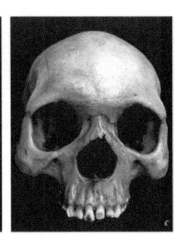

(d) Nasal Aperture Width (NAW)
The width of the nasal aperture is assessed relative to the facial skeleton. It is scored as narrow (1), medium (2), or broad (3).

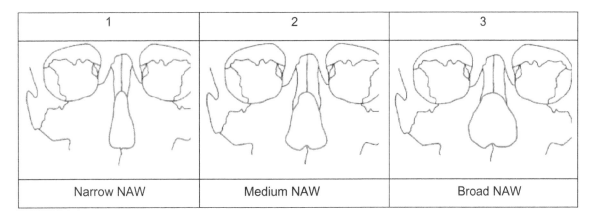

1	2	3
Narrow NAW	Medium NAW	Broad NAW

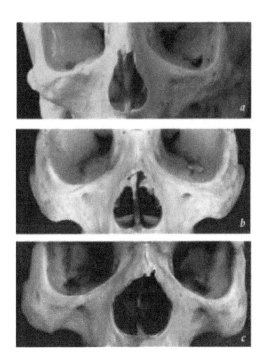

(e) Nasal Bone Structure (NBS)

Nasal Bone Contour (NBC) is defined as the contour of the midfacial region (particularly the contour of the nasal bones and the frontal process of the maxilla) approximately 1 cm below nasion. A contour gage should be used to assist in examining the shape of the nasal bone counter when possible.

0	1	2
Low and rounded nasal bone contour, lacking steep walls.	An oval contour, with elongated, high, and rounded lateral walls.	Steep lateral walls and a broad (roughly 7 mm or more), flat superior surface plateau.
3	**4**	
Steep-sided lateral walls and a narrow superior surface plateau.	Triangular cross section, lacking a superior surface plateau.	

(f) Post-Bregmatic Depression (PBD)

PBD is a slight to broad depression along the sagittal suture, posterior to bregma, which is not the result of pathology. Observed in lateral profile, the trait is scored as either absent (0) or present (1).

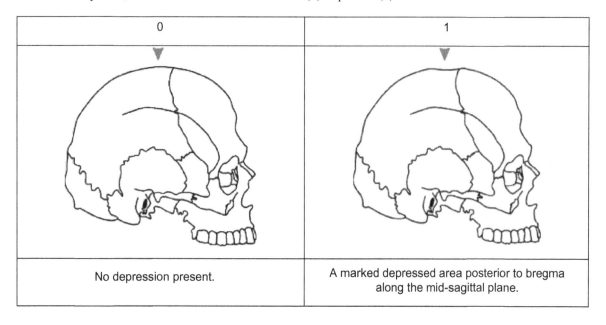

0	1
No depression present.	A marked depressed area posterior to bregma along the mid-sagittal plane.

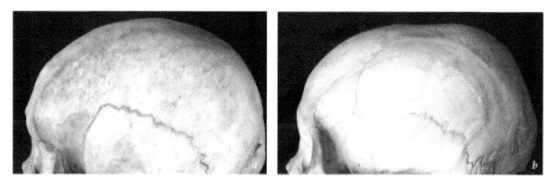

(From Hefner, J.T., 2009. Cranial nonmetric variation and estimating ancestry. J. Forensic Sci. 54(5), 985–995; Hefner, J.T., 2011. Chapter 9: macromorphoscopics. In: Osteoware Software Manual Volume I. Repatriation Osteology Lab Smithsonian Institution. https://osteoware.si.edu.)

Binary Transformation of OSSA Scores

Trait **Anterior Nasal Spine (ANS)**		Expression			
	Slight	Intermediate	Marked		
Character State Score	1	2	3		
OSSA Score	0	1	1		
Inferior Nasal Aperture (INA)					
	Pronounced Slope	Moderate Slope	Straight	Partial Sill	Sill
Character State Score	1	2	3	4	5
OSSA Score	0	0	0	1	1
Interorbital Breadth (IOB)					
	Narrow	Intermediate	Wide		
Character State Score	1	2	3		
OSSA Score	1	1	0		
Nasal Aperture Width (NAW)					
	Narrow	Medium	Broad		
Character State Score	1	2	3		
OSSA Score	1	1	0		
Nasal Bone Structure (NBS)					
	Low/Round	Oval	Marked Plateau	Narrow Plateau	Triangular
Character State Score	0	1	2	3	4
OSSA Score	0	0	1	1	1
Post-Bregmatic Depression (PBD)					
	Absent	Present			
Character State Score	0	1			
OSSA Score	1	0			

(Modified from Hefner, J.T., 2009. Cranial nonmetric variation and estimating ancestry. J. Forensic Sci. 54(5), 985–995.)

OSSA Trait	Character State/Score	OSSA Score
ANS		
INA		
IOB		
NAW		
NBS		
PBD		
	Sum:	

Sum of 0–3 = American Black

Sum of 4+ = American White

A spreadsheet to facilitate calculations is also available at: http://math.mercyhurst.edu/~sousley/Workshops/Spreadsheets/HefnerNonMetricAncestry-OSSA2.1.xls.

APPENDIX O: ANCESTRY ESTIMATION USING A DECISION TREE OF MORPHOSCOPIC TRAITS

Decision tree of morphoscopic traits (refer to Appendix N for traits and scoring)

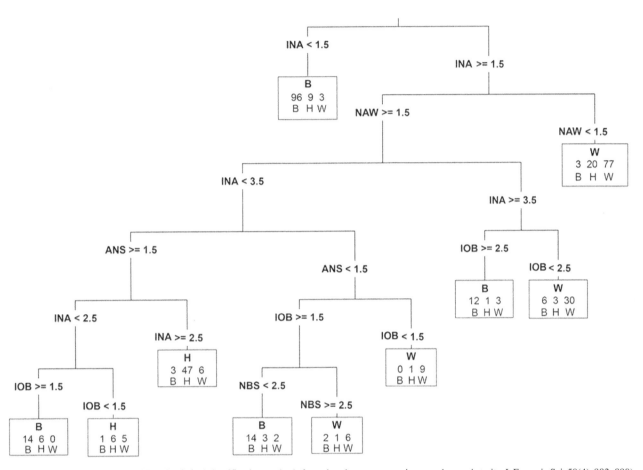

(From Hefner, J.T., Ousley, S.D., 2014. Statistical classification methods for estimating ancestry using morphoscopic traits. J. Forensic Sci. 59(4), 883–890)

APPENDIX P: ANCESTRY ESTIMATION USING DENTAL METRIC ANALYSIS

Tooth Measurements and Definitions	
Measurement	**Definition**
Buccolingual (BL) crown breadth (diameter)	The greatest distance between the buccal/labial and lingual surfaces of the crown, taken at right angles to the plane in which mesiodistal crown length was taken
Mesiodistal (MD) crown length (diameter)	The greatest mesiodistal dimension, taken parallel to the occlusal and buccal/labial surfaces of the tooth crown
(Modified from Hillson, S., 1996. Dental Anthropology. Cambridge University Press, Cambridge.)	

Tooth measurements. Left: Mesiodistal (MD) crown length (diameter); right: Buccolingual (BL) crown breadth (diameter)

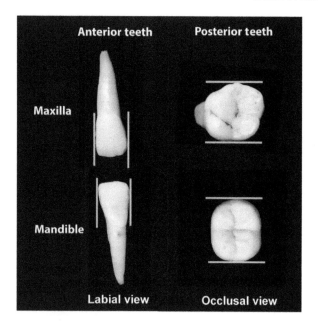 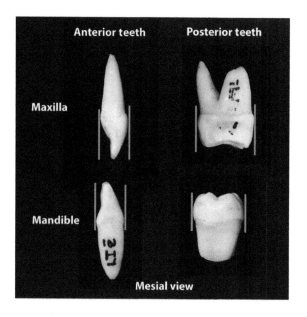

(From Pilloud, M.A., Kenyhercz, M.W., 2016. Dental metrics in biodistance analysis. In: Pilloud, M.A., Hefner, J.T. (Eds.), Biological Distance Analysis: Forensic and Bioarchaeological Perspectives, first ed. Academic Press, London; San Diego, CA.)

Dental Measurements Form							
Tooth	**Side**	**MD**	**BL**	**Tooth**	**Side**	**MD**	**BL**
UI1				LI1			
UI2				LI2			
UC				LC			
UP3				LP3			
UP4				4LP			
UM1				LM1			
UM2				LM2			

U, upper; L, lower; I, incisor; C, canine; P, premolar; M, molar.

Discriminant Function Equations to Distinguish Between Africans/Asians and Europeans

Equation 1. Females

UI1_MD	UI2_MD	UC_MD	UP3_MD	UP4_MD	UM1_MD	UM2_MD	LI1_MD	LI2_MD	LC_MD	LP3_MD	LP4_MD	LM1_MD	LM2_MD
-0.765	1.265	0.156	0.003	0.560	-0.316	-0.195	-0.155	0.920	-1.297	-0.155	-0.087	1.236	0.456

UI1_BL	UI2_BL	UC_BL	UP3_BL	UP4_BL	UM1_BL	UM2_BL	LI1_BL	LI2_BL	LC_BL	LP3_BL	LP4_BL	LM1_BL	LM2_BL
0.440	-0.855	-0.157	1.373	-0.322	0.996	-0.178	0.297	-0.316	-0.183	1.120	-0.844	-0.746	-0.564

Equation 1. Males

UI1_MD	UI2_MD	UC_MD	UP3_MD	UP4_MD	UM1_MD	UM2_MD	LI1_MD	LI2_MD	LC_MD	LP3_MD	LP4_MD	LM1_MD	LM2_MD
-.330	.229	.542	-.204	.384	-.349	.118	.120	.049	.321	.111	.254	.597	-.002

UI1_BL	UI2_BL	UC_BL	UP3_BL	UP4-BL	UM1_BL	UM2_BL	LI1_BL	LI2_BL	LC_BL	LP3_BL	LP4_BL	LM1_BL	LM2_BL
.176	-.074	-.895	1.350	-.603	.060	-.480	-.226	.360	-.226	1.273	-1.080	.335	.158

U, upper; L, lower; I, incisor; C, canine; P, premolar; M, molar; BL, buccolingual; MD, mesiodistal.

Female: Constant = -17.870; Wilk's lambda significance = 0.000; 95.0% of original grouped cases correctly classified; 91.2% of cross-validated grouped cases correctly classified; Functions at group centroids: African/Asian = 0.240, European = -3.224; Results > -1.492 indicate African/Asian ancestry.

Male: Constant = -15.949; Wilk's lambda significance = 0.000; 90.5% of original grouped cases correctly classified; 86.2% of cross-validated grouped cases correctly classified; Functions at group centroids: African/Asian = 0.237, European = -2.194; Results > -0.979 indicate African/Asian ancestry.

(From Pilloud, M.A., Hefner, J.T., Hanihara, T., Hayashi, A., 2014. The use of tooth crown measurements in the estimation of ancestry. J. Forensic Sci. 59(6), 1493–1501.)

Discriminant Function Equations to Distinguish Between Africans and Asians

Equation 2. Females

UI1_MD	UI2_MD	UC_MD	UP3_MD	UP4_MD	UM1_MD	UM2_MD	LI1_MD	LI2_MD	LC_MD	LP3_MD	LP4_MD	LM1_MD	LM2_MD
.303	.531	.960	.216	-.203	1.124	.295	.451	-1.082	-2.210	1.013	-.096	-1.220	-.030

UI1_BL	UI2_BL	UC_BL	UP3_BL	UP4-BL	UM1_BL	UM2_BL	LI1_BL	LI2_BL	LC_BL	LP3_BL	LP4_BL	LM1_BL	LM2_BL
.206	.060	-.022	-.174	.192	1.033	-1.091	1.067	.782	-1.171	.886	-2.096	.414	.152

Equation 2. Males

UI1_MD	UI2_MD	UC_MD	UP3_MD	UP4_MD	UM1_MD	UM2_MD	LI1_MD	LI2_MD	LC_MD	LP3_MD	LP4_MD	LM1_MD	LM2_MD
1.125	-.476	-1.184	.555	-.529	.577	.789	-.713	-.669	.510	.742	.173	-.640	.207

UI1_BL	UI2_BL	UC_BL	UP3_BL	UP4-BL	UM1_BL	UM2_BL	LI1_BL	LI2_BL	LC_BL	LP3_BL	LP4_BL	LM1_BL	LM2_BL
.098	.543	.515	-.696	.028	-.584	.012	-1.526	.472	.096	.519	.141	-.043	-.869

U, upper; L, lower; I, incisor; C, canine; P, premolar; M, molar; BL, buccolingual; MD, mesiodistal.

Females: Constant = -1.003; Wilk's lambda significance = 0.221; 98.6% of original grouped cases correctly classified; 95.3% of cross-validated grouped cases correctly classified; Functions at group centroids: African = -4.553, Asian = 0.062; Results > -2.246 indicate Asian ancestry.

Males: Constant = 5.322; Wilk's lambda significance = 0.000; 83.5% of original grouped cases correctly classified; 79.4% of cross-validated grouped cases correctly classified; Functions at group centroids: African = 1.745, Asian = -0.177; Results > 0.784 indicate African ancestry.

(From Pilloud, M.A., Hefner, J.T., Hanihara, T., Hayashi, A., 2014. The use of tooth crown measurements in the estimation of ancestry. J. Forensic Sci. 59(6), 1493–1501.)

APPENDIX Q: AGE ESTIMATION USING DENTAL DEVELOPMENT

Tooth formation stages for single-rooted teeth

	ci: Initial cusp formation			Ri: Initial root formation with diverge edges
	Cco: Coalescence of cusps			R 1/4: Root length less than crown length
	Coc: Cusp outline complete			R 1/2: Root length equals crown length
	Cr 1/2: Crown half completed with dentine formation			R 3/4: Three quarters of root length developed with diverge ends
	Cr 3/4: Crown three quarters completed			Rc: Root length completed with parallel ends
	Crc: Crown completed with defined pulp roof			A 1/2: Apex closed (root ends converge) with wide PDL
				Ac: Apex closed with normal PDL width

(From AlQahtani, S.J., Hector, M.P., Liversidge, H.M., 2010. Brief communication: the London atlas of human tooth development and eruption. Am. J. Phys. Anthropol. 142, 481–490.)

Tooth formation stages for multi-rooted teeth

	Ci: Initial cusp formation		
	Cco: Coalescence of cusps		R 1/4: Root length less than crown length with visible bifurcatio area
	Coc: Cusp outline complete		R 1/2: Root length equals crown length
	Cr 1/2: Crown half completed with dentine formation		R 3/4: Three quarters of root length developed with diverge ends
	Cr 3/4: Crown three quarters completed		Rc: Root length completed with parallel ends
	Crc: Crown completed with defined pulp roof		A 1/2: Apex closed (root ends converge) with wide PDL
	Ri: Initial root formation with diverge edges		Ac: Apex closed with normal PDL width

(From AlQahtani, S.J., Hector, M.P., Liversidge, H.M., 2010. Brief communication: the London atlas of human tooth development and eruption. Am. J. Phys. Anthropol. 142, 481–490.)

Root resorption stages for single and multi-rooted teeth

	Ac: Apex closed with normal PDL width	
	Res 1/4: Resorption of apical quarter of the root	
	Res 1/2: Resorption of half the root	
	Res 3/4: Resorption of three quarters of the root	

(From AlQahtani, S.J., Hector, M.P., Liversidge, H.M., 2010. Brief communication: the London atlas of human tooth development and eruption. Am. J. Phys. Anthropol. 142, 481–490.)

Tooth eruption stages

	Position 1: When the occlusal or incisal surface is covered entirely by bone	
	Position 2: When the occlusal or incisal surface breaks through the crest of the alveolar bone	
	Position 3: When the occlusal or incisal surface is midway between the alveolar bone and the occlusal plane	
	Position 4: Occlusal or incisal surface is in the occlusal plane	

(From AlQahtani, S.J., Hector, M.P., Liversidge, H.M., 2010. Brief communication: the London atlas of human tooth development and eruption. Am. J. Phys. Anthropol. 142, 481–490.)

Atlas of human tooth development and eruption

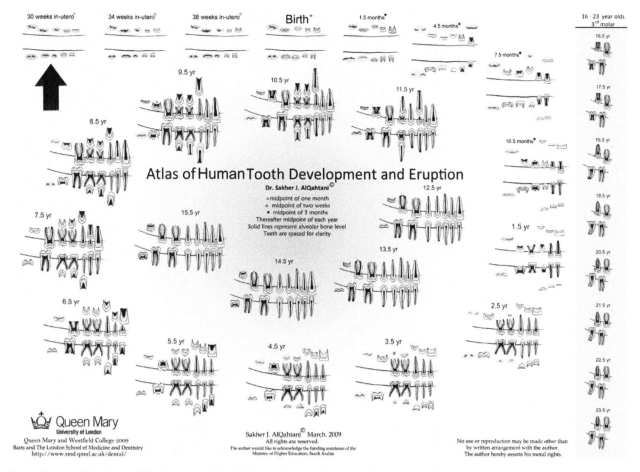

(From AlQahtani, S.J., Hector, M.P., Liversidge, H.M., 2010. Brief communication: the London atlas of human tooth development and eruption. Am. J. Phys. Anthropol. 142, 481–490.)

Tooth Development Data From Autopsied Infants[a] (Combined Sex)

		Maxilla					Mandible			
		Number	Tooth Formation Stage				Number	Tooth Formation Stage		
Age	Tooth	of Teeth	Minimum	Median	Maximum	Tooth	of Teeth	Minimum	Median	Maximum
30 Weeks in utero[b]	i^1	12	Coc	Cr $\frac{1}{2}$	Cr $\frac{3}{4}$	i_1	12	Coc	Cr $\frac{1}{2}$	Cr $\frac{3}{4}$
	i^2	12	Cco	Coc	Cr $\frac{3}{4}$	i_2	12	Cco	Coc	Cr $\frac{3}{4}$
	c'	12	Ci	Ci	Coc	c'	12	Ci	Ci	Coc
	m^1	12	Ci	Cco	Coc	m_1	12	Ci	Cco	Coc
	m^2	12	Ci	Ci	Cco	m_2	12	Ci	Ci	Cco
34 Weeks in utero[b]	i^1	13	Cr $\frac{1}{2}$	Cr $\frac{3}{4}$	Cr $\frac{3}{4}$	i_1	15	Cr $\frac{1}{2}$	Cr $\frac{3}{4}$	Crc
	i^2	13	Cr $\frac{1}{2}$	Cr $\frac{1}{2}$	Cr $\frac{3}{4}$	i_2	7	Cr $\frac{1}{2}$	Cr $\frac{3}{4}$	Cr $\frac{3}{4}$
	c'	13	Ci	Ci	Coc	c'	12	Ci	Ci	Coc
	m^1	15	Cco	Cco	Coc	m_1	14	Cco	Cco	Coc
	m^2	13	Ci	Ci	Cco	m_2	12	Ci	Ci	Cco
38 Weeks in utero[b]	i^1	26	Cr $\frac{1}{2}$	Cr $\frac{3}{4}$	Crc	i_1	23	Cr $\frac{1}{2}$	Cr $\frac{3}{4}$	Crc
	i^2	20	Cr $\frac{1}{2}$	Cr $\frac{1}{2}$	Cr $\frac{3}{4}$	i_2	15	Cr $\frac{1}{2}$	Cr $\frac{3}{4}$	Crc
	c'	26	Ci	Ci	Coc	c'	26	Ci	Cco	Coc
	m^1	29	Cco	Cco	Cr $\frac{1}{2}$	m_1	29	Cco	Cco	Cr $\frac{1}{2}$
	m^2	27	Ci	Ci	Cco	m_2	26	Ci	Ci	Cco
Birth[c]	i^1	23	Cr $\frac{3}{4}$	Cr $\frac{3}{4}$	Crc	i_1	27	Cr $\frac{3}{4}$	Crc	Crc
	i^2	20	Cr $\frac{1}{2}$	Cr $\frac{3}{4}$	Cr $\frac{3}{4}$	i_2	18	Cr $\frac{3}{4}$	Cr $\frac{3}{4}$	Crc
	c'	30	Ci	Coc	Cr $\frac{1}{2}$	c'	28	Ci	Coc	Coc
	m^1	25	Cco	Coc	Cr $\frac{1}{2}$	m_1	29	Cco	Coc	Cr $\frac{1}{2}$
	M^2	29	Ci	Cco	Coc	m_2	26	Ci	Ci	Coc

[a]Twelve children from 28 to <32 weeks in utero, 15 children from 32 to <36 weeks in utero, 30 children from 36 to 39 weeks in utero, and 30 children from >39 weeks in utero to <1 week after birth.
[b]Midpoint of 4 weeks.
[c]Midpoint of 2 weeks.
(From AlQahtani, S.J., Hector, M.P., Liversidge, H.M., 2010. Brief communication: the London atlas of human tooth development and eruption. Am. J. Phys. Anthropol. 142, 481–490.)

Tooth Development Data From Skeletal Remains[a] (Combined Sex)

Age (Months)	Tooth	Number of Teeth	Tooth Formation Stage			Tooth	Number of Teeth	Tooth Formation Stage		
			Minimum	Median	Maximum			Minimum	Median	Maximum
			Maxilla					**Mandible**		
1.5[b]	i^1	34	$Cr\,\frac{3}{4}$	Crc	Ri	i_1	29	$Cr\,\frac{3}{4}$	Crc	Ri
	i^2	31	$Cr\,\frac{1}{2}$	$Cr\,\frac{3}{4}$	Crc	i_2	25	$Cr\,\frac{3}{4}$	Crc	Ri
	c'	34	Coc	Coc	$Cr\,\frac{1}{2}$	c'	29	Coc	Coc	$Cr\,\frac{1}{2}$
	m^1	33	Cco	Coc	$Cr\,\frac{1}{2}$	m_1	28	Cco	Coc	$Cr\,\frac{1}{2}$
	m^2	27	Ci	Cco	Coc	m_2	25	Ci	Cco	$Cr\,\frac{1}{2}$
	M^1	4	–	–	Ci	M_1	3	–	–	Cco
4.5[b]	i^1	13	Crc	Ri	$R\,\frac{1}{4}$	i_1	11	Crc	Ri	$R\,\frac{1}{4}$
	i^2	11	Crc	Crc	Ri	i_2	13	$Cr\,\frac{3}{4}$	Ri	$R\,\frac{1}{4}$
	c'	14	Coc	$Cr\,\frac{1}{2}$	$Cr\,\frac{3}{4}$	c'	16	Coc	$Cr\,\frac{1}{2}$	$Cr\,\frac{3}{4}$
	m^1	7	$Cr\,\frac{1}{2}$	$Cr\,\frac{1}{2}$	$Cr\,\frac{3}{4}$	m_1	11	$Cr\,\frac{1}{2}$	$Cr\,\frac{3}{4}$	Crc
	m^2	8	Coc	$Cr\,\frac{1}{2}$	$Cr\,\frac{3}{4}$	m_2	11	$Cr\,\frac{1}{2}$	$Cr\,\frac{3}{4}$	Crc
	I^1	4	Ci	Ci	Coc	i_1	1	–	–	Ci
	M^1	4	Ci	Ci	Ci	M_1	5	Ci	Ci	Cco
7.5[b]	i^1	6	Ri	$R\,\frac{1}{4}$	$R\,\frac{1}{2}$	i_1	5	$R\,\frac{1}{4}$	$R\,\frac{1}{2}$	$R\,\frac{1}{2}$
	i^2	6	Crc	$R\,\frac{1}{4}$	$R\,\frac{1}{4}$	i_2	4	Ri	$R\,\frac{1}{4}$	$R\,\frac{1}{4}$
	c'	8	$Cr\,\frac{3}{4}$	Crc	Crc	c'	6	$Cr\,\frac{1}{2}$	$Cr\,\frac{3}{4}$	Crc
	m^1	9	Crc	Ri	$Cr\,\frac{1}{2}$	m_1	10	$Cr\,\frac{3}{4}$	Crc	Ri
	m^2	5	$Cr\,\frac{3}{4}$	Crc	Crc	m_2	10	$Cr\,\frac{1}{2}$	$Cr\,\frac{3}{4}$	$Cr\,\frac{3}{4}$
	I^1	4	Coc	Coc	$Cr\,\frac{1}{2}$	I_1	3	Coc	Coc	$Cr\,\frac{1}{2}$
	C'	4	Ci	Ci	Ci	C'	1	–	–	Ci
	M^1	4	Cco	Cco	Coc	M_1	4	Cco	Coc	Coc
10.5[b]	i^1	5	Ri	$R\,\frac{1}{2}$	$R\,\frac{1}{2}$	i_1	9	$R\,\frac{1}{4}$	$R\,\frac{3}{4}$	$R\,\frac{3}{4}$
	i^2	4	Ri	$R\,\frac{1}{4}$	$R\,\frac{1}{2}$	i_2	10	Ri	$R\,\frac{1}{2}$	$R\,\frac{1}{2}$
	c'	6	$Cr\,\frac{3}{4}$	Crc	Ri	c'	12	$Cr\,\frac{3}{4}$	Crc	Crc
	m^1	4	Crc	$R\,\frac{1}{4}$	$R\,\frac{1}{4}$	m_1	12	Crc	$R\,\frac{1}{4}$	$R\,\frac{1}{2}$
	m^2	6	$Cr\,\frac{3}{4}$	Crc	Ri	m_2	12	$Cr\,\frac{3}{4}$	Crc	Ri
	I^1	4	Coc	$Cr\,\frac{1}{2}$	$Cr\,\frac{1}{2}$	I_1	5	$Cr\,\frac{1}{2}$	$Cr\,\frac{1}{2}$	$Cr\,\frac{1}{2}$
	C'	4	Ci	Ci	Ci	C'	4	Ci	Ci	Ci
	M^1	4	Cco	Coc	Coc	M_1	10	Cco	Coc	Coc

[a]Thirty-four children from 1 week to <3 months, 14 children from 3 to <6 months, 10 children from 6 to <9 months, and 14 children from 9 to <12 months.
[b]Midpoint of 3 months.
(From AlQahtani, S.J., Hector, M.P., Liversidge, H.M., 2010. Brief communication: the London atlas of human tooth development and eruption. Am. J. Phys. Anthropol. 142, 481–490.)

Combined Sex Tooth Development Data for 17 Children (Skeletal Remains) From 1 to <2 Years, 24 Children From 2 to <3 Years, and 24 Children From 3 to <4 Years

Age (Years)	Maxilla					Mandible				
	Tooth	Number of Teeth	Tooth Formation Stage			Tooth	Number of Teeth	Tooth Formation Stage		
			Minimum	Median	Maximum			Minimum	Median	Maximum
1.5[a]	i¹	5	$R\frac{1}{4}$	$R\frac{3}{4}$	$R\frac{3}{4}$	i₁	7	$R\frac{3}{4}$	$R\frac{3}{4}$	Rc
	i²	6	Ri	$R\frac{1}{2}$	$R\frac{3}{4}$	i₂	7	$R\frac{3}{4}$	$R\frac{3}{4}$	Rc
	c′	6	Crc	Ri	$R\frac{1}{2}$	c′	7	$Cr\frac{3}{4}$	Ri	$R\frac{1}{2}$
	m¹	7	Ri	$R\frac{1}{2}$	$R\frac{3}{4}$	m₁	8	Ri	$R\frac{1}{2}$	$R\frac{3}{4}$
	m²	8	Crc	Ri	$R\frac{1}{4}$	m₂	8	$Cr\frac{3}{4}$	Ri	$R\frac{1}{4}$
	I¹	6	$Cr\frac{1}{2}$	$Cr\frac{1}{2}$	$Cr\frac{1}{2}$	I₁	6	$Cr\frac{1}{2}$	$Cr\frac{1}{2}$	$Cr\frac{3}{4}$
	I²	4	–	Coc	Coc	I₂	6	Coc	$Cr\frac{1}{2}$	$Cr\frac{1}{2}$
	C′	8	Coc	Coc	Coc	C′	4	–	Coc	Coc
	M¹	4	–	Coc	$Cr\frac{1}{2}$	M₁	8	Cco	Coc	$Cr\frac{1}{2}$
2.5[a]	i¹	24	Rc	Ac	Ac	i₁	24	Rc	Ac	Ac
	i²	24	Rc	Ac	Ac	i₂	24	Rc	Ac	Ac
	c′	24	$R\frac{3}{4}$	Rc	Rc	c′	24	$R\frac{3}{4}$	Rc	Rc
	m¹	24	$R\frac{3}{4}$	Rc	Ac	m₁	24	$R\frac{3}{4}$	Rc	Ac
	m²	24	$R\frac{1}{4}$	$R\frac{3}{4}$	Ac	m₂	24	$R\frac{1}{2}$	$R\frac{3}{4}$	Ac
	I¹	24	$Cr\frac{1}{2}$	$Cr\frac{3}{4}$	$Cr\frac{3}{4}$	I₁	24	$Cr\frac{1}{2}$	$Cr\frac{3}{4}$	Crc
	I²	24	Coc	$Cr\frac{1}{2}$	$Cr\frac{3}{4}$	I₂	24	$Cr\frac{1}{2}$	$Cr\frac{3}{4}$	Crc
	C′	21	–	$Cr\frac{1}{2}$	$Cr\frac{1}{2}$	C′	24	Coc	$Cr\frac{1}{2}$	$Cr\frac{1}{2}$
	P¹	19	–	Ci	Cco	P₁	20	–	Cco	Cco
	P²	10	–	–	Ci	P₂	18	–	Ci	Ci
	M¹	24	$Cr\frac{1}{2}$	$Cr\frac{3}{4}$	$Cr\frac{3}{4}$	M₁	24	$Cr\frac{1}{2}$	$Cr\frac{3}{4}$	Crc
	M²	16	–	Ci	Ci	M₂	15	–	Ci	Ci
3.5[a]	i¹	24	Ac	Ac	Ac	i₁	24	Ac	Ac	Ac
	i²	24	Ac	Ac	Ac	i₂	24	Ac	Ac	Ac
	c′	24	Ac	Ac	Ac	c′	24	Ac	Ac	Ac
	m¹	24	Ac	Ac	Ac	m₁	24	Ac	Ac	Ac
	m²	24	Ac	Ac	Ac	m₂	24	Ac	Ac	Ac
	I¹	24	$Cr\frac{3}{4}$	$Cr\frac{3}{4}$	Ri	I₁	24	$Cr\frac{3}{4}$	Crc	Ri
	I²	24	$Cr\frac{1}{2}$	$Cr\frac{1}{2}$	Crc	I₂	24	$Cr\frac{1}{2}$	$Cr\frac{3}{4}$	Crc
	C′	24	$Cr\frac{1}{2}$	$Cr\frac{1}{2}$	$Cr\frac{3}{4}$	C′	24	Coc	$Cr\frac{1}{2}$	Crc
	P¹	24	Ci	Coc	$Cr\frac{1}{2}$	P₁	24	Ci	$Cr\frac{1}{2}$	$Cr\frac{1}{2}$
	P²	20	–	Ci	Cco	P₂	22	–	Ci	Coc
	M¹	24	$Cr\frac{1}{2}$	Crc	$R\frac{1}{4}$	M₁	24	$Cr\frac{1}{2}$	Ri	Ri
	M²	20	–	Cco	Coc	M₂	22	–	Cco	Coc

[a]*Midpoint of 1 year.*

(From AlQahtani, S.J., Hector, M.P., Liversidge, H.M., 2010. Brief communication: the London atlas of human tooth development and eruption. Am. J. Phys. Anthropol. 142, 481–490.)

Tooth Development Data (Combined Sex) for 24 Children in Each Age Group: 4 to <5 Years, 5 to <6 Years, and 6 to <7 Years

Age (Years)		Maxilla					Mandible			
	Tooth	Number of Teeth	Tooth Formation Stage			Tooth	Number of Teeth	Tooth Formation Stage		
			Minimum	Median	Maximum			Minimum	Median	Maximum
4.5[a]	i^1 to m^2	24 each	Ac	Ac	Ac	i_1 to m_2	24 each	Ac	Ac	Ac
	I^1	24	Cr $\frac{3}{4}$	Crc	Ri	I_1	24	Cr $\frac{3}{4}$	Ri	R $\frac{1}{4}$
	I^2	24	Cr $\frac{3}{4}$	Cr $\frac{3}{4}$	Ri	I_2	24	Cr $\frac{3}{4}$	Ri	Ri
	C'	24	Cr $\frac{3}{4}$	Cr $\frac{3}{4}$	Ri	C'	24	Cr $\frac{1}{2}$	Cr $\frac{3}{4}$	Ri
	P^1	24	Cr $\frac{1}{2}$	Cr $\frac{1}{2}$	Cr $\frac{3}{4}$	P_1	24	Cr $\frac{1}{2}$	Cr $\frac{1}{2}$	Crc
	P^2	24	Coc	Cco	Cr $\frac{3}{4}$	P_2	24	Ci	Coc	Cr $\frac{1}{2}$
	M^1	24	R $\frac{1}{4}$	R $\frac{1}{4}$	R $\frac{1}{2}$	M_1	24	R $\frac{1}{4}$	R $\frac{1}{4}$	R $\frac{1}{2}$
	M^2	24	Ci	Coc	Cr $\frac{1}{2}$	M_2	24	Cco	Coc	Cr $\frac{1}{2}$
5.5[a]	i^1	24	Ac	Ac	Res $\frac{1}{4}$	i_1	24	Ac	Ac	Res $\frac{1}{2}$
	i^2	24	Ac	Ac	Res $\frac{1}{4}$	i_2	24	Ac	Ac	Res $\frac{1}{4}$
	c' to m^2	24 each	Ac	Ac	Ac	c' to m_2	24 each	Ac	Ac	Ac
	I^1	24	Crc	Ri	R $\frac{1}{4}$	I_1	24	Ri	R $\frac{1}{4}$	R $\frac{1}{2}$
	I^2	24	Crc	Crc	Ri	I_2	24	Crc	R $\frac{1}{4}$	R $\frac{1}{4}$
	C'	24	Cr $\frac{3}{4}$	Crc	Ri	C'	24	Cr $\frac{3}{4}$	Crc	Ri
	P^1	24	Cr $\frac{1}{2}$	Cr $\frac{3}{4}$	Crc	P_1	24	Coc	Cr $\frac{3}{4}$	Crc
	P_2	24	Cco	Cr $\frac{1}{2}$	Cr $\frac{3}{4}$	P_2	24	Cco	Cr $\frac{3}{4}$	Cr $\frac{3}{4}$
	M^1	24	R $\frac{1}{4}$	R $\frac{1}{4}$	R $\frac{1}{2}$	M_1	24	R $\frac{1}{4}$	R $\frac{1}{4}$	R $\frac{1}{2}$
	M^2	24	Coc	Cr $\frac{1}{2}$	Cr $\frac{3}{4}$	M_2	24	Coc	Cr $\frac{1}{2}$	Cr $\frac{3}{4}$
6.5[a]	i^1	14	Ac	Res $\frac{3}{4}$	–	i_1	11	Ac	–	–
	i^2	22	Ac	Res $\frac{1}{4}$	Res $\frac{3}{4}$	i_2	13	Ac	Res $\frac{1}{2}$	–
	c'	24	Ac	Ac	Ac	c'	24	Ac	Ac	Ac
	m^1	24	Ac	Ac	Res $\frac{1}{4}$	m_1	24	Ac	Ac	Res $\frac{1}{4}$
	m^2	24	Ac	Ac	Ac	m_2	24	Ac	Ac	Res $\frac{1}{4}$
	I^1	24	Crc	R $\frac{1}{4}$	R $\frac{3}{4}$	I_1	24	R $\frac{1}{4}$	R $\frac{1}{2}$	Rc
	I^2	24	Crc	Ri	R $\frac{1}{2}$	I_2	24	Ri	R $\frac{1}{4}$	R $\frac{3}{4}$
	C'	24	Crc	Ri	R $\frac{1}{4}$	C'	24	Cr $\frac{3}{4}$	Ri	R $\frac{1}{4}$
	P^1	24	Cr $\frac{3}{4}$	Crc	Ri	P_1	24	Cr $\frac{1}{2}$	Crc	Ri
	P_2	24	Cr $\frac{1}{2}$	Crc	Crc	P_2	24	Coc	Crc	Ri
	M^1	24	R $\frac{1}{4}$	R $\frac{1}{2}$	R $\frac{3}{4}$	M_1	24	R $\frac{1}{4}$	R $\frac{1}{2}$	R $\frac{3}{4}$
	M^2	24	Coc	Cr $\frac{1}{2}$	Crc	M_2	24	Coc	Cr $\frac{1}{2}$	Crc

[a]*Midpoint of 1 year.*
(From AlQahtani, S.J., Hector, M.P., Liversidge, H.M., 2010. Brief communication: the London atlas of human tooth development and eruption. Am. J. Phys. Anthropol. 142, 481–490.)

Tooth Development Data (Combined Sex) for 24 Children in Each Age Group: 7 to <8 Years, 8 to <9 Years, and 9 to <10 Years

Age (Years)	Maxilla					Mandible				
	Tooth	Number of Teeth	Minimum	Median	Maximum	Tooth	Number of Teeth	Minimum	Median	Maximum
7.5^a	i^1	2	Res $\frac{3}{4}$	–	–	i_1	–	–	–	–
	i^2	13	Res $\frac{1}{2}$	Res $\frac{3}{4}$	–	i_2	2	Ac	–	–
	c'	24	Ac	Ac	Ac	c'	24	Ac	Ac	Ac
	m^1	24	Ac	Ac	Res $\frac{1}{2}$	m_1	24	Ac	Ac	Res $\frac{1}{2}$
	m^2	24	Ac	Ac	Res $\frac{1}{2}$	m_2	24	Ac	Ac	Res $\frac{1}{4}$
	I^1	24	R $\frac{1}{4}$	R $\frac{3}{4}$	Rc	I_1	24	R $\frac{3}{4}$	Rc	A $\frac{1}{2}$
	I^2	24	R $\frac{1}{4}$	R $\frac{1}{2}$	Rc	I_2	24	R $\frac{1}{4}$	R $\frac{3}{4}$	A $\frac{1}{2}$
	C'	24	Ri	R $\frac{1}{4}$	R $\frac{1}{2}$	C'	24	Ri	R $\frac{1}{4}$	R $\frac{1}{4}$
	P^1	24	Cr $\frac{3}{4}$	Ri	R $\frac{1}{4}$	P_1	24	Ri	Ri	R $\frac{1}{4}$
	P^2	24	Cr $\frac{3}{4}$	Crc	R $\frac{1}{4}$	P_2	24	Crc	Crc	R $\frac{1}{4}$
	M^1	24	R $\frac{1}{4}$	R $\frac{3}{4}$	A $\frac{1}{2}$	M_1	24	R $\frac{3}{4}$	R $\frac{3}{4}$	A $\frac{1}{2}$
	M^2	24	Cr $\frac{1}{2}$	Cr $\frac{3}{4}$	R $\frac{1}{4}$	M_2	24	Cr $\frac{1}{2}$	Cr $\frac{3}{4}$	R $\frac{1}{4}$
	M^3	4	–	–	Ci	M_3	8	–	–	Ci
8.5^a	i^2	6	Res $\frac{3}{4}$	–	–	i_2	–	–	–	–
	c'	24	Ac	Ac	Res $\frac{1}{4}$	c'	24	Ac	Ac	Res $\frac{1}{2}$
	m^1	24	Res $\frac{1}{4}$	Res $\frac{1}{2}$	Res $\frac{1}{2}$	m_1	24	Res $\frac{1}{4}$	Res $\frac{1}{4}$	Res $\frac{1}{2}$
	m^2	24	Ac	Res $\frac{1}{2}$	Res $\frac{1}{2}$	m_2	24	Ac	Ac	Res $\frac{1}{4}$
	I^1	24	R $\frac{1}{2}$	Rc	A $\frac{1}{2}$	I_1	24	R $\frac{3}{4}$	Ac	Ac
	I^2	24	R $\frac{1}{4}$	R $\frac{3}{4}$	Rc	I_2	24	R $\frac{1}{4}$	A $\frac{1}{2}$	Ac
	C'	24	Ri	R $\frac{1}{4}$	R $\frac{3}{4}$	C'	24	R $\frac{1}{4}$	R $\frac{1}{4}$	R $\frac{3}{4}$
	P^1	24	Ri	Ri	R $\frac{1}{2}$	P_1	24	Ri	R $\frac{1}{4}$	R $\frac{1}{2}$
	P^2	24	Ri	Ri	R $\frac{1}{2}$	P_2	24	Crc	Ri	R $\frac{1}{4}$
	M^1	24	R $\frac{1}{2}$	Rc	Ac	M_1	24	R $\frac{3}{4}$	R $\frac{3}{4}$	A $\frac{1}{2}$
	M^2	24	Crc	Ri	R $\frac{1}{4}$	M_2	24	Cr $\frac{3}{4}$	Ri	R $\frac{1}{4}$
	M^3	13	–	Ci	Coc	M_3	20	–	Ci	Cco
9.5^a	c'	22	Ac	Ac	–	c'	22	Ac	Res $\frac{1}{4}$	–
	m^1	24	Res $\frac{1}{4}$	Res $\frac{1}{2}$	Res $\frac{3}{4}$	m_1	24	Res $\frac{1}{4}$	Res $\frac{1}{4}$	Res $\frac{3}{4}$
	m^2	24	Res $\frac{1}{4}$	Res $\frac{1}{2}$	Res $\frac{3}{4}$	m_2	24	Ac	Res $\frac{1}{4}$	Res $\frac{1}{2}$
	I^1	24	R $\frac{3}{4}$	Rc	A $\frac{1}{2}$	I_1	24	Rc	Ac	Ac
	I^2	24	R $\frac{1}{2}$	Rc	A $\frac{1}{2}$	I_2	24	Rc	A $\frac{1}{2}$	Ac
	C'	24	R $\frac{1}{4}$	R $\frac{1}{2}$	R $\frac{3}{4}$	C'	24	R $\frac{1}{4}$	R $\frac{1}{2}$	R $\frac{3}{4}$
	P^1	24	R $\frac{1}{4}$	R $\frac{1}{4}$	R $\frac{3}{4}$	P_1	24	R $\frac{1}{4}$	R $\frac{1}{2}$	R $\frac{3}{4}$
	P^2	24	Ri	R $\frac{1}{4}$	R $\frac{3}{4}$	P_2	24	Ri	R $\frac{1}{4}$	R $\frac{3}{4}$
	M^1	24	Rc	Ac	Ac	M_1	24	R $\frac{3}{4}$	A $\frac{1}{2}$	Ac
	M^2	24	Ri	R $\frac{1}{4}$	R $\frac{1}{2}$	M_2	24	Ri	R $\frac{1}{4}$	R $\frac{1}{2}$
	M^3	17	–	Coc	Cr $\frac{3}{4}$	M_3	22	–	Cco	Cr $\frac{3}{4}$

[a]Midpoint of 1 year.

(From AlQahtani, S.J., Hector, M.P., Liversidge, H.M., 2010. Brief communication: the London atlas of human tooth development and eruption. Am. J. Phys. Anthropol. 142, 481–490.)

Tooth Development Data (Combined Sex) for 24 Children in Each Age Group: 10 to <11 Years, 11 to <12 Years, and 12 to <13 Years

Age (Years)	Tooth	Maxilla				Tooth	Mandible			
		Number of Teeth	Tooth Formation Stage				Number of Teeth	Tooth Formation Stage		
			Minimum	Median	Maximum			Minimum	Median	Maximum
10.5[a]	c'	20	Ac	Res $\frac{1}{4}$	–	c'	–	–	–	–
	m^1	17	Res $\frac{1}{4}$	Res $\frac{1}{2}$	–	m$_1$	16	Res $\frac{1}{4}$	Res $\frac{1}{2}$	–
	m^2	21	Res $\frac{1}{4}$	Res $\frac{1}{2}$	–	m$_2$	18	Ac	Res $\frac{1}{4}$	–
	I^1	24	Rc	A $\frac{1}{2}$	Ac	I$_1$	24	A $\frac{1}{2}$	Ac	Ac
	I^2	24	Rc	A $\frac{1}{2}$	Ac	I$_2$	24	Rc	Ac	Ac
	C'	24	R $\frac{1}{2}$	R $\frac{3}{4}$	R $\frac{3}{4}$	C'	24	R $\frac{3}{4}$	R $\frac{3}{4}$	Rc
	P^1	24	R $\frac{1}{4}$	R $\frac{1}{2}$	Rc	P$_1$	24	R $\frac{1}{4}$	R $\frac{1}{2}$	Rc
	P^2	24	Ri	R $\frac{1}{2}$	Rc	P$_2$	24	R $\frac{1}{4}$	R $\frac{1}{2}$	R $\frac{3}{4}$
	M^1	24	Rc	Ac	Ac	M$_1$	24	Rc	Ac	Ac
	M^2	24	R $\frac{1}{4}$	R $\frac{1}{2}$	R $\frac{1}{2}$	M$_2$	24	R $\frac{1}{4}$	R $\frac{1}{2}$	R $\frac{1}{2}$
	M^3	23	–	Coc	Cr $\frac{1}{2}$	M$_3$	23	–	Cco	Cr $\frac{1}{2}$
11.5[a]	c'	17	Ac	Res $\frac{3}{4}$	–	c'	4	Res $\frac{1}{4}$	–	–
	m^1	8	Res $\frac{1}{2}$	–	–	m$_1$	6	Res $\frac{1}{4}$	–	–
	m^2	17	Res $\frac{1}{4}$	Res $\frac{3}{4}$	–	m$_2$	18	Ac	Res $\frac{1}{2}$	–
	I^1	24	Rc	Ac	Ac	I$_1$	24	Rc	Ac	Ac
	I^2	24	R $\frac{3}{4}$	Ac	Ac	I$_2$	24	A $\frac{1}{2}$	Ac	Ac
	C'	24	R $\frac{1}{2}$	R $\frac{3}{4}$	Rc	C'	24	R $\frac{3}{4}$	R $\frac{3}{4}$	A $\frac{1}{2}$
	P^1	24	R $\frac{1}{2}$	R $\frac{3}{4}$	A $\frac{1}{2}$	P$_1$	24	R $\frac{1}{2}$	R $\frac{3}{4}$	A $\frac{1}{2}$
	P^2	24	R $\frac{1}{4}$	R $\frac{3}{4}$	Rc	P$_2$	24	R $\frac{1}{4}$	R $\frac{3}{4}$	A $\frac{1}{2}$
	M^1	24	A $\frac{1}{2}$	Ac	Ac	M$_1$	24	A $\frac{1}{2}$	Ac	Ac
	M^2	24	R $\frac{1}{4}$	R $\frac{1}{2}$	Rc	M$_2$	24	R $\frac{1}{4}$	R $\frac{1}{2}$	R $\frac{3}{4}$
	M^3	24	Ci	Cr $\frac{1}{2}$	Ri	M$_3$	24	Ci	Coc	R $\frac{1}{4}$
12.5[a]	m^2	2	Res $\frac{3}{4}$	–	–	m$_2$	10	Res $\frac{1}{4}$	–	–
	I^1	24	Rc	Ac	Ac	I$_1$	24	A $\frac{1}{2}$	Ac	Ac
	I^2	24	Rc	Ac	Ac	I$_2$	24	A $\frac{1}{2}$	Ac	Ac
	C'	24	R $\frac{3}{4}$	Rc	Rc	C'	24	R $\frac{3}{4}$	A $\frac{1}{2}$	Ac
	P^1	24	R $\frac{3}{4}$	Rc	A $\frac{1}{2}$	P$_1$	24	R $\frac{3}{4}$	Rc	Ac
	P^2	24	R $\frac{1}{2}$	R $\frac{3}{4}$	A $\frac{1}{2}$	P$_2$	24	R $\frac{1}{2}$	Rc	Ac
	M^1	24	Ac	Ac	Ac	M$_1$	24	Ac	Ac	Ac
	M^2	24	R $\frac{1}{4}$	R $\frac{3}{4}$	Rc	M$_2$	24	R $\frac{1}{4}$	R $\frac{3}{4}$	Rc
	M^3	24	Cco	Cr $\frac{3}{4}$	R $\frac{1}{4}$	M$_3$	24	Ci	Cr $\frac{1}{2}$	R $\frac{1}{4}$

[a]Midpoint of 1 year.
(From AlQahtani, S.J., Hector, M.P., Liversidge, H.M., 2010. Brief communication: the London atlas of human tooth development and eruption. Am. J. Phys. Anthropol. 142, 481–490.)

Tooth Development (Combines Sex) for 24 Children in Each Age Group: 13 to <14 Years, 14 to <15 Years, 16 to <17 Years, and 17 to <18 Years

Age (Years)	Tooth	Number of Teeth	Minimum	Median	Maximum	Tooth	Number of Teeth	Minimum	Median	Maximum
			Maxilla — Tooth Formation Stage					**Mandible — Tooth Formation Stage**		
13.5[a]	I^1	24	Ac	Ac	Ac	I_1	24	Ac	Ac	Ac
	I^2	24	Ac	Ac	Ac	I_2	24	Ac	Ac	Ac
	C′	24	Rc	Rc	A ½	C′	24	Rc	A ½	Ac
	P^1	24	Rc	A ½	Ac	P_1	24	R ¾	A ½	Ac
	P^2	24	R ½	Rc	Ac	P_2	24	R ¾	Rc	Ac
	M^1	24	Ac	Ac	Ac	M_1	24	Ac	Ac	Ac
	M^2	24	Coc	R ¾	A ½	M_2	24	R ½	R ¾	A ½
	M^3	24	Ci	Cr ¾	R ¼	M_3	24	Ci	Cr ½	R ¼
14.5[a,b]	C′	24	Rc	A ½	Ac	C′	24	A ½	Ac	Ac
	P^1	24	A ½	Ac	Ac	P_1	24	A ½	Ac	Ac
	P^2	24	Rc	Ac	Ac	P_2	24	Rc	Ac	Ac
	M^2	24	Rc	Rc	Ac	M_2	24	Rc	Rc	Ac
	M^3	24	Cr ¾	R ¼	R ¼	M_3	24	Cr ½	R ¼	R ¼
15.5[a,b]	C′	24	R ¾	Ac	Ac	C′	24	Ac	Ac	Ac
	P^1	24	Ac	Ac	Ac	P_1	24	Ac	Ac	Ac
	P^2	24	Ac	Ac	Ac	P_2	24	Ac	Ac	Ac
	M^2	24	Rc	A ½	Ac	M_2	24	Rc	A ½	Ac
	M^3	24	Cr ½	R ¼	R ¾	M_3	24	Cr ½	R ¼	R ¾
16.5[a,c]	C′	24	Ac	Ac	Ac	C′	24	Ac	Ac	Ac
	M^2	24	A ½	Ac	Ac	M_2	24	A ½	Ac	Ac
	M^3	24	Ri	R ½	R ¾	M_3	24	Crc	R ½	R ¾
17.5[a,c]	M^2	24	Ac	Ac	Ac	M_2	24	Ac	Ac	Ac
	M^3	24	Crc	R ½	Rc	M_3	24	R ¼	R ½	Rc

[a]Midpoint of 1 year.
[b]Teeth that reached radiographic apical closure stage (Ac) are permanent upper and lower incisors and first molars.
[c]Teeth that reached radiographic apical closure stage (Ac) are permanent incisors, premolars, and first molars.
(From AlQahtani, S.J., Hector, M.P., Liversidge, H.M., 2010. Brief communication: the London atlas of human tooth development and eruption. Am. J. Phys. Anthropol. 142, 481–490.)

Third Molar Development for 24 Individuals (Combined Sex) From 18 to <24 Years

		Maxilla						Mandible			
Age (Years)	Tooth	Number of Teeth	Tooth Formation Stage			Tooth	Number of Teeth	Tooth Formation Stage		
			Minimum	Median	Maximum			Minimum	Median	Maximum
18.5^a	M^3	24	Crc	$R\frac{3}{4}$	Rc	M_3	24	$R\frac{1}{4}$	$R\frac{3}{4}$	Rc
19.5^a	M^3	24	$R\frac{1}{4}$	Rc	$A\frac{1}{2}$	M_3	24	$R\frac{1}{4}$	Rc	$A\frac{1}{2}$
20.5^a	M^3	24	$R\frac{1}{2}$	$A\frac{1}{2}$	$A\frac{1}{2}$	M_3	24	$R\frac{3}{4}$	$A\frac{1}{2}$	$A\frac{1}{2}$
21.5^a	M^3	24	Rc	$A\frac{1}{2}$	Ac	M_3	24	Rc	$A\frac{1}{2}$	Ac
22.5^a	M^3	24	Rc	$A\frac{1}{2}$	Ac	M_3	24	Rc	$A\frac{1}{2}$	Ac
23.5^a	M^3	24	Ac	Ac	Ac	M_3	24	Ac	Ac	Ac

Teeth that reached radiographic apical closure stage (Ac) are permanent incisors, canines, premolars, first, and second molars.
[a]*Midpoint of 1 year.*
(From AlQahtani, S.J., Hector, M.P., Liversidge, H.M., 2010. Brief communication: the London atlas of human tooth development and eruption. Am. J. Phys. Anthropol. 142, 481–490.)

Median Age of Eruption for Deciduous Teeth (Combined Sex)[a]

	Maxilla				Mandible		
Tooth	Alveolar Eruption	Clinical Emergence[b]	Full Eruption	Tooth	Alveolar Eruption	Clinical Emergence[b]	Full Eruption
i^1	4.5 months	9.96 months	10.5 months	i_1	4.5 months	8.04 months	10.5 months
i^2	7.5 months	11.4 months	1.5 years	i_2	7.5 months	1.08 years	1.5 years
c'	10.5 months	1.58 years	2.5 years	$c,$	10.5 months	1.67 years	2.5 years
m^1	10.5 months	1.33 years	1.5 years	m_1	10.5 months	1.33 years	1.5 years
m^2	1.5 years	2.42 years	2.5 years	m_2	1.5 years	2.25 years	2.5 years

[a]*Midpoint of 3 months for younger than 1 year and midpoint of 1 year otherwise.*
[b]*From Lysell et al. (1962).*
(From AlQahtani, S.J., Hector, M.P., Liversidge, H.M., 2010. Brief communication: the London atlas of human tooth development and eruption. Am. J. Phys. Anthropol. 142, 481–490.)

Median Age (Years) of Eruption for Permanent Teeth (Combined Sex)[a]

	Maxilla				Mandible			
Tooth	Alveolar Eruption	Clinical Emergence[b]		Full Eruption	Tooth	Alveolar Eruption	Clinical Emergence[b]		Full Eruption
		Boys	Girls				Boys	Girls	
I^1	6.5	6.9	6.7	7.5	I_1	5.5	6.3	6.2	7.5
I^2	7.5	8.3	7.8	9.5	I_2	6.5	7.3	6.8	7.5
C'	11.5	12.1	10.6	12.5	C'	9.5	10.4	9.2	11.5
P^1	10.5	10.2	9.6	11.5	P_1	10.5	10.3	9.6	11.5
P^2	11.5	11.4	10.2	12.5	P_2	11.5	11.1	10.1	12.5
M^1	5.5	6.4	6.4	6.5	M_1	5.5	6.3	6.3	6.5
M^2	10.5	12.8	12.4	13.5	M_2	10.5	12.2	11.4	12.5
M^3	16.5	–	–	20.5	M_3	16.5	–	–	20.5

[a]*Midpoint of 1 year.*
[b]*From Haavikko (1970).*
(From AlQahtani, S.J., Hector, M.P., Liversidge, H.M., 2010. Brief communication: the London atlas of human tooth development and eruption. Am. J. Phys. Anthropol. 142, 481–490.)

Stages of third molar development

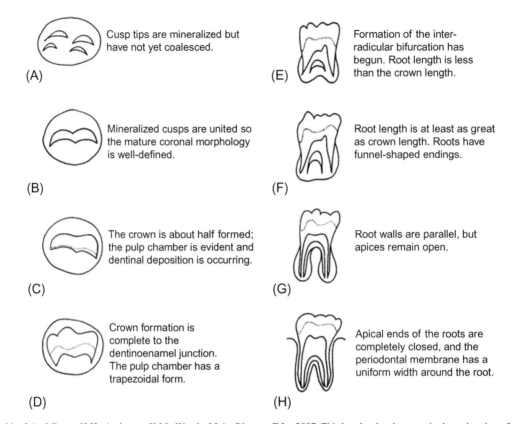

(A) Cusp tips are mineralized but have not yet coalesced.

(B) Mineralized cusps are united so the mature coronal morphology is well-defined.

(C) The crown is about half formed; the pulp chamber is evident and dentinal deposition is occurring.

(D) Crown formation is complete to the dentinoenamel junction. The pulp chamber has a trapezoidal form.

(E) Formation of the inter-radicular bifurcation has begun. Root length is less than the crown length.

(F) Root length is at least as great as crown length. Roots have funnel-shaped endings.

(G) Root walls are parallel, but apices remain open.

(H) Apical ends of the roots are completely closed, and the periodontal membrane has a uniform width around the root.

(From Blankenship, J.A., Mincer, H.H., Anderson, K.M., Woods, M.A., Biurton, E.L., 2007. Third molar development in the estimation of chronological age in American blacks as compared with whites. J. Forensic Sci. 52(2), 428–433.)

Mean Ages (in Years) of Attainment of Third Molar Stages

Group	Stage				
	D	E	F	G	H
Maxilla					
White Males	x̄: 16.0	x̄: 16.6	x̄: 17.7	x̄: 18.2	x̄: 20.2
	SD: 1.97	SD: 2.38	SD: 2.28	SD: 1.91	SD: 2.09
1SD range	14.03–17.97	14.22–18.98	15.42–19.98	16.29–20.11	18.11–22.29
2SD range	12.06–19.94	11.84–21.36	13.14–22.26	14.38–22.02	16.02–24.38
White Females	x̄: 16.0	x̄: 16.9	x̄: 18.0	x̄: 18.8	x̄: 20.6
	SD: 1.55	SD: 1.85	SD: 1.95	SD: 2.27	SD: 2.09
1SD range	14.45–17.55	15.05–18.75	16.05–19.95	16.53–21.07	18.51–22.69
2SD range	12.9–19.1	13.2–20.6	14.1–21.9	14.26–23.34	16.42–24.78
Black Males and Females				x̄ 19.3	x̄: 20.4
				SD: 3.37	SD: 3.14
1SD range				15.93–22.67	17.26–23.54
2SD range				12.56–26.04	14.12–26.68
Mandible					
White Males	x̄: 15.5	x̄: 17.3	x̄: 17.5	x̄: 18.3	x̄: 20.5
	SD: 1.59	SD: 2.47	SD: 2.14	SD: 1.93	SD: 1.97
1SD range	13.91–17.09	14.83–19.77	15.33–19.67	16.37–20.23	18.53–22.47
2SD range	12.32–18.68	12.36–22.24	13.16–21.84	14.44–22.16	16.56–24.44
White Females	x̄: 16.0	x̄: 16.9	x̄: 17.7	x̄: 19.1	x̄: 20.9
	SD: 1.64	SD: 1.64	SD: 1.80	SD: 2.18	SD: 2.01
1SD range	14.36–17.64	15.26–18.54	15.9–19.5	16.92–21.28	18.89–22.91
2SD range	12.72–19.28	13.62–20.18	14.1–21.3	14.74–23.46	16.88–24.92
Black Males and Females				x̄: 17.2	x̄: 21.4
				SD: 3.14	SD: 2.34
1SD range				14.06–20.34	19.06–23.74
2SD range				10.92–23.48	16.72–26.08

(Modified from Mincer, H.H., Harris, E.F., Berryman, H.E., 1993. The ABFO study of third molar development and is use as an estimator of chronological age. J. Forensic Sci. 38(2), 379–390.)

Probability of Being At Least 18 Years of Age Based on Third Molar Stage

Group	Stage				
	D	E	F	G	H
Maxilla					
Males	15.9	27.8	44.0	46.8	85.3
Females	9.7	28.4	50.4	63.3	89.6
Mandible					
Males	6.1	69.4	40.5	56.0	90.1
Females	11.3	27.4	43.2	69.8	92.2

(Modified from Mincer, H.H., Harris, E.F., Berryman, H.E., 1993. The ABFO study of third molar development and is use as an estimator of chronological age. J. Forensic Sci. 38(2), 379–390.)

Probability of Being At Least 18 Years Based on Third Molar Stage for American Blacks and Whites

	Males			Females		
	N	Proportion	95% CI	N	Proportion	95% CI
American Blacks						
D	0	–	–	63	0.048	0.012–0.116
E	76	0.132	0.068–0.185	82	0.024	0.004–0.079
F	80	0.150	0.083–0.200	86	0.186	0.113–0.231
G	205	0.634	0.564–0.644	80	0.325	0.227–0.366
H	343	0.927	0.893–0.928	125	0.840	0.761–0.847
American Whites						
D	60	0.033	0.006–0.106	88	0.182	0.111–0.226
E	57	0.246	0.145–0.308	91	0.297	0.208–0.334
F	69	0.319	0.215–0.367	108	0.472	0.376–0.497
G	117	0.479	0.386–0.501	14	0.693	0.599–0.707
H	169	0.899	0.841–0.903	166	0.934	0.882–0.936

(Modified from Blankenship, J.A., Mincer, H.H., Anderson, K.M., Woods, M.A., Biurton, E.L., 2007. Third molar development in the estimation of chronological age in American blacks as compared with whites. J. Forensic Sci. 52(2), 428–433.)

APPENDIX R: AGE ESTIMATION USING LONG BONE DIAPHYSEAL LENGTH

Age and Length (in mm) of Fetal Long Bone Diaphysis

Age (Weeks)	12	14	16	18	20	22	24	26	28	30	32	34	36	38	40
Humerus	8.8	12.4	19.5	25.8	31.8	34.5	37.6	39.9	44.2	45.8	50.4	53.1	55.5	61.3	64.9
Radius	6.7	10.1	17.2	21.5	26.2	28.9	31.6	33.4	35.6	38.1	40.8	43.3	45.7	48.8	51.8
Ulna	7.2	11.2	19.0	23.9	29.4	31.6	35.1	37.1	40.2	42.8	46.7	49.1	51.0	55.9	59.3
Femur	8.5	12.4	20.7	26.4	32.6	35.7	40.3	41.9	47.1	48.7	55.5	59.8	62.5	69.0	74.4
Tibia	6.0	10.2	17.4	23.4	28.5	32.6	35.8	38.0	42.0	43.9	48.6	52.7	54.7	60.1	65.2
Fibula	6.0	9.9	16.7	22.6	27.8	31.1	34.3	36.5	40.0	42.8	46.8	50.5	51.6	57.6	62.0

(Adapted from Fazekas, I.Gy., Kosa, F., 1978. Forensic Fetal Osteology. Akademiai Kaido, Budapest.)

Diaphyseal Lengths (Without Epiphyses) of the Humerus and Femur (in mm) From 2 Months to 12 Years

	Males			Females		
Age (Years)	N	Mean	SD	N	Mean	SD
			Humerus			
0.125	59	72.4	4.5	69	71.8	3.6
0.25	59	80.6	4.8	65	80.2	3.8
0.5	67	88.4	5	78	86.8	4.6
1	72	105.5	5.2	81	103.6	4.8
1.5	68	118.8	5.4	84	117.0	5.1
2	68	130	5.5	84	127.7	5.8
2.5	72	139	5.9	82	136.9	6.1
3	71	147.5	6.7	79	145.3	6.7
3.5	73	155	7.8	78	153.4	7.1
4	72	162.7	6.9	80	160.9	7.7
4.5	71	169.8	7.4	78	169.1	8.3
5	77	177.4	8.2	80	176.3	8.7
5.5	73	184.6	8.1	74	182.6	9
6	71	190.9	7.6	75	190.0	9.6
6.5	72	197.3	8.1	81	196.7	9.7
7	71	203.6	8.7	86	202.6	10
7.5	76	210.4	8.9	83	209.3	10.5
8	70	217.3	9.8	85	216.3	10.4
8.5	72	222.5	9.2	82	221.3	11.2
9	76	228.7	9.6	83	228	11.8

Diaphyseal Lengths (Without Epiphyses) of the Humerus and Femur (in mm) From 2 Months to 12 Years—cont'd

Age (Years)	Males			Females		
	N	Mean	SD	N	Mean	SD
9.5	78	235.1	10.7	83	234.2	12.9
10	77	241	10.3	84	239.8	13.2
10.5	76	245.8	11	75	245.9	14.6
11	75	251.7	10.7	76	251.9	14.7
11.5	76	257.4	11.9	75	259.1	15.3
12	73	263	12.8	71	265.6	15.6
Femur						
0.125	59	86	5.4	68	71.8	4.3
0.25	59	100.7	4.8	65	80.2	3.6
0.5	67	112.2	5	78	86.8	4.6
1	72	136.6	5.8	81	103.6	4.9
1.5	68	155.4	6.8	84	117	6.4
2	68	172.4	7.3	84	127.7	7.1
2.5	72	187.2	7.8	82	136.9	7.7
3	71	200.3	8.5	79	145.3	8.7
3.5	73	212.1	11.4	78	153.4	10
4	72	224.1	9.9	80	160.9	10.1
4.5	71	235.7	10.5	78	169.1	11.4
5	77	247.5	11.1	80	176.3	11.5
5.5	73	258.2	11.7	74	182.6	12.2
6	71	269.7	12	75	190	13.5
6.5	72	280.3	12.6	81	196.7	13.8
7	71	291.1	13.3	86	202.6	13.6
7.5	76	301.2	13.5	83	209.3	15.2
8	70	312.1	14.6	85	216.3	15.6
8.5	72	321	14.6	82	221.3	15.8
9	76	330.4	14.6	83	228	16.8
9.5	78	340	15.8	83	234.2	18.6
10	77	349.3	15.7	84	239.8	19.1
10.5	76	357.4	16.2	75	245.9	21.4
11	75	367	16.5	76	251.9	22.4
11.5	76	375.8	18.1	75	259.1	23.4
12	74	386.1	19	71	265.6	22.9

(Adapted from Scheuer, L., Black, S., 2000. Developmental Juvenile Osteology. Academic Press, San Diego, CA.)

APPENDIX S: AGE ESTIMATION USING OSSIFICATION AND EPIPHYSEAL UNION

Age (in Years) of Ossification and Epiphyseal Union in Males

Bone	Epiphysis	Open	Partial	Complete
Humerus	Proximal	<20	16–21	>18
	Medial	<18	16–18	>16
	Distal	<15	14–18	>15
Radius	Proximal	<18	14–18	>16
	Distal	<19	16–20	>17
Ulna	Proximal	<16	14–18	>15
	Distal	<20	17–20	>17
Hand	MCs & Phalanges	<17	14–18	>15
Femur	Proximal	<18	16–19	>16
	Greater Trochanter	<18	16–19	>16
	Lesser Trochanter	<18	16–19	>16
	Distal	<19	16–20	>17
Tibia	Proximal	<18	16–20	>17
	Distal	<18	16–18	>16
Fibula	Proximal	<19	16–20	>17
	Distal	<18	15–20	>17
Foot	Calcaneus	<16	14–20	>16
	MTs & Phalanges	<17	14–16	>15
Scapula	Coraco-Glenoid[a]	<16	15–18	>16
	Acromion	<20	17–20	>17
	Inferior Angle	<21	17–22	>17
	Medial Border	<21	18–22	>18
Innominate	Triradiate Complex[b]	<16	14–18	>15
	Ant Inf Iliac Spine	<18	16–18	>16
	Ischial Tuberosity	<18	16–20	>17
	Iliac Crest	<20	17–22	>18
Sacrum	Auricular Surface	<21	17–21	>18
	S1–S2 Bodies	<27	19–30+	>25
	S1–S2 Alae	<20	16–27	>19
	S2–S5 Bodies	<20	16–28	>20
	S2–S5 Alae	<16	16–21	>16
Vertebrae[c]	Annular Rings	<21	14–23	>18
Ribs[c]	Heads	<21	17–22	>19
Clavicle	Medial	<23	17–30	>21
Manubrium	1st Costal Notch	<23	18–25	>21

[a]Includes union of coracoid process, and the subcoracoid and glenoid epiphyses.
[b]Includes union of primary elements on both pelvic and acetabular surfaces and the acetabular epiphyses.
[c]At least one vertebra or one rib displays this type of activity.
(From Schaefer, M., Black, S., Scheuer, L., 2009. Juvenile Osteology: A Laboratory and Field Manual. Academic Press, San Diego, CA.)

Age (in Years) of Ossification and Epiphyseal Union in Females

Bone	Epiphysis	Open	Partial	Complete
Humerus	Proximal	<17	14–19	>16
	Medial	<15	13–15	>13
	Distal	<15	11–15	>12
Radius	Proximal	<15	12–16	>13
	Distal	<18	14–19	>15
Ulna	Proximal	<15	12–15	>12
	Distal	<18	15–19	>15
Hand	MCs & Phalanges	<15	11–16	>12
Femur	Proximal	<15	14–17	>14
	Greater Trochanter	<15	14–17	>14
	Lesser Trochanter	<15	14–17	>14
	Distal	<16	14–19	>17
Tibia	Proximal	<17	14–18	>18
	Distal	<17	14–17	>15
Fibula	Proximal	<17	14–17	>15
	Distal	<17	14–17	>15
Foot	Calcaneus	<12	10–17	>14
	MTs & Phalanges	<13	11–13	>11
Scapula	Coraco-Glenoid[a]	<16	14–18	>16
	Acromion	<18	15–17	>15
	Inferior Angle	<21	17–22	>17
	Medial Border	<21	18–22	>18
Innominate	Tri-radiate Complex[b]	<14	11–16	>14
	Ant Inf Iliac Spine	<14	14–18	>15
	Ischial Tuberosity	<15	14–19	>16
	Iliac Crest	<16	14–21	>18
Sacrum	Auricular Surface	<20	15–21	>17
	S1–S2 Bodies	<27	14–30+	>21
	S1–S2 Alae	<19	11–26	>14
	S2–S5 Bodies	<20	12–26	>19
	S2–S5 Alae	<14	10–19	>13
Vertebrae[c]	Annular Rings	<21	14–23	>18
Ribs[c]	Heads	<21	17–22	>19
Clavicle	Medial	<23	17–30	>21
Manubrium	1st Costal Notch	<23	18–25	>21

[a]Includes union of coracoid process and the subcoracoid and glenoid epiphyses.
[b]Includes union of primary elements on both pelvic and acetabular surfaces and the acetabular epiphyses.
[c]At least one vertebra or one rib displays this type of activity.
(From Schaefer, M., Black, S., Scheuer, L., 2009. Juvenile Osteology: A Laboratory and Field Manual. Academic Press, San Diego, CA.)

APPENDIX T: AGE ESTIMATION USING PUBIC SYMPHYSEAL MORPHOLOGY

Mean and Observed Ages (in Years) by Phase for the Pubic Symphysis in Males and Females

		Males				Females		
Phase	N	Mean	SD	Observed	N	Mean	SD	Observed
1	14	19.29	1.93	18–22	5	19.8	1.33	18–22
2	14	22.14	1.86	20–26	5	23.2	2.38	20–25
3	36	29.53	6.63	21–44	25	31.44	5.12	24–44
4	69	42.54	8.8	27–61	35	43.26	6.12	33–58
5	90	53.87	8.42	37–72	32	51.47	3.94	44–60
6	34	63.76	8.06	51–83	35	72.34	7.36	56–86
7	96	77	9.33	58–97	56	82.54	7.41	62–99

(Modified from Hartnett, K.M., 2010a. Analysis of age-at-death estimation using data from a new, modern autopsy sample—part I: pubic bone. J. Forensic Sci. 55, 1145–1151.)

Pubic Symphysis Phase Descriptions

Phase 1   A clear ridge and furrow system extends from the pubic tubercle onto the inferior ramus. Ridges and furrows are deep and well-defined and do not look worn down. There is no dorsal lipping. Bone is of excellent quality and is firm, heavy, dense, and smooth on the ventral and dorsal body. There is no rim formation. The dorsal plateau is not formed. The ridges and furrows extend to the dorsal edge

Phase 2   The rim is in the process of forming but mainly consists of a flattening of the ridges on the dorsal aspect of the face and ossific nodules present along the ventral border. Ridges and furrows are still present. The ridges and furrows may appear worn down or flattened, especially on the dorsal aspect of the face. The furrows are becoming shallow. The upper and lower rim edges are not formed. There is no dorsal lipping. The bone quality is very good and the bone is firm, heavy, dense, and smooth on the ventral and dorsal body, with little porosity. The pubic tubercle may appear separate from the face

Phase 3   The lower rim is complete on the dorsal side of the face and is complete until it ends approximately halfway up the ventral face leaving a medium to fairly large gap between the lower and upper extremities on the ventral face. This enlarged "V" is longer on the dorsal side than the ventral side. Some ridges and shallow furrows are still visible but appear worn down. In some cases, the face is becoming slightly porous. The rim is forming both on the dorsal aspect of the face and the upper and lower extremities. In some cases, there is a rounded buildup of bone in the gap between the upper and lower extremities above the enlarged "V." Bone quality is good; the bone is firm, heavy, dense, and has little porosity. The dorsal surface of the body is smooth, and there are small bony projections near the medial aspect of the obturator foramen. The ventral aspect of the body is not elaborate. Very slight to no dorsal lipping. Quality of bone and rim completion are important deciding factors. Variant: In some cases, a deep line or epiphysis is visible on the ventral aspect parallel to and adjacent to the face (males only)

Phase 4   In most cases, the rim is complete at this stage but may have a small ventral hiatus on the superior and ventral aspect of the rim. The face is flattened and not depressed. Remnants of ridges and furrows may be visible on the face, especially on the lower half. The quality of bone is good, but the face is beginning to appear more porous. The dorsal and ventral surfaces of the body are roughened and becoming coarse. There is slight dorsal lipping. In females with parturition pits, dorsal lipping can be more pronounced. The ventral arc may be large and elaborate in females

Pubic Symphysis Phase Descriptions—cont'd

Phase 5	The face is becoming more porous and is depressed but maintains an oval shape. The face is not irregularly shaped or erratic. The rim is complete at this stage. In general, the rim is not irregular. Ridges and furrows are absent on the face. There may be some breakdown of the rim on the ventral border, which appears as irregular bone (not rounded/solid). The ventral surface of the body is roughened and irregular, with some bony excrescences. The dorsal surface of the body is coarse and irregular. Projections are present on the medial aspect of the obturator foramen. Bone quality is good to fair; it is losing density and is not smooth. The bone is moderately light in weight. In females the ventral arc is prominent
Phase 6	The face is losing its oval shape and is becoming irregular. The rim is complete, but breaking down, especially on the ventral border. The rim and face are irregular, porous, and macroporous. Bone quality is fair, and the bone is lighter and more porous, even with bony buildup on the ventral body surface. The rim is eroding. The dorsal surface of the bone is rough and coarse. There are no ridges and furrows. Dorsal lipping is present. Projections are present at the medial aspect of the obturator foramen. Bone weight is a major deciding factor between phases 6 and 7
Phase 7	The face and rim are very irregular in shape and are losing integrity. The rim is complete but is eroding and breaking down, especially on the ventral border. There are no ridges and furrows. The face is porous and macroporous. Dorsal lipping is pronounced. Bone quality is poor, and the bone is very light and brittle. Bone weight is an important deciding factor. The dorsal surface of the bone is roughened. The ventral surface of the body is roughened and elaborate. Projections are present at the medial wall of the obturator foramen. The pubic tubercle is elaborate and proliferative. Bone weight is a major deciding factor between phases 6 and 7
Variant	The rim is complete except for a lytic/sclerotic appearing hiatus at the superior ventral margin that extends toward the pubic tubercle and sometimes underneath the ventral rim, which should not be confused with a hiatus

(From Hartnett, K.M., 2010a. Analysis of age-at-death estimation using data from a new, modern autopsy sample—part I: pubic bone. J. Forensic Sci. 55, 1145–1151.)

APPENDIX U: AGE ESTIMATION USING AURICULAR SURFACE MORPHOLOGY

Regions of the auricular surface assessed for age estimation. (1) Apex, (2) superior demiface, (3) inferior demiface, and (4) retroauricular area

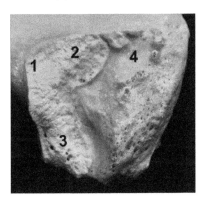

(From Christensen, A.M., Passalacqua, N.V., Bartelink, E.J., 2014. Forensic Anthropology: Current Methods and Practice. Academic Press, Amsterdam.)

Mean Ages (in Years) and 95% Prediction Intervals by Phase for the Auricular Surface

Phase	N	Mean	SD	Suggested Age Range
1	11	21.1	2.98	≤27
2	13	29.5	8.20	≤46
3	37	42.0	13.74	≤69
4	82	47.8	13.95	20–75
5	17	53.1	14.14	24–82
6	102	58.9	15.24	29–89

(Adapted from Osborne, D.L., Simmons, T.L., Nawrocki, S.P., 2004. Reconsidering the auricular surface as an indicator of age at death. J. Forensic Sci. 49(5), 768–773.)

Auricular Surface Phase Descriptions

Phase 1	Billowing with possible striae; mostly fine granularity with some coarse granularity possible
Phase 2	Striae; coarse granularity with residual fine granularity; retroauricular activity may be present
Phase 3	Decreased striae with transverse organization; coarse granularity; retroauricular activity present beginnings of apical change
Phase 4	Remnants of transverse organization; coarse granularity becoming replaced by densification; retroauricular activity present; apical change; macroporosity is present
Phase 5	Surface becomes irregular; surface texture is largely dense; moderate retroauricular activity; moderate apical change; macroporosity
Phase 6	Irregular surface; densification accompanied by subchondral destruction; severe retroauricular activity; severe apical change; macroporosity

(Adapted from Osborne, D.L., Simmons, T.L., Nawrocki, S.P., 2004. Reconsidering the auricular surface as an indicator of age at death. J. Forensic Sci. 49(5), 768–773.)

APPENDIX V: AGE ESTIMATION USING STERNAL RIB END MORPHOLOGY

Mean and Observed Ages (in Years) by Phase for the Sternal Rib End in Males

Phase	Males				Females			
	N	Mean	SD	Observed	N	Mean	SD	Observed
1	20	20.00	1.45	18–22	7	19.57	1.67	18–22
2	27	24.63	2.00	21–28	7	25.14	1.67	24–27
3	27	32.27	3.69	27–37	22	32.95	3.17	27–38
4	47	42.43	2.98	36–48	21	43.52	3.08	39–49
5	76	52.05	3.50	45–59	32	51.69	3.31	47–58
6	61	63.13	3.53	57–70	18	67.17	3.41	60–73
7	75	80.91	6.60	70–97	71	81.20	6.95	65–99

(Modified from Hartnett, K.M., 2010b. Analysis of age-at-death estimation using data from a new, modern autopsy sample—part 2: sternal end of first rib. J. Forensic Sci. 55, 1152–1156.)

Sternal Rib End Phase Descriptions

Phase 1	The pit is shallow and flat, and there are billows in the pit. The pit is shallow and U-shaped in cross section. The bone is very firm and solid, smooth to the touch, dense, and of good quality. The walls of the rim are thick. The rim may show the beginnings of scalloping
Phase 2	There is an indentation to the pit. The pit is V-shaped in cross section, and the rim is well defined with round edges. The rim is regular with some scalloping. The bone is firm and solid, smooth to the touch, dense, and of good quality. There is no flare to the rim edges; they are parallel to each other. The pit is still smooth inside, with little to no porosity. In females, the central arc, which manifests on the anterior and posterior walls as a semicircular curve, is visible
Phase 3	The pit is V-shaped, and there is a slight flare to the rim edges. The rim edges are becoming undulating and slightly irregular, and there may be remnants of scallops, but they look worn down. There are no bony projections from the rim. There is porosity inside the pit. The bone quality is good; it is firm, solid, and smooth to the touch. The rim edges are rounded, but sharp. In many females, there is a build-up of bony plaque, either in the bottom of the pit or lining the interior of the pit, creating the appearance of a two-layer rim. An irregular central arc may be apparent
Phase 4	The pit is deep and U-shaped. The edges of the pit flare outward, expanding the oval area inside the pit. The rim edges are not undulating or scalloped but are irregular. There are no long bony projections from the rim, and the rim edges are thin, but firm. The bone quality is good but does not feel dense or heavy. There is porosity inside the pit. In some males, two distinct depressions are visible in the pit. In females, the central arc may be present and irregular; however, the superior and inferior edges of the rim have developed, decreasing the prominence of the central arc
Phase 5	There are frequently small bony projections along the rim edges, especially at the superior and inferior edges of the rim. The pit is deep and U-shaped. The rim edges are irregular, flared, sharp, and thin. There is porosity inside the pit. The bone quality is fair; the bone is coarse to the touch and feels lighter than it looks
Phase 6	The bone quality is fair to poor, light in weight, and the surfaces of the bone feel coarse and brittle. There are bony projections along the rim edges, especially at the superior and inferior edges, some of which may be over 1 cm long. The pit is deep and U-shaped. The rim is very irregular, thin, and fragile. There is porosity inside the pit. In some cases, there may be small bony extrusions inside the pit. In females, the central arc is not prominent

Sternal Rib End Phase Descriptions—cont'd

Phase 7	The bone is very poor quality, and in many cases, translucent. The bone is very light, sometimes feeling like paper, and feels coarse and brittle to the touch. The pit is deep and U-shaped. There may be long bony growths inside the pit. The rim is very irregular with long bony projections. In some cases, much of the cartilage has ossified and window formation occurs. In some females, much of the cartilage in the interior of the pit has ossified into a bony projection extending more than 1 cm in length
Variant	In some males, the cartilage has completely or almost completely ossified. The ossification tends to be a solid extension of bone, rather than a thin projection. All of the bone is of very good quality, including the ossification. It is dense, heavy, and smooth. In these instances, bone quality should be the determining factor. There are probably other factors, such as disease, trauma, or substance abuse that caused premature ossification of the cartilage. When the individual is truly very old, the bone quality will be very poor. Be aware of these instances where a rib end may appear very old because of ossification of the cartilage but is actually a young individual, which can be ascertained by bone quality. In these cases, consult other age indicators in conjunction with the rib end

(From Hartnett, K.M., 2010b. Analysis of age-at-death estimation using data from a new, modern autopsy sample—part 2: sternal end of first rib. J. Forensic Sci. 55, 1152–1156.)

APPENDIX W: AGE ESTIMATION USING RIB HISTOMORPHOMETRY

The following guidelines assume that rib sections have already been prepared and mounted onto microscope slides, and calibrations have already been performed. For guidance on slide preparation and microscope calibration, see Crowder et al. (2012). For additional guidance on histomorphometric data collection, see Crowder et al. (2012) and Robling and Stout (2000). The sixth rib is preferentially used, but ribs between four and seven are considered to have comparable OPD.

Histological data collection guidelines

- Place a Merz reticule in the eyepiece of the microscope. A Merz reticule creates a region of interest (ROI) for assessment, which is delineated by a square with six parallel wavy lines with tick marks at regular intervals. These tick marks are used for counting within the ROI. Each ROI evaluated comprises a separate "field," and structures falling on one of the reticule ticks are called a "hit."
- When possible, evaluate 100% of the bone sample. Evaluating two thin sections is typically adequate to account for microstructure variation within the bone. Evaluation of at least 50% of the sample using a checkerboard pattern may be used in cases where portions of the section are taphonomically compromised or have missing/cracked portions. Use a systematic pattern to ensure that fields do not overlap. The positioning of the reticule and path of data collection should be planned before analysis begins.
- Sections should be evaluated slowly, using polarized and nonpolarized light, and frequent manipulation of microscope focus and light.
- The following variables should be collected/calculated when using the published rib methods. (Note that the method being used should be followed carefully and may involve slight differences in definitions.)

Data Collection for Histomorphometric Age Estimation	
Total area of bone sampled (Sa.Ar.) (in mm^2)	Total number of "hits" overlaying cortical bone for each field, multiplied by the area represented by one hit in the reticule
Number of intact osteons (N.On)	Number of secondary osteons with at least 90% of their perimeters intact or unremodeled
Number of fragmentary osteons (N.On.Fg)	Secondary osteons in which 10% or more of their perimeters have been remodeled by subsequent osteons
Osteon population density (OPD) (per mm^2)	The sum of N.On and N.On.Fg. divided by Sa.Ar
Relative cortical area (Ct.Ar./Tt.Ar.)	The ratio of cortical bone area (Ct.Ar) to total area (Tt.Ar.), including the meduallary cavity, of the rib cross section
Mean osteonal cross-sectional area (On. Ar.) (in mm^2)	The average cross-sectional area of a minimum of 25 complete osteons per cross section

Example of path of data collection

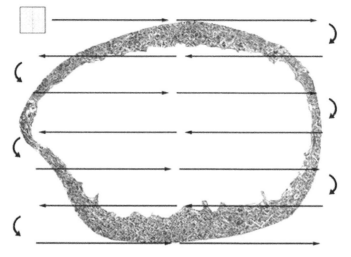

(From Crowder, C.M., Stout, S., 2012. Bone Histology: An Anthropological Perspective. CRC Press, Boca Raton, FL.)

Examples of intact (A) and fragementary (B) secondary osteons in a rib thin section

(From Crowder, C.M., Stout, S., 2012. Bone Histology: An Anthropological Perspective. CRC Press, Boca Raton, FL.)

Histomorphology Data Collection Table

Field#	#Hits	#Intact	#Fragmentary

Sum:

(Modified from Crowder, C.M., Stout, S., 2012. Bone Histology: An Anthropological Perspective. CRC Press, Boca Raton, FL.)

Age Estimation Equations

African-American	Age (in years) = 38.029 + 1.603(OPD) − 51.228(Ct.Ar/Tt.Ar.)
European-American	Age (in years) = 38.029 + 1.603(OPD) − 88.210(On.Ar) − 51.228(Ct.Ar/Tt.Ar.) + 57.441(Ct.Ar/Tt.Ar.)
Unknown ancestry	Age (in years) = 29.524 + 1.560(OPD) + 4.786(Ct.Ar/Tt.Ar) − 592.899(On.Ar)
Unknown ancestry and incomplete cross section	Age (in years) = 37.982 + 1.375(OPD) − 699.581(On.Ar)

(From Cho, H., Stout, S.D., Madsen, R.W., Streeter, M.A., 2002. Population-specific histological age estimating method: a model for known African-American and European-American skeletal remains. J. Forensic Sci. 47(1), 12–18.)

APPENDIX X: ODONTOSEARCH DENTAL CODING FORM

Dental Coding Form (Refer to Appendix C for Tooth Numbering)

Tooth	Code	Tooth	Code
1		17	
2		18	
3		19	
4		20	
5		21	
6		22	
7		23	
8		24	
9		25	
10		26	
11		27	
12		28	
13		29	
14		30	
15		31	
16		32	

Odontoseach Coding Definitions

General Guidelines and Definitions

All codes apply to permanent teeth; retained deciduous teeth are coded as permanent, and supernumerary teeth are not coded.

M=mesial; D=distal; F=facial; L=lingual; O=occlusal; X=missing antemortem; V=unrestored/virgin; R=restored

Teeth exhibiting active decay should be coded as unrestored (V)

Multiple restorations on a single surface are assigned a single code

Teeth with restorations on all surfaces are coded the same as a crown

In the generic/simplified dataset, all filled surface are condensed to a single code, R

Odontosearch Detailed and Generic Codes

Condition	Code in Detailed Dataset	Code in Generic Dataset
Restoration (anterior teeth)	Any combination of M (mesial), D (distal), F (facial), L (lingual)	R
Restoration (posterior teeth)	Any combination of M, O (occlusal), D, F, L	R
Crown (anterior teeth)	MDFL	R
Crown (posterior teeth)	MODFL	R
Missing antemortem	X	X
Unrestored/Virgin	V	V
Unrestored Decay	V	V

APPENDIX Y: NOTES FORMS

Date:
Case Number:
Preparer:

Methods should include any instruments, exemplars, reference data, and citations, as appropriate. Use additional pages as necessary.

---

*Minimum number of individuals (MNI):*_____

Method(s) used and/or basis for conclusion:

---

*Sex estimate:*_____

Method(s) used and/or basis for conclusion:

---

*Age estimate:*_____

Method(s) used and/or basis for conclusion:

Page ____ of ____

*Ancestry estimate:*_____

Method(s) used and/or basis for conclusion:

*Stature estimate:*_____

Method(s) used and/or basis for conclusion:

Observations of trauma, taphonomy, variations, other alterations, etc.:

Page ____ of ____

Additional observations and examination notes:

APPENDIX Z: CHAIN OF CUSTODY FORM

Agency:		Case Number:	
Item Number	*Date/Time of Transfer*	*Reason for Transfer*	*Signature*

Page _____ of _____

APPENDIX AA: EXAMPLE REPORTS

Skeletons, Inc. Forensic Anthropology Laboratory
123 Osteon Drive
Biomechanicsburg, VA 12345
777-555-4321

FORENSIC ANTHROPOLOGY REPORT

Case Number: 999-55444

09 August 2017

To: Sheriff John Johnson
       456 Main Street
       Springfield, CA 67890

Examination Results

A small fragment of suspected human bone was submitted to the laboratory on 01 June 2017. The item was examined visually and using low-powered microscopy, but no features or characteristics indicative of origin were observed.

The item was examined using X-ray fluorescence spectrometry (XRF). Results indicate levels of calcium and phosphorus consistent with skeletal tissue.

The item was then sectioned for histological analysis and examined using polarized light microscopy. The results indicate the presence of plexiform bone which is inconsistent with the microstructure of human bone. Human origin can therefore be excluded for this item.

If you have any questions about the content of this report, please contact me at 777-555-4321.

Oz Teology

Oz Teology, PhD, D-ABFA
Forensic Anthropologist

Page 1 of 1

Skeletons, Inc. Forensic Anthropology Laboratory
123 Osteon Drive
Biomechanicsburg, VA 12345
777-555-4321

FORENSIC ANTHROPOLOGY REPORT

Case Number: 999-55777

01 August, 2017

To: Mr. David Davidson
       100 First Street
       Newtown, IL 90123

Examination Results

Skeletal remains suspected to be those of Sally Smith were submitted to the laboratory on 30 June 2017. Specifically, the skeletal items consist of the following elements:

Cranium	Left innominate
Mandible	Right innominate
Right femur	Sacrum
Left tibia	Left clavicle
Left fibula	Right clavicle
Left humerus	Right scapula
Right humerus	

Prior to analysis, the skeletal remains were cleaned with soft bristle brushes and cold water to remove adhering sediment.

Minimum Number of Individuals
One. The remains are consistent in anatomical representation, taphonomic features, and biological indicators with originating from one (1) individual.

Sex
Female. Morphoscopic analysis of the left and right *os coxae* following the criteria of Phenice (1979) indicate that the remains are most likely those of a female.

Page 1 of 2

Ancestry

European (white). Metric analysis of the cranium using Fordisc 3.0 (Jantz and Ousley 2005) indicates the measurements of the remains most closely resemble those of individuals of White ancestry using a three group comparison of White Females, Black Females and Hispanic Females (posterior probability of WF 0.925, BF 0.050, HF 0.025).

Age

24-29 years. Skeletal development, specifically the complete fusion of the epiphyses of the long bones with incomplete fusion of the epiphysis of the clavicle, indicates an age 24-29 years (McKern and Stewart, 1957).

Stature

5'1"-5'9". Metric analysis of the maximum length of the right femur (448 mm) using Fordisc 3.0 for White females (95% confidence interval) results in an estimate of 65.1 +/- 4 inches.

Trauma and Other Alterations

No evidence of antemortem or perimortem trauma was noted. Many of the skeletal elements present display pitting and scoring consistent with postmortem carnivore scavenging.

Identification Comparison

This biological profile is consistent with that of Sally Smith, reported to be a female of European ancestry, 28 years of age, with a height of 5'4". If antemortem records of Smith (such as radiographic medical or dental records) become available for comparison, these may be helpful in confirming whether the remains are those of Sally Smith.

If you have any questions about the content of this report, please contact me at 777-555-4321.

Oz Teology

Oz Teology, PhD, D-ABFA
Forensic Anthropologist

Page 2 of 2

References

Adams, B., Crabtree, P., 2012. Comparative Osteology: A Laboratory and Field Guide of Common North American Animals. Academic Press, Oxford.

Adams, B.J., Konigsberg, L.W., 2004. Estimation of the most likely number of individuals from commingled human skeletal remains. Am. J. Phys. Anthropol. 125, 138–151.

AlQahtani, S.J., Hector, M.P., Liversidge, H.M., 2010. Brief communication: the London atlas of human tooth development and eruption. Am. J. Phys. Anthropol. 142, 481–490.

American Academy of Forensic Sciences, www.aafs.org, Accessed May 13, 2017.

American Board of Forensic Anthropology, www.theabfa.org, Accessed May 13, 2017.

Aschheim, K.W., Adams, B.J., 2015. OdontoSerach. www.odontosearch.com.

Bailey, L., 2014. As a Forensic Artists: Skulls, Suspects, and the Art of Solving Crime. Honeybee Media. www.aksaforensicartist.com.

Barnes, E., 1994. Developmental Defects of the Axial Skeleton in Paleopathology. University Press of Colorado, Niwot, CO.

Barnes, E., 2012. Atlas of Developmental Field Anomalies of the Human Skeleton: A Paleopathology Perspective. Wiley-Blackwell, Hoboken, NJ.

Bass, W.M., 2004. Human Osteology: A Laboratory and Field Manual, fifth ed. Missouri Archaeology Society, Columbia.

Behrensmeyer, A.K., 1978. Taphonomic and ecological information from bone weathering. Paleobiology 4, 150–162.

Black, S., Agarwal, A., Payne-James, J. (Eds.), 2010. Age Estimation in the Living: The Practitioner's Guide. John Wiley & Sons, Winchester.

Blankenship, J.A., Mincer, H.H., Anderson, K.M., Woods, M.A., Biurton, E.L., 2007. Third molar development in the estimation of chronological age in American blacks as compared with whites. J. Forensic Sci. 52 (2), 428–433.

Boldsen, J.L., Milner, O.R., Konigsberg, L.K., Wood, J.W., 2002. Transition analysis: a new method for estimating age from skeletons. In: Hoppa, R.D., Vaupel, J. (Eds.), Palcodemography: Age Distributions From Skeletal Samples. Cambridge University Press, Cambridge, pp. 73–106.

Brogdon, B.G., Vogel, H., McDowel, J.D., 2003. A Radiologic Atlas of Abuse, Torture, Terrorism and Inflicted Trauma. CRC Press, Boca Raton, FL.

Brooks, S., Suchey, J.M., 1990. Skeletal age determination based on the os pubis: a comparison of the Acsadi-Nemeskeri and Suchey-Brooks methods. Hum. Evol. 5, 227–238.

Buikstra, J.E., Ubelaker, D.H., 1994. Standards for Data Collection From Human Skeletal Remains. Archaeological Survey Research Seminar Series, vol. 44. Archaeological Survey, Fayetteville, AR.

Cho, H., Stout, S.D., Madsen, R.W., Streeter, M.A., 2002. Population-specific histological age estimating method: a model for known African-American and European-American skeletal remains. J. Forensic Sci. 47 (1), 12–18.

Christensen, A.M., 2003. An Empirical Examination of Frontal Sinus Outline Variability Using Elliptic Fourier Analysis: Implications for Identification, Standardization, and Legal Admissibility (PhD dissertation). The University of Tennessee, Knoxville, TN.

Christensen, A.M., Anderson, B.E., 2013. Personal identification. In: Tersigni-Tarrant, M.T., Shirley, N. (Eds.), Forensic Anthropology: An Introduction. CRC Press, Boca Raton, FL, pp. 397–420.

Christensen, A.M., Hatch, G.M., 2016. Quantification of radiologic identification and development of a population frequency data repository. J. Forensic Radiol. Imaging 7, 14–16.

Christensen, A.M., Passalacqua, N.V., Bartelink, E.J., 2014. Forensic Anthropology: Current Methods and Practice. Academic Press, San Diego.

Christensen, A.M., Smith, M.A., Cunningham, D. Wescott, D., Glieber, D. 2018. The use of industrial X-ray computed tomography technologies in forensic anthropology. Forensic Anthropology (in press).

Christensen, A.M., Smith, M.A., Thomas, R.M., 2012. Validation of X-ray fluorescence spectrometry for determining osseous or skeletal origin of unknown material. J. Forensic Sci. 57 (1), 6–11.

Claes, P., Hill, H., Shriver, M.D., 2014. Toward DNA-based facial composites: preliminary results and validation. Forensic Sci. Int. Genet. 13, 208–216.

Crowder, C., Heinrich, J., Stout, S.D., 2012. Rib histomorphometry for adult age estimation. In: Bell, L.S. (Ed.), Forensic Microscopy for Skeletal Tissues: Methods and Protocols, Methods in Molecular Biology, vol. 915, pp. 109–127.

Crowder, C.M., Stout, S., 2012. Bone Histology: An Anthropological Perspective. CRC Press, Boca Raton, FL.

Daubert v. Merrell Dow Pharmaceuticals, Inc. 509 U.S. 579, 1993.

Fazekas, I.G., Kosa, F., 1978. Forensic Fetal Osteology. Akademiai Kaido, Budapest.

Federal Rules of Evidence, 1975; 2000.

Forensic Anthropology Society of Europe, www.forensicanthropology.eu, Accessed May 13, 2017.

France, D.L., 2011. Human and Non-Human Bone Identification: A Concise Field Guide. CRC Press, Boca Raton, FL.

Frye v. United States, 54 App. D.C. 46, 293 F. 1013, 1923.

Gray, H., 1918. Anatomy of the Human Body. Lea & Febiger, Philadelphia, PA.

Haglund, W.D., 1997. Dogs and coyotes: postmortem involvement with human remains. In: Haglund, W.D., Sorg, M.H. (Eds.), Forensic Taphonomy: The Postmortem Fate of Human Remains. CRC Press, Boca Raton, FL, pp. 367–382.

Hartnett, K.M., 2010a. Analysis of age-at-death estimation using data from a new, modern autopsy sample—part I: pubic bone. J. Forensic Sci. 55, 1145–1151.

Hartnett, K.M., 2010b. Analysis of age-at-death estimation using data from a new, modern autopsy sample—part 2: sternal end of first rib. J. Forensic Sci. 55, 1152–1156.

Hatch, G.M., Dedouit, F., Christensen, A.M., Thali, M.J., Ruder, T.D., 2014. RADid: a pictorial review of radiologic identification using postmortem CT. J. Forensic Radiol. Imaging 2, 52–59.

Hefner, J.T., 2009. Cranial nonmetric variation and estimating ancestry. J. Forensic Sci. 54 (5), 985–995.

Hefner, J.T., 2011. Chapter 9: macromorphoscopics. In: Osteoware Software Manual Volume I. Repatriation Osteology Lab Smithsonian Institution, Washington, DC. https://osteoware.si.edu.

Hefner, J.T., Ousley, S.D., 2014. Statistical classification methods for estimating ancestry using morphoscopic traits. J. Forensic Sci. 59 (4), 883–890.

Hillson, S., 1996. Dental Anthropology. Cambridge University Press, Cambridge.

Iscan, M.Y., 1989. Age Markers in the Human Skeleton. Charles C. Thomas, Springfield, IL.

Jantz, R.L., Ousley, S.D., 2005. FORDISC 3.0: Personal Computer Forensic Discriminant Functions. The University of Tennessee, Knoxville, TN.

Klales, A.R., Ousley, S.D., Vollner, J.M., 2012. A revised method of sexing the human innominate using Phenice's nonmetric traits and statistical methods. Am. J. Phys. Anthropol. 149 (1), 104–114.

Langley, N.R., Jantz, L.M., Ousley, S.D., Jantz, R.L., Milner, G., 2016. Data Collection Procedures for Forensic Skeletal Material 2.0. Department of Anthropology, University of Tennessee; Anatomy Department, Lincoln Memorial University, Knoxville, TN.

Latham, K.E., Finnegan, M. (Eds.), 2010. Age Estimation of the Human Skeleton. CC Thomas, Springfield, IL.

Lewis, C.J., Garvin, H.M., 2016. Reliability of the walker cranial nonmetric method and implications for sex estimation. J. Forensic Sci. 61 (3), 743–751.

Megyesi, M.S., Nawrocki, S.P., Haskell, N.H., 2005. Using accumulated degree-days to estimate the postmortem interval from decomposed human remains. J. Forensic Sci. 50 (3), 1–9.

Mincer, H.H., Harris, E.F., Berryman, H.E., 1993. The ABFO study of third molar development and is use as an estimator of chronological age. J. Forensic Sci. 38 (2), 379–390.

Moore-Jansen, P.M., Ousley, S.D., Jantz, R.L., 1994. Data collection procedures for forensic skeletal material. Report of investigations no. 48. Department of Anthropology, University of Tennessee, Knoxville, TN.

Moorrees, C.F.A., Fanning, E.A., Hunt Jr., E.E., 1963a. Formation and resorption of three deciduous teeth in children. Am. J. Phys. Anthropol. 21, 205–213.

Moorrees, C.F.A., Fanning, E.A., Hunt Jr., E.E., 1963b. Age variation of formation stages for ten permanent teeth. J. Dent. Res. 42, 1490–1502.

Murray, E.A., Anderson, B.E., 2007. In: Forensic anthropology in the courtroom: trends in testimony. Presented at the 59th Annual Meeting of the American Academy of Forensic Sciences, San Antonio, TX.

NamUs, www.namus.org.

National Institute of Standards and Technology, Organization of Scientific Area Committees, www.nist.gov/forensics/osac, Accessed May 13, 2017.

Ortner, D.J., 2003. The Identification of Pathological Conditions in Human Skeletal Remains, second ed. Academic Press, San Diego, CA.

Osborne, D.L., Simmons, T.L., Nawrocki, S.P., 2004. Reconsidering the auricular surface as an indicator of age at death. J. Forensic Sci. 49 (5), 768–773.

Ousley, S.D., 2010. Threeskull. Version 2.0.

Ousley, S.D., Jantz, R.L., 2012. Fordisc 3 and statistical methods for estimating sex and ancestry. In: Dirkmaat, D.C. (Ed.), A Companion to Forensic Anthropology. Wiley-Blackwell, Chichester, pp. 311–329.

Passalacqua, N.V., 2010. The utility of the Samworth and Gowland age-at-death "look-up" tables in forensic anthropology. J. Forensic Sci. 55 (2), 482–487.

Phenice, T.W., 1969. A newly developed visual method of sexing the Os pubis. Am. J. Phys. Anthropol. 30, 297–302.

Pilloud, M.A., Hefner, J.T., Hanihara, T., Hayashi, A., 2014. The use of tooth crown measurements in the estimation of ancestry. J. Forensic Sci. 59 (6), 1493–1501.

Pilloud, M.A., Kenyhercz, M.W., 2016. Dental metrics in biodistance analysis. In: Pilloud, M.A., Hefner, J.T. (Eds.), Biological Distance Analysis: Forensic and Bioarchaeological Perspectives, first ed. Academic Press, San Diego.

RADid Resource, 2016. http://cfi.unm.edu/rad-id-index.html (Accessed 19 May 2017).

Raxter, M.H., Auerbach, B.M., Ruff, C.B., 2006. Revision of the fully technique for estimating statures. Am. J. Phys. Anthropol. 130, 374–384.

Robling, A.G., Stout, S.D., 2000. Histomorphometry of human cortical bone: applications to age estimation. In: Katzenburg, M.A., Saunders, S.R. (Eds.), Biological Anthropology of the Human Skeleton. Wiley-Liss, New York, NY.

Ruder, T., Brun, C., Christensen, A.M., Thali, M., Gascho, D., Schweitzer, W., Hatch, G.M., 2016. Comparative radiologic identification with CT images of paranasal sinuses—development of a standardized approach. J. Forensic Radiol. Imaging 7, 1–9.

Samworth, R., Gowland, R., 2007. Estimation of adult skeletal age-at-death: statistical assumptions and applications. Int. J. Osteoarchaeol. 17, 174–188.

Schaefer, M., Black, S., Scheuer, L., 2009. Juvenile Osteology: A Laboratory and Field Manual. Academic Press, San Diego, CA.

Scheuer, L., Black, S., 2000. Developmental Juvenile Osteology. Academic Press, San Diego, CA.

Smith, B.H., 1991. Standards of human tooth formation and dental age assessment. In: Kelly, M.A., Larsen, C.S. (Eds.), Advances in Dental Anthropology. Wiley-Liss, New York, NY, pp. 143–168.

Society of Forensic Anthropologists, www.sofainc.org, Accessed May 13, 2017.

Spradley, M.K., Jantz, R.L., 2011. Sex estimation in forensic anthropology: skull versus postcranial elements. J. Forensic Sci. 56 (2), 289–296.

Steadman, D.W., DiAntonio, L.L., Wilson, J.J., Sheridan, K.E., Tammariello, S.P., 2006. The effects of chemical and heat maceration techniques on the recovery of nuclear and mitochondrial DNA from bone. J. Forensic Sci. 51 (1), 11–17.

Stewart, T.D., 1979. Essentials of Forensic Anthropology. Charles C. Thomas, Springfield, IL.

Trotter, M., Gleser, G.C., 1952. Estimation of stature from long bones of American Whites and Negroes. Am. J. Phys. Anthropol. 10, 463–514.

Ubelaker, D.H., 1989. Human Skeletal Remains: Excavation, Analysis, Interpretation, second ed. Taraxacum, Washington, DC.

Ubelaker, D.H., Buchholz, B.A., Stewart, J.E.B., 2006. Analysis of artificial radiocarbon in different skeletal and dental tissue types to evaluate date of death. J. Forensic Sci. 51 (3), 484–488.

Walker, P.L., 2008. Sexing skulls using discriminant function analysis of visually assessed traits. Am. J. Phys. Anthropol. 136, 39–50.

White, T.D., Black, M.T., Folkens, P.A., 2011. Human Osteology, third ed. Academic Press, San Diego, CA.

White, T.D., Folkens, P.A., 2005. The Human Bone Manual. Academic Press, San Diego, CA.

Willey, P., Falsetti, T., 1991. Inaccuracy of height information on driver's licenses. J. Forensic Sci. 36 (3), 813–819.

Yoder, C., Ubelaker, D.H., Powell, J.F., 2001. Examination of variation in sternal rib end morphology relevant to age assessment. J. Forensic Sci. 46, 223–227.

List of Photo Credits

Index

Note: Page numbers followed by *f* indicate figures and *t* indicate tables.